Literature and Identity in
The Golden Ass of Apuleius

Literature and Identity in *The Golden Ass* of Apuleius

Luca Graverini

Translated from the Italian by
Benjamin Todd Lee

The Ohio State University Press • Columbus

Copyright © 2007 by Pacini Editore S.p.A.
All rights reserved.
English translation published 2012 by The Ohio State University Press.

Library of Congress Cataloging-in-Publication Data
Graverini, Luca.
 [Metamorfosi di Apuleio. English]
 Literature and identity in The Golden Ass of Apuleius / Luca Graverini ; translated by Benjamin Todd Lee.
   p. cm.
 Includes bibliographical references and index.
 ISBN 978-0-8142-1191-5 (cloth : alk. paper) — ISBN 0-8142-1191-7 (cloth : alk. paper) — ISBN 978-0-8142-9292-1 (cd-rom)
 1. Apuleius. Metamorphoses. 2. Latin fiction—History and criticism. I. Lee, Benjamin Todd. II. Title.
 PA6217.G7313 2012
 873'.01—dc23
                          2012004578
Paper (ISBN: 978-0-8142-5638-1)
Cover design by Jerry Dorris, AuthorSupport.com
Type set in Adobe Garamond Pro
Text design by Juliet Williams

contents

Translator's Note	vii
Author's Note to the English Translation	ix
Preface and Acknowledgments	xi

Chapter 1 • A Sweet Poetics — 1
- 1.1 "But I..." — 2
- 1.2 The ass and the cicada — 10
- 1.3 A sweet and misleading whisper — 12
- 1.4 Between philosophy and entertainment: Astonishment (*ut mireris*) — 36
- 1.5 The poetics of the novel — 38
- 1.6 Lucius of Patrae and Aristides of Miletus — 42

Chapter 2 • Old Wives' Tales and Servile Pleasures — 51
- 2.1 Entertainment, initiation, *aporia*, and satire — 52
- 2.2 Dissonances — 57
- 2.3 Greedy priests — 69
- 2.4 Isis and her sisters — 75
- 2.5 Lucius' shaven head — 82
- 2.6 Horizons of expectation — 89
- 2.7 An old wives' tale (*anilis fabula*) — 95
- 2.8 Paradox, satire, and levels of reading — 118
- 2.9 Lucius, before and after — 131

Chapter 3 • Metamorphoses of Genres — 133
    3.1 Philosophers on the road — 134
    3.2 Eyes and ears as criteria for truth — 141
    3.3 Lucius and his Sirens — 146
    3.4 Readers, listeners, and spectators — 154

Chapter 4 • Greece, Rome, Africa — 165
    4.1 On the road with Lucius — 166
    4.2 The reputation of Corinth — 169
    4.3 Romanization — 175
    4.4 Romanocentrism — 179
    4.5 The readership of the novel — 198
    4.6 Between Rome and the provinces — 200

Bibliography — 209
Index locorum — 228
General Index — 236

translator's note

I volunteered to translate this book because, as a classicist interested in Apuleius, I found it to be one of the most useful and stimulating pieces of Apuleian scholarship I had come across in years. Above all it synthesizes and makes reference to many European studies of Apuleius that are not always easily accessible to the American reader. I hope this translation will help narrow the gap between European and American studies of Apuleius.

I have tried to give a lucid approximation of Graverini's text, but many Italian idioms do not have precise equivalents in English. The relative poverty of my own prose style must be held responsible if the translation presented here turns out, in some places, to be less elegant than the original. Nevertheless, I will be happy if the reader will be able to understand what the author meant in the Italian.

All translations of Greek and Latin passages come from the Loeb series, except the following:

- Greek novels, which come from the collection edited by Reardon 1989
- Apuleius' rhetorical works (*Apologia, Florida, De deo Socratis*), which come from Harrison-Hilton-Hunink 2001

Other sources of translations are mentioned when I use them. Minor changes have been introduced to all these translations when necessary.

Translations of ancient works that are not included in the Loeb series or in the collections cited above are my own, unless otherwise indicated in the text.

Lastly, I would like to thank Christopher Trinacty and Victoria Neuman for their help editing and proofreading this book. Any errors that remain are solely my responsibility. I would also like to thank Eugene O'Connor and Marian Rogers for their help with the formidable task of editing and formatting the manuscript.

Benjamin Todd Lee
Oberlin, March 2012

author's note to the english translation

There is no rest, it seems, for Apuleian scholarship, and indeed this widespread interest testifies to the appeal of studying the *Metamorphoses*. In the few years since the original publication of this volume, several important monographs and journal papers have appeared, and even more are expected in the near future. Besides all these published and forthcoming studies, more occasions for illuminating discussions with several colleagues have been provided by several conferences on the ancient novel—let me mention only two recent ones here: *Apuleius and Africa*, held at Oberlin College in April–May 2010 and organized by the translator of this volume, with some help by the author and other distinguished colleagues; and *ISIS: The Religious Ending of the Golden Ass,* organized in Rostock in November 2008 by Wytse Keulen, the proceedings of which have been published as volume 3 of *Aspects of Apuleius'* The Golden Ass (*AAGA* 2012). Equally invaluable have been the meetings of the team that is producing the next Groningen commentary on the last book of the *Metamorphoses;* I have greatly enjoyed the opportunity to discuss different views on the novel with learned friends and colleagues like Wytse Keulen, Stephen Harrison, Lara Nicolini, Stelios Panayotakis, Danielle van Mal-Maeder, Ulrike Egelhaaf-Gaiser, Stefan Tilg, Friedeman Drews, and Warren Smith. I am also most grateful to Roberto Nicolai for the instructive and helpful conversations we had when we met in Cordoba (Argentina) for a double event (both the Curso de posgrado *Apuleyo y la novella antigua* and *II Jornadas Internacionales de Estudios Clasicos*), which was organized by Marcos Carmignani, Guillermo De Santis, and Gustavo Veneciano, the editors of the journal *Ordia Prima.*

And so it seems that a great deal has happened in a short time. Nevertheless, though I could not abstain from some very small changes and additions, I limited myself to a bare minimum; I have already confessed to being *pervicax pertinax* in the introduction to the original Italian edition, so I think it will be no surprise that my positions have not changed after only five years. On the contrary, I have even tried to restate them with further support in a few papers that the reader might find of interest; these are cited in the bibliography as Graverini 2009, 2010, 2012, and 2013a and b. Of course, nobody is ever going to have the final word on the interpretation of the *Metamorphoses* (or, indeed, of any first-rate literary work), and this book is certainly not an exception. But I still think it will have something to say for some time at least in regard to its main points: that is, to give a better understanding of the literary and cultural identity of Apuleius' novel, and to challenge John Winkler's conclusions about its general "meaning." While Winkler's methods still stand, and are his most valuable legacy together with his illuminating discussions on so many aspects of the *Metamorphoses,* my hope is that I can incite at least some discussion about the nearly general consensus, reached in the last two decades, about his "comic" interpretation of the novel.

Last but not least, a few words are needed to express my deep gratitude. Ben, the reason you offered to undertake the daunting task of translating my difficult and sometimes too Byzantine Italian into good English still escapes me: all the more reason to say a very heartfelt thank-you.

preface and acknowledgments

For many years now, the *Metamorphoses* of Apuleius has garnered a remarkable degree of critical attention that, with an ever-increasing emphasis, has demonstrated the highly sophisticated literary nature of the work, as well as its many considerable hermeneutic difficulties. Apuleius' pursuit of a highly complex and elaborate narrative style is in fact combined with a sort of essential ambiguity, which seems to leave the greatest diversity of interpretive possibilities open to the contemporary reader: and so it is that the *Metamorphoses* can be read as a sophisticated and detached narrative *divertissement;* or as an allegorical novel (*roman à clef*), whose goal is religious and/or philosophical propaganda; as a satire of fatuous belief in otherworldly powers; or even, for all intents and purposes, as an utterly aporetic text in its own right, a detective novel that presents its case to the reader in the form of a mystery that s/he alone can solve. Similarly, different genres of readings, as we shall see, are to be found not only among modern scholars, but ancient readers as well. At least to some degree, then, one might think that such a broad spectrum of interpretive choices and possibilities is the result of a certain ambiguity inherent in the text and cannot have been caused merely by the extreme diversity found in the cultural settings of its critics—a span that finds, to cite only two examples, Fulgentius at one end, and John Winkler at the other. In the case of a narrative text, moreover, this ambiguity takes on a special significance, since the possible transmission of any message (whether religious, philosophical, or of some other sort) becomes subordinated to the act of narration. To extrapolate any meaning from that narration is, consequently, somehow random, an act inevitably determined by the exegetic whim of the reader, as much as by the intentions of the author.

Albeit pleasant to read, the *Metamorphoses* presents itself to the critic as a deeply tangled knot; and to confront it, in the first two chapters of this book I have tried to analyze not only the text of the novel, but also the cultural and literary contexts that are responsible for the novel's production. I did this to find some firm points to which I might anchor a possible interpretation. I am well aware that I have utilized only a selection of many possible texts and contexts, so that here too there might be some arbitrariness in my method. Yet every critical method must make such selections, and so I can hope—if my choices show their relevance and prove convincing—that they will have been worthwhile.

The first chapter addresses the prologue of the novel, the inevitable point of departure for this type of analysis. I aim to clarify Apuleius' terminology, and explore its significance in several contexts: the self-styling of Hellenistic and Augustan poets in terms of genres and styles; the polemic among rhetors on the correct declamatory style (*pronuntiatio*); and finally, the idea of enchantment, connected in epic (and not in epic alone) with singing, music, and the rhetoric of heroes. I utilize these successive approximations, as well as an analysis of the programmatic statements found in other Greek and Latin narrative texts, in order to delineate the poetics of the ancient novel, in which the prologue shows itself to be a vigorous participant. This poetics is the "sweet" and seductive character of fictional narration, far removed from the programmatic "usefulness" (*utilitas*) that characterizes a great portion of the literature produced in antiquity. When he involved himself in these kinds of literary programmatics, Apuleius chose a route that had already been plotted out by his immediate literary models, namely, the *Metamorphoses* of Lucius of Patrae and the *Milesian Tales* of Aristides of Miletus (texts about which we can venture to make hypotheses, even though they are irrecoverably lost). However that may be, it is important to stress that we are dealing with a provocative literary program, one that seems to condemn Apuleius' novel to a marginal position and an inferior rank in the ancient literary system. In fact, to judge by the surviving ancient and late antique evidence, it seems that the *Metamorphoses* did not enjoy any great prestige, at least not in the most elite and conservative literary circles (which is not to say, however, that it remained unread by that audience).

But to what extent is our faith in the prologue of the novel justified? Do we have a reliable exegetical guide on our hands? Or does the prologue present a vision that is biased, even mystifying? The second chapter aims to verify whether the text itself maintains its own faith in this literary program, by taking into account the profusion of hermeneutic possibilities mentioned above. Taking for granted the inapplicability of the most excessive mysteriophilosophical interpretations, which are generally discredited today, I will review, and partially refute, the positions of those scholars who consider the *Metamorphoses* an aporetic text, one that leaves to the reader the responsibility of determining its significance; I will also differ with those who prefer to read the novel as a satire of religious fatuousness. The analysis found in the first part of the chapter is confined mainly to an internal investigation of Apuleius' text. What follows is based instead (as I emphasized above) on a literary and cultural contextualization of several key phrases in the novel, such as the words *anilis fabula* ("an old wives' tale") as they are applied to the Cupid and Psyche episode, and the expression *serviles voluptates* ("servile pleasures"), adopted by the priest Mithras in book 11. The cultural and literary contexts to which I refer in the analysis of these passages are the Platonic dialogues, as well as satire and folktale. According to these, the *Metamorphoses* should be placed in the sphere of the *spoudogeloion*, a literary posture that links (not without a certain taste for paradox) comic entertainment and self-irony with higher moral, philosophical, and religious aims. This designation in part reengages earlier scholarly positions, which have required reexamination in the light of objections raised by Winkler and successive literary criticism. Above all, the term *spoudogeloion* has the advantage of allowing a complete valorization of the links between Apuleius' novel and the genre of Latin satire. Despite the *aporiai* and ambiguities that derive from the separation of the poet and his satirical persona, Latin satire succeeds in joining comic elements (and, occasionally, also the narrative form itself) with the transmission of a certain moral or philosophical message. The designation "satirical" in a broad sense can also differentiate the Latin novel from the Greek tradition of narrative, even if, inevitably, these kinds of distinctions can never be entirely neat and are compromised by our incomplete knowledge of the ancient novels. After the analysis of the prologue offered in the first chapter, which emphasizes the underlying affinity between the *Metamorphoses* and the Greek novels, the second chapter helps construct a more complete representation of Apuleius' novel and of the dialectic between *utile* and *dulce* characteristic of it. This chapter also emphasizes the self-ironic, and to a certain degree provocative, nature of the words spoken by the *ego* that utters the prologue.

Certainly, all this does not yet suffice to represent the literary complexity of a text like the *Metamorphoses*, a protean work that finds one of its greatest strengths in its mixture of styles, and in the freedom with which it traverses the confines of literary genres. Beyond the dialectic between pleasing entertainment and philosophical engagement, we must remember that the novel is, perhaps above all, a sophisticated literary product. The third chapter confronts the theme of the interactions between the *Metamorphoses* and other literary genres, often absorbed and metabolized by the novel through parodic hyperbole. This analysis considers not so much the great number of allusions or imitations offered in the text, as those pieces that, through the investigation of intertextuality, allow a study of these interactions between genres from a structural and not merely episodic point of view, sometimes nearly suggesting the reflex of a conscious meditation of the author on this theme. The points of reference in this case are made up of the genres of philosophical dialogue, historiography, epic poetry, and drama.

Finally, the last chapter investigates the more general theme of cultural identity that emerges from Apuleius' novel. It deals with an argument that inevitably assumes a definite significance in the case of an African author, whose work is essentially an adaptation of a Greek original, and that has a Greek from Corinth for its protagonist and narrative voice, who puts an end to his own wanderings in the capital of the Empire and lays the foundation for a solid career in the field of rhetoric. From this vantage point, the *Metamorphoses* takes its place at the crossroads of three diverse cultures that did not always interact peacefully with each other throughout the course of history. To ask oneself if and to what degree the text encourages a conflicting vision of these interactions means to ask questions not only about the personality of Apuleius and the context in which the work was produced, but also regarding the social composition and geographic distribution of the public of readers for whom his work was conceived.

This book gathers the fruit of studies undertaken in the past few years, some of them unpublished, and some that have already appeared in journals and edited volumes. The material utilized in the previously published articles has been thoroughly revised, expanded, and redistributed across the four chapters of this book, with the result that there can be no precise correspondence between the pagination of this and of earlier versions.

> Chapter 1 incorporates material found in three articles: "Sweet and Dangerous? A Literary Metaphor (*aures permulcere*) in Apuleius' Prologue," pages 177–196 in *Metaphor and the Ancient Novel (Ancient Narrative* supplement 4), edited by S. J. Harrison, M. Paschalis, and S. Frangoulidis (Groningen, 2005); "A *lepidus susurrus:* Apuleius and the Fascination of Poetry," pages 1–18 in *Desultoria Scientia: Genre in Apuleius'* Metamorphoses *and Related Texts,* edited by R. R. Nauta (Leuven, 2006); "The Ass's Ears and the Novel's Voice: Orality and the Involvement of the Reader in Apuleius' *Metamorphoses*," pages 138–167 in *Seeing Tongues, Hearing Scripts: Orality and Representation in the Ancient Novel*

(*Ancient Narrative* supplement 7), edited by V. Rimell (Groningen, 2007).

Chapter 2 is composed of new material, but an article based on what is now § 2.7 has appeared in "An Old Wife's Tale," pages 86–110 in *Lectiones Scrupulosae: Essays on the Text and Interpretation of Apuleius' Metamorphoses* (*Ancient Narrative* supplement 6), edited by W. Keulen, R. R. Nauta, and S. Panayotakis (Groningen, 2006).

Chapter 3 incorporates material found in "The Ass's Ears and the Novel's Voice: Orality and the Involvement of the Reader in Apuleius' *Metamorphoses*" (cited just above), and in "La scena raccontata: teatro e narrativa antica," pages 1–24 in *La scena assente. Realtà e leggenda sul teatro nel Medioevo,* edited by F. Mosetti Casaretto (Alessandria, 2006).

Chapter 4 provides an extended revision of "Corinth, Rome, and Africa: A Cultural Background for the Tale of the Ass," pages 58–77 in *Space in the Ancient Novel* (*Ancient Narrative* supplement 1), edited by M. Paschalis and S. Frangoulidis (Groningen, 2002).

In hindsight, I would like to think that this book is the result of a research project begun some time ago and carried forward coherently up to this point in time. Nevertheless, although I am convinced that my studies over the past few years have enabled me to offer a sufficiently accurate and well-rounded picture of Apuleius' novel, this coherence has emerged gradually over the course of time. For the most part, the articles listed above owe their origins to disparate stimuli that must be attributed above all to the untiring organizers of the Rethymno International Conferences on the Ancient Novel, Michael Paschalis and Stavros Frangoulidis; and likewise to the team of the journal *Ancient Narrative,* who in addition to their annual journal publish the useful *Supplementa* dedicated to specific themes. Both *RICAN* and *AN* are by now essential and fertile junctures of exploration and debate for anyone who is involved with ancient narrative.

I have had the good fortune to work in the Dipartimento di Teoria e Documentazione delle Tradizioni Culturali, of the Facoltà di Lettere e Filosofia di Arezzo (University of Siena), which has provided another important source of inspiration and cultural investigation. Thanks to the financial support of the department I have had the opportunity to participate in the series *Arti Spazi Scritture,* conceived and organized by its director, Francesco Stella, whom I am also happy to call my friend, and to whom I would like to convey my gratitude here.

Whatever good points may be found in this book, it would surely have been much worse without the invaluable help of a great number of other colleagues and friends. I owe a particularly heartfelt debt of gratitude to Alessandro Barchiesi, Marco Fucecchi, and Wytse Keulen, who, in addition to having read and discussed earlier drafts of this book with me, never failed to offer advice as I was preparing the works cited above. I have also benefited from the many useful suggestions and provocative criticisms offered by the editors of the volumes in which my articles have appeared. On several specific subjects I have enjoyed a most useful exchange of ideas with Roberto Bigazzi, Ken Dowden, Kirk Freudenberg, Ann Kuttner, Thomas McCreight, and Niall Slater. Naturally, *pervicax pertinax,* as if I were some sort of dodgy Apuleian character, I have not always followed their suggestions: any errors or infelicities that might remain (in spite of the contributions these people have offered) must be attributed to me alone.

There are also a few people whom I have never met, but whose work, without a doubt, has improved my own. It seems only proper then that I express my gratitude to those who have developed the non-proprietary software that I have utilized over the years: the Kubuntu Linux operating system (www.kubuntu.org), the suite Openoffice.org (www.openoffice.org), and the unicode font Titus Cyberbit Basic (titus.fkidg1.uni-frankfurt.de/unicode/tituut.asp). When I used commercial software, I found AtticGreek (based on the Keyman program by Tavultesoft, www.tavultesoft.com) invaluable for entering Greek texts. Among many websites, I should at least make mention of the *Rassegna degli strumenti informatici per lo studio dell'antichità classica* ("review of information tools for the study of classical antiquity") found at www.rassegna.unibo.it, and the Perseus Digital Library (www.perseus.tufts.edu). Considering the instability of website addresses, I can only hope that the information provided in this paragraph might maintain its usefulness for some time to come—and that the usefulness of this book will last just a bit longer.

Finally, one must acknowledge that a work of this kind involves a notable commitment on the part of those closest to the author undertaking it. I should confess that I have thought on several occasions that, without my family, this work would have been finished much more quickly; but it is very likely that, without them, it would never have been finished at all.

My heartfelt thanks, then, to Angela, Elena, and Daniele.

1

A Sweet Poetics

THERE ARE many things we do not know about the ancient novel. For example, we can only make conjectures about the circumstances of its birth or about its audience, not to speak of the dense fog that shrouds the biographies of most of its authors. Even its correct name is obscure: as far as we know, there was no single term, unambiguously used by ancient readers and authors, to identify those works we normally define as "novels"—a term which is, indeed, an anachronism, albeit a happy one.[1] This ambiguity is mainly due to two causes: the late birth of the genre, which prevented Hellenistic grammarians and philologists from considering it in their investigations; and the very low esteem in which prose narrative was held by ancient cultural elites. Be that as it may, the novel in antiquity apparently occupied a loosely defined space, a sort of no man's land between other literary genres, and is usually defined by analogy with those genres. Thus, we find names drawn from theatrical literature, like δρᾶμα ("drama," or more generally "fictive account"), κωμωδία ("comedy"), ὑπόθεσις and *argumentum* ("plot, subject"), and the Latin term *fabula* ("tale"), which may define both theatrical plays and prose narratives.[2] Another semantic group highlights the narrative and/or fictional character of the novel: for example, μῦθος and μύθευμα ("imaginary story"), or πλάσμα ("unreal, invented story"). Then we have definitions such as ἱστορία and *historia* ("history, tale") that sug-

---

1. For a more extensive overview of these subjects, see my introductory chapter in Graverini-Keulen-Barchiesi 2006. On the ancient name of the novel, see Kuch 1989, 13–18; Marini 1991; Dostálová 1996, 181.
2. See p. 163 and n. 82.

gest an overlap with historiography; finally, some authors refer more or less explicitly to the elusive genre of the *fabula Milesia*, to which I will return in § 1.6.

Of course, if there was no standard definition for the novel, this does not necessarily mean that authors and readers had no awareness of the novel as a literary genre, or of its features. In the Byzantine age, for example, Photius reconstructs a short literary history of the novel, and gathers together as many as seven different authors under the rubric of πλάσις, "fiction":

> It is in this way and on these subjects that Antonius Diogenes has contrived his work of fiction (ἡ τῶν δραμάτων πλάσις). It seems that he is earlier than those who have made it their business to write this kind of fiction (τὰ τοιαῦτα ... διαπλάσαι), such as Lucian, Lucius, Iamblichus, Achilles Tatius, Heliodorus, and Damascius. In fact this romance seems to be the fount and the root of Lucian's *True Story* and Lucius' *Metamorphoses*. Moreover, Dercyllis, Ceryllus, Thruscanus, and Dinias seem to have been the models for the romances (πλάσματα) about Sinonis and Rhodanes, Leucippe and Clitophon, Chariclea and Theagenes, and for their wanderings, love affairs, capture, and dangers. (*Bibliotheca* 166.111b)

We will see later (§1.5) that some Latin authors, when referring to Petronius and Apuleius' novels, employed rhetorical terminology very similar to that expressed in Greek. But, by way of beginning, it is a matter of greater interest to examine the terms used by the authors themselves as they refer to their own work. In fact, they often used prologues and metaliterary passages to offer their readers points of reference, thereby allowing them to properly set what they were reading into a contemporary literary and rhetorical context. Here I will try to investigate the literary identity of the ancient novels by starting from the text of the novels themselves. Apuleius' *Metamorphoses* offers a complex but intriguing starting point to perform this task.

1.1 "But I..."

The prologue to the *Metamorphoses* is not easy to interpret, and in the last decades scholars have attached a very wide range of hermeneutic possibilities to it.[3] In the following pages, I will extend this range even further; I hope,

---

[3] An entire volume is now available on this prologue (Kahane-Laird 2001); see there for further bibliography, with a few supplements in my review (Graverini 2002a). The text continues to stimulate scholarly interest: see now Drews 2006, Keulen 2007a and Tilg 2007.

however, that it will be a useful exercise, and that my analysis will shed light on some issues that up to this point have not been fully investigated. In order to do this, I will need to devote the next pages only to the first words—or, better, only to the first syllables—of the novel: *at ego.*

The speaking *ego*[4] begins by making a very specific promise to the reader:

> At ego tibi sermone isto Milesio varias fabulas conseram auresque tuas benivolas lepido susurro permulceam. (1.1.1)[5]

> But I would like to tie together different sorts of tales for you in that Milesian style of yours, and to caress your ears into approval with a sweet whisper.

Why the initial *at?* The particle implies some sort of transition or opposition, but its appearance at the very beginning of our text is rather astonishing: the reader, of course, cannot know from what point of origin this dialogic transition (or opposition) originates. Nevertheless, its highly relevant position at the very beginning of the novel forces us to formulate at least some hypotheses, which will be useful for our comprehension of the prologue and consequently of the whole novel. John Morgan argues that "the emphatic position of *at ego tibi* implies a previous storytelling *tu mihi* . . . we are plunged into the position of overhearing part of a larger narrative exchange already in progress."[6] This suggestion is perfectly consistent with the fact that, after just a few words, the novel is labeled as a *sermo Milesius,* a "talk in the Milesian style"; and the prologue to the pseudo-Lucianic *Amores* suggests that Aristides, in his *Milesian Tales,* introduced himself not only as a narrator, but also as a listener:

> This morning I have been quite gladdened by the sweet winning seductiveness of your wanton stories (αἱμύλη καὶ γλυκεῖα πειθὼ τῶν ἀκολάστων σου διηγημάτων), so that I almost thought I was Aristides being enchanted (ὑπερκηλούμενος) by those Milesian Tales.

We will have an opportunity to analyze the relevance of this text to Apuleius' prologue in greater detail below (§ 1.6), but let us linger here for

---

4. His identity is possibly the most difficult enigma of this short text, but there is no need to find an answer here. For some bibliography see below, p. 52 n. 1.
5. Apuleius' text, here and throughout this book, is from Robertson 1971–72[4].
6. Morgan 2001, 161.

a moment over *at ego tibi*. Alexander Scobie[7] argues that the parallelism between *at* in the prologue and *sed* in the introduction of *Cupid & Psyche* (4.27.8 *sed ego te* . . .) could suggest that Apuleius here "temporarily casts off the guise of Platonist and assumes that of a *fabulator*," and that "the opening sentence of the prologue was possibly a formula used by story-tellers." He also points out that beginning a literary work with the word *at* is almost unparalleled, the only precedents being in Greek—Xenophon's *Symposium* and *Constitution of the Spartans* (which begin respectively with ἀλλ' ἐμοὶ δοκεῖ and ἀλλ' ἐγὼ ἐννοήσας). He attributes such strange openings to a "naïveté real or assumed," or to an attempt to make the two works appear as parts of a larger project. Wytse Keulen suggests that "perhaps . . . *at* is merely a colloquial particle," noting that "the combination *at ego* is characteristic of dialogue and occurs very frequently in comedy, sometimes to emphasize a promise or proposal."[8] But Scobie also points out that an initial *at* is a feature of some Latin poetic texts, starting with the famous opening of Virgil's *Aeneid* book 4, *At regina* . . . .[9] At this point, we need to add that this usage has roots in epic, since several books of the *Iliad* and of the *Odyssey* begin with αὐτάρ:[10] after all, it is not inappropriate to Apuleius' style that the *Metamorphoses* begins with a combination of words that is suspended between conversational and epic language. The prologue as a whole suggests, as we will shortly see, that the style of the novel it introduces is halfway between prose and poetry.

We can, however, also try to set this problematic *incipit* in a different context, one that not only can define its style, but also adheres to the general design of the prologue. The speaking *ego*, whoever he is, invites the reader to listen to an account,[11] or to take part in a dialogue, the subject of which is

---

7. Scobie 1975, 66.

8. Keulen 2007b, 63; see also Harrison 2003, 240–1. According to Tatum 1979, 26–7. "the *ego tibi* with which the novel opens . . . resembles the *sermo* or conversation typical of Roman verse satire."

9. Cf. also Propertius 2.27.1; Ovid, *Epist.*12.1; *Met.* 4.1; Lucan 4.1 and 9.1; Silius Italicus 15.1; Statius, *Theb.* 3.1; Valerius Flaccus 6.1 (with the commentary by Fucecchi 2006) and 8.1. Dowden 2001, 132 points out the "eye-catching use of *at* to announce the subject of this . . . work," and compares the beginning of the *Metamorphoses* with the lines that, according to Servius, opened the *Aeneid* (*at nunc horrentia Martis / arma virumque cano* . . .).

10. *Iliad* 3 and 15; *Odyssey* 11, 12, 14, 19, 20; cf. also *Il.* 9, 22, 23 and *Od.* 6. The fact that several books of Homer begin with αὐτάρ is probably significant for his readers and imitators, but it might not signal a sharp break for Homer himself; for a discussion (and further bibliographical references) on the divisions between books in Homer and in the ancient novels, see Nimis 2004. It is also useful to remember that the epigrammatist Pollianus in *Anthologia Graeca* 11.130.1 defines the epic poets as τοὺς αὐτὰρ ἔπειτα λέγοντας: even though αὐτὰρ ἔπειτα is never placed at the beginning of a book, Pollianus' text shows that the use of adverbs and particles in Homer and his imitators was considered significant.

11. That a reader is invited to listen to something is a paradox, recurring also at other points in the novel: see more thoroughly on this below, § 3.2.

going to be defined in the next sentences: the *ego* is going to give the reader some preliminary information about the novel before it begins. Taking only the first sentence into account, he tells us that the story will be "in the Milesian style," that it will be composed of "different sorts of tales" narrated by a "sweet whisper," and that it will be able to "caress the ears" of those who listen to it. All these pieces of information deserve careful consideration, but, for the moment, I only point out that they concern the literary genre ("Milesian"),[12] contents ("different sorts of tales"), and style (the "sweet whisper" that "caresses the ears") of the *Metamorphoses*. For the moment, then, we could overlook the fact that the words *at ego* open the novel, and instead place more emphasis on their function: namely, to introduce a statement on the literary genre, the style, and the contents of what is about to begin. In this context, we should take into account the possibility that *at ego tibi* does not imply a preceding *tu mihi*, as Morgan says, but rather *alii tibi*: it could stress the difference between the prologue speaker's literary choices and other genres and/or styles that other speakers could offer to the same audience.[13] From this perspective, we can also reappraise the *sed ego te* that, as we have seen, introduces *Cupid and Psyche*. What the old narrator is saying is that it would be possible for her to comfort Charite, who has been shocked by a bad dream, by offering rational reasons for consolation, "but she" will rather try to relax her with a nice tale:

> ... even dreams at night sometimes predict opposite outcomes. For instance, weeping and being beaten and occasionally having your throat cut announce some lucrative and profitable outcome. Conversely, laughing and stuffing the belly with honey-sweet pastries or joining in Venus'

---

12. Dowden 2001, 126 claims that it is not appropriate to speak about a "Milesian genre," since all we know about it are the extremely scanty fragments of Aristides' *Milesian Tales* and of Sisenna's translation (a cautious and conservative position, already adopted by Erwin Rohde and Aragosti 2000, 4 ff.). However, Keulen 2007b, 64f. demonstrates that the word *milesia* can also mean, more generically, "popular fiction," especially in polemical contexts: see below, § 1.6 pp. 48–49. Cf. also Moreschini 1994a, 87 (for whom Apuleius uses *fabula Milesia* to define what we call a 'novel' today); Jensson 2004, 267 ff. (at p. 270 he lists other possible examples of Milesian works, about which we are informed by the indirect tradition and by papyri). Of course, it is also possible that *sermo Milesius* is simply a stylistic indication: for example, a reference to Sisenna's archaizing style (cf. Callebat 1968, 478; Dowden 2001, 127), or to the explicit and "risqué" language adopted in some scenes. For the *Metamorphoses* as *fabula Milesia*, see esp. Harrison 1998a, 68 ff., with further bibliography.

13. Gowers 2001, 85 ff. similarly suggests that "Apuleius' *at ego* ... in the Prologue can be read in two ways, either as a distraction ('... Now, let me tell you a story') or as a pointed interaction with something outside ('... But this is *my* kind of story')." I am not totally convinced that in Apuleius' prologue there is an "unspoken contrast" with Persius; but I certainly agree that "for Apuleius the deceptions of flattery and fiction that Persius condemns are an essential part of the tactics of philosophical initiations (even if he fails eventually to deliver the reader into the innermost *penetrale*)." We will return to these themes again in the first two chapters of this book.

pleasure will foretell that one is going to be harassed by mental depression and physical weakness and every other sort of loss. But right now I shall divert you with a pretty story and an old wives' tale (4.27.6–7: *sed ego te narrationibus lepidis anilibusque fabulis . . . avocabo*).

I will not try to offer alternative interpretations of this prologue that are absolutely contrary to what others have already suggested. This is a narrative prologue and not a rhetorical treatise, and looking for clear-cut definitions in it would be unwise. It is an enigmatic text, one that manages to create several kinds of generic expectations for its reader—perhaps even false or incomplete expectations;[14] for precisely this reason, I think that the wisest approach is to try to understand as many facets of the prologue as possible.

At ego is clearly a very common word sequence. The fact that it recurs in particular contexts is significant only if we decide *a priori* that those contexts are relevant to our understanding of the prologue—a clear example of implicitly circular reasoning. For example, it is true that *at ego* is frequently found in the language of comic writers, but we only consider this fact remarkable because we start from the hypothesis, or rather from the observation, that Plautine language and the *sermo cotidianus* are important elements in Apuleius' complex style. Yet we can also start from a completely different hypothesis, that this odd *incipit* is meant to aid the reader in discerning the metaliterary significance of the prologue (which, as we have seen, is especially concerned with defining the style and genre of the novel). Therefore, *at ego* could also be a first indicator of a very complex style that exploits the language of comedy and the *sermo cotidianus* in the context of a larger and more sophisticated literary project.

In fact, there was a widespread tradition of beginning a programmatic statement about the choice of a subject, a style, or a literary genre (or *tout court* about the choice of giving oneself to literature) with something like "but I." The ancient historians offer several examples of this practice. Sallust had to account for his decision to write history instead of devoting himself to his country: "And for myself (*ac mihi quidem*), although I am well aware that by no means equal repute attends the narrator and the doer of deeds, yet I regard the writing of history as one of the most difficult of tasks" (*Catil.* 3.2). Livy had the less essential (but still very important) problem of justifying the choice of the subject matter for his first chapters, the very ancient and mythical past of Rome: 1 *pr.* 5 "I myself (*ego contra*), on the contrary, shall seek in this an additional reward for my toil." Proudly claim-

---

14. Cf. § 1.4.

ing his own impartiality and disinterest in writing history, Tacitus stresses in his prologues the opposition between himself (*Hist.* 1.1.3 and *Ann.* 1.1.3 *mihi*) and the other historians (*Hist.* 1.1.1 *multi auctores; Ann.* 1.1.1 *clari scriptores*). Among Greek historians see e.g. Polybius, who at 12.12.3, begins a polemic statement against Timaeus' methods with ἐγὼ δέ.

For the Augustan poets, too, who had a strong preference for a personal, lyric and/or elegiac Muse, subject matter and literary genre were also common and highly important issues, while their patrons tried to promote a more politically committed poetry. In Propertius, for example, metapoetical statements often take the form of a *recusatio*, a refusal to engage in "civic" or epic poetry.[15] The "but I" form explicitly appears at 2.1.45 f.: "the soldier counts his wounds, the shepherd his sheep; I for my part (*nos contra*) wage wars within the narrow confines of a bed," but it is clearly present also at 4.1.61 f. "let Ennius crown his verse with a ragged garland: Bacchus, give me leaves of your ivy" (*Ennius . . . mi*). If we consider similar adversative uses of first-person pronouns without *at* or *contra*, the examples from Augustan poetry might easily be multiplied. See for example Ovid, *Fast.* 1.13 "let others sing of Caesar's wars; let my theme be Caesar's altars" (*alii . . . nos*); and several passages in Horace, such as *Carm.* 1.7.1–10: "let others praise famed Rhodes. . . . As for me, not hardy Lacedaemon . . . has so struck my fancy . . . (*alii . . . me*).[16] An explicit *at*, such as we find in Apuleius, recurs in the lengthy *recusatio* that opens the third book of Manilius' *Astronomica*. After enumerating a series of topics he is not going to discuss, the poet concludes: "it is a hackneyed task to write poems on attractive themes and compose an uncomplicated work. But I (*at mihi*) must wrestle with numerals and names of things unheard of" (3.29 ff.).[17] Later *recusationes* also reiterate this

---

15. See Graverini 1997a, 236–243 for an initial bibliography on *recusationes;* and Nauta 2006a for the afterlife of this literary form in Flavian times.

16. See also *Carm.* 1.6.1–9 *scriberis Vario fortis . . . Nos, Agrippa, neque haec dicere . . . conamur;* 1.31.9–15 *premant Calena falce quibus dedit / fortuna vitem . . . me pascunt olivae;* 4.2.25–32 *multa Dircaeum levat aura cycnum . . . ego apis Matinae / more modoque . . . carmina fingo.* Such antitheses based on first-person pronouns are common in *recusationes* and metapoetic statements: cf. Nisbet-Hubbard 1970, 85 commenting on *Carm.* 1.6.5 *nos.*

17. Manilius' *recusatio* (on which see Liuzzi 1988, 85–88) provides an extremely interesting comparand to Apuleius' prologue, with which it shares some key features; there is probably no direct relationship between the two texts, but the correspondences suggest that both Manilius and Apuleius resort to stock themes in their prologues. After the *recusatio* proper with *at mihi,* the poet urges the reader to watch and to listen attentively (3.36 f. *huc ades, o quicumque meis advertere coeptis / aurem oculosque potes, veras et percipe voces. / impendas animum . . .*). Then he takes a stand in the debate between *utile* and *dulce* in poetry, declaring that he will not offer *dulcia carmina,* but useful teachings, since truth (*res ipsa*) needs no embellishment (3.38 f.). Finally, he justifies the presence of foreign terms in his poem (*et, si qua externa referentur nomina lingua / hoc operis, non vatis erit:* 3.40 f.). For the first point, cf. *Met.* 1.1.6 *lector intende* (and for the appeal to the reader's ears and eyes, cf. 1.1.1 *aures*

pattern. For example, in Martial 8.3.17–19 the ninth Muse incites the poet with these words: "let those themes be written by men grave overmuch, and overmuch austere, whom at midnight their lamp marks at their wretched toil. But do you (*at tu*) dip your little Roman books in sprightly wit. . . . To a thin pipe you may appear to sing, if only your pipe outblow the trump of many."

Of course, this is not the place for a thorough review of the theme of *recusatio* in Augustan poetry, but the picture would not be complete without a look at Hellenistic Greek authors, who frequently adopted the same rhetorical gesture. To begin with minor texts, my first example is an epigram attributed to Theocritus in the *Anthologia Graeca* (9.434.1–2): "The Chian Theocritus is another, but I (ἐγὼ δέ), the Theocritus who wrote these poems, am one of the many Syracusans." This is a problematic text; its attribution to Theocritus is only conjectural, and Wilamowitz's identification of the "Chian" with Homer, which would allow us to interpret the epigram as a contrast between epic and bucolic poetry, is probably to be rejected: the anonymous epigrammatist aims rather at differentiating Theocritus of Syracuse, the bucolic poet, from another Theocritus, a sophist of Chios.[18] The first two verses seem primarily interested in distinguishing the two Theocrituses, but in the fourth and last verses, an important literary statement occurs, where the epigrammatist points out the difference between the Muses that inspired the two authors bearing the same name: Μοῦσαν δ' ὀθνείαν οὔ τιν' ἐφελκυσάμαν, "I have adopted no alien Muse." Another relevant apocryphal text is the *Epitaphium Bionis*, ascribed to Moschus. After enumerating a series of cities and places that lament Bion's death far more than the loss of the famous poets to whom they gave birth (Ascra/Hesiod, Boeotia/Pindar, Lesbos/Alcaeus, Teos/Anacreon, Paros/Archilochus, Mytilene/Sappho, Syracuse/Theocritus), the poet says that he, for his part (αὐτὰρ ἐγώ), sings Ausonia's lament for Bion as a bucolic poet (93 f.): just as the author of the epigram quoted above does with Theocritus, Pesudo-Bion differentiates himself from other poets in regard to both birthplace and poetic genre.

The most celebrated text, however, as well as the most relevant for my purposes, must be the prologue of Callimachus' *Aitia*, which Margaret Hubbard defined as "possibly more significant for Latin poetry than any other single page of Greek,"[19] and which has certainly influenced many of the pas-

---

and *inspicere*); for the second, cf. 1.1.1 *lepido susurro permulceam;* for the third, cf. 1.1.5 *en ecce praefamur veniam, siquid exotici ac forensis sermonis rudis locutor offendero*. These points will be discussed further in the pages immediately below.

18. See Cameron 1995, 422–426; Rossi 2001, 344.

19. Hubbard 1974, 73; see also Thomas 1993, 199, who stresses that "Callimachus does in fact

sages quoted above. The poet proclaims that he prefers the "shrill cry" (λιγὺς ἦχος)[20] of the cicadas to the "din" (θόρυβος) of the ass. Both the chirp of the cicadas and the bray of the ass are clearly symbols of different kinds of poetry: letting other poets bray like the long-eared beast, Callimachus prefers to be like the slight and winged cicada (1.31 f. θηρὶ μὲν οὐατόεντι πανείκελον ὀγκήσαιτο / ἄλλος, ἐγὼ δ' εἴην οὐλαχύς, ὁ πτερόεις). At the end of the *Aitia* a similar pattern, αὐτὰρ ἐγώ, announces a transition to a new work and a new genre, the *Iambi:* the poet says his farewell to Zeus and commends the royal house to his protection, while he, he says, is heading to the pasture where the Muses walk (112.8 f. χαῖρε, Ζεῦ, μέγα καὶ σύ, σάω δ' ὅλον οἶκον ἀνάκτων·/ αὐτὰρ ἐγὼ Μουσέων πεζὸν ἔπειμι νομόν).[21] In these closing verses we can read, I think, a sort of metaliterary *sphragis*, a further differentiation between the activities of the poet and those of Zeus and the kings (this contrast was a convention found already in Hesiod, *Th.* 94–96: "it is from the Muses . . . that men are poets . . . but it is from Zeus that they are kings"); this could be an echo of the prologue, where he says that "it is not mine to thunder; that belongs to Zeus" (1.20 βροντᾶν οὐκ ἐμόν, ἀλλὰ Διός).

In these texts, Callimachus employs ἐγὼ δέ and αὐτὰρ ἐγώ to set himself and his poems apart from other literary traditions, and, as we have seen, it is possible to find similar expressions in similar contexts among later Hellenistic and Latin poets. It could, of course, be mere coincidence: "but I" is a common and natural way to begin a statement about one's originality. Propertius 2.1.45, however, provides an example to the contrary. Callimachus' poetry is an inescapable model for the Roman poet, and the context of Propertius' *recusatio* is not far from that of the prologue of the *Aitia;* and if we take into account that, only five verses before *nos contra*, "Callimachus with a narrow breast" had been explicitly mentioned as a model of Propertius' anti-epic poetry, the parallelism between *nos contra* and ἐγὼ δέ appears to be more than mere coincidence.

In other words, Propertius' poem offers a sort of "collective security"[22] that allows us to imagine intertextual connections even in words or phrases

---

deserve, from a number of aspects, the prominent position accorded him by relatively recent criticism."

20. Or, more probably, "sweet cry": see below, p. 19 n. 52.

21. Pfeiffer 1949, 125 *ad loc.* points out that this is a variation on a standard closure in the *Homeric Hymns:* cf. e.g. *H. Cer.* 495; *H. Ap.* 546; *H. Merc.* 580; *H. Ven.* 293.

22. For the terminology see Hinds 1998, 28. I also refer to Hinds' discussion of *me miserum* in Ovid and Propertius (pp. 29–34) as a theoretical background to the interpretability of such "loose" intertexts. On the relationship between Propertius 2.1 and Callimachus' poetry, see the recent commentary by Fedeli 2005.

that have no eye-catching peculiarity by themselves. What I am suggesting is that ἐγὼ δὲ, *nos contra*, and similar expressions could be regarded as stylized rhetorical gestures that recur with some frequency in metapoetic contexts, especially in the Hellenistic and Augustan authors.

This "collective security" does help us with Propertius, but the situation is seemingly different for Apuleius' prologue. It is true our passage contains a programmatic statement on style, subject, and literary genre; but can we place on it the same emphasis we usually attribute to similar statements made by Callimachus and other poets—and even think that Apuleius is consciously shaping his poetics through a comparison with those texts? After all, some would argue that Apuleius' *Metamorphoses* is a prose narrative, and it does not seem that Hellenistic and Augustan poets can offer a useful context to interpret its prologue. Yet I intend to refute this statement in the pages below.

1.2 The ass and the cicada

As we have seen, in the prologue of his *Aitia* Callimachus used the braying of the ass and the songs of the cicadas as metaphors for bad and good poetry respectively.[23] These same voices seem to reverberate in our prologue. The prologue speaker defines himself as a *rudis locutor*, a "raw speaker": these words refer *prima facie* to a (feigned) poor command of the Latin language by a speaker who locates his "ancient stock" in the renowned lands of the Hymettus, of the Isthmus, and of the Spartan Taenarus (referring, as it seems, also to literary representations of these places);[24] but most scholars also read *rudis locutor* as a playful reference to a "braying" speaker that foreshadows Lucius' transformation into an ass, at least for a reader who already knows the plot of the novel (a "second reader," in Winkler's terms).[25] This idea fits Apuleius' typical wit very well: he was a "juggler of words,"[26] who certainly had no problems playing on an implicit connection of *rudis* with *rudere*. It should also be noted that the connection between *rudis locutor* and

---

23. The voices of the ass and of the cicada are compared also in Aesop, 195 Hausrath. Callimachus uses the braying ass as a figure for the bad poet in frg. 192.11 Pfeiffer.

24. *Hymettos Attica et Isthmos Ephyrea et Taenaros Spartiatica, glebae felices aeternum libris felicioribus conditae, mea vetus prosapia est* (1.1.3).

25. Cf. e.g. Winkler 1985, 196 f.; Gianotti 1986, 106; Mazzoli 1990, 77. James 2001, 259 and n. 8 highlights the contrast between *lepidus susurrus* and *rudis locutor*, on which see below in the text. See also the phrase *rudis ... historia* at 6.29.3: it is a tale written *doctorum ... stilis*, but that has an ass as its main character.

26. *Iam haec equidem ipsa uocis immutatio desultoriae scientiae stilo quem accessimus respondet* (1.1.6).

rudere is a pun that, in the light of ancient rhetoric, fits very well with the interpretation of the prologue that I will present in the following pages. It was a common *topos* to compare an orator's voice to the cry of an animal: the barking of the dog was, as it seems, the most common metaphor,[27] but at least one orator was unlucky enough to be described as a braying ass by Lucilius (frg. 261 M. *haec . . . rudet ex rostris*).[28]

An attentive reader of the prologue could therefore hear the faint resonance of a braying donkey. The chirp of cicadas could also be heard (admittedly, even more weakly) in the *lepidus susurrus* that describes the prologue speaker's voice, but I will delay discussion of this point for a few pages. For the moment, it is important to point out that, if all this is true, it would be easy to interpret the prologue, at least partially and tentatively, as a reaction to Callimachus' poetics: a prologue speaker who tries to speak with a cicada-like *lepidus susurrus* and ends up as a braying ass is contrasted with a poet who refuses to speak like an ass, and identifies himself with a slender cicada. However, I do not believe that we really need to read anti-Callimacheanism into Apuleius' text. The prologue speaker, with wordplay and by the use of significant keywords derived from ancient literary and rhetorical polemic, adopts instead an inclusive strategy: the novel is announced as a work that will have both Callimachean and anti-Callimachean features (an elaborate style, but also a long book that, at times, shows both epic and colloquial language).[29] We will repeatedly see in this book that a constant feature of Apuleius' style is how he crosses boundaries that divide different literary genres; furthermore, this feature is enhanced by the literary nature of the novel, a truly "mixed" genre, where even the difference between prose and poetry is often blurred.[30]

---

27. Cf. e.g. Cic. *Brut.* 58 *latrant enim iam quidam oratores, non loquuntur;* also Sallust, *frg.* 4.54 Maurenbrecher (Nonius I 60 M. = 84 L.) *canina, ut ait Appius, facundia exercebatur*. On this passage see La Penna 1973; the metaphor is adopted also by Quintilian, *Inst.* 12.9.9 and Hieronymus, *Epist.* 119.1. Cf. also Ovid, *Ib.* 232 *latrat et in toto verba canina foro* and several other passages quoted by La Penna 1973, 189 n. 2.

28. In Persius 3.9 *rudere* qualifies the nonsensical talk of the lazy young man. The metaphor was adopted also by some detractors of Apuleius' style in the sixteenth century: see Harrison 2002a, 148.

29. On the presence of Callimachean motives and phraseology in anti-Callimachean programmatic statements (Persius and others), see Thomas 1993, 202 f. There is a vast bibliography concerning the relationship between the *Metamorphoses* and epic literature: in this book, also see §§ 1.3.4 and 3.2; for a general overview, see e.g. Harrison 2000, 222 f.: "though . . . the *Metamorphoses* is full of literary allusions to many kinds of writing, it seems to be particularly concerned with highlighting its similarities with and differences from the epic in particular."

30. On the difference between prose and poetry, blurred by the novel, see § 1.5 p. 41 n. 125; and cf. the first chapter of Graverini-Keulen-Barchiesi 2006, 18 f. (with bibliography at p. 56), which addresses the novel as a 'mixed' genre. See also below, § 3; on the Greek novel I cite here only Fusillo 1989, 17–109.

The latest critical approaches to the *Metamorphoses* have begun to offer some "collective security" that makes the hypothesis of a connection between Apuleius and Callimachus (as well as with the canons of Hellenistic and Augustan poetry) less hazardous. For example, Ellen Finkelpearl has shown that we can effectively adapt critical methodologies originally developed for Augustan poetry to Apuleius' novel, and that there is often "much to gain by . . . seeing many allusions as, in part, literary criticism and replies to stylistic statements of earlier writers."[31] Relying on this background, in the pages below I will try to show that the chirp of the cicadas is indeed relevant to Apuleius' prologue. We will also see how this speaker with an asinine voice offers the reader some clues toward the identification of an appropriate literary context for the novel, by echoing in his language several elements of stylistic and rhetorical polemics that, though centuries old, were still of great concern in the second century.

1.3 A sweet and misleading whisper

The formulation I offered above of the relationship between the prologues of Apuleius and Callimachus implies some sort of connection between the prologue speaker's *lepidus susurrus* and the voice of the cicadas. My starting point in demonstrating this connection is a suggestion by Bruce Gibson,[32] who argues that Apuleius' *lepidus susurrus* is a hint at the first verse of Theocritus' *Idyll* 1 (ἁδύ τι τὸ ψιθύρισμα . . .), used to describe the soft rustle of the wind through the branches of a pine. Indeed, the similarity is striking (also with regard to the sound of the words), and Gibson reinforces it with two further remarks: 1) the prologue also mentions the *calamus* with which the book has been written: *calamus*, here "stylus," can also mean "reed

---

31. Finkelpearl 1998, 17; she refers to programmatic statements by Callimachus and some Augustan poets at pp. 62–67 ("Hair, Elegy, and Style"). The Groningen commentators credit the tale of *Cupid and Psyche* with "an almost 'Alexandrian' feel" (*GCA* 2004, 3) that derives from its various levels of irony and humor, as well as from its rich intertextuality: and we can certainly say that these features are not limited to *Cupid and Psyche* but can be found throughout the novel. Mattiacci 1985, 249 states that in Apuleius' poetic production we can see a strong influence of Hellenistic and Neoteric models. Harrison 1997, 56–57 suggests that the name of Lucius' father, Theseus (*Met.* 1.23.6), reflects the author's intention of alluding to Callimachus' *Hecale*. More generally, on Apuleius' Greek culture (he was proud of practicing all the literary genres *tam Graece quam Latine*: see *Flor.* 9.14; 9.27–29), see Sandy 1997. In Apuleius' times, Gellius 9.9.3 ff. shows that a thorough comparison between the Augustan poets and their Hellenistic models was common practice in the second century: *scite ergo et considerate Vergilius, cum aut Homeri aut Hesiodi aut Apollonii aut Parthenii aut Callimachi aut Theocriti aut quorundam aliorum locos effingeret, partem reliquit, alia expressit . . .*

32. Gibson 2001, 71 ff.

pipe," and hence might hint at the Pan-pipe, whose sound is compared in Theocritus to the ψιθύρισμα of the pine branches (vv. 2–3 ἁδὺ δὲ καὶ τύ / συρίσδες, "sweetly, too, do you play the syrinx");[33] 2) the prologue mentions Egypt with some emphasis, the source of both the *calamus* and the papyrus on which the tale is written. According to Gibson "an Egyptian mode of composition could suggest Theocritus, a poet of Alexandria."[34]

Unfortunately, Gibson fails to specify what this "Egyptian mode of composition" consists of, and to what extent an allusion to Theocritus in the prologue is significant for the characterization of the novel's style, genre, or contents: should we think that the style of the whole novel is thereby characterized as Theocritean? This would, of course, seem too far-fetched; the adjectives "pastoral" or "bucolic" could not adequately describe the *Metamorphoses* as a whole.

Even if a simplistic form of literary exhibitionism would certainly not be out of place in Apuleius, we should not reject a potentially significant intertext merely because we do not yet know what to make of it. I would also point out that Theocritus is not an unlikely source for an allusion in the *Metamorphoses,* and I will substantiate this statement with a new proposal. At *Met.* 8.1.3 one of Charite's slaves reports the death of his masters to an audience consisting of grooms, shepherds, and herdsmen (and of course the ass); this character has been frequently compared to a tragic messenger,[35] and the comparison accounts very well for the pathetic tone of his speech. But the choice of words does not seem to adhere to the tragic genre: the messenger's opening, *equisones opilionesque, etiam busequae* ("grooms and shepherds, and herdsmen, too"), fully qualifies as an imitation of Theocritus, *Idyll* 1.80 ἦνθον τοὶ βοῦται, τοὶ ποιμένες, ᾡπόλοι ἦνθον ("the herdsmen came, and shepherds and goatherds too"), while Virgil, *Ecl.* 10.16 and 19 *stant et oves circum . . . venit et upilio, tardi venere subulci* ("the sheep stand around . . . and the shepherds came, and the slow swineherds too") seem to

---

33. Cf. also the *dolciloquus calamus* at the end of Apuleius' elegy quoted in *Apol.* 9.

34. Gibson's paper, in general, aims at demonstrating that the phrase *papyrum Aegyptiam argutia Nilotici calami inscriptam* does not only refer to the act of writing, but also contains "possible auditory elements" (2001, 68; on this see also Finkelpearl 2003, 47 f.). Gibson also keenly notes (p. 71 n. 12) that "beguiling whisperings are not always agreeable . . . quite apart from the possibly dangerous implications of *lepido susurro* . . . compare also the insidious qualities of *permulceo* at Quintilian, *Inst.* 2.12.6 *nihilque aliud quam quod vel pravis voluptatibus aures adsistentium permulceat quaerunt.*" His observation is developed by Keulen 2003a, 8–19 and 2007b, 8–26 and will be thoroughly treated in the following pages.

35. Cf. López 1976, 338; and more recently Nicolini 2000, who points out several features of the slave's speech that recall and possibly parody the typical announcement of a tragic ἄγγελος. See also *GCA* 1985, 29 *ad loc.*; and May 2007, 90. More generally, on messengers in Euripides, see the comprehensive study by I. J. F. de Jong 1991.

echo less distinctly in Apuleius' text. This is due to the different composition of the triad of characters that are mentioned,[36] and the fact that they suffer a form of "dilution" as they are spread apart in non-adjacent verses. The context is instead fully relevant, in both Theocritus and Virgil, to the Apuleian messenger's account of Charite's tragic death: the shepherds and the others are called to participate in the mourning for the deaths, real or figurative, of Thyrsis and Gallus respectively. This direct allusion to bucolic poetry is part of a sophisticated literary apparatus, which successfully adapts a tragic narrative to a rustic setting inhabited by slaves and humble farmers.[37]

The likelihood of a Theocritean echo in the prologue, however, is a different case. First, in spite of the parallels highlighted by Gibson (the term *calamus* and an implicit reference to Egypt), the similarity of *lepido susurro* with ἁδύ . . . ψιθύρισμα is not strongly supported by any contextual relationship between the prologue and Theocritus' *Idylls*—in other words, there is no real "collective security." Secondly, and perhaps most importantly, a prologue is always a text that has been constructed with care, and we need to consider with equal care the meaning of a particular choice of words. A direct comparison with Theocritus leaves this question unanswered, but an analysis of Apuleius' mediation with Virgil's *Eclogues* and other texts will offer us several useful routes of interpretation.

1.3.1 THE CICADA'S HYPNOTIC SONG

The leaves of the Theocritean pine gently rustle in the wind; their sound is compared by Thyrsis to the sound of the *syrinx* of his unnamed fellow goatherd. Virgil takes up Theocritus' imagery and wording in his first *Eclogue*: besides the first verses of the poem, where Tityrus plays the flute under the beech and teaches the woods to sing with him, we ought to recall *Ecl.* 1.53–55, in which Meliboeus enviously tells Tityrus *hinc tibi, quae semper, vicino ab limite saepes / Hyblaeis apibus florem depasta salicti / saepe levi somnum suadebit inire susurro* ("on this side, as aforetime, on your neighbor's

---

36. It is well known (cf. e.g. Clausen 1994, 299 *ad loc.*) that the swineherds mentioned by Virgil are alien to the traditional bucolic world. Here we are forced into an intriguing but insoluble dilemma: Apuleius is perhaps "correcting" Virgil, by returning to Virgil's model, and replacing the swineherds with the more common literary choice of cowherds, such as are found in Theocritus. Apuleius' text could also be used (together with *Flor.* 3.3 *nihil aliud plerique callebant quam Vergilianus upilio seu busequa;* and *Apol.* 10.6 *Aemilianus, vir ultra Virgilianos opiliones et busequas rusticanus*) to support La Cerda's reading of the text of the *Eclogues* (bibliographical references are quoted by Clausen *ad loc.*), with *bubulci* instead of the transmitted *subulci*.

37. Cf. Finkelpearl 1998, 147: "The messenger's announcement underlines the uncertainty of literary genre . . . is this a tale, tragedy (drama), pastoral, or epic?"

border, the hedge whose willow blossoms are sipped by Hybla's bees shall often with its gentle hum soothe you to slumber"). In the immediately preceding lines (51–52), Meliboeus had imagined Tityrus enjoying the cool shade in his familiar spots along the streams and sacred springs; and Michael Putnam has shown that this *frigus* is "figurative for one aspect of the pastoral myth—the soul's absorption by poetry and spiritual calm . . . Tityrus' domain . . . is one of *fontis sacros*, of fountains sacred to the water nymphs, but also sources, perhaps, of that song which forms, with the landscape, an extended metaphor for the imagination itself."[38] The light drone of the bees is an important element in Meliboeus' description of Tityrus' pastoral song; as we are going to see shortly, this *levis susurrus*, once connected with the Theocritean picture of Nature signing alongwith the shepherds, has a metapoetic significance even stronger than the *frigus* mentioned above.

In contrast to Theocritus' ἁδὺ ψιθύρισμα, Virgil's *levis susurrus* obviously lacks any connection with Egypt; it is not strictly associated with the sound of a pipe (but cf. line 1 *avena*); nor does it appear in the very first verse of an entire poetic collection, which would be a highly prominent position. It consequently lacks the contextual elements that, for Gibson, had suggested a parallel with Apuleius' prologue. But, perhaps more importantly, the Virgilian *susurrus* puts Tityrus to sleep, and thus shares an element of enchantment with the Apuleian *susurrus*, since in the *Metamorphoses* the *levis susurrus* also has the purpose of enchanting the listeners' ears (*permulcere aures*). The verb *mulceo* is frequently connected with sleep;[39] and as we will see later, the expression *permulcere aures* is often used to describe the psychagogic effects of music and rhetoric. This all would seem to encourage us to place more emphasis on Virgil's first *Eclogue* than the Theocritean intertext. Another possible Virgilian element in the prologue, though it is less obvious, might be the phrase *Hymettos Attica*, one of the three elements of the prologue speaker's *vetus prosapia:* Mount Hymettos was renowned for honey and bees.[40] But while this hierarchy might clarify the intertextual structure of the phrase, it is certainly not enough to solve our problem: why should Apuleius hint at a bucolic author, be it Theocritus or Virgil, in the very beginning of his prologue?

---

38. Putnam 1970, 47 f. (cf. Hor. *Carm.* 3.13.9–12 and 1.17.17–20).

39. Cf. e. g. Virg. *Aen.* 7.754 f.; Ov. *Ep.* 18.27; *Met.* 8.824; 11.625; Plin. *Nat.* 10.136; Sil. 7.293; Stat. *Theb.* 2.30 f.; V. Fl. 1.299 f.; 2.140. In Apuleius, the case of Thelyphron at *Met.* 2.25.1 (*animum meum permulcebam cantationibus*) is exemplary: see Graverini 1998, 134.

40. See the commentary by Keulen 2007b, 76 *ad* 1.1.3 *Hymettos Attica* for sources on the metaphorical use of Hymettos and its honey in connection with the 'sweetness' of Attic oratory; in Apuleius' day it is also used satirically, to denounce "an excessively abundant and effeminately ornamental style."

To answer this question, let us focus for a moment on some significant innovations introduced by Virgil in his Theocritean description. Virgil's *susurrus* comes, like Theocritus' ψιθύρισμα, from a plant (a willow hedge in Virgil, a pine in Theocritus), but it is actually produced by the bees; it is not only sweet (ἁδύ in Theocritus, loosely echoed by *levis* in Virgil), but it also has a concrete effect on those who listen to it, since, as we have seen, it induces sleep (*somnum suadebit*). Bees and sleep are two important details that highlight the metapoetic character of Meliboeus' speech. At the beginning of Callimachus' *Aitia* and of Ennius' *Annales* (and cf. also Propertius 3.3) sleep and dreams are places of poetic initiation.[41] As for bees and honey, they were typically connected with poetry and with the Muses. For example, the bees are *Musarum volucres* in Varro, *Res rusticae* 3.16.7; and Plato, *Ion* 534a-b, exploiting the easy pun μέλη/μέλιτται, compares them to the poets: "the poets tell us . . . that the songs they bring us are the sweets they cull from honey-dropping founts . . . like the bees."[42] The bucolic setting and the welcoming landscape, resonating with many voices (the bees' drone, but also the song of the *frondator* and the cries of the *turtur* and *palumbae*), allow Tityrus to continue composing poetry, since music seems to be the result of the mutual efforts of shepherd and pastoral landscape (v. 5 *formosam resonare doces Amaryllida silvas*); Meliboeus, banished from this environment, will see his poetic spring dry up (v. 65 *carmina nulla canam*).[43]

Thus, there are several features, including Tityrus' sleep, that imbue Virgil's verses with metapoetic significance. The shepherd's sleep is induced by the bees, and this seems to be an unprecedented detail in ancient literature; but a comparison with another text will reveal the topical nature of many elements in Meliboeus' description of Tityrus and the peaceful countryside, and will also help us to establish a bridge between Virgil's first *Eclogue* and the *Metamorphoses*. In Chapter 6 of the *Vita Aesopi* (rec. G), Aesop, hot and tired from the hard work he has been doing, lies down under a tree. He ends up falling asleep after he has been enchanted (ψυχαγωγούμενος) by the sounds of nature (the gurgling of a stream, the songs of a nightingale and a blackbird, the rustle of the wind among the branches of olive and pine trees), which are all diffused with the echo of a melodious whisper

---

41. See Ennius, *Ann.* 1.5; on Callimachus' dream cf. also e.g. *AP* 7.42; Propertius 2.34.32. Pausanias 2.31.3 reports that "sleep is considered the god that is dearest to the Muses." Useful references and further bibliography on the topos in Massimilla 1996, 233–237. See Fantuzzi-Hunter 2004, 4 ff. on the dream in Herondas, *Mim.* 8.

42. See Scarcia 1964, 19–24 and Waszink 1974 for further occurrences of the topos.

43. Gutzwiller 1991, 85 (on Theocritus' first *Idyll*) points out that "the herdsmen through their music are not just in harmony with nature, but part of a continuum that fails to distinguish the two."

(εὐμελὲς ψιθύρισμα). In his sleep (Chapter 7), Aesop receives from Isis and the Muses the gift of speech and the ability to weave tales together (μύθων . . . πλοκήν).⁴⁴ This important passage in the *Vita*—where Aesop's future career as an orator and storyteller is established—appears to be curiously similar to Apuleius' prologue; and it would be easy to connect ψυχαγωγεῖν with *permulcere*, ψιθύρισμα with *susurrus*, and μύθων πλοκή with *fabulas conserere*. Yet I do not want to go so far as to suppose a direct link between the *Vita Aesopi* and Apuleius' prologue: just as in Virgil, here we have to deal with standard descriptive elements, and for most of them the obvious common source could be Theocritus' *Idylls* 1, 5, and 7. There is only one detail for which Theocritus offers no parallel: the psychagogic power of the *susurrus*/ψιθύρισμα, which induces Tityrus and Aesop to sleep, and enchants the reader of Apuleius (*aures permulcere*, on which see § 1.3.2 and 1.3.3). It is also worth noting that both Virgil and the *Vita Aesopi* describe the drone of bees and cicadas in their *loci amoeni*, so clearly investing them with symbolic value.

The image of insects provoking sleep and offering poetic inspiration, though absent in Theocritus, saw a wide diffusion in Hellenistic epigrams.⁴⁵ Both the grasshopper (ἀκρίς) and the cicada appear in an epigram by Anyte (*AG* 7.190), in which the maiden Myro cries over their death; Kathryn Gutzwiller suggests that Myro is a figure for the poetess, and the two insects symbolize her poetic inspiration.⁴⁶ The grasshopper is παραμύθιον ὕπνου ("persuading sleep") and λιγυπτέρυγος ("sweet-winged") in an epigram by Meleager (*AG* 7.195), where it inspires the poet, almost as a sort of Muse (v. 3 κρέκε μοί τι ποθεινόν, "play for me a love tune"). In another epigram (*AG* 7.196) Meleager prays to the cicada to put him to sleep and ease his suffering in love, while he takes shelter from the midday sun in the shade of a plane tree. These epigrams and others similar to them⁴⁷ confirm that insects such as grasshoppers and cicadas were commonly used as symbols for poetic inspiration in Hellenistic poetry; this symbolic value is clearly also present in Virgil's first *Eclogue*⁴⁸ and, with some differences, in the *Vita Aesopi*.

---

44. See Mignogna 1992 for a commentary on these chapters of the *Vita Aesopi*; for connections between the *Vita* and Apuleius' *Metamorphoses*, see Winkler 1985, 283–285 and Finkelpearl 2003, with further references; cf. below, § 2.6 pp. 89 f.
45. Cf. Gutzwiller 1998, 65–67, 113, 160–161, 320–321. A wealth of information on insects in ancient culture (including of course bees, cicadas, and grasshoppers) is offered by Davies-Kathirithamby 1986 and Beavis 1988.
46. Gutzwiller 1998, 66.
47. Cf. also *AG* 7.192; 193; 194; 197; 198; 6.120; 9.92.
48. Gutzwiller 1998, 320–321 suggests that the first verses of Virgil's first *Eclogue* echo Meleager's second epigram, quoted above. The Hellenistic poet imagines himself (v. 8) ὑπὸ σκιερᾷ κεκλιμένος

Meleager's poem contains a clue that leads us to an earlier text, itself probably the common source of some important details in these descriptions; this is none other than Plato's *Phaedrus*. Virgil introduces an innovation to the bucolic tradition not only by choosing bees instead of other insects, but also by placing Tityrus in the shade of a beech tree[49] instead of a pine or an oak; Meleager, with his plane tree, goes back to the very origins of the topos, to a text that we can consider as the archetype of most bucolic and non-bucolic *loci amoeni*. But in the *Phaedrus* a plane tree is the hallmark of the pleasant landscape that surrounds Phaedrus and Socrates (230 b–c).[50] This landscape also resonates with the sounds of nature, particularly the chirp of the cicadas. These insects are more than decorative elements; as Socrates will explain at 258e ff., they also represent a temptation and a warning for the two philosophers. Socrates tells Phaedrus that the cicadas were once men who, enchanted by the songs of the Muses, neglected food and drink until they died; afterwards, the cicadas were born from them and the Muses granted that they live without any food or drink, devoting all their time to songs and music. After the death of a mortal man, they report to the Muses how much and in what way he honored each of them. But, Socrates says, they are also dangerous: in the midday heat, with their mesmerizing voice, they can distract the philosopher so that he abandons his thought and nods off to sleep, just like the slaves who sit nodding under a shady tree, or the sheep that rest near a cool spring at noon. Philosophers must avoid being enchanted by the song of the cicada (remaining steadfastly ἀκηλήτους),

---

πλατάνῳ, and Tityrus is *patulae recubans sub tegmine fagi;* most of all, Meleager's cicada sings an ἀγρονόμαν . . . μοῦσαν, that corresponds very well to Tityrus' *silvestrem Musam*. In fact, Virgil's verbal choices might also be influenced by Theocritus (see the commentary by Clausen 1994, 34–35 *ad loc.*); yet, it is extremely likely that Meleager's epigram had a programmatic value, and maybe even the function of a proem to his whole poetic collection, as Gutzwiller suggests.

49. The beech was typical of Northern Italy and had no poetic pedigree: cf. Clausen 1994, 35.

50. On the almost automatic connection between the plane tree and Plato's dialogue, see Scaevola's words in Cicero, *De orat.* 1.28: "cur non imitamur, Crasse, Socratem illum, qui est in Phaedro Platonis? Nam me haec tua platanus admonuit, quae non minus ad opacandum hunc locum patulis est diffusa ramis, quam illa, cuius umbram secutus est Socrates." Crassus agrees, but he wishes to be more comfortable than Socrates, who sat on the grass, and so offers chairs and pillows to his guests: an overly primitive bucolic setting does not fit Cicero's characters. Cf. also *Leg.* 2.7, where the origin of the Muses is mentioned by people conversing under a plane tree, as in the *Phaedrus*. In Latin bucolic poetry, the plane tree reappears in Calpurnius Siculus 4.2; cf. Martial 3.58 on this tree as a feature of "artificial" landscapes. In the Greek novel, see the highly allusive passage in Achilles Tatius 1.2.3 (on which see Graverini 2010). See also Borghini 1991 on the chthonic symbolism attached to the plane tree. On the importance of Plato's *Phaedrus* for bucolic poetry, and more generally for descriptions of *loci amoeni*, cf. e.g. Hunter 1999, 14 and 145 f.; Gutzwiller 1991, 233 n. 18; Fantuzzi-Hunter 2004, 143 ff., with further references.

just as Odysseus resisted the enchanting song of the Sirens.[51] We should note that Plato attributes an hypnotic power to the cicadas: although their chirp is sometimes referred to as a *cantus* (as at Apuleius, *Flor.* 13.1), other traditions characterize it as annoying, and as preventing sleep instead (e.g. Phaedrus 3.16).[52]

The cicadas then, like the bees, are closely connected to poetry and to the Muses.[53] The two insects are explicitly associated to each other, for example, in Virgil's fifth *Eclogue*, in which Menalcas says that Daphnis' praises will be sung "so long as the bees feed on thyme and the cicadas on dew" (1.77): this clearly signifies "so long as there will be (bucolic) poetry." Aelianus (*NA* 5.13) claims that "what the divine Plato says of cicadas and their love of song and music one might equally say of the choir of bees."[54] The function of the cicadas is ambiguous in Plato, as a consequence of the philosopher's dubious appraisal of artistic activities. Thanks to the report the insects give to the Muses at their death, men can obtain a valuable gift that is probably to make them even more skilled and inspired in the arts they practice;[55] but the cicadas are also compared to the Sirens, whose sweet and melodious voice

---

51. Plato, *Phdr.* 258e–259a. Ferrari 1987, 27 comments: "Phaedrus . . . as cultural 'impresario' . . . has a tendency to promote clever talk for its own sake, indiscriminately. I propose that through the myth of the cicadas Plato takes his stand against this tendency in such a way as to admonish the readers that they too . . . must beware of careless discrimination among the breeds of intellectual discourse." For Gutzwiller 1991, 77 divine possession and poetic inspiration are "a danger as well as a necessity in the philosopher's search for the truth" in the *Phaedrus*. The myth of the cicadas is usually considered to be Plato's own invention: see e.g. White 1993, 183.

52. The same ambiguity is attached to the bees: Pliny, who defines the chirp of the cicadas with the noun *stridor*, uses *murmur* for the drone of the bees (*Nat.* 11.266), and so seems to consider the latter more agreeable. At *Aen.* 7.65 Virgil uses *stridor* for the drone of the bees. Leaving aside for the moment such subjective assessments as the pleasant or hypnotic character of the sounds produced by cicadas and bees, it must be noted that the sweetness and shrillness of a sound seem to be closely connected qualities in ancient Greek literature. We find in Callimachus' *Aitia* that cicadas sing with a λιγὺς ἦχος (1.29); Trypanis 1958 translates "shrill voice," and D'Alessio 1996 a "sharp sound" (*suono acuto*), but λιγύς contains also the notion of "melodious" and "sweet": see e.g. Stephanus s.v. ("Stridulus, Argutus, s. Argutum stridens: interdum et Canorus, Iucundus . . . Suaviter loquens"), and especially Hesychius' lemma λιγυρόν· ἡδύ, γλυκύ. Λιγύς is also used to describe the Muses in Homer, *Od.* 24.62, and Plato, *Phdr.* 237a; cf. Virgil, *Georg.* 2.475 (quoted also by Tacitus, *Dial.* 13.5) *dulces . . . Musae*. Λιγυρός describes the Sirens' song in Homer, *Od.* 12.44 and 183, while Apollonius Rhodius 4.893 f. ἡδείῃσι / θέλγουσαι μολπῇσιν corresponds to Homer's λιγυρῇ θέλγουσιν ἀοιδῇ.

53. As we have seen, this connection also exists in Callimachus; cf. also Theocritus 1.148 "your singing is as delightful as the cicada's chirping in spring."

54. On the symbolic value of both bees and cicadas, see Roscalla 1998, 60–75; and cf. above, n. 43.

55. Cf. White 1993, 184–185.

represents a dangerous temptation.⁵⁶ Cicadas—that is, music and art—can be an incitement to philosophy, but also a deadly risk if they are appreciated *per se*.

While Socrates and Phaedrus want to resist sleep and not to yield to the enchanting power of the cicadas, Meliboeus envies Tityrus precisely because he will be allowed to sleep, lulled by the sweet *susurrus* of the bees; and Aesop will obtain the gift of speech only when he sleeps, under the hypnotic effect of a ψιθύρισμα to which the chirp of the cicadas also contributes. The *locus amoenus* described by Plato is undoubtedly an inescapable model for later philosophical and literary texts, but in a somewhat paradoxical fashion, it is by resorting to Plato's imagery that some authors—among them Virgil, the author of the *Vita Aesopi*, and the authors of several Greek epigrams—confer on literary and poetic production a higher and autonomous value, one that is not a consequence of its usefulness to philosophical reasoning or to the life of the *polis*.⁵⁷

In sum, when he describes the speaking voice of the prologue as a *lepidus susurrus*, Apuleius possibly has in mind the *levis susurrus* of Virgil's bees and the literary tradition that, starting with Plato, charged a *locus amoenus* with literary and philosophical significance. Whether or not we have such a direct allusion on our hands here, the background I have outlined for *lepidus susurrus* (indeed, a curious way in itself of describing the narrator's voice)

---

56. See Capra 2007 on Plato's complex attitude towards poetry; Capra 2000 is especially helpful on the myth of the cicadas. Nehamas 1999, 329–330 suggests that the fact that Socrates leaves Athens together with Phaedrus (and Socrates, it is well known, did not at all like to leave the city) is a sort of variation on the theme of Odysseus reluctantly leaving Ithaca to join the Achaean army; from this point of view, the mention of the Sirens in the *Phaedrus* contributes to Socrates' Odyssean quality (a feature that will be inherited by the homonymous character in Apuleius: cf. Münstermann 1995, 8–26). On the ambiguous role of the cicadas in Plato's dialogue, see also White 1993, 190: "To be enamored of the Muses to such an extent that one ceases to be concerned with the body is a vice rather than a virtue, and the fact that human beings who lived their lives this way were reborn as cicadas testifies to this one-dimensional and inferior mode of existence."

57. The prologue to Callimachus' *Aitia* can also be interpreted as a sort of reaction to Plato's stance towards poetry and poets. Hunter 1989, 1, commenting on the poet's desire to be a slight and winged insect (frg. 1.32 οὐλαχύς, ὁ πτερόεις), notes that "the reference is to the cicada, but the language can hardly be other than a reworking of the famous words which Plato puts in Socrates' mouth at *Ion* 534b: κοῦφον γὰρ χρῆμα ποιητής ἐστιν καὶ πτηνὸν καὶ ἱερόν." It is possible that the locus amoenus from the Phaedrus played a role in Callimachus' text, perhaps connecting Callimachus' dream to the polemic against the Telchines; and if the dream was set in the midday heat, then the chirp of the cicadas might have linked the first fragment to the second (Hunter 1989, 2). If this conjecture is correct, then Callimachus' *Aitia* might have been an intermediary between Plato's *Phaedrus* and Moelibeus' description of Tityrus sleeping while the bees drone around him (*Ecl.* 1.53 ff.).

allows us to catch a glimpse of its implicit metaliterary significance.[58] In the following pages I will attempt to confirm and qualify this claim.

1.3.2 Between *utile* and *dulce*

A *susurrus* can be a magic spell pronounced in a low voice,[59] and this is the meaning of the term *susurramen* derived from it, appearing at 1.3.1 (where Aristomenes' skeptical fellow traveler claims that Aristomenes' tale is a lie, just as if someone said that a magic *susurramen* can reverse the flow of a river). But even in less extreme cases, a *susurrus* often implies some form of danger or deception: at 5.6.1 Cupid, finally defeated by his wife's *Venerius susurrus*, allows her sisters to visit her, even though he knows what dangers could come out of it (she is clearly well-conscious of persuasive power, as is Venus with Vulcan in *Aen.* 8.370 ff.); and at 8.10.1 Thrasyllus tries to entice Charite with his *susurri improbi*. By using this terminology, the speaking *ego* of the prologue tries to secure the complete and undivided attention of his reader, who is lured into joining a potentially dangerous narrative project. Lucius himself, the main character of the novel, is the best example of hazardous abandon to the seduction of magic and love; the pleasure of listening to good stories also puts him in danger, since Aristomenes' tale is one of the reasons listed at 2.1.2 for his growing curiosity in magic.[60] The prologue is

---

58. Trapp 2001, 41 already suggested, but very hesitantly, that Apuleius' prologue hints at Plato's description of the "bewitching buzz of the cicadas": "I would like to be able to see another echo of this scene [*sc. Phdr.* 258e–259d] in Apuleius' soothingly sibilant *aures . . . lepido susurro permulceam . . . ,* but I am not sure that I can." Of course I support his hypothesis; and I also share his opinion that, in Apuleius' prologue, "the Plato of the *Phaedrus* is . . . invoked not as an ally but as an adversary" (p. 41): Apuleius seems to adopt the poetics of the cicadas (that is, a poetics mostly concerned with musical and magical incantation) here, rather than that of Socrates (a truthful and useful poetics). Schlam 1992, 46 f. offers another Platonizing interpretation, but a very different one: "*permulcere . . .* recurs in the *Metamorphoses* with the sense of offering verbal therapy," just as according to Plato, some myths can ἐπᾴδειν, produce a positive enchantment that leads to wisdom, like the καλοὶ λόγοι in *Charm.* 157a. However, the argumentation in the *Charmides* has nothing to do with the narration of myth: curiously, Schlam is quoting tendentiously a passage from Plato that is quoted tendentiously (though in a different way) by Apuleius himself at *Apol.* 26.5 (see Hunink 1997, 2: 90 *ad loc.*). In any case, Plato is obviously an important model for Apuleius, who had renown as *philosophus Platonicus*: see e.g. Harrison 2000, 252–259, who however warns that the primary function of Platonic allusions in the novel is "that of entertaining literary and cultural display" (p. 255), and not of offering the reader a sketch of Platonic philosophy. The *Phaedrus*, in particular, is also a model for the ending of the story of Socrates: see § 3.1. In general, Trapp 1990, 141 states that "few works were more firmly entrenched in the 'cultural syllabus' of Hellenic *paideia* by the second century A.D. than Plato's *Phaedrus*."

59. On the magic meaning of *murmur*, see Baldini Moscadi 2005, 165–174.

60. This establishes an important parallel between Lucius and the reader of the novel: see below, n. 69.

therefore both an invitation and a warning; but even more than that, it is, as I have shown in the previous pages, an initial outline offered to the reader, describing what kind of literary product he holds in his hands.

If we put this terminology into the appropriate context, the novel's self-presentation appears to be a form of provocation. Any literate second century reader would be well aware of the never-ending debate, dating back to Plato, between the supporters of a psychagogic approach to literature and rhetoric, and those who preferred to stress the moral and pedagogical purposes of the work of cultured men. In the *Phaedrus,* the cicadas have the power to induce sleep, a power that clearly antagonizes the philosopher, and that he must fight to overcome, since his main concern is truth, not enchantment. On the other hand, different texts, such as Virgil's *Eclogues* and the *Vita Aesopi,* apparently suggest a very different perspective. Of course, there were also attempts at finding a happy medium. Horace, for example, is well aware of the psychagogic power of poetry, as he expresses in the *Ars poetica* lines 99–100: "it is not enough for poems to have beauty (*pulchra esse*): they must have charm (*dulcia sunto*), and lead the hearer's soul where they will."[61] At lines 333 f. he depicts a form of compromise between the two positions: "poets aim either to benefit, or to amuse (*prodesse aut delectare*), or utter words at once both pleasing and helpful to life"; and at 343 f. he continues "he has won every vote who has blended profit and pleasure (*qui miscuit utile dulci*), at once delighting and instructing the reader."[62] By way of contrast, bucolic poetry defines its literary space as closer to *utile* than to *dulce*. In this vein Richard Hunter, commenting on the adjective ἁδύ that tellingly opens Theocritus' first *Idyll,* points out that

> the pleasure (τὸ τερπνόν, *dulce, iucundum*) that poetry brings had been a battleground for Plato and Aristotle, and one branch of Hellenistic theory . . . privileged poetry's emotional appeal, its ψυχαγωγία, over any moral or educational claims it might have. On this view, 'bucolic poetry' will have no effect in the world in which it is performed—goats go on being goats, and Daphnis' *pathos* will become . . . purely a subject for our aesthetic appreciation.[63]

---

61. See Brink 1971, 182 on the distinction between *pulchrum* and *dulce,* καλόν and ἡδύ.

62. Boethius is implicitly trying to find the same balance when after a speech by Philosophy, he comments *iam cantum illa finiverat cum me audiendi avidum stupentemque arrectis adhuc auribus carminis mulcedo defixerat* (*De consolatione philosophiae* 3.1).

63. Hunter 1999, 70.

In other contexts, Apuleius himself strikes a different sort of balance. At *Florida* 17.9–10 he compares the human voice to the sound of several musical instruments, and at first the human voice seems not to fare well: the trumpet has a more powerful and fierce sound, the lyre offers more harmonic possibilities, the flute is more moving, the pan-pipe is more agreeable, and the horn can be heard from farther off (and note that the wording seems to recall the prologue of the novel: *tuba rudore torvior . . . fistula susurru iucundior*). Yet although it is inferior in so many respects, the human voice has the advantage of being "more useful to the mind than agreeable to the ear" (13): it can therefore be used to declaim an *utile carmen* in front of large audiences, especially like the one Apuleius will present as a panegyric to the proconsul Scipio Orfitus.[64] This *carmen* will be, in Horace's manner, *nec minus gratum quam utile* (19).

The prologue to the *Metamorphoses* leads us into a totally different literary space. The voice that addresses us is a sweet *susurrus*, and the speaking *ego* of the prologue seems not to take into account the element of the *utile*, which for a large part of ancient culture might have colored literary endeavors with at least a patina of dignity. Several of Apuleius' ancient readers did not follow Fulgentius in an attempt to rehabilitate the novel through an allegorical interpretation, and drew conclusions from the prologue that reflected their disapproval of literature without *utilitas*; needless to say, this strategy is clearly not the one and only way we can reach a "true" interpretation of the *Metamorphoses*. Macrobius (*Somn.* 1.2.8) set out to make a clear distinction between *fabulae* (that is, false tales) that are told only to offer pleasure to the ears of their audience (*tantum conciliandae auribus voluptatis . . . gratia*) and those that have moral or philosophical merits. Apuleius' novel, together with Petronius' *Satyricon* and Menander's comedies, is among the tales that *auditum mulcent:* they stimulate the ear, but have nothing to do with *sapientia*. They are pastimes for children, Macrobius says, like the stories told by wet nurses.[65] According to the *Historia Augusta* (*Alb.* 12.12), in a letter to the Senate Septimius Severus referred to Apuleius' novel with the phrases *Punicae Milesiae* and *neniae aniles*, "old women's lullabies." Both Macrobius and Septimius Severus voice the contempt that philosophy and "serious" literature traditionally held for fictional narrative, on the grounds that it had no educational purpose. Most interestingly, they do so with words that seem to have been taken from Apuleius' novel: the prologue's *aures permulcere*

---

64. For more on Scipio Orfitus, proconsul of Africa in 163/4, see the *Florida* commentaries by Hunink 2001, A. La Rocca 2005, and Lee 2005.

65. On some interpretive problems in Macrobius' passage, see § 2.7.1 p. 97 n. 134.

appears in Macrobius, and in the text of Septimius' letter from the *Historia Augusta* one finds the term *anilis fabula,* used by Apuleius at 4.27.8 for the tale of *Cupid and Psyche* (itself a topical definition for false myths and tales with no rational basis, whose history goes as far back as Plato).[66]

Whoever enjoys this kind of literature, whether as an author or as a reader, exposes himself to some risk, symbolized by the possibility of undergoing an unpleasant metamorphosis. First, his reputation is in jeopardy, as is well shown by the contempt Macrobius and the *Historia Augusta* clearly feel for authors and readers of fictional narrative.[67] The literary tradition offers several instructive stories about what can happen to readers or listeners who cannot make intelligent choices and distinguish what is important from what is pointless. In Ovid's *Metamorphoses,* king Midas is the prototype of the incompetent listener, who prefers the *leve carmen* Pan plays on his *calamum agreste* to the solemn notes Apollo raises with his precious ivory lyre inlaid with gems: as a punishment, he grows the ears of a donkey (*induitur . . . aures lente gradientis aselli:* 11.179). Midas' ears were already proverbial in Aristophanes (*Pl.* 287), and were a natural metaphor for those who listen and do not understand.[68] In light of this, perhaps, the prologue speaker's emphasis on the ears of his audience (*aures tuas . . . permulceam*) might raise some suspicion; especially since it urges the audience to listen attentively to a literary work of a rather ambiguous nature, whose main character is going to be transformed into an ass. The reader (or listener) might indeed be taking the same risk as Lucius, since the novel could have the same effect on him as magic will have on the main character.[69] But it is not only a matter of reputation, bad literary choices, and inattentive reception of stories: an animal metamorphosis can serve as a metaphor for the

---

66. See § 2.7. This topos is wittily exploited by Margaret Doody, *Poison in Athens* (London: 2004), ch. 6, p. 99: the hetaira Phrines, when she is about to tell the patrons of a brothel a story whose main character is a Milesian woman, says: "Just pretend I'm your old nurse, my little babes."

67. The same contempt for "Milesian" narrative is shown by several texts quoted below, § 1.6 pp. 48–49; see also Keulen 2007b, 64 f. for *Milesio* as "generic term for popular fiction of doubtful literary quality."

68. See e.g. Aelius Aristides 28.144; Dio Chrysostom 32.101; Persius 1.121; Horace, *Epist.* 2.1.199 f. compares an incompetent audience to a deaf donkey. Cf. pseudo-Plutarch, *De proverbiis Alexandrinorum* 32: "somebody told a tale, a μῦθος, to a donkey: and it only shook its ears."

69. See below, pp. 138–40 on Lucius' dangerous *curiositas,* which has been piqued by Aristomenes' story. James 2001, 260 claims that the promise to "stroke the ears" of the listeners to the prologue "implies an asinine but attentive audience." For Gowers 2001, 78 the expression *permulcere aures* places emphasis "on the reader's most *asinine* [author's emphasis] characteristic, his ears—ears which are slow to respond unless they are repeatedly cajoled, or excited into curiosity. So it comes about that the reader is transformed into a forerunner for the narrator Lucius." See also Krabbe 1989, 13–14; James 1991, 170; Münstermann 1995, 70, following Schlam 1970, 179 f.; Graverini 2005a, 177 and 193 f.; and cf. below, § 3.4 pp. 154 ff.

wrong moral and philosophical positions that could be derived from reading and interpretation. A codex of Heliodorus (*Ven. Marc. gr.* 410) preserves, together with the novel, the beginning of an allegorical interpretation of the novel itself, attributed to an otherwise unknown "Philip the philosopher."[70] The introduction to this small treatise uses an allegorical interpretation of the Homeric episode of Circe to describe the *Aithiopika* as follows:[71]

> This book, my friends, is very much like Circe's brew: those who take it in a profane manner, it transforms into licentious pigs, but those who approach it in a philosophical way, in the manner of Odysseus, it initiates into higher things.

In sum, the prologue offers us a "sweet" and psychagogic kind of literature, apparently unconcerned with anything *utile,* and able to entice its reader with an almost magical and possibly dangerous power; Lucius' asinine metamorphosis seems to symbolize the perils connected with a total and irresponsible abandon to the enchantments of narrative. In the next section we will see that this literary program is linked to a discussion concerning the correct attitude of the rhetor and the ultimate significance of his actions, one that was well-attested and of great importance in ancient culture. This debate presents the concrete aspect of a more general problem: the correct balance of *utile* and *dulce.*

1.3.3 An alluring rhetoric

At first glance, rhetoric would not necessarily appear to be helpful in constructing a hermeneutic approach to the prologue. *Ego tibi* seems to describe a very private, one-to-one relationship between speaker and listener—quite

---

70. The text of Philip's *Hermeneuma* has been published by Hercher 1869; Aristide Colonna includes it among Heliodorus' *testimonia* in his edition (Colonna 1938, 365–370). Lamberton 1986, 306–311 gives the English translation from which I quote. According to Acconcia Longo 1991, Philip is to be placed in Constantinople, in the fifth century; for more information, and different hypotheses, see Stramaglia 1996a, 141–143; MacAlister 1996, 108–112; Sandy 2001; Hunter 2005. See also below § 2.8 p. 130.
71. Cf. also Porphyry in Stobaeus, *Ecl.* 1.49.60; while commenting on Circe's episode, he says (I quote the English translation by Lamberton 1986, 115–117) that "those who are taken over and dominated by the appetitive part of the soul, blossoming forth at the moment of transformation and rebirth, enter the bodies of asses and animals of that sort (ὀνώδη σώματα) to lead turbulent lives made impure by love of pleasure and by gluttony." In pseudo-Plutarch, *De vita Homeri* 126, Circe is a symbol for the cycle of metensomatosis, to which Odysseus, being an ἔμφρων ἀνήρ, is immune.

different from *ego vobis,* a standard opening addressed to an audience.[72] In the passage from the *Florida* I have quoted above (17.9–10) Apuleius says that, since the human voice is such an important divine gift, it needs to be constantly exercised, especially in front of large audiences (17.4); and "he who is going to produce a song that will benefit men, adults, and the elderly should sing before thousands" (17.18). The voice of a good rhetor needed to be loud and clear enough to be heard by a large audience,[73] even though its volume had to be varied in accordance with the *pathos* of the speech; some sources attest that the volume of the voice was a subject for discussion and polemics among rhetors. A Sallustian fragment preserved by Fronto is an accusation against those who *murmurantium voculis in loco eloquentiae oblectantur,* "take delight by way of eloquence in the soft notes of whisperers";[74] and Fronto himself reproaches his august disciple because he prefers "a whisper and a mumble to a trumpet-note," *murmurare et friguttire potius quam clangere.*[75] On the contrary, the voice that narrates the *Metamorphoses* is, at least at the beginning, a weak whisper.

Nevertheless, rhetorical polemic becomes extremely important if we take into account the verbal expressions used by the prologue to describe its narrative style and voice, since the passage suggests an ambiguous pretense of orality.[76] Wytse Keulen has clearly shown that the prologue presents the *Metamorphoses* as a narration whose style is effeminate and theatrical, in strong contrast to the traditional rules of rhetoric: "it seems that the *ego* in the prologue avows exactly the kind of rhetoric against which professors of rhetoric warned."[77] In the next few pages I will generally adhere to Keulen's line of reasoning, but will also add several parallels, and include a survey of the evidence from Greek rhetoric.

The key issue here is the prologue speaker's promise "to caress your ears" (*aures tuas . . . permulceam*). According to Cicero, the good orator should

---

72. Cf. e.g. Cicero, *Agr.* 2.102; *Caec.* 9; *Mur.* 90.

73. At *Met.* 3.29.3 the donkey tries in vain to speak as an orator in the Forum, and his hee-haw is *disertum ac validum.*

74. *Ant.* 4.3 pp. 143,15 f. VdH (the fragment has not been included in Sallust's editions so far), on which see La Penna 1973. Sophocles gives a whispering voice to Odysseus, who in the Homeric tradition was a skilled orator (see § 1.3.4), when he needs to highlight his skills as a dangerous deceiver: *Ajax* 148 f. Τοιούσδε λόγους ψιθύρους πλάσσων / εἰς ὦτα φέρει πᾶσιν Ὀδυσσεύς, / καὶ σφόδρα πείθει. On Odysseus as a liar, see below, § 3.2 p. 144 n. 26.

75. *Ant.* 2.16 p. 140,4 VdH.

76. Cf. § 3.3.

77. Keulen 2003a, 18; cf. also 2007a and 2007b, 21f. His point is anticipated in Trapp 2001, esp. 44 f.; Nicolai 1999, 145 points out that the phrase *lepido susurro permulceam* "brings us us into a lexical space in between literary criticism (hence the use of rhetorical terminology) and the psychagogic effects of music." For a slightly different perspective, see Schlam 1992, 50f.

not completely avoid the search for auditory pleasure: in *Orator* 163, for example, he says that "there are two things that charm the ear (*quae permulceant auris*), sound and rhythm"; and soon after (164) he considers the *iudicium . . . aurium* as an important criterion for evaluating the *numerosa oratio*. And yet Cicero's relatively tolerant position did not become an unchallenged standard in later rhetorical treatises, and may have had no formative influence on the most common trends of thought on this subject. Quintilian, in particular, allows his orator to offer auditory pleasure only in epideictic speeches, which are written *ad delectationem audientium* and can show off more grace and sophistication (11.1.48); but generally speaking Quintilian uses *aures (per)mulcere* to describe the effect of a corrupt and reprehensible rhetorical style, used by incompetent orators to please a foolish audience.[78]

At 11.3.57–60 he provides us with more details about this degenerate rhetoric. The worst habit of his contemporaries, he says, was the so-called "singing style" adopted by rhetors who declaimed in a melodious, almost singsong tone; their attitude, Quintilian argues, is more appropriate to the stage or to drunken rants than to a courtroom. This ear-soothing style, although reprimanded by old-fashioned teachers, was widely accepted, and this fact explains why Quintilian condemns it so insistently and so harshly, going so far as to say that it reflects a moral flaw in its practitioners. Acting in this case as the defender of the traditional austerity of Rome against the laxity of the East, he condemns this style as foreign (since it originated in Lycia and Caria)[79] and as unworthy of the Forum and Roman courthouses.[80]

This "singing style," as Maud Gleason has pointed out, was widely perceived as a threat to the *Romanitas* and even to the masculinity of orators.[81]

---

78. Quintilian, *Inst.* 2.12.6; 9.4.116; 11.3.60; 12.10.52. More generally, the phrase *aures (per)mulcere* is often linked to literary and rhetorical criticism: see Cicero, *Orat.* 163; Fronto, *Aur.* 1.9.3 pp. 17–18 Van den Hout; Gellius 20.9.1. In different contexts, it is mainly poetic: Horace, *Epist.* 1.16.26; Ovid, *Met.* 5.561; *Trist.* 2.1.358; Silius Italicus 11.288 ff.
79. Phrygia and Caria for Cicero, *Orat.* 57 *est autem etiam in dicendo quidam cantus obscurior, non hic e Phrygia et Caria rhetorum epilogus paene canticum, sed ille quem significat Demosthenes et Aeschines*. However, Cicero was careful not to generalize and not to censure this style as only Greek: *Orat.* 25 *Caria et Phrygia et Mysia, quod minime politae minimeque elegantes sunt, adsciverunt aptum suis auribus opimum quoddam et tanquam adipale dictionis genus quod eorum vicini non ita lato interiecto mari Rhodii nunquam probaverunt, Graeci autem multo minus, Athenienses vero funditus repudiaverunt*.
80. *Inst.* 11.3.57–60.
81. Gleason 1995, xxvii, 112 f., 117 f., 124 f. A large collection of sources for such rhetorical polemics was offered first by Norden 1898, 294 f., 372 ff. Of course, the debate on singsong *pronuntiatio* is an aspect of the more general polemic on the usage of psychagogic stratagems that stir up the passions of the audience without using reason to convince them; on the earliest examples of this polemic in Republican Rome, see G. Moretti 2002. This debate is often connected with larger concerns about the penetration of Greek culture into Rome. On the rhetoric and cultural conflict between Greece and Rome in the second century C.E., see Norden 1898, 362, for whom "the influence of Greek upon

Quintilian, for example, clearly states that he does not wish "the boy ... to talk with the shrillness of a woman or in the tremulous accents of old age" (1.11.1; cf. also 11.3.91). This polemic is so pervasive that it makes even Quintilian and Seneca (two otherwise antithetical personalities) agree with each other: the philosopher writes to his friend Lucilius against the "degenerate style of speech ... modulated like the music of a concert piece" (*Epist.* 114.1: *corrupti generis oratio ... in morem cantici ducta*) so popular in his day. A letter to Marcus Aurelius from Fronto also testifies to the persistence of this view in the second century, albeit in less heated language.[82]

In this context, the prologue speaker's promise to *permulcere aures* and the following mention of a *vocis immutatio* (1.1.6), for which he feels obliged to apologize,[83] seem to manifest a deliberate stance in an ancient, but still relevant dispute. We can also say that these phrases contribute to the Greek coloring of the prologue, since in Rome such rhetorical characteristics were cast as typical of Greece and Asia.[84] Other Greek elements in the prologue are suggested also by the mention of *sermo Milesius* (1.1.1), by the speaking *ego*'s Greek origins (1.1.3 *Hymettos Attica* ...), and by the definition of *fabula Graecanica* applied to the novel (1.1.6). After all, the *vocis immutatio* seems to be one of the features in the prologue that makes the narrator's Latin an *exoticus sermo* (1.1.5). Yet we should also recall that the polemic against the "singing style," and more generally against the psychagogic powers of rhetoric, was by no means limited to the Roman world.

Aelius Aristides, for example, harshly criticizes rhetors who exploit the most sophisticated tricks of rhetoric but lose sight of the higher goals of their trade—in a word, the "sophists."[85] Their main purpose is, according

---

Latin was never greater." See also e.g. Walker 2000, 94; G. Anderson 1990, 99; according to Russell 1990b, 17 in the second century "*Graecia victa* was establishing her victory more and more securely"; and for Whitmarsh 2001, 10 "Hellenism is both a resource and a threat."

82. *Aur.* 1.9.3 pp. 17–18 VdH: *Hic summa illa virtus oratoris atque ardua est, ut non magno detrimento recta eloquentia auditores oblectet; eaque delenimenta, quae mulcendis volgi auribus conparat, ne cum multo ac magno dedecore fucata sint: potius ut in conpositionis structuraeque mollitia sit delictum quam in sententia inpudentia: vestem quoque lanarum mollitia delicatam esse quam colore muliebri, filo tenui aut serico, purpuream ipsam, non luteam nec crocatam.*

83. On *vocis immutatio* as a "modulation of the voice" that is connected with the singing style mentioned above, see Keulen 2007a and 2007b, 88 f. *ad loc.*, with several parallels and a thorough bibliography. However, I would not exclude, as Keulen does in his commentary, the possibility that the phrase is *also* a metaphor for the "translation" of the ass-story from Greek to Latin (he is more receptive to alternative interpretations in the second study I have quoted). Note that *immutare* also has magic overtones: cf. Bettini 1991, 26 ff. on Plautus, *Amph.* 456 *ubi immutatus sum?* Therefore, the phrase might have an implicit "metamorphical" meaning, similar to that probably implied by *rudis locutor* (cf. above, pp. 10–11).

84. See again Keulen 2007a; 2007b, 88 f.

85. On Aristides' polemic against the "sophists," see Behr 1994, 1163–1223; Moreschini 1994b,

to Aristides, γαργαλίσαι τὰ ὦτα, "to titillate the ears" of their audience,[86] rather than to convince them with reason (34.17 ἄγειν καὶ πείθειν); in so doing, they disclose their weak and limp nature (34.16 μαλακίζεσθαι), and end up seeming effeminate or, even worse, like eunuchs (34.18).[87] The same terminology recurs in the works of the Christian rhetor Clement of Alexandria and in several other Greek authors:[88] in Greek as well as in Latin, it seems, to "stroke" or to "soothe" the ears was adopted as a technical term in the arsenal of rhetorical polemics. But the criticism of overly musical rhetoric was widespread, even beyond the use of this polemical phrase; see for example Plutarch, for whom many sophists "sweeten their voice by certain harmonious modulations and softenings and rhythmic cadences, as to ravish away and transport their hearers" (*de recta ratione audiendi* 41d).

As for Aristides, the target of his attacks was probably Favorinus of Arles,[89] who provided the most notorious Greek example of an effeminate, musical, and enchanting voice. According to Philostratus (*VS* 491), when Favorinus "delivered discourses in Rome . . . even those who did not understand the Greek language shared in the pleasure that he gave," since "he fascinated (ἔθελγε) even them by the tones of his voice." In the same passage, Philostratus disapproves of Favorinus' singsong declamatory style that let him have such a great effect on his large audiences. In the *Demonax* (12), Lucian connects Favorinus' "sweet" rhetoric with his effeminacy. Demonax ridiculed the "singing style" exhibited by Favorinus, criticizing it as effeminate and shameful for a philosopher. Favorinus asks Demonax just who he thought he was to make fun of him, and he answered "a man with an ear that is not easy to cheat." The eunuch rhetor was not yet satisfied, and asked Demonax exactly what one needed to become a philosopher; with wit (if without grace) Demonax answered "ὄρχεις"—"balls."

1235 f.

86. On this invective by Aelius Aristides, see Norden 1898, 374 f.

87. Quintilian, *Inst.* 1.8.2 recommends a *lectio* that is not *in cantico dissoluta nec plasmate . . . effeminata*.

88. Clement of Alexandria, *Strom.* 1.3.22.5. Cf. also Epiphanius, *Haer.* 3.333; Joannes Chrysostomos, *De sancta Thecla martyre* 50.748; Theodoretus, *Interpretatio in Ezechielem* 81.917. Cf. also Suidas, delta 1603, where γαργαλίζειν is explained as "to make laugh and to persuade"; and Anon. *In Aristotelis artem rhetoricam commentarium* 161, which describes the rhetors' temptation to titillate the listener with flowery diction. Similar phrases are constructed with less colorful verbs than γαργαλίζειν, such as κηλεῖν; there are other texts worth mentioning, e.g. Eusebius' *De laudibus Constantini*, on which see §1.6.

89. Or, according to Behr 1981, 399 n. 34, Polemo of Thasos. On the contraposition between Aristides and Favorinus, see Gleason 1995, 125 (and 122 on Aristides' speech quoted in the text). On the contrary, some scholars highlight a sort of spiritual affinity between Favorinus and Apuleius: cf. below, p. 173 and n. 23.

The prologue, then, heralds a fascinating, musical style, which could certainly appear "Greekish" to a Roman, but which generally speaking was unwelcome to anyone who held a more conservative view of rhetoric, whether Greek or Roman. This style has also been denigrated in the modern era: Eduard Norden, for example, deplores the fact that Apuleius "applies in the most extravagant ways all the antics that serve the softest melodiousness," and censures "the immoderate use of the most striking and spicy figures that resonate in the ears like the jingling of bells";[90] and Giuseppina Magnaldi, in a study on the Apuleian edition *in usum Delphini*, reminds us that there was a general prejudice against the *horror affectatae compositionis qui aures laedere poterat*.[91] The phrase *aures laedere* represents a similar acoustic stylistic assessment, guarding, as it were, against such rhetoric. Across the centuries rhetorical polemics show a surprising stability in regard to their imagery and the terminology used to express it.

There is also a certain consistency in Apuleius' programmatic statements. The text suggests a striking parallel between the prologue speaker and the old woman who narrates the tale of *Cupid and Psyche:* compare *Met.* 1.1.1 *at ego tibi . . . varias fabulas conseram auresque tuas . . . lepido susurro permulceam* ("but I would like to tie together different sorts of tales for you . . . and to caress your ears into approval with a sweet whisper") with 4.27.8 *sed ego te narrationibus lepidis anilibusque fabulis protinus avocabo* ("but right now I shall divert you with a pretty story and an old wife's tale").[92] We might wonder whether the prologue speaker is supposed to have the same trembling and feminine voice that we might expect of the old woman (the same kind of voice, in fact, that Quintilian *Inst.* 1.11.1 advised his pupils not to imitate, as we have seen above); but the analogies go well beyond this point. I have suggested elsewhere that this delirious and drunken old woman (6.25.1 *delira et temulenta . . . anicula*) is characterized as a degraded epic storyteller, since the adjectives *delira et temulenta* represent two common features of the poet, especially the epic poet: *furor* and Bacchic intoxication.[93]

---

90. Norden 1898, 601 and 603.

91. Magnaldi 2000, 97.

92. On the parallels between the two passages see Winkler 1985, 53; Kenney 1990, 13 and 22 f.; and cf. above, pp. 4–6. It is not by chance, I think, that both the prologue and the introduction to *Cupid and Psyche* are alluded to in the preface to Fulgentius' *Mitologiae* (1, p. 3,13 Helm): cf. Mattiacci 2003, 232–234.

93. Graverini 2003a, 214. On the epic poet's madness, cf. e.g. Plato, *Phdr.* 245a ὃς δ' ἂν ἄνευ μανίας Μουσῶν ἐπὶ ποιητικὰς θύρας ἀφίκηται, πεισθεὶς ὡς ἄρα ἐκ τέχνης ἱκανὸς ποιητὴς ἐσόμενος, ἀτελὴς αὐτός τε καὶ ἡ ποίησις ὑπὸ τῆς τῶν μαινομένων ἡ τοῦ σωφρονοῦντος ἠφανίσθη; on his drunkenness, Horace, *Epist.* 1.19.6–8 *ut male sanos / adscripsit Liber Satyris Faunisque poetas, / vina fere dulces oluerunt mane Camenae. / laudibus arguitur vini vinosus Homerus: / Ennius ipse pater numquam nisi potus ad arma / prosiluit dicenda.*

We will see shortly that the speaker of the prologue could be described in similar terms. After all, we already know from Plutarch's passage quoted above that a "Bacchic" style was not limited to descriptions of poetry, but was also applied to orators who blurred the boundaries between rhetoric and poetry (especially the "Asianist" orators). For example, Philostratus (*VS* 1.511) says of Nicetes of Smyrna that "his type of eloquence forsook the antique political convention and is almost bacchic and like a dithyramb."[94] Eduard Norden was certainly not an enthusiastic admirer of Apuleius' style, but he described it not inappropriately as "a style frenzied with Bacchic furor."[95]

Therefore, in spite of the fact that many did not approve of their contiguity, rhetoric and poetry can be very closely related to each other; this is especially true for a 'musical' rhetoric like the one adopted by Apuleius' prologue.

1.3.4 BETWEEN RHETORIC AND POETRY: THE SIRENS

With a few exceptions, tradition seems not to have offered rhetoric a specific Muse for protection;[96] oratory was not a "Musical" activity, and its task—especially in a traditional, classical perspective—was to persuade, not to enchant, hence Quintilian's and Aristides' disapproval of an alluring or singsong rhetorical style. At the same time, the psychagogic power of arousing passions and conjuring up fictional worlds is important in other genres, especially for drama: see for example Horace, *Epist.* 2.1.210–213:

> ille per extentum funem mihi posse videtur
> ire poeta meum qui pectus inaniter angit
> inritat mulcet, falsis terroribus implet,
> ut magus, et modo me Thebis, modo ponit Athenis.

> That poet seems able to walk a tightrope, who with airy nothings wrings my heart, inflames, soothes, fills it with vain alarms like a magician, and sets me down now at Thebes, now at Athens.

---

94. "Dithyrambic" is also used to describe Socrates' inspired speech on love in *Phaedrus* 238d, a speech that will even become "epic" at 241e; yet we must also remember that in Socrates' estimation it is a "foolish and somewhat impious speech" (242d), which will require a palinode guided by reason to balance its inadequate regard for the truth.

95. Norden 1898, 600 f.

96. Cf. Murray 2002, 42 ("rhetoric is always regarded as a *techne* . . . designed to be teachable, and *technai* do not need Muses . . . the art of speech, in contrast to music and poetry, is thus seen as an entirely human activity").

Even long before the "singing" rhetors like Favorinus, the theoretical division between "Musical" and alluring poetry on one side, and "technical" and convincing rhetoric on the other, was never completely observed in practice.[97] In Homer (*Od.* 8.169 ff.), Odysseus describes eloquence as a gift of the Gods and not as a *techne;* it concerns itself not so much with truth and intellectual persuasion as with the emotions and auditory pleasures: the listeners are τερπόμενοι, and the speaker's words are honey-sweet.[98] Indeed, in Odysseus himself, it seems we find a complete convergence of theory and practice. He is a fascinating orator: he lies, but his words hold the audience spellbound (θέλγει) like the songs of an epic poet (so says Eumeus at *Od.* 17.514 and 521; cf. also 14.387). In fact, elsewhere in the *Odyssey* a speaker who charms his audience is often associated with lies, deception, and danger (cf. e.g. *Od.* 3.264; 16.195; 18.282).[99] A sweet and charming voice seems to be a necessary quality for all good orators in ancient epic. The best representative of them is Nestor, who is (*Il.* 1.248) ἡδυεπής, λιγύς ἀγορητής, "sweet of speech, . . . a clear-voiced orator."[100] Virgil, on the other hand, seems to endow none of his orators with honey-sweet voices to enchant their listeners.[101] This is a telling absence: in Rome, during the Augustan age, rhetoric was supposed to be quite different from the psycha-

---

97. Eduard Norden was a fierce opponent of the "marriage" of rhetoric and poetry; but despite much grumbling, he nonetheless assembled a useful collection of passages on the subject (Norden 1898, 883 ff.). Aristotle (*Rh.* 1405a) and Isocrates (*Evag.* 9 ff.), it seems, were the first to differentiate rhetoric and poetry on a theoretical level (on Isocrates, see e.g. Nicolai 2004, 89 f.); in Cicero, *Orat.* 65 ff. the distinction is too soft for Norden's tastes, but it nevertheless exists, and sophists, historians, and poets are all evaluated in terms of *eloquentia.* In Tac. *Dial.* 20.5–7 the "modernist" Aper recommends a blend of rhetoric and poetry that can satisfy the audience's ears without undermining the effectiveness of the speech; and even the traditionalist Maternus acknowledges that the *primordia eloquentiae* are the same for poetry and oratory (12.1–2). The inextricable connection between poetry and rhetoric is the main subject of Walker 2000 (who appears to have overlooked Norden's work); but in my opinion he probably goes too far in silencing some rhetors' complaints about this marriage. On a theoretical level, too, poetry seems to have given a warmer reception to rhetoric than it received in return.

98. Cf. also Hesiod, *Th.* 92. Kennedy 1963, 36 says that "speech in the epic is generally treated as an irrational power, seen in the ability to move an audience and in its effects on a speaker himself, and is thus inspiration, a gift of the gods."

99. On the meaning of θέλγειν in Homer, see Marsh 1979; Ritook 1989, 335; Goldhill 1991, 60–66.

100. On the ambiguous meaning of λιγύς ("shrill" but also "sweet"), see above, n. 52. On the "sweetness" of Nestor's rhetoric, see also Cicero, *Brut.* 40; *Sen.* 31; *Laus Pisonis* 64; Quintilian, 12.10.64; Valgius Rufus 2.4. In Tacitus, *Dial.* 16.5, Nestor, together with Odysseus, provides an *exemplum* of oratory.

101. Virgil uses the word *mulcent* several times to describe the effect on the audience made by a speaker; but in these cases the meaning of *mulcere* is not "to enchant," but has the more general sense of appeasing anger or grief: see *Aen.* 1.153; 5.464; 7.754.

gogic, poetic and "Musical" art practiced by Homeric heroes.[102] It is also significant that in Petronius' *Satyricon* (1.3) Encolpius, while deploring the decadence of rhetoric, says that in school young students are accustomed to *mellitos verborum globulos*, "honey-balls of phrases."[103] Agamemnon quickly adds that good rhetoric (*ars severa*, "stern art") should be *Graio exonerata*[104] *sono*, "unburdened from the music of Greece" (5.1.15 f.). Honey and Greece are for Petronius' characters symbols of the decadence of rhetoric. In Apuleius, the origins of the prologue speaker are clearly set in Greece, and there is mention of Mount Hymettos, an area which was particularly famous for bees and honey.

In some cases, the semantic range of the verb θέλγειν includes magic and supernatural powers. At *Od.* 1.57 Calypso "enchants" (θέλγει) Odysseus with her sweet words, so as to make him forgetful of his homeland. At 12.40 and 44 the Sirens λιγυρῇ θέλγουσιν ἀοιδῇ, "beguile ... with their sweet song" the passing sailors, and their songs have an even more drastic outcome than the words of Calypso. From a certain point of view, there is not much difference between the Sirens and an epic bard. The Sirens seem to describe themselves as such at 12.189–90: "we know all the toils that in wide Troy the Argives and Trojans endured through the will of the Gods."[105] It would also seem that Calypso and the Sirens, whose voices are honey-sweet (μελίγηρυς: 12.187), are the best practitioners of the art of epic narration. For example, there is not so much difference between the Sirens and Nestor: his speech is an ἀοιδή ("word," but also "song") and his voice is λιγύς, "clear-toned." Nestor himself, like the Sirens, is a kind of substitute for a bard: in *Od.* 3.103 ff. he recapitulates the events of the Trojan War and of several *nostoi*. In Hesiod, *Th.* 98–103 the ἀοιδός is able to enchant

---

102. Of course, there were exceptions: Seneca's invective in *Epist.* 114 (cited above in the discussion of *corrupti generis oratio*) was directed against Maecenas.

103. Encolpius also has something to say about the sound of the voice: *levibus enim atque inanibus sonis ludibria quaedam excitando effecistis ut corpus orationis enervaretur et caderet* (2.2).

104. The text of this passage (*hinc Romana manus circumfluat, et modo Graio / exonerata sono mutet suffusa saporem*) is uncertain. For Müller 1995⁴ *exonerata* represents a textual crux, while the phrase did not seem problematic to Ernout 1922. For an overview see Pellegrino 1986, 160–162; however, I am not inclined to agree with him in considering *exonerata* as a neuter accusative plural, the direct object of *mutet* (which requires, consequently, an emendation of *saporem*); it is far more natural and economical to read *exonerata* as feminine in agreement with *Romana manus*. The text seems to offer an acceptable meaning, and Heseltine 1956 translates it "then let the company of Roman writers pour about him, and, newly unburdened from the music of Greece, steep his soul and transform his taste." *En passant*, it is worth mentioning that this lamentation on excessively Greekish tastes is put into the mouth of a character named Agamemnon.

105. According to Segal 1983, 39 "to remain and listen to their song would be to yield to the seduction of a heroic tradition rendered in its most elegant, attractive, and deadly form." Cf. below, § 3.3 p. 150.

his listeners and to make them forgetful of their sorrows (ἐπιλήθεται, just like Calypso). In the epic tradition, it seems, there is no clear distinction between speech and song: both are the gifts of the Muses, honey-sweet, and enchanting to the listener.[106]

When Apuleius uses the verb *permulcere* in his prologue to describe the narrative art of the *Metamorphoses*, he connects it with the standard rhetorical polemic against poetic diction (qualified in the epic tradition by adjectives like ἡδύς or λιγύς, and the verb θέλγειν). Indeed, it seems that *permulcere* and θέλγειν are used as keywords in rhetorical polemic precisely because they can suggest these kinds of associations. By using this verb Apuleius gives us the first indication that poetry, and in particular epic poetry, will provide an important model for our novel; it is well known, after all, that there is some measure of continuity between epic and novel, since in the Imperial period "prose genres such as the novel . . . tend to replace conventional poetic genres such as the epic."[107]

The literary tradition of the Sirens offers excellent testimony as to the close connection between the Latin *(per)mulcere* and the Greek θέλγειν. As we have seen, in Homer *Od.* 12.44 the Sirens λιγυρῇ θέλγουσιν ἀοιδῇ, "beguile . . . with their sweet song"; the expression is taken up again by Apollonius 4.893–4, where the Sirens ἡδείῃσι / θέλγουσαι μολπῇσιν. The act of θέλγειν was so closely connected to the Sirens that one of them was even called Θελξιέπεια, "Word-enchanter."[108] Ovid, who certainly knew these poetic models, described the voice of the Sirens (*Met.* 5.561) as a *canor mulcendas natus ad aures*, a "tuneful voice, so soothing to the ear." *(Per)mulcere aures* translates θέλγειν, and conveys the same associations of enchantment and possible deception.[109] In Apuleius' prologue, *permulcere aures* defines the novel's genre and style as a hybrid of both prose and poetry, dangerously

---

106. Walker 2000, 4: "Hesiod considers both the *aoidos* and the good *basileus* to be engaged in essentially the same activity. Both acquire their gift of eloquence from the Muses, and both are gifted with the power of persuasion, here depicted as the ability to deflect or 'turn aside' the listener's mind from its current state or path."

107. Harrison 2002a, 161. There is of course a wealth of studies on the contiguity of novel and epic; a classic is for example Perry 1967, 44–54, while among the more recent studies see for example Fusillo 2002 (which is not limited to the ancient novel). Cf. also my § 1.4 in Graverini-Keulen-Barchiesi 2006, and § 3.3 in this volume.

108. On the names of the Sirens, see Scarcia 1964, 41 n. 30; De Sanctis 2003.

109. Philostratus and Gellius use this terminology when they describe Favorinus' charming rhetorical style. The former, as we have seen, said that Favorinus ἔθελγε τῇ τε ἠχῇ τοῦ φθέγματος (*VS* 1.491); the latter, that he *sermonibus . . . amoenissimis demulcebat* (16.3.1). On Gellius and Favorinus see Gleason 1995, 138 ff. Naturally the semantic field of *(per)mulceo* included magic and the supernatural as well, so that the verb shows a nearly perfect correspondence to θέλγειν: see e.g. Horace, *Epist.* 2.1.212; Seneca, *Herc. f.* 575; Ovid, *Met.* 1.716. On the great variety of meanings—magical and poetic—of the verb θέλγειν, see Parry 1992.

hovering between persuasion and enchantment, teaching and deception, truth and fiction.

The phrase *aures mulcere* is used both to describe a rhetorical style and to define the contents and the literary genre of a book; it is also easy to associate it with fictitious and false plots. For example, the word appears in a passage in Ovid's *Tristia*, where the poet tries to show that the *delicias* and *mollia carmina* he has written are not evidence of his personal corruption, since "my life is moral, my muse is playful" (2.354). He claims that, although he "presents very many things suited to charm the ear" (*plurima mulcendis auribus apta feret:* 2.358), the majority of his writing is "unreal and fictitious" (2.355), and has no autobiographical or didactic significance.[110]

We could even imagine—if somewhat boldly and fancifully—that the speaking voice of the prologue presents itself as a Homeric Siren. The text offers a series of clues: we find a sweet and hypnotic voice (*lepido susurro permulceam*), the promise of a marvelous tale (*figuras fortunasque hominum in alias imagines conversas . . . ut mireris*), and the invitation—in fact, practically a command—to listen to a story that will bring pleasure to its audience. In Homer, as we have seen, the Sirens have a sweet and alluring voice, one that enchants (θέλγει, parallel to *permulcet*) the sailors who pass by them; they invite Odysseus to stop and listen (12.185), promising that he will be delighted (τερψάμενος: 12.188); they also offer a short outline of what they are going to tell Odysseus ("we know all the toils that in wide Troy the Argives and Trojans endured through the will of the gods": 12.189–90). Of course, even more than in Apuleius, the Sirens urge their audience to listen to something that could have very unpleasant consequences if they prove to be naïve; and Homer seems to display a similar focus on the ears of the Sirens' audience.

Needless to say, the danger presented by the Sirens is far more serious and concrete than the danger encountered by those who give themselves over to reading texts like Apuleius' novel, namely a metaphorical metamorphosis into an ass.[111] Furthermore, seductive as it may be, the parallel between our prologue and the descriptions of the Sirens in Homer is certainly not a case of plain and unambiguous allusion.[112] It is true, in any case, that

---

110. More examples at § 1.5 p. 41 and n. 125.

111. See above, p. 24 and n. 68.

112. Of course it is only a very abstract speculation, but it may be that a veiled reference to the Sirens is well suited to a prologue (a literary space normally occupied by the Muses) because Muses and Sirens had so much in common in ancient culture. The latter are even defined by Doherty 1995, 85 as "unauthorized Muses." On the periodically competitive relationship between Muses and Sirens, see Scarcia 1964, 17 and *passim;* Pucci 1979, 126–129; Murray 2002, 33–37; Tentorio 2009, 33 n. 52 and *passim.* It is noteworthy that Ovid (*Met.* 5,555) uses *doctae* to describe the Sirens, an epithet

rhetors employed the Sirens (in addition to the notion of "titillating" or "enchanting" the ear) as part of a standard repertory of images to describe a melodious and seductive style. One of the most polemical instances of this topos occurs in Themistius (*Or.* 28.341C): he contrasts his style with that of the sophists, and says that, like the Sirens (πάσας ἵεντες φωνάς καὶ ᾄσματα ὥσπερ Σειρῆνες), their speeches are seductive (οἱ λόγοι αἵμυλοι εἰσί), and that they utter every word with a sensual melody. Themistius is a much later author than Apuleius, but this topos can be traced back many centuries. Demosthenes, for example, made a similar claim about Aeschines, suggesting that he was like a Siren and that his speeches "have proved the ruin of those who have listened to him" (Aeschines, *In Ctes.* 228). Dionysius of Halicarnassus (*De Demosthenis dictione* 35) tells us that Aeschines in turn adopted the same image referring to Demosthenes. Dionysius seems to interpret this comparison as laudatory, but in light of the passages I have just cited, I think we should be skeptical of this conclusion, given the hostility between the two rhetors, and the fact that Dionysius was a passionate defender of Demosthenes. It is true, however, that a comparison with a Siren was not necessarily negative for an orator: Plutarch (*Vitae X orat.* 838c) and Philostratus (*VS* 1.503), for example, relate that the image of a Siren stood on the grave of Isocrates.[113]

1.4 Between philosophy and entertainment: Astonishment (*ut mireris*)

The first conclusion we can draw from all this is that the prologue of the *Metamorphoses* evokes the same auditory seduction that was typical of music and poetry; a seduction that, for many conservative theorists of rhetoric, was incompatible with oratory. Plato considered this form of rhetoric just as dangerous for men seeking the truth as the voices of Sirens and cicadas. But Apuleius' audience is urged to a reading (or listening) practice that not only involves their intellect and reason; they will also feel surprise and astonish-

---

usually reserved for the Muses. According to Plutarch, *Quaest. conv.* 9.14.745f (Ammonius is speaking) Plato, in *Resp.* 10.617b–c, would use "Sirens" in place of "Muses."

113. According to De Romilly 1975, 83 Philostratus here adapts the connection between magic and rhetoric that was typical of the Second Sophistic and applies it to Isocrates. Cf. also Eunapius, *VS* 6.5.1–2 on the rhetor Eustathius: he was κάλλιστος, and the fascinating power of his speech seemed to be almost magical; his voice was so honey-sweet that the listener completely surrendered, like the Lotus-eaters, and hung on his lips; he differed little from the Sirens. In Philostratus, *Heroikos* 43.1 the Phoenician listens to the vine-dresser's speech with such rapt attention that he depends on his tales like the Lotus-eaters on their drugs. See further pp. 128 ff. for parallels between Socrates and the Sirens.

ment (*ut mireris:* 1.1.2). This might be considered another good reason to make a clear distinction between the novel and "useful" literature. Plutarch's *De recta audiendi* seems to echo this sentiment, concluding "philosophic reasoning, through knowledge and acquaintance with the cause in every case, does away with the wonder and amazement (θαῦμα καὶ θάμβος) that spring from blindness and ignorance."[114]

Indeed, this is a rather provocative stance, one that can even baffle readers of the novel—at least those who already know Apuleius as a successful *philosophus Platonicus*, and know that he took great pride in that title.[115] What is the place of the *Metamorphoses* in the career of a philosopher and orator who had clearly always done everything he could to present himself as something more than a simple entertainer?[116]

A broader perspective can render this question less paradoxical. We can see, for example, that not all philosophers shared Plutarch's understanding of amazement. Plato, for one, who considered philosophy not as something acquired once and for all but as a dialectical process that leads to contemplation of the Beautiful and the Good, claimed that "the feeling of wonder (τὸ θαυμάζειν) shows that you are a philosopher, since wonder is the only beginning of philosophy."[117] Thus, there is at least the possibility of a complex, dialectical opposition between seduction and teaching, between enchantment and philosophy, and between *utile* and *dulce*. The prologue, while presenting us with several important features of the novel, may offer us only a partial and perhaps provocative representation of it, one that we will need to refine and complete as we continue.

This is clearly a problem that involves a general interpretation of the whole novel, which will be the subject of Chapter 2 of this book; for the moment, suffice it to say that the conclusions I have just reached can only

---

114. *De recta ratione audiendi* 44b. On the contrary, ἔκπληξις was often connected with a musical and fascinating poetic style (see Keulen 2007b, 72, with further references): as we have seen, this is exactly the style that Apuleius adopts in his novel. I would also add that astonishment is a typical feature of narrative literature: in Antonius Diogenes the box containing the cypress tablets on which Dercyllis' story is written bears the inscription "stranger, whoever you are, open this box to learn things that will amaze you (ἵνα μάθῃς ἃ θαυμάζεις)"; and in Longus (prol. 1.2) the author decides to write his novel out of a sense of astonishment in front of a painting. I have offered a more thorough treatment of philosophy and astonishment in Apuleius and more generally in the ancient novel in Graverini 2010; see also the collection of studies published in Morgan-Jones 2007.

115. Cf. *Apol.* 10.6. See Hijmans 1987, 416 for other useful passages; and p. 470 on the "disappointment" that those inevitably feel who try to place the "many-leveled subtle ironies" of the novel in the context of Apuleius' oeuvre as a whole.

116. Even in the *Florida*, where he is constantly trying to entertain his audience, Apuleius does not abandon his philosophical image: see § 4.5.

117. *Tht.* 155d; cf. also *Symp.* 208b on Socrates' astonishment after Diotima's teachings.

be provisional. To complete the literary analysis I have carried out in this chapter, I will investigate how the prologue serves to define the literary genre of the *Metamorphoses*.

1.5 The poetics of the novel

Apuleius' rhetorical stance will appear less isolated, if not less provocative, once it is set in the context of the prologues and programmatic statements of the extant Greek novels. In fact, in the wide spectrum of choices between the opposing poles of *utile* and *dulce,* the novel as a genre finds its place nearer to the latter.

Chariton's novel has an extremely short prologue in the manner of Herodotus and Thucydides,[118] but the beginning of the last book seems to offer more metaliterary remarks. There, Chariton says he believes that "this last chapter will prove very agreeable (ἥδιστον) to its readers" (8.1.4). Lucian's *True Story,* on the other hand, has a rather extensive prologue, in which the author places his novel halfway between *utile* and *dulce*. Even men of culture, he says, need some rest from their serious work:

> They will find this interlude agreeable if they choose as company such works as not only afford wit, charm, and distraction pure and simple (ἐκ τοῦ ἀστείου τε καὶ χαρίεντος ψιλὴν παρέξει τὴν ψυχαγωγίαν), but also provoke some degree of cultured reflection (θεωρία οὐκ ἄμουσος: 1.2).

The "cultured reflection" offered by the *True Story* concerns the spectacular lies of certain historiographers, and Lucian is clearly trying to reconcile the *dulce* of a fantastic tale with the *utile* that comes from a satirical outlook.[119] Achilles Tatius' prologue is narrative and dialogic: the main narrator arrives in Sidon, where he meets Clitophon and hears the story of his adventures. At 1.2.2 the dialogue lets the reader determine the features of the novel that, thanks to its fictional contents, will "give pleasure" to the audience (ἥσειν, a verb connected with the adjective ἡδύς, "sweet"):

> "What have you suffered, my friend?" . . . "You are stirring up a wasps' nest of narrative. My life has been very storied."[120] "Well sir, by Zeus and

---

118. Cf. e.g. F. Zimmerman 1961, 345.
119. On satire in the *True Story,* see Georgiadou-Larmour 1998, esp. 44 f., with further bibliography.
120. "Stirring up a wasps' nest of narrative" is a quotation from Plato, *Resp.* 450b. The Platonic

by Eros himself, please don't hesitate. Your account will give me even more pleasure, if it is more storied" (μὴ κατοκνήσῃς . . . ταύτῃ μᾶλλον ἥσειν, εἰ καὶ μύθοις ἔοικε).

Longus' prologue also contains a dialectic between *utile* and *dulce* in the form of a very clear allusion to Thucydides:

> I . . . produced the four volumes of this book, as an offering to Love, the Nymphs, and Pan, and something for mankind to possess and enjoy (κτῆμα . . . τερπνόν: *praef.* 3).

Thucydides proudly defined his work as a "possession for all time" (1.22.4 κτῆμα ἐς αἰεί), and rejected any possibility of a compromise between narrative and auditory pleasure: "it may well be that the absence of the fabulous from my narrative will seem less pleasing to the ear" (καὶ ἐς μὲν ἀκρόασιν ἴσως τὸ μὴ μυθῶδες αὐτῶν ἀτερπέστερον φανεῖται, 1.22.4). Longus makes a sort of Copernican leap by placing pleasure (τὸ τερπνόν) at the center of his novel, and makes the Thucydidean virtues of utility and universality stem from the same "pleasure" that Thucydides himself despised.[121] We have no prologues or programmatic statements by Xenophon of Ephesus or Heliodorus, nor do any appear in the novels we only know through indirect tradition or papyrus fragments; there are, however, some remarks by late antique or Byzantine readers that are of great interest. We have already seen that Macrobius mentions Petronius and Apuleius as authors of *fabulae* that *auditum mulcent* (*Somn.* 1.2.8). According to Photius, Antonius Diogenes'

---

elements of the dialogue are also emphasized by the *locus amoenus* described slightly later in the introduction, recalling the famous setting of Plato's *Phaedrus* (230b–c: see Graverini 2010, 62–68). The *Phaedrus* is also an important intertext at the beginning of Apuleius' novel, on which see below § 3.1.

121. Cf. e.g. the commentary by Morgan 2004, 147 *ad loc.;* Cueva 2004, 54–61. This "Copernican leap" does not mean that there is a direct and complete opposition between historiography and Longus' novel. Hunter 1983, 48 rightly notes that Polybius makes an attempt to reconcile utility and pleasure, since he mentions at 1.4.11 τὸ χρήσιμον καὶ τὸ τερπνόν of historiography (and cf. also Xenophon, *Hier.* 11.15 κάλλιστον καὶ μακαριώτατον κτῆμα). From this point of view, then, Longus' novel could be viewed as part of the trend of Hellenistic (or Herodotean) historiography. And yet the two audiences differ greatly. Thucydides addresses an audience who wants to know the truth, in order to draw from past events models of conduct for the future; and Polybius claims that history provides "education and training for a life of active politics" (1.1.2). By way of contrast Longus says that his novel is meant as consolation and teaching for those who suffer the pangs of love. Hunter compares Longus' programmatic statement with Achilles Tatius 1.2.2 and with Apuleius' prologue, but considers Chariton in opposition to these three authors, since "he begins his narrative by announcing its strict historicity (πάθος ἐρωτικὸν ἐν Συρρακούσαις γενόμενον διηγήσομαι)" (p. 48). See, however, Chariton's statement at 8.1.4, quoted above in the text. On γλυκύτης as an important feature of Longus' style and narrative, see Hunter 1983, 92–98; cf. below, n. 127.

novel is "most agreeable" (πλεῖστον ἔχει τοῦ ἡδέος: 166.109a); and the patriarch says that Iamblichus' style is

> flowing and gentle (ῥέουσα καὶ μαλακή). As for its sonorous qualities, the words have not been given rhythmical force so much as titillating and, so to speak, mincing movement. (ἐπὶ τὸ γαργαλίζον, ὡς ἄν τις εἴποι, καὶ βλακῶδες παρακεκίνηται: 94.73b)

Here we find γαργαλίζειν again, a verb that we have already encountered as one of the Greek equivalents of Apuleius' *permulcere*. Of course, it is impossible for us to know whether Photius has drawn his critical terminology from the very text he is discussing (as is most likely the case with Macrobius' assessment of Apuleius' novel[122]), but we should not rule out this possibility: for example, it is very likely that Photius' short account of Lucius of Patrae closely reflects the prologue to his lost *Metamorphoseis*.[123] In any case, Photius provides us with a good example (*e contrario*) of the thematic connection between fictional narrative and the idea of "soothing the ears" of an audience. The greatest merit of Eudocia's *Metaphrasis of the Octateuch*, he says, is that

> this book does not try to soothe the ears of young people by distorting the truth with fictional tales, as the poets do (οὔτε γὰρ ἐξουσίᾳ ποιητικῇ μύθοις τὴν ἀλήθειαν τρέπων ἡδύνειν σπουδάζει μειρακίων ὦτα: 183.128a).

We can say, then, that the ancient novel (a well-defined though nameless literary genre) advertizes its proximity to *dulce* rather than to *utile*. This is a "generic" definition of its literary space, and great variation can be found in individual cases. Nevertheless, the novel marks its divergence from older and more classical literary and rhetorical canons by advertising the "sweet" nature of its psychagogic entertainment.

The notion that prose fiction (here in form of the ancient novel) can seduce its audience challenges the traditional division between prose and poetry. Thucydides, as we have seen, made the ideas of "fiction" (τὸ μυθῶδες), and "pleasure" (τὸ τερπνόν) overlap at 1.22.4: only poets and

---

122. Cf. pp. 23 and 96–97. On the adjective μαλακός used by Photius to describe Iamblichus' style, cf. Isocrates, *Panath.* 4, where it defines a kind of discourse more suited to the orator's advanced age and different from those he had published in his younger years.

123. Cf. below, pp. 43–44. On Photius' methods and practice, and his possible use of the prologues of the works he reviews, see Mazza 1999, 92 n. 41 and 134 n. 33.

logographers should resort to fictional narratives, told only to win an audience. Of course this is a common distinction drawn by historians who claim that they adhere strictly to the truth: Polybius, for example, adopts the same categories to criticize the careless historian Timaeus,[124] and Livy feels he needs to apologize for including in his *Historiae* the narration of Rome's mythical history, that is, a subject matter that is "rather adorned with poetic legends than based upon trustworthy historical proofs" (*praef.* 6).[125] But the connection between fiction and pleasure was a common topos in ancient literary culture as a whole. For example, at Ovid *Trist.* 2.354 ff.[126] (mentioned above) and Seneca, *Ben.* 1.4.5–6, false and imaginary subjects go hand in hand and with the idea of soothing the ear (or in any case the more general emphasis on the "sweetness" of the text).[127] Plutarch (*Quomodo adulescens poetas audire debeat* 17a) says that a tragedy by Aeschylus is "a mythical fabrication which has been created to please or astound the hearer (μυθοποίημα καὶ πλάσμα ... πρὸς ἡδονὴν ἢ ἔκπληξιν ἀκροατοῦ)." Photius, in his short account of Lucius of Patrae, relates his taste for telling fairy-tales (τερατεία) and the sweetness (γλυκύτης) of his style;[128] Eusebius, at the beginning of the *De laudibus Constantini*, claims he will avoid exploiting these same devices.[129] The association of sweet or mythical qualities with narration is also attested in rhetorical treatises: according to Hermogenes of Tharsus, "mythic thoughts (αἱ μυθικαί) are especially sweet (γλυκεῖαι) and pleasurable (ἡδονὴν ἔχουσαι)." Of course, no novels are to be found among the examples provided by the rhetor, but the myth of the cicadas in Plato's *Phaedrus* (259a–d) holds a place of honor in his list.[130]

In sum, the prologue speaker's promise to "titillate the ears of the reader with a sweet whisper" can also be read as a genre marker that prepares

---

124. 12.27.2; cf. below, p. 142.
125. According to Lucian, "the poets flavor their writings with the delectability that the fable yields, a most seductive thing" (*Philops.* 4, τὸ ἐκ τοῦ μύθου τερπνὸν ἐπαγωγότατον: what follows clearly opposes μῦθος to τἀληθές). Of course, we need to emphasize that the distinction between prose and poetry was not a specific "rule": Aristotle, for example, had no problem admitting that Empedocles, even though he used the same meter as Homer, was not an epic poet but a scientist (*Poet.* 1447b); and Quintilian could claim that historiography was very close to poetry (10.1.31). On the distinction between prose and poetry, see above, p. 11 n. 30.
126. Cf. above, p. 35.
127. Cf. p. 100.
128. 109.96b: see p. 44.
129. Cf. § 1.6 p. 46.
130. περὶ τῶν ἰδεῶν λόγου 2,4 (330 Rabe). On this section of Hermogenes' treatise, see Hunter 1983 92–98, and especially p. 47 for more useful examples on the thematic connection between fiction, pleasure, and sweetness. I would add the beginning of Isocrates' *Panathenaicus*, where μυθώδες, τερατεία, and ψευδολογία are the features that offer the most delight to an audience, instead of "that which is devoted to their welfare and safety" (*Panath.* 1).

the audience for an entertaining work of narrative literature. Possessed of a strong psychagogic power, similar to the power of music, poetry, and magic, the novel leads the reader into an imaginary world where it will evoke powerful emotions.[131] Finally, the prologue connects the novel closely to its Greek counterparts, which represented themselves in similar terms.[132] This connection will be the subject of the next few pages, where I will suggest more elusive analogies with two lost narrative texts.

1.6 Lucius of Patrae and Aristides of Miletus

The verbal affinities that link Apuleius' prologue to the programmatic statements of the Greek novels and to the reports of some late readers reveal Apuleius' acute awareness of genre. But we should not forget that Apuleius is actually *translating* and *adapting* a story that is Greek in origin: some analogies, therefore, may owe their origin to his lost Greek model (I would hasten to add that this does not detract from the "awareness of genre" mentioned above: Apuleius was careful about what parts of his model he would translate, neglect, or modify).[133]

It is not clear whether Lucius of Patrae's *Metamorphoseis* had a prologue or not. The pseudo-Lucianic *Onos* has none, but this absence could be due to the intervention of the epitomator. Most scholars today agree that the *Metamorphoseis* did indeed have a prologue, and that it was remarkably similar to that of Apuleius. This can be surmised from the short account Photius offers of that novel at 129.96b, in which we can see several resemblances to

---

131. For more on this see § 3.3. The emotions one could feel while reading a novel were so strong that the physician Theodorus Priscianus (fourth–fifth century) prescribed reading erotic novels as a remedy for impotence: "it is advisable to read what drives one's soul towards love (*ad delicias animum pertrahentibus*): for example Philippus of Amphipolis or Herodian or Iamblichus the Syrian, or the others who tell love stories in a sweet style (*ceteris suaviter amatorias fabulas describentibus*)" (*Euporista* 2.11.34 p. 133 Rose). Longus claims in his prologue that his novel has a "propaedeutic" function for erotic experiences, while in Achilles Tatius Clitophon says that "stories of love stir feelings of lust" (1.5.6). The reader, therefore, is inclined to identify with the characters in the narrative, and to live their adventures vicariously. As I have already noted, in the case of Apuleius' Lucius this identification has several unpleasant implications.

132. For this reason I cannot agree with Scobie 1975, 64, who claims that "the most unusual feature of the preface of the *Met*. is the fact that it contains no hint of an apology or justification for the programme of entertainment it advertises." The parallels I have highlighted do not mean, of course, that Apuleius' prologue and the programmatic statements of the Greek novels completely overlap (they are themselves in fact highly diverse): for such differences see e.g. Morgan 2001.

133. There is nowadays a scholarly consensus on the common derivation of Apuleius' novel and of the pseudo-Lucianic *Onos* from the lost novel by Lucius of Patrae. For an overview of the question, see Harrison 1996, 500 f. or, more thoroughly, Mason 1994.

the opening of the Latin *Metamorphoses*. Below is Photius' text, and I have placed after it a table originally compiled by Alexander Scobie[134] that compares some of its phraseology to similar terms in Apuleius' prologue.

Read the various stories of *Metamorphoses* (μεταμορφώσεων λόγοι διάφοροι) by Lucius of Patrae. The style is clear, pure, and agreeable (ἔστι δὲ τὴν φράσιν σαφής τε καὶ καθαρὸς καὶ φίλος γλυκύτητος); avoiding innovations in language, the author carries to excess his tales of marvels (τὴν ἐν τοῖς διηγήμασι τερατείαν), so that he may be called a second Lucian. The first two books are almost translations from Lucian's *Lucius* or *The Ass*, unless Lucian borrowed from Lucius, which, if I may hazard the conjecture, is the case, although I have not been able to find out for certain which wrote first. For it seems that Lucian, having cut down the more copious work of Lucius and removed all that seemed unsuitable for his purpose, combined what was left into a single composition, in which the words and arrangement of the original were preserved, and gave the title of *Lucius* or *The Ass* to what he had borrowed. Both works are full of mythical fictions and disgraceful indecency. The only difference is that Lucian, as in all his other writings, ridicules and scoffs at heathenish superstitions, whereas Lucius, taking quite seriously and believing the transformations of men into other men and brutes, and of brutes into men (τὰς ἐξ ἀνθρώπων εἰς ἀλλήλους μεταμορφώσεις τάς τε ἐξ ἀλόγων εἰς ἀνθρώπους καὶ ἀνάπαλιν), and all the idle talk and nonsense of ancient fables, set them down in writing and worked them up into a story (γραφῇ παρεδίδου ταῦτα καὶ συνύφαινεν. Trans. J.H. Freese 1920).

Table of comparison:

Photius' account	Apuleius 1.1
λόγοι διάφοροι	*varias fabulas* (1.1.1)
συνύφαινεν	*conseram* (1.1.1)[135]
τὰς ἐξ ἀνθρώπων εἰς ἀλλήλους μεταμορφώσεις τάς τε ἐξ ἀλόγων εἰς ἀνθρώπους καὶ ἀνάπαλιν	*figuras fortunasque hominum in alias imagines conversas et in se rursum mutuo nexu refectas* (1.1.2)

---

134. Scobie 1975, 65; see also Winkler 1985, 183, with further bibliography.
135. On the possibility that *consero* means not "weave" but "sew" here, see Thibau 1965, 94; James 2001, 258; Dowden 2006, 47.

Τερατείαν	*ut mireris* (1.1.2)
φίλος γλυκύτητος	*lepido susurro* (1.1.1)

The last point in the comparative table is, in this context, the most important: according to Photius, the style (φράσις) of Lucius of Patrae is agreeable, φίλος γλυκύτητος, and it is not at all unlikely that, according to what I have shown in the previous section, the lost *Metamorphoseis* had some programmatic statement (probably in the prologue) as to its inclination towards the *dulce*. This would match its explicitly stated tendency towards fantastic and implausible narration, τὴν ἐν τοῖς διηγήμασι τερατείαν.[136]

Besides Lucius of Patrae, there is another Greek model for the *Metamorphoses;* it is even explicitly mentioned by Apuleius, but we cannot define its exact role in the genesis of the novel. The prologue says that the *Metamorphoses* are a *sermo Milesius*, and therefore it is somehow connected to Aristides' *Milesian Tales;* this connection is restated with the mention of a *Milesiae conditor* at 4.32.6,[137] a passage that associates the tale of *Cupid and Psyche* (or possibly the entire novel) with the "Milesian genre."[138] Another interesting detail is the Milesian origin of Thelyphron (2.21.3), which can be considered as a genre marker that connects the tale told by this character to Milesian tales.[139] Finally, we have already seen that in the *Historia Augusta* (*Alb.* 12.12) the emperor Septimius Severus refers to Apuleius' work with the words *Milesiae Punicae*. If we consider that the mention of *sermo Milesius* in the prologue is perhaps the most explicit mention of a literary model in the whole novel, we certainly have very good reason to think that the *Metamorphoses* is closely connected to the work of Aristides or to its Latin translator, Sisenna. According to Gottskálk Jensson, the author of the most recent and informed study of Milesian narratives, "the classification of the *Metamorphoses* as *Milesia* defines the literary project of Apuleius as the re-enactment of the earlier performance of Sisenna."[140]

Unfortunately, we only have scant fragments of Sisenna and Aristides, preserved in the form of single words or very short phrases quoted by ancient grammarians;[141] for this reason it would seem impossible to try and define

---

136. Cf. above, pp. 40–41.
137. It is not clear whether the *conditor* is Apuleius, or the speaking *ego* of the prologue. On the tangle of hermeneutic problems in this passage, see *GCA* 2004, 84 f. *ad loc.;* Harrison 1998a, 70.
138. On the "Milesian genre" see above, pp. 5 and n. 12.
139. See *GCA* 2001, 311 *ad loc.*, with ample bibliography.
140. Jensson 2004, 267.
141. We have just a word of Aristides' *Milesian Tales,* quoted by Harpocration, frg. 29 in FHG 4.326; Aragosti 2000 provides a text with extensive commentary on Sisenna's fragments.

precisely how these two obscure authors could have influenced Apuleius' prologue. Yet the indirect tradition allows a few conjectures.

An interesting mention of Aristides' work is found in the prologue of the pseudo-Lucianic *Amores:*

Ἐρωτικῆς παιδιᾶς, ἑταῖρέ μοι Θεόμνηστε, ἐξ ἑωθινοῦ πεπλήρωκας ἡμῶν τὰ κεκμηκότα πρὸς τὰς συνεχεῖς σπουδὰς ὦτα, καί μοι σφόδρα διψῶντι τοιαύτης ἀνέσεως εὔκαιρος ἡ τῶν ἱλαρῶν σου λόγων ἐρρύη χάρις· ἀσθενὴς γὰρ ἡ ψυχὴ διηνεκοῦς σπουδῆς ἀνέχεσθαι, ποθοῦσι δ' οἱ φιλότιμοι πόνοι μικρὰ τῶν ἐπαχθῶν φροντίδων χαλασθέντες εἰς ἡδονὰς ἀνίεσθαι. πάνυ δή με ὑπὸ τὸν ὄρθρον ἡ τῶν ἀκολάστων σου διηγημάτων αἱμύλη καὶ γλυκεῖα πειθὼ κατεύφραγκεν, ὥστ' ὀλίγου δεῖν Ἀριστείδης ἐνόμιζον εἶναι τοῖς Μιλησιακοῖς λόγοις ὑπερκηλούμενος.

Theomnestus, my friend, since dawn your sportive talk about love has filled these ears of mine that were weary of unremitting attention to serious topics. As I was parched with thirst for relaxation of this sort, your delightful stream of merry stories was very welcome to me. For the human spirit is too weak to endure serious pursuits all the time, and ambitious toils long to gain some little respite from tiresome cares and to have freedom for the joys of life. This morning I have been quite gladdened by the sweet winning seductiveness of your wanton stories, so that I almost thought I was Aristides being enchanted beyond measure by those Milesian Tales.

Jensson and others have already discussed this passage as a means of reconstructing the narrative structure of the *Milesian Tales;*[142] but I would hasten to point out that the prologue to the *Amores* of Pseudo-Lucian seems to recapitulate the same thematic features I have identified in the programmatic statements from the Greek novels and from Apuleius' prologue. Lycinus, the character who makes the speech I have quoted above, thanks his friend Theomnestus for the stories he has told him, highlighting the "sweet, winning seductiveness" of those stories, as well as the relaxation and rest they offer from more serious intellectual efforts.[143] With regard to lexicography

---

142. Jensson 2004, 263 ff.; cf. also Harrison 1998a, 65; Aragosti 2000, 36 ff. (pp. 86 ff. on the possibility that the *Milesian Tales* contained a version of the ass-story).

143. There is a close verbal affinity here with the prologue to Lucian's *True Story:* note the opposition between σπουδή and ἄνεσις/ἀνίημι in the *Amores,* and between ἄνεσις/ἀνίημι and σπουδάζω in *True Story* 1.1. The need for relaxation after an intellectual effort was a topos: several parallels (but not the pseudo-Lucianic *Amores*) are listed in the commentary on Lucian's *True Story* by Georgiadou-Larmour 1998.

we ought to note the phrase "to fill the ears," and especially the picture of Aristides as "charmed past measure" (ὑπερκηλούμενος) by the Μιλεσιακοῖ λόγοι: there is an evident parallelism with Apuleius' *at ego tibi sermone isto Milesio varias fabulas conseram auresque tuas lepido susurro permulceam*. Among the several Greek equivalents of *permulcere*, we should pay particular attention to the pseudo-Lucianic ὑπερκηλούμενος, which deserves particular emphasis because of the structural parallel in the prefix *per-*/ὑπερ-.[144]

It is by no means unlikely that the prologue to the *Amores* of pseudo-Lucian is imitating the prologue to Aristides' *Milesian Tales:* at this point, then, we need to seriously consider the possibility that the same prologue had an influence on the prologue of the *Metamorphoses*—either directly, or through the mediations of Lucius of Patrae and/or of Sisenna. This hypothesis can receive indirect confirmation from a much later text that shows, very unexpectedly, some close similarities to all the others I have quoted above. At the beginning of his *De laudibus Constantini*, Eusebius claims that he will resist the temptation of inventing stories to win his audience; he will not worship a "sweet and vulgar Muse" (μοῦσάν . . . ἡδεῖαν καὶ πάνδημον)[145] but, following the true path to wisdom, he will discuss the virtues and exploits of the emperor Constantine. Here are his words:

Ἀλλ' οὐκ ἐγὼ μύθους, οὐκ ἀκοῆς θήρατρα, λόγων εὐγλωττίαν πλασάμενος πάρειμι κηλήσων ὦτα φωνῇ Σειρήνων . . .

But I am not appearing in front of you to make up fantastic tales, enticing speeches, and musical words to enchant your ears with a Siren's voice. . . .

Here again we find the image of an audience whose ears have been enchanted by invented stories, μῦθοι. This similarity to Apuleius' prologue is not surprising, since we have already seen the same terminology adopted in rhetorical polemics, and used as a recurrent genre marker for prose narratives. Eusebius is simply distancing himself from the genre of fictional prose narrative by claiming (in spite of its sometimes miraculous character) that what he is about to say is not fiction; further, Eusebius' goal is not to offer pleasure to those who listen to him (he says that his words are not ἡδονῆς φάρμακα), but to teach and to improve them—that is, Eusebius' speech is *utile* and not *dulce*.

---

144. On *mulcere*/κηλεῖν see above, p. 29 n. 98.

145. The implicit distinction between a πάνδημος and a "serious" Muse clearly echoes the opposition between Aphrodite Ourania and Aphrodite Pandemos in Plato's *Symposium* (180d ff.); in this case, too, Plato seems to play a role.

But the first words of Eusebius' panegyric, Ἀλλ' οὐκ ἐγώ, offer us an opportunity for further consideration, as we discover yet another form of *at ego*, the words that began Apuleius' prologue. As we have seen, this is a very peculiar way of beginning a speech or a literary work, and only in Apuleius do we find it linked to the idea of enchanting the ears of an audience. It is unlikely, though not impossible, that Eusebius knew Apuleius well enough to allude to the opening of his novel;[146] perhaps more to the point, it is extremely unlikely that, when Eusebius delivered this speech in 335 for the emperor's *tricennalia*, his audience would have known Apuleius' *Metamorphoses* so well that they could recognize such an allusion to the prologue. Of course it might be a simple verbal coincidence, but a more plausible explanation might be that Eusebius' model was Aristides' *Milesian Tales*, a Greek text that would probably have enjoyed a wide circulation in Eusebius' day: as we will see shortly, Aristides' work enjoyed a widespread and sinister notoriety among the Latin fathers of the church. This suggestion is only an hypothesis, but it allows us to imagine an even closer relationship between the prologue to the *Metamorphoses* and what may have been the opening of Aristides work, or Sisenna's version of it. From the *Milesian Tales*, then, Apuleius could have taken not only the idea of the almost magical seduction to which the audience of fictional tales is exposed, but also the peculiar *incipit* I have discussed at the beginning of this chapter.[147]

It may be that a link between Apuleius' *Metamorphoses* and Aristides' *Milesian Tales* produces more problems than solutions, as a consequence of the irremediably slippery character of the "Milesian genre." In what sense are the *Metamorphoses* a "Milesian tale"?[148] And how can we define as "Milesian"

---

146. On Apuleius' renown in the East, see Stramaglia 1996b, 141 ff. Eusebius, in his works, mentions Latin authors (such as Tertullian, Cyprian, and Virgil), but this is not enough to demonstrate that he had an extensive knowledge of Latin literature: on the contrary, according to Barnes 1981, 142, "of Latin writers Eusebius knew virtually nothing." For an overview of the extent to which Greek authors in the Imperial age were familiar with Latin literature, see e.g. Hunter 1983, 76–83 (with further bibliography at p. 123 n. 73).

147. A passage in Pliny's *Epistles* is also worth quoting, even though it is not particularly significant, since an (almost) initial *at ego* introduces a work that appeared exotic, "sweet" and lascivious to a Latin audience: *tu fortasse orationem, ut soles, et flagitas et exspectas; at ego quasi ex aliqua peregrina delicataque merce lusus meos tibi prodo* (14.1: it is a collection of hendecasyllables written as a pastime, containing several passages that show varying degrees of obscenity).

148. This definition seems to make a pointed reference to the contents of the *Milesian Tales* (non-idealized stories, sometimes rather bawdy, and with low-life characters: even though, from this point of view, *Cupid and Psyche* is certainly not very "Milesian") and to its narrative structure (first-person narration, with several secondary stories framed in the main tale): cf. Harrison 1998a, 70 ff.; Jensson 2004, 263 ff. On the contrary, Walsh 1970 was very skeptical about the presence of a unifying narrative structure; he considered the *Milesian Tales* "a collection of lubricious anecdotes without a fictional framework" (p. 17). In general, it is necessary to be cautious when we speak of a "Milesian genre": see above, n. 12.

the tale of *Cupid and Psyche*, which certainly has nothing of the transgressive qualities we usually attribute to Aristides' collection of stories?[149] Perhaps the *Milesian Tales* (either Aristides' original tales, or more generally the "Milesian genre") were defined less by their lewdness, than by their nature as entertaining literature and fictional narrative, with no moral or didactic goal: a kind of literature, therefore, that was often looked at with suspicion by conservative or "committed" intellectuals, even if they were appreciated from time to time by more transgressive personalities. The Latin literary tradition provides us with a number of testimonia, in which the term "Milesian tales" is used to refer not to Aristides' *Milesian Tales* in particular, but more generally to a narrative tradition characterized by the features I have just outlined. Wytse Keulen has collected the following relevant testimonia in his commentary,[150] to which I would add a final supplement:

> The Valentinians put the germ of Sophia in the soul, by which they recognise the stories and Milesian tales (*historias atque Milesias*) of their Eons in the visible things. (Tertullian, *De anima* 23.4)

> It is even a greater source of chagrin, that some of you thought he should be praised for his knowledge of letters, when in fact he is busied with old wives' songs, and grows senile amid the Milesian stories from Carthage that his friend Apuleius wrote and such other learned nonsense (*neniis quibusdam anilibus occupatus inter Milesias punicas Apulei sui et ludicra litteraria*). (*Historia Augusta, Alb.* 12.12: it is the text of a letter from Septimius Severus addressed to the Senate. Cf. also 11.5)

> No writer is so incompetent as not to find a reader who is like him: and those who leaf through the Milesian stories (*Milesias fabellas*) are much more than those who read Plato's books. The former provide entertainment and distraction (*ludus et oblectatio*), the latter difficulty and hard work. (Hieronymus, *Commentaria in Isaiam*, PLD 24.409d)

> As if crowds of curly-haired boys did not recite Milesian fictions (*Milesiarum . . . figmenta*) in their schools . . . and as if this kind of nonsense was

---

149. On the transgressive character of the *Milesian Tales*, see esp. Ovid, *Trist.* 2.413 f. *iunxit Aristides Milesia crimina secum / pulsus Aristides nec tamen urbe sua est*, and 2.443 f. *vertit Aristiden Sisenna, nec obfuit illi / historiae turpis inseruisse iocos;* cf. also the prologue to pseudo-Lucian's *Amores* quoted above in the text, or Petronius' stories of the *Matron of Ephesus* and the *Boy of Pergamon*, defined as "Milesian anecdotes" by Walsh 1970, 15.

150. Keulen 2007b, 64 f.

not popular in the banquets of the fools. (Hieronymus, *Contra Rufinum* 1.17)

Here is the story of an accomplished young man, as good as a Milesian tale or an Attic comedy. (*habetis historiam iuvenis eximii, fabulam Milesiae vel Atticae parem:* Sidonius Apollinaris, *Epist.* 7.2.9)

(Philology) was afraid that after she had ascended among the immortals, she would need to completely abandon the myths (*mythos*), the delights of the Milesian stories' poetic variety (*poeticae . . . diversitatis delicias Milesias*), and the histories (*historias*) of the mortals. (Martianus Capella 2.100)

And so it appears that "Milesian" could describe several kinds of prose fiction, regardless of the immorality or indecency of its contents; it is impossible (and perhaps even pointless) for us to decide whether Aristides' own *Milesian Tales* created the basis for this generic significance[151] or whether it was created by a later tradition.[152]

In conclusion, it is possible and even likely that, as he composed his own prologue, Apuleius used both the lost Greek *Metamorphoseis* and the chimerical *Milesian Tales* of Aristides. These two models allowed him to fit his novel into a well-defined narrative tradition, whose features we can at least partially reconstruct. Given the present condition of the evidence, however, it is impossible to say more than that, or to describe in more minute detail the relationship between Apuleius and his immediate models. Nevertheless

---

151. On this "generic" significance, in addition to the commentary by Keulen (2007b), cf. Moreschini 1990, 124 ff. and 1994a, 87. According to Aragosti 2000, 8 f. the main features of the Milesian 'genre' were a variety of contents including eroticism, and the frequent use of fantastic elements. If we want to go beyond the scant evidence available to us to look for a "complete" definition for *fabula Milesia*, we could also consider a passage from the *Adagia* published by Paolo Manuzio while he was reworking Erasmus' work of the same title: *Fabulae Milesiae proverbio dicuntur sermones nec veri, nec verisimiles, nec in aliquem vitae usum parati et congruentes: sed tantum ad voluptatem et extrahendum tempus, vel in conviviis, vel in coetibus virorum ac feminarum, qualia sunt etiam amatoria omnia. Ideoque Lucianus sermones amatorios vocat Milesios, et Capella quasdam poetarum fabulas. Scripsit nominatim de Milesiis Aristides libros aliquos:* μιλησιακῶν, *et Apuleius asinum, ex Lutiani asino desumptum et concinnatum. Eiusmodi narrant vetulae pueris ad focum ne plorent, aut molesti sint. Milesiae a Mileto Ioniae, quae de luxu, et deliciis male audivit, dicuntur* (I quote from the posthumous edition of Oberursel [1603], p. 1403, available on the web at http://www.uni-mannheim.de/mateo/camenaref/manuzio.html). Under the entry *Domi Milesia* (pp. 162 f.) Manutius offers a slightly more detailed description of Apuleius' novel: *quin et Apuleius in carmine iambico, quo asinum suum auspicari voluit, demulcentes, et prurientes narrationes suas sermonem Milesium vocat.*

152. It may have been influenced by Apuleius' usage: according to Mazzarino 1950 Apuleius himself would have modified the erotic character of the original "Milesian" genre, adapting it to be a vehicle for conveying symbolic meanings.

it is now clear that the "Milesian" character of Apuleius' *Metamorphoses* is completely consistent with the features of the novel I have identified so far: it is a fictional and fantastic story that provides a pleasant pastime, similar to the tales told by old women to young children; it is also a sophisticated literary production characterized by a poetic and "sweet" style.

2

Old Wives' Tales and Servile Pleasures

WE HAVE DETERMINED what sort of images and ideas are suggested by the prologue, but it remains to be seen whether we ought to allow ourselves to fall under its spell. For we know by now that the fascination of a sweet voice can be dangerous, something which it might be better to resist. As I already noted in § 1.4, we need to take into account the possibility that the prologue offers only an incomplete or biased representation of what follows it. Those who consider the novel in the broader context of Apuleius' career as a *philosophus Platonicus* might well object that a more ambitious text is concealed under the mask of an entertaining story, a text that aims to communicate philosophical and religious ideas. This is, as is well known, a very controversial subject, and there seems to be no scholarly consensus on it.

I will deal with this problem here by analyzing several short passages, which I will consider in the broader contexts of literary self-representation in the novel and the novel's relationship to its cultural milieu. I will not try to offer a comprehensive interpretation of the novel or examine in detail all its possible hidden meanings; rather, I will focus on a question that is at the root of any hermeneutic engagement with the *Metamorphoses:* does Apuleius somehow urge his reader to a reading practice that goes beyond the purely aesthetic and musical pleasure promised by the prologue? The answer to this question will provide a more precise definition of the literary identity of the novel and will refine the conclusions I have outlined in the first chapter.

2.1 Entertainment, initiation, *aporia*, and satire

We can begin our investigation into the meaning of Apuleius' novel by focusing on Lucius' own description of his final metamorphosis, through which he regains his human form:

> at ego stupore nimio defixus tacitus haerebam, animo meo tam repentinum tamque magnum non capiente gaudium, quid potissimum praefarer primarium, unde novae vocis exordium caperem, quo sermone nunc renata lingua felicius auspicarer, quibus quantisque verbis tantae deae gratias agerem. (11.14.1)

> As for me, I was completely dumbfounded and stood speechless, rooted to the spot. My mind could not comprehend this great and sudden joy. I did not know what would be most appropriate to say first, where to find opening words for my new-found voice, what speech to use in making an auspicious inaugural of my tongue born anew, or with what grand words to express my gratitude to so great a goddess.

Two key words, *praefarer* and *exordium*, suggest that—even though the passage is in the middle of the last book—we can consider this sentence as a sort of new prologue, the starting point of a new narrative segment. The phraseology of the first or "true" prologue (at 1.1) is extensively echoed in this passage: first of all, *at ego* (which in this case establishes an opposition between Lucius' silence and the noisy crowd who praise Isis at 11.13.6 *clara . . . et consona voce*); but also *gaudium* (cf. 1.1.6 *laetaberis*), *praefarer* (1.1.5 *praefamur*), *novae vocis* (1.1.5 *rudis locutor;* 1.1.6 *vocis immutatio*), *exordium* (1.1.3 *exordior*), *quo sermone* (1.1.1 *sermone . . . Milesio;* 1.1.4 *indigenam sermonem*), *lingua* (1.1.4 *linguam Atthidem,* though with a different meaning), and *felicius* (1.1.3 *glebae felices*).

These lexical echoes establish analogies, but also important differences, with the "true" prologue. In this passage, we have silence, instead of enchanting words; a human voice, instead of braying; a grateful adept of Isis, instead of a brilliant entertainer. All of these differences demonstrate that Lucius, after his retransformation, is not the old Lucius any more, and that he is no longer identical to the prologue speaker.[1] What should we deduce from

---

1. The identity of the prologue-speaker is in fact somewhat ill-defined, but most interpreters identify him with Lucius: see e.g. the (rather humorous) report of a poll carried out by Ahuvia Kahane and Andrew Laird in the introduction to Kahane-Laird 2001. This is certainly the most reasonable and direct hypothesis, but one is left wondering whether a direct and reasonable answer is really

these differences? Should one Lucius prevail over the others? Should it be the religious Lucius of the last book, who as the main character completes a journey and goes beyond the light-hearted thoughtlessness that he showed at the beginning of the novel? Or, the opposite: should it be the brilliant entertainer of the prologue, the curious Lucius of the first books, a choice which would cast a shadow of suspicion over the final conversion? But we should also take into account the possibility that a combination of these two different personalities serves to shape a single and coherent figure, even if it is a complex one.

If we place the two *Lucii* side by side, we can visualize the highly problematic interaction in the novel between the element of entertainment on the one hand and of religious-philosophical commitment on the other. Such a juxtaposition ultimately urges us to find a dependable interpretive key to the novel that can guide us through the reading of Lucius' story. It is a fundamental and all-important quest, but I have to start off by saying that it will not offer us a definite answer or an interpretation that everyone will be forced to share. Any interpretation of a text, whether literary or non-literary, is provisional to some degree; it is inevitably conditioned by the clues offered in the text itself, by the cultural climate of the text, and also by the outlook of the interpreter. This is all the more true for narrative texts, which are usually by nature much less explicit than philosophical or historiographical works in their attempts to lead readers towards a given interpretation.[2] In spite of this difficulty, at the end of this chapter I will try to suggest a possible answer to the "problem of the two *Lucii*." It will not be a particularly innovative solution, but, during the long journey that will lead us to it, I hope I will be able to offer a better understanding of some very important issues regarding Apuleius' novel and its literary identity.

---

appropriate to the question of the prologue-speaker's identity. The identification of the *ego* of the prologue with Lucius becomes objectively difficult with the (in)famous *Madaurensem* at 11.27.9 (on which see below, § 4.4. p. 186); but already in the prologue it is difficult to definitively rule out other possible identities (e.g. Apuleius, a personified *Prologus*, or the book itself). Winkler 1985, 203 for example defined *ego* as a "nexus of connected identities"; the need to think of a multiple personality has been restated by Dowden 2001, 129; and according to Too 2001, 187 "identity is an aggregation" in the *Metamorphoses*. Deremetz 2002, 141 identifies the prologue-speaker with "le genre milésien dans sa plénitude, venu de Grèce et désormais passé à Rome." I have treated this subject more thoroughly in Graverini 2005a (and cf. also Rosati 2003, not available when I was writing the 2005 article, esp. 271 ff.); see also below, p. 174. In any case, Lucius certainly plays an important role in this complex of identities; consequently, for the purposes of this chapter, we should keep him at the forefront of the discussion.

2. This can be considered as an aspect, or a consequence, of the fact that the genre of the novel occupies a position in between poetry and prose: on this see above, p. 11 n. 30.

The history of the problem[3] is easily outlined. A convenient starting point is offered by Ben Edwin Perry in his monograph of 1967:

> Structurally considered in relation to the *Metamorphoses* as a whole, Book XI is an artistic unit standing apart by itself in strong contrast to the preceding ten books, with which it is only loosely and outwardly connected, and in which, by contrast, the real nature and *raison d'être* of the *Metamorphoses*—primarily a series of mundane stories exploited on their own account as such for the reader's entertainment—is to be seen. . . . The real purpose [*sc.* of Book XI] . . . was to redeem his book from the appearance of complete frivolity. To publish for sheer entertainment a lengthy work of fiction . . . was something that Apuleius really *wanted* [emphasis by the author] to do, but did not *dare* to do, without qualifying his work in such a way as would leave the impression that he had, after all, something of serious importance to convey by it. . . . Instead of building into the framework of his story-book as a whole an ostensible meaning in terms of satire, philosophical critique, or allegory which would be evident from start to finish. . . . Apuleius is content merely to tack on at the end a piece of solemn pageantry as ballast to offset the prevailing levity of the preceding ten books.[4]

Other scholars are more inclined to highlight the unity of the novel and understand it as a complete narration of Lucius' fall and redemption. For them, Book 11 offers an inexorable key to fully understanding what comes before it, and the first ten books introduce several themes that anticipate, and even demand, the religious conclusion of the last book (for example, Lucius' *curiositas* and his excessive inclination towards sensual pleasures, or the verbal and thematic parallelisms that connect the maidservant Photis to the goddess Isis). From this point of view, the true goal of the novel is not to entertain the reader, but rather to divulge a hidden religious or philosophical message.[5]

---

3. Useful overviews are offered by Harrison 1999, xxxii–xxxviii; 2000, 238–259; 2002a. A thoroughly annotated bibliography can be found in Schlam-Finkelpearl 2000, 45–117. Here, I will limit myself to the most salient references.

4. Perry 1967, 242–245.

5. For a Platonic reading of the novel, see Wlosok 1969; Penwill 1975; Dowden 1982 and 1998; O'Brien 2002 (and Hijmans 1987 for a good overview of Apuleius' philosophical works); on Lucius' *curiositas*, DeFilippo 1990, with further references. For a religious approach, see Grimal 1971; Griffiths 1975 and 1978; on Photis and Isis, Alpers 1980 and De Smet 1987. Münstermann 1995 tries to reconcile Platonism and Hermeticism in his interpretation. The most "extreme" religious readings, such as Merkelbach 1962, have fallen out of favor with most contemporary critics. A well-balanced overview can be found in Beck 1996, esp. 146 ff. Of course, it is also possible (though potentially hazardous) to read Book 11 as an essentially faithful account of Isiac religion that reflects the historical reality of the second century C.E.: see recently Egelhaaf-Gaiser 2000.

Both these interpretations clearly demand that Lucius' final conversion to the Isiac faith be taken seriously. On this point, and on many other aspects of the novel, John Winkler signaled a momentous turning point with the publication of his book in 1985, in which the *Metamorphoses* is considered as a sort of detective story without a final solution. He argues that the novel is an open text, which allows different and even opposite readings and does nothing to urge the reader in one direction or the other; therefore, it can be read as both a genuine aretalogy of Isis and a worldly-wise satire of religious credulity. Lucius' shaven head at the very end of the novel is a sort of icon of this ambiguity: it can signal both the Isiac adept's devotion and the buffoonery of a comic actor. The last scene of the *Metamorphoses* thus presents us with

> a picture of exquisite ambiguity. Those readers who are inclined to share with sympathy Lucius' commitment to his dreams and his priests will have no trouble with his bold, almost defiant and obviously joyous display of his naked head. Those others who are inclined to doubt the claims of priests and the business of shrines will find just as much justification in the *A*[*sinus*] *A*[*ureus*] for their murmurs "What a fool this Lucius is."[6]

According to Winkler, the true "key" to the text is not any religious message that can be extracted from it, but the "hermeneutic pleasure" that results from the need of interpreting it.

Though it is impossible to understate Winkler's influence on modern Apuleian scholarship, there have been some significant scholarly innovations since 1985. Several contemporary critics see the novel as a coherent structure with a well-defined goal; however, the consistency of the *Metamorphoses* emerges not as a consequence of religious or philosophical messages hidden in the first ten books, but as the result of an unambiguous interpretation of the last book as a satire of religious credulity. This interpretation culminates in the description of a deceptive cult managed by a rapacious priesthood, to whom Lucius falls victim. In this view, then, the novel has an ironic and entertaining tone from beginning to end; even after his retransformation and "conversion," Lucius is still the same naïve, curious, and gullible young man who fell victim to witchcraft in Book 3.[7]

---

6. Winkler 1985, 226 f.

7. See e.g. Van Mal-Maeder 1997a and 2001 (esp. 14–16 and 409–411); Harrison 1996, 510–516; 2000, 235–259; 2000–2001; Murgatroyd 2004. Also according to Shumate 1996, 325 "Lucius is a dupe, a gullible sucker who is so enamored of his new love that it blinds him to the possibility that he is in the hands of religious charlatans." Cf. also Habinek 1990. Van Mal-Maeder 1997a, 10 proceeds with some caution: "It would go too far, however, to define Book 11 as nothing but a

Several studies from the last few decades have suggested good reasons not to read the *Metamorphoses* as a fundamentally committed text that constantly requires a symbolic or allegorical reading, or as a text whose main goal is to divulge philosophical or religious ideas (a goal that, moreover, would be elusive for the vast majority of its readers). Hence I think that we should resist the temptation to read the "new prologue" at 11.14.1 as a sort of palinode that wishes to reveal the new and true stance of the narrator, and that consequently directs the reader towards a new and different reading practice. As I will argue at greater length here, this does not necessarily mean that we should read the last book as a satire of religious credulity, or that the novel as a whole has no protreptic aim at all. In my view, the main problem of post-Winklerian criticism is that it makes no attempt to recognize or explain the simultaneous presence of comic and serious elements in the novel.[8] A credible interpretation of the *Metamorphoses* must be able to highlight and to explain the interaction between comic and serious intentions.

To this end I will reconsider here the arguments of those critics who consider Book 11 a satire of religious credulity; then, from § 2.7 onwards, I will examine some passages that seem to articulate a seriocomic reading. We will see that this perspective does not obliterate the "satiric" features of the novel; on the contrary, it allows us to appreciate the satiric elements of the novel in a new way. Above all, a seriocomic perspective shows a greater degree of coherence with Apuleius' literary and cultural milieu.

---

parody. To be recognized as such, a text must caricature to the utmost the things it wants to denounce. Such is not the case here. . . . And though the contrast in relation to the first ten books does seem less pronounced than is generally stated, the 'book of Isis' nevertheless remains a curious appendix, whose overall tonality differs from the one dominating the Milesian books." The position of Kenney 2003, though similar in many respects to those of Harrison and Van Mal-Maeder, offers an original point of view: "over the voice of Lucius . . . we are hearing that of Apuleius admitting that he had once experimented with combining Plato and Isis *à la* Plutarch, but had later realized that after all it would not work" (pp. 185 f.). Therefore, the novel is "a retrospective assessment of a fruitless attempt to reconcile Egyptian religion with Platonism" (p. 159); Kenney himself, however, admits that it is a rather elusive message, which can be understood only by a small fraction of the readers of the novel (pp. 188 f.). Slater 2003 suggests yet another perspective: Lucius, who at the beginning of the novel was often a spectator of various events, ends up as a character in a performance staged for others: a situation that, if we consider the various allusions to and descriptions of (amphi)theater performances in the novel, "seems more terrifying than comforting" (p. 100). According to Keulen 2003c, 130 Lucius is a victim of superstition in the last book, but "it is not the intrinsic aim of the *Metamorphoses* to attack superstition. . . . Rather, superstition is used as a foil, as a conventional literary means of exposing corrupt rhetoric. . . . Thus, addiction to superstitious (Isiac) cult becomes one of the paradigms of false rhetoric."

    8. Of course there are some exceptions, before and after Winkler: see e.g. Walsh 1970, Tatum 1979, Gianotti 1986, and Schlam 1992. See also the thorough and well-balanced introductions to the translated editions by Fo 2002 and Nicolini 2005.

2.2 Dissonances

The hypothesis that Lucius is a gullible victim of the greedy priests of Isis is usually based on the last chapters of Book 11. The intense lyricism of Lucius' prayer at 11.2 and his intense emotions at 11.7, for example, do not cast any suspicion on Lucius or on the Isiac cult: the first real doubts emerge when Lucius meets the Egyptian priests, who would seem to exploit his naivety and gullibility to their material advantage. Nevertheless, some interpreters have also drawn attention to a few dissonances in the first chapters of Book 11 that would undermine the serious tone of the novel's ending and support a satirical reading.

2.2.1 Desecrating details

At 11.1 the ass wakes up in the night and loses himself in the contemplation of the moon and the silence that surrounds him. He hopes that Fate is at last fed up with his misfortunes and decides to pray to the nocturnal goddess; but before doing that, he dips his head in the sea seven times, since Pythagoras regards that number as "most fitting for rituals" (*religionibus aptissimum*). The scene is full of mystery and expectation. Stephen Harrison and Danielle Van Mal-Maeder have pointed out, however, that its solemnity is challenged by the fact that Lucius is still an ass, and not yet a man, when he purifies himself in the water and prays to the Moon.[9] Wytse Keulen adds that this purification rite resembles the superstitious practices described by Plutarch in *De superstitione* 3.166a.[10] Similarly, after Lucius' retransformation at 11.13–14, the crowd is awe-struck and praises Isis' power and mercy; and yet the comic description of Lucius standing naked before them, "pressing my thighs tightly together, and placing my hands carefully in front of me as to protect myself properly" (11.14.4), seems to provide a sharp contrast to the solemnity of the crowd.[11]

These solemn scenes do contain some comic elements, but it should be noted that this mixture is a constant feature recurring throughout the novel, and not solely in the last book. In fact, we can only draw conclusions that are somewhat obvious from this heterogeneous blend of the comic and the

---

9. Harrison 1999, 239 f.; for Van Mal-Maeder 1997a, 106 "the simple fact that the glory of Isis' omnipotence is to be revealed through an asinine character like Lucius" is a discordant element.

10. Keulen 2003c, 126.

11. See Van Mal-Maeder 1997a, 108 f.; a similar point is made by Murgatroyd 2004, 320 on the abundant sweating of the ass at 11.7.1, immediately after Isis' apparition.

serious: Apuleius wrote a novel, not an Isiac catechism or a philosophical treatise. Furthermore, he decided to translate and rework a Greek novel that certainly contained a number of comic elements such as those described above (e.g., Lucius' nudity after his retransformation).[12] Finally, we can conclude that he consciously decided to retain many of these comic elements in his translation. The presence of comic elements helps shape the literary identity of the novel, both as a single text and within its genre; what we have to decide here is whether the presence of these elements in Book 11 is specifically intended to cast suspicion on Egyptian cults and on Lucius' conversion.

In my opinion, the text provides no clues to this effect; a comic and satirical reading is still possible, but cannot rely on the passages mentioned above. Lucius' nudity in the middle of the crowd is certainly ridiculous: it might even remind us of the description of Socrates in Book 1. Aristomenes finds him dressed in rags, and his miserable cloak is so short that when he covers his head with it, he is left naked beneath his navel (1.6.4).[13] But we should resist the temptation to consider this parallel as one of the proofs that witchcraft and Isiac religion are similar, rather than opposed to one another.[14] The text does not blame Lucius' nudity on Isis or on her adepts (no one notices the irony of his condition, and a priest immediately offers him a linen tunic to cover himself), while Socrates' miserable state, explicitly deplored by Aristomenes, is a consequence of the witch Meroe's rapacity (1.7.10).

We can say the same for Lucius' purification ritual. It is true that Plutarch describes a similar ceremony as an example of superstitious practice, and in addition to Plutarch we could add the testimony offered by satirical poems of Horace, Persius and Juvenal.[15] But does the text urge the reader toward a satirical reading? Once again, a comparison with another scene will prove useful. At 9.4.1 the ass needs to demonstrate that he is not affected with rabies, so he approaches a large pot full of water, drinks, and even dips his head in it. This last act is completely unnecessary: at 9.3.3 it is very clear that Lucius' persecutors want only to make sure he does not refuse to drink. Lucius is plainly acting according to the principle "better safe than sorry," but there is also a clear allusion to ritual purification: the water he drinks is

---

12. *Onos* 54.
13. On Socrates in Book 1 see below, pp. 134 ff..
14. Cf. below, § 2.4.
15. Hor. *Sat.* 2.3.291 f.; Pers. 2.15 f.; Juv. 6.522 ff.; cf. Griffiths 1975, 113 *ad* 11.1.4, who compiles a list of non-satirical texts that describe purification rituals involving water.

the "water of salvation," *salutares vere equidem . . . aquas*.[16] This salvation, however, is only temporary: the ass remains an ass and is still in the hands of the corrupted priests of the Dea Syria. He must give further proof of his tameness immediately after his "purification" by enduring several trials. Conversely, on a narrative level, the episode at 11.1.4 is well integrated into the plot without superfluous content, and is described in a wholly different register. Lucius' misfortunes are about come to an end, and have already ended when, at 11.23.1, another purifying bath is necessary before his initiation.

Nonetheless, there is something surprising and subversive in the description of an ass engaging in religious ceremonies. But the point of such a subversive description is still unclear.

2.2.2 LUCIUS, THE PRIEST, AND THE MOB

Immediately after his retransformation, Lucius stands petrified, mute, and completely naked in the middle of the crowd. The priest of Isis (at 11.22.3 we will be informed that his name is Mithras) rejoices at Lucius' salvation, and takes the opportunity to praise the goddess Isis for granting it. He then gives a teleological reading of Lucius' vicissitudes:

> Multis et variis exanclatis laboribus magnisque Fortunae tempestatibus et maximis actus procellis ad portum Quietis et aram Misericordiae tandem, Luci, venisti. Nec tibi natales ac ne dignitas quidem, vel ipsa, qua flores, usquam doctrina profuit, sed lubrico virentis aetatulae ad serviles delapsus voluptates curiositatis inprosperae sinistrum praemium reportasti. Sed utcumque Fortunae caecitas, dum te pessimis periculis discruciat, ad religiosam istam beatitudinem inprovida produxit malitia. . . . In tutelam iam receptus es Fortunae, sed videntis, quae suae lucis splendore ceteros etiam deos illuminat. . . . Videant inreligiosi, videant et errorem suum recognoscant: en ecce pristinis aerumnis absolutus Isidis magnae providentia gaudens Lucius de sua Fortuna triumphat. (11.15.1–4)

> Finally, Lucius, you have reached the harbor of Peace and the altar of Mercy. Not your birth, nor even your position, nor even your fine education (*doctrina*) has been of any help whatever to you; but on the slippery path of headstrong youth you plunged into slavish pleasures and reaped the perverse

---

16. On the comic elements of this scene, see Mattiacci 1996, 119, who attributes them to a typically Apuleian sense of humor. A similarly ironic ordeal is described in Achilles Tatius 8.14.2–4: Melites corroborates her captious oath on her chastity by lowering herself into sacred waters.

reward of your ill-starred curiosity. Nevertheless the blindness of Fortune, while torturing you with the worst of perils, has brought you in its random wickedness to this holy state of happiness . . . now you have been taken under the protection of a Fortune who can see, and who with the brilliance of her own light illumines all the other gods as well . . . let the unbelievers see; let them see and recognize their errant ways. Behold! Lucius, set free from his tribulations of old and rejoicing in the providence of great Isis, triumphs over his Fortune.

Mithras' speech summarizes Lucius' adventures as a story of fall and redemption. It is of course an important passage for the interpretation of the novel, and, not surprisingly, every scholar who attempts to give an overall interpretation of the *Metamorphoses* must deal with it. Winkler,[17] in particular, points out that Mithras' speech is only *one* of the interpretations of Lucius' adventures provided by the text, even though the text itself confers authority on it in several ways (the speech, ultimately inspired by the goddess Isis, is pronounced by a high priest and is followed by exhaustion and silence). Other interpretations are offered by Lucius himself (who keeps silent), and most notably, by the crowd:

> Exin permixtus agmini religioso procedens comitabar sacrarium totae ciuitati notus ac conspicuus, digitis hominum nutibusque notabilis. Omnes in me populi fabulabantur: "Hunc omnipotentis hodie deae numen augustum reformavit ad homines. Felix hercules et ter beatus, qui vitae scilicet praecedentis innocentia fideque meruerit tam praeclarum de caelo patrocinium ut renatus quodam modo statim sacrorum obsequio desponderetur." (11.16.2–4)

> At once I joined the ceremonial procession and walked along in attendance to the shrine. The whole city knew about me and I was the center of attention as people pointed their fingers and nodded at me. Everyone was talking about me, saying: "He is the one who was transformed back into a human being today by the majestic force of the all-powerful goddess. How fortunate he is, by Hercules, and thrice blessed! It is doubtless because of the innocence and faithfulness of his past life that he has earned such remarkable patronage from heaven, and was in a manner reborn and immediately engaged to the service of her cult."

---

17. Winkler 1985, 209–215.

This "popular" interpretation, according to Winkler, is incompatible with Mithras' speech. The priest had condemned Lucius because he was dominated by *serviles voluptates* and *curiositas improspera,* and presents Isis' intervention as an act of benevolence; the crowd, instead, praises Lucius' *innocentia* and *fides*,[18] and here Isis is depicted as having rewarded Lucius with her help. Hence, there are two incompatible interpretations of this key event. The text attributes some characteristics of orthodoxy to one of them, but does nothing to prove the other wrong—and Lucius himself, the main interested party, does nothing but keep silent. All this, Winkler says, suggests that this is an "unauthorized" text. No clear preference for an interpretive approach is expressed; the reader is left completely free to choose his own reading.

Winkler's fully aporetic perspective has been mostly abandoned by subsequent critics, who see in the text a more decidedly parodic and satirical stance:

> Like the epiphany of Isis, the speech [*sc.* of Mithras] shows elevation and dignity. But the reaction of the crowd at 11.16.3, as Winkler has crucially stressed, injects a note of complexity and a suggestion of parodic or satirical interpretation. . . . The gap between these two interpretations, as Winkler has stressed, encourages the reader to think that not everything in the narrative of the Isis-cult is to be taken at face value. Every time an elevated and dignified religious moment is narrated, it is followed by material which suggests another approach.[19]

Indeed, there is some difference between the point of view of Mithras, for whom Lucius is a sinner saved by divine Providence, and that of the crowd, for whom Lucius deserves salvation because of his *innocentia* and *fides*. Some scholars, however, have tried to mitigate this difference. Gwyn Griffiths,[20] for example, suggests that the phrase "innocence and faithfulness of his past life" is a reference to Lucius' life *before* the events narrated in the novel, and that the novel relates his subsequent fall from grace. Griffiths also argues that the *makarismos* of the crowd is constructed with standard formulae, whose significance we should not overestimate. As for Mithras'

---

18. Winkler 1985, 212 f., with further references at n. 12.
19. Harrison 2000, 244.
20. Griffiths 1975, 257 *ad* 11.16.4. S. Heller 1983, 330 f. goes as far as to state that "the priest's speech is an invective against *saeva Fortuna,* not a statement of censure against Lucius. While Lucius' curiosity and involvement with magic were indeed the occasion of his transformation into an ass, the transformation is not said by the priest to be a punishment for his curiosity."

speech, I would add that although the priest does not pass over Lucius' sins in silence, he does all he can to present Lucius to the crowd in a favorable light. For this reason, Mithras acknowledges Lucius' *natales, dignitas,* and *doctrina*. These are external virtues, different from the *innocentia* and *fides* attributed to him by the crowd, but they are positive traits all the same (and, like *innocentia* and *fides,* they refer to Lucius' life *before* the novel). The priest also provides an extenuating circumstance for Lucius, his *virens aetatula:* in the first part of Mithras' speech, Lucius' youthful ignorance was the cause of his downfall and merited his unfortunate metamorphosis.

It is worth noting that there are contradictions within Mithras' speech, as well. He presents seemingly incompatible images of Lucius: he is simultaneously a sinner and a young man oppressed by *Fortuna*. Mithras' speech also suggests that *Fortuna* is "blind" not so much because she shoots her arrows at random (on the contrary, her obstinacy in persecuting Lucius is constant and deliberate), but because she fails to realize that her persecution will only lead Lucius towards Isis. Unless we want to consider the blind *Fortuna* (against whom Mithras rails so scornfully) as a sort of sidekick who chastises sinners on behalf of Isis, we have to admit that the priest's speech is not a monolithic condemnation of Lucius' faults. The young, unfortunate sinner is easy to forgive, and easy to like.

Be it great or small, the difference between Mithras' perspective and the perspective of the crowd cannot completely be explained away by identifying the crowd itself with the *inreligiosi* who are admonished in Mithras' speech. Winkler himself points out that

> It would have been easy enough for Apuleius to specify that the second interpretation comes from the *profani*. What the text offers us, however, is simply an incorrect general opinion, proreligious in content, not specifically attached to anyone or undercut in any way by the narrator's authority.[21]

The text suggests a simpler reason for this difference: those who speak at 11.16.3–4 could probably *not* be present at Lucius' retransformation, and thus could not have heard Mithras' speech. When the priest finishes speaking, the procession, which had stopped in astonishment at the miracle, starts up again, and Lucius walks along with it. While he moves on, it is clear that Lucius becomes a great spectacle. The account of his metamorphosis and of Mithras' speech follows him, passing from mouth to mouth.[22] The crowd,

---

21. Winkler 1985, 213.

22. It is easy to imagine that the procession was not compact, and that the participants had different vantage points, depending on where they were positioned at the moment of Lucius' transforma-

therefore, can only conjecture about what lay behind the grace received by Lucius, since, unlike Mithras, they have not been divinely informed in advance (11.6.3; 11.13.1). They know of the miraculous event only by hearsay: indeed, the text itself emphasizes the subjectivity of the crowd's interpretation with a telling *scilicet*. Consequently, it seems perfectly natural that the narrator lets the crowd offer a "vulgarized" version of the facts, different from that of Mithras.[23] The text, in my opinion, offers no real basis for a theological debate on the reasons for Lucius' salvation.

Last, but not least, is Lucius' reaction. According to Winkler, "Mithras steps in exactly at the moment when Lucius is trying to decide what to say" (p. 214), but this is not correct. Lucius, petrified with astonishment, is still speechless, but he already knows perfectly well what he wants to say: he is searching for how to convey his "gratitude to so great a goddess" (11.14.2). Some scholars point out that Lucius could have gotten the much-coveted roses on his own, without the intervention of Isis, since by that point in the narrative it was finally spring.[24] Nevertheless, I still think that Lucius has good reason to be grateful to Isis. It is true that at 10.29.2 the ass voices his faint hope (*tenuis specula*) that his miseries can come to an end with the springtime arrival of blooming roses, but it is also true that he has had roses within reach many times before, to no avail.[25] His problem is not the availability of roses, but rather that evil fortune always prevents him from getting hold of any. Moreover, he would need to eat the roses in secret, so as not to be accused of practicing magic by a witness to his retransformation. Isis eliminates both of these obstacles with her intervention.

To conclude, we cannot positively speak of an Isiac *Summa Theologiae* in Book 11 of the novel. Mithras' sermon is slightly ambiguous, and the comments of the crowd are not much more than rumors. Moreover, there is no

---

tion. At 11.9.1 *oblectationes ludicras popularium* (the *anteludia* described at the previous chapter) are wandering here and there while Isis' *peculiaris pompa* is starting out; the crowd is dense everywhere, requiring a group of men at the front of the procession to clear a way through it (11.9.6).

23. Such is the case if we consider that the astonishment and the comments of the crowd seem to have been caused by Lucius' immediate acceptance into the group of Isiac devotees, and not so much by Lucius' retransformation (at which most of them, as we have seen, had not been present). The bandit's speech at 7.1.5–6 provides a good example of an account that has suffered extreme deformation as it is passed from mouth to mouth: *Nec argumentis dubiis, sed rationibus probabilibus congruo cunctae multitudinis consensu nescio qui Lucius auctor manifestus facinoris postulabatur, qui proximis diebus fictis commendaticiis litteris Miloni sese virum commentitus bonum artius conciliaverat, ut etiam hospitio susceptus inter familiaris intimos haberetur, plusculisque ibidem diebus demoratus falsis amoribus ancillae Milonis animum inrepens ianuae claustra sedulo exploraverat et ipsa membra in quis omne patrimonium condi solebat curiose perspexerat.*

24. Winkler 1985, 213; Van Mal-Maeder 1997a, 100 f.

25. Cf. 3.27.2–3; 3.29.5–8; at 4.2 the search for roses is fruitless; at 7.15.2 the hope of finding roses is short-lived.

good reason to read these passages as an ironic demystification of superstitious beliefs. At this point, it seems that the novel thoroughly exploits religious elements for its narrative purposes, but not to the point of becoming a work of propaganda, or of hagiography.

2.2.3 His Holiness Martin Luther

Mithras himself has been considered an ambiguous figure for other reasons, as well. Winkler points out that

> To give the name Mithras to the high priest of Isis, whose role is to reveal to the first-reader a startling new meaning for *The Golden Ass,* is like introducing the pope in the last chapter of a detective novel and calling him Martin Luther . . . the mythology, cult, and aspirations of militaristic Mithras and maternal Isis have so little in common that it is hard to imagine how a single person could take them both seriously—that is, with the fervor and dedication illustrated by the prayers of Book 11.[26]

In this view, the name of the priest, who appears in the narrative at 11.12.1 (though Isis mentions him already at 11.2.2–3), would be withheld until 11.22.3 precisely in order to ease the shock resulting from an Isiac priest bearing the name of a Persian god; this would maintain "the discrete balance of Book 11's hermeneutic comedy."[27]

The "ideological" incompatibility between the cults of Isis and Mithras, on which Winkler's argumentation rests, is mostly taken for granted by the historians of Eastern religions in the Roman Empire.[28] However, it is also possible to consider the two cults as complementary, rather than vying with each other.[29] Inasmuch as one cult identified the supreme god as the Moon, and the other the Sun, a syncretistic outlook would consider them akin to one another. But other elements contributed to an easy interaction between the two religions, such as the presence of the goddess Anāhitā in the Per-

---

26. Winkler 1985, 245 and 247.
27. Winkler 1985, 246.
28. See e.g. Cumont 1896, 1: 332: "The ancient religious hostility of the Egyptians and Persians endured even in Imperial Rome, and the Iranian mysteries seem to have been separated from those of Isis by a quiet rivalry, if not an open opposition."
29. See e.g. Witt 1975. Turcan 2003 states that there are no grounds for connecting initiation cults with ethnic or cultural identity (an assumption often made by scholars), and suggests that in Rome and in the other large cities of the Empire "the coexistence of foreign cults contributed . . . to a sort of ecumenical paganism" (p. 556).

sian pantheon (who bears a close resemblance to Isis in regard to mythical functions and iconographical features), and the common identification of Mithras with Sarapis. The role of conciliator and peacemaker played by Mithras himself may also have facilitated an interaction between the two religions.

A brief glance at the historical evidence confirms that contact and communication between the cults, though not always simple, was not only possible, but actually took place. Winkler adduces two examples as evidence to the contrary. First, he cites a dedicatory inscription "to the only god Zeus, Sarapis, Helios" where the name of Sarapis has been erased and replaced by Mithras.[30] The second example appears in Eunapius (*VS* 7.3.4 p. 476 Wright). The text contains an account of the repression of the cult of Demeter by a certain Eleusinian hierophant, who was also a devotee of Mithras. Exceptions to this supposed opposition of the two cults are rare and come late, but in the fourth century C.E. we know of a Ceionius Rufius Volusianus who held various sacerdotal offices; he was a *pater* of Mithras and *propheta* of Isis.[31] In the late third century C.E. a slave named Mithres makes a dedication to Sarapis.[32] Now, Winkler rightly emphasizes the difference between a slave named Mithres and the priest Mithras' very prominent position in the Isiac ending of the *Metamorphoses*. Nonetheless, we should not expect to find a perfect epigraphic parallel for the character in Apuleius' novel.

Moreover, a few more cases of interaction between the two cults are attested. The temple of Iuppiter Dolichenus on the Aventine, for example, contained sacred images of both Isis and Mithras.[33] At Nersae, in central Italy, there is a Mithraic bas-relief dated 172 C.E. and paid for by a Marcus Apronianus; another inscription attributes two statues of Serapis and Isis

---

30. Winkler 1985, 246; cf. Vidman 1969, 196 n. 389. But Becatti 1954, 81 deems the same inscription a good example of syncretism, rather than opposition between the two cults, since the stone "had been placed by the Mithraic priests in the temple of Carcalla devoted to the Alexandrian divinities, thus putting Mithras in a rank below Serapis; and after the death of Caracalla, perhaps under Commodus (who was a protector of Mithraism), the priests wanted to correct the primary inscription by explicitly identifying Mithras with Zeus Helios." In fact, on the back side of the inscription there is a dedication to "Zeus Helios Sarapis Mithras"—a clear example of syncretism between Persian and Egyptian cults (the text could be read also as a dedication to "Zeus Helios Sarapis" made by a person named Mithras: in this case we would have an instance of a theophoric name that seems to clash with the cult, just as is the case of Apuleius' Mithras).
31. Vidman 1969, 212 n. 434. More fourth-century followers of both Isis and Mithras are listed at pp. 457 and 450. On Ceionius Rufius Volusianus see also Mora 1990, 402.
32. Vidman 1969, 196 n. 388; see also Mora 1990, 398.
33. See Chini 1996. More continuities between Egyptian and Persian cults can be found in Witt 1975, 483 ff., with examples from Memphis, Tarsus, Doura-Europos, Athens, and Palaiopolis (on the island of Andros), as well as several other towns both in Italy (including Rome itself) and the Roman provinces.

to the same person.³⁴ Attilio Mastrocinque points out that "in Mithraism the influx of Egyptian elements, and in particular themes from the Osiris-cycle . . . defined the doctrine at the base of Mithraism itself, as demonstrated by the statues, reliefs, and inscriptions of Sarapis, found in the Mithraea in London (Walbrook), Emerita, Poetovio, and Rome (the Mithraeum of Santa Prisca and the baths of Caracalla)."³⁵ Cupid and Psyche are portrayed on a Mithraic gem used for magic, and in a bas-relief of the Mithraeum of Santa Prisca. This testifies to the fact that the myth of Cupid and Psyche, a tale that shows links to Egyptian mythology and to the Platonic myth of Eros, had been somehow "adopted" by Mithraic religion, as well.³⁶

It is true that the Isiac cult seems to be exclusive and intolerant of other cults: this is shown by the external marks symbolizing membership in the cult, such as the shaven head of adepts. The evidence I have listed above, however, demonstrates that this sense of exclusiveness was not universal. Such external marks of membership may simply suggest that "the cult of Isis much more regularly offered a religious status that could also be paraded as a marker of social and public status," rather than suggesting a sharp disinclination to syncretism in comparison with other cults.³⁷

Among the literary sources it is worth mentioning the prayer to *Phoebus parens,* which appears at the end of the first book of Statius' *Thebaid.* In this passage, Osiris and Mithras are two of the names that can be used to address Apollo (1.718–720).³⁸ Another text, though it lacks evidential force (owing to the fact that it appears in a fictional narrative), could suggest an even tighter connection: at the end of Heliodorus' *Aithiopika,* as in the *Metamorphoses,* a priest summarizes the vicissitudes of Theagenes and Charikleia. His account is somewhat biased, and he says that the story of

---

34. Beard-North-Price 1998, 307; sources in vol. II at 12.5b. See also Mora 1990, 393; Vidman 1969, 224 n. 477. On an unnamed priest of Isis active in Rome in 376, who had also celebrated a *taurobolium* and held an office in the cult of Mithras, see Mora 1990, 441. The double priesthood of Isis and Cybeles/Magna Mater is not infrequent: see again Mora 1990, 400 (*Cantria P. fil. Longina,* priestess of *Mater deum Magna Idaea,* and priestess of *Isis regina,* from Apulia at the end of the first century C.E.); 423 (*L. Pacilius Taurus,* priest of *Magna Mater, dea Suria* and *sacrorum Isidis,* mentioned in a first- or second-century funeral inscription from Brundisium); 416 (*C. Iulius C. f. Horatia Severus,* priest of Isis and of Magna Mater); 435 (*L. Valerius L. f. Fyrmus,* second–third century, priest of Isis of Ostia, and of the Transtiberine Magna Mater).

35. Mastrocinque 1998, 92; cf. Witt 1975, 486.

36. Mastrocinque 1998, 100 f.; cf. Witt 1975, 490.

37. Beard-North-Price 1998, 309. They also point out that the archaeological evidence, from which much of our knowledge of these cults derives, requires close scrutiny: "if only objects with a strongly Egyptian style are associated with Isiac shrines, then Isiac shrines will inevitably appear exclusively Egyptian" (p. 282). The impression of exclusivity of Isiac cult could be, at least in part, the result of such a "circular" interpretation of archaeological findings.

38. See Witt 1975, 482. A large collection of Greek and Roman literary sources on Oriental cults can be found in Sanzi 2003.

the two characters has followed a previously unsuspected divine plan. The priest's name is Sisimithres, and Ken Dowden has suggested that it might not be a coincidence that it is the result of a fusion of the names Isis and Mithras (the former spelled in reverse).[39] Although it is only hypothesis, this could be another instance of the novel's tendency toward religious syncretism.

To sum up, it seems to me that, in spite of Winkler's arguments, it is not overly difficult to think that somebody could seriously follow both Isiac and Mithraic religions. In fact, emperors like Trajan, Commodus, Caracalla, Galerius and Julian clearly had no problem in supporting and even following both Egyptian and Persian cults.[40] The fact that Mithras' name is disclosed so late in Book 11 is certainly not due to Apuleius' fear of disrupting the narrative illusion with a sudden and violent "theological" shock. In my opinion, Mithras is called by name at 11.22.3 and 11.25.7 to highlight his increased familiarity with Lucius: after being Isis' instrument for Lucius' salvation, the priest is now also the minister of his initiation (moreover, he is also *divino quodam stellarum consortio . . . mihi coniunctum*), and even a sort of surrogate father, to whom Lucius shows his fondness with hugs and kisses.[41]

But even if the choice of the name Mithras is not desecrating, as Winkler claimed, the question still stands: why "Mithras"? While the name has the effect of inhibiting a purely Isiac interpretation of the final book, it does nothing to encourage us to think that the priests of Isis are deceitful and exploitative. On the contrary, it reflects the syncretistic tendencies typical of the religious practice in the second century C.E., and which, moreover, are clearly attested by Apuleius himself;[42] it prevents us from reading the novel as propaganda for a specific mystery cult and urges us to search for a more general and inclusive meaning.[43]

---

39. Heliodorus 10.39; cf. Dowden 1996, 270. Note, however, that Sisimithres was also the name of a general whom Alexander met in battle, and therefore is not Heliodorus' invention: see e.g. Strabo 11.11.4; Plut. *Alex.* 58.3–5; Curt. 8.2.19–8.4.20.

40. Sources and further bibliography in Witt 1975, 487 f.

41. 11.25.7: *ad istum modum deprecato summo numine complexus Mithram sacerdotem et meum iam parentem colloque eius multis osculis inhaerens veniam postulabam, quod eum condigne tantis beneficiis munerari nequirem*. With a rather irreverent analogy, we could point out that we meet the old *cinaedus*, follower of the Dea Syria, at the beginning of his negotiation to buy the ass at 8.24.2, but his name (Philebus, a "speaking name" like many others in the novel—Mithras' too, in a different way) is revealed only at 8.24.6 when the negotiation is over and Lucius definitively belongs to him. On the name of Philebus, perhaps a playful reference to the beginning of Plato's *Philebus* (11b: Φίληβος μὲν τοίνυν ἀγαθὸν εἶναί φησι τὸ χαίρειν πᾶσι ζῴοις καὶ τὴν ἡδονὴν καὶ τέρψιν), see Hijmans 1978, 112.

42. See *Apol.* 55,8 *sacrorum pleraque initia in Graecia participavi*, with the commentary by Hunink 1997 *ad loc.;* Lucius himself, in the novel, is *sacris pluribus initiatus* (3.15.4).

43. According to Dowden 1998, 3 "the priest Mithras is a deliberately dissonant note to emphasize the broader applicability of these cults when correctly understood in establishment language."

Before moving on, it is worth mentioning another theory concerning the appearance of the name Mithras in the novel. Filippo Coarelli[44] has suggested that the author of the *Metamorphoses* was a certain L. Apuleius Marcellus, who, according to an inscription found on two lead water pipes, owned an Ostian *domus* around the middle of the second century C.E. He presents a variety of circumstantial evidence to support this theory. Near the house, in a public area closely connected with it, the base of a monument has been discovered; if the dedication found nearby belonged to this monument, as seems likely, then it was dedicated to a Quintus Asinius Marcellus, a consul and patron of Ostia,[45] whose family conducted business in Africa. Asinius Marcellus is also the name of the priest of Isis who awaits the visit of the "man from Madauros" at 11.27.2–9 and will lead Lucius toward his second initiation. If Coarelli's hypothesis is true, then the passage contains not one, but two ruptures in the dramatic pretense of the novel. First, Lucius becomes for an instant a "man of Madauros," and thus is identified with Apuleius. Second, the character of the priest is given the name of an important person from Apuleius' period, perhaps the friend or patron who had introduced him into the best social circles in the capital.[46] But more important is the so-called "Mithraeum of the seven spheres," found near the Ostian house and connected to it. Coarelli places the construction of this building in the same period as Lucius Apuleius Marcellus' restoration of the *domus* and suggests that Apuleius himself had the Mithraeum built. The iconography of this room is remarkable. Coarelli points out the syncretistic nature of the Mithraic cult as it is represented there, and its Platonizing overtones;[47] and some details, like the order of the planetary gods, seem to correspond closely to two passages in Apuleius' *de mundo* and *de Platone*—and only to them.[48]

It is well known that there is no trace of an initiation of Apuleius into the cult of Isis. But, if Coarelli is right,[49] there is concrete evidence of a connec-

---

44. Coarelli 1989.

45. For Coarelli 1989, 41 f. he is the Asinius Marcellus who was consul under Hadrian, and not one of his sons.

46. Coarelli 1989 dates his death around 148, when the monument in Ostia was dedicated to him. This date could be used (but Coarelli does not venture this far) to set a *terminus ante quem* for the chronology of the novel, that therefore would have been written during Apuleius' stay at Rome (between 145 and 152 for Coarelli, p. 39). Such a tight chronology, even though it is accepted by some scholars, is far from certain and is problematic in several respects. The mention of Asinius Marcellus in the novel could be just an homage paid by Apuleius to his old patron's family (or, *pace* Coarelli, p. 41 and n. 76, it could be interpreted as a reference to a son of the consul). On the chronology of the novel see below, pp. 192 ff.

47. Coarelli 1989, 36.

48. Coarelli 1989, 36 f.

49. Indeed, there is still open controversy about Coarelli's conclusions. D'Asdia 2002 dates the

tion between Apuleius and the cult of Mithras, filtered through an *interpretatio platonica*.⁵⁰ The choice of Isis as Lucius' savior was almost unavoidable, due to his asinine shape, and the connection in Isiac cult of the ass to Seth/Typhon.⁵¹ Nonethelesss, we can imagine that Apuleius, when he had to choose a name for his priest, slipped into the novel at least a mention of the god to whom he was personally tied.

2.3 Greedy priests

Admittedly, all the texts I have analyzed so far do not yield evidence that would force us in one direction or the other. According to Winkler himself,

> The swelling rise of chapters 1–26 of Book 11 can only be read as a joyful hymn to the saving goddess, with Mithras's speech setting a tone that overwhelms the tiny dissonance of the crowd's misinterpretation. But . . . that same Lucius whom we are constrained to view as a providentially saved man in chapters 1–26 also has the unmistakable look of a fool in the last four chapters of the book. The effect and intent is to make us see Lucius two ways—as a redeemed Isiac and a dupe—and to be unable to decide *on the author's authority* which is finally correct.⁵²

It is therefore only in the last four chapters of the novel that the ambiguous character of Book 11 would become unmistakable, in the form of repeated and increasingly large expenditures that mark Lucius' progression through the three initiations. The greed of Isis' priests is the first of the three strongest arguments used by several scholars, especially after Winkler,⁵³ who

---

Mithraeum much later than the middle second century, on the basis of a study of the stonework and of the mosaics; therefore, it would be incompatible with Apuleius' biography. Beck 2000 disproves Coarelli's statements on the connection between the order of the planets in the Mithraeum and Apuleius' Platonic writings (see also Beck 1979); however, he still believes in the possible identification of Lucius Apuleius Marcellus with the novelist and points out several "Mithraic" elements in the novel. It must be noted, in any case, that Beck does not consider the *Metamorphoses* a "roman à clef," whose hidden meaning would be understandable only to a narrow circle of initiates. On the contrary, he states that "the audience of *The Golden Ass* is the sympathetic outsider" (p. 560); and that there is no reason to imagine that Apuleius himself was "a full-blown Mithraic initiate" (p. 563).

50. On this, see Turcan 1975 and Beck 2000.
51. Cf. 11.6.2, where Isis defines the ass as *mihi . . . iam dudum detestabilis belua*, with Griffiths 1975, 162 *ad loc.*
52. Winkler 1985, 215 f. (his emphasis).
53. Of course there are some precedents. See e.g. Griffiths 1978, 152 f.: " . . . there are several hints in Book 11 that the priests of Isis in Rome, when they urge Lucius to undertake the Second and Third Initiations, do so in a rather mercenary spirit, compelling him to sell even his wardrobe. Yet

consider the main character of the *Metamorphoses* to be the gullible victim of a rapacious cult.

The first expense Lucius has to meet to carry on his religious practices is to rent an *aedes* near Isis' temple at 11.19.1.[54] The initiation at 11.23.1 seems to require even more money, and Isis herself reveals its exact amount to Lucius (11.21.4; 11.22.3). After his initiation, Lucius laments his poverty, since it does not allow him to show his complete gratitude to the goddess and her priest Mithras (11.24.6; 11.25.6–7). Up to this point we could say that nothing terribly strange has occurred, but all of this will be repeated with the second and third initiations, both of which will take place in Rome, and which are described in the last four chapters. At 11.27.8 the priest Asinius Marcellus says that he has been forewarned by Osiris in a dream of the visit of a "man of Madauros, but very poor" who should be initiated; Osiris also announces *studiorum gloriam* for the Madauran and a large reward for Asinius himself (but no further mention of this reward is to be found in the novel). At 11.28.1 Lucius again laments his indigence, complaining that it is delaying the ceremonies he has longed for. The god urges him on, chiding him that he is afraid when it comes to paying for the initiation, but would not have hesitated to sell even his clothing to give himself up to pleasure. Lucius follows the god's advice, collects the necessary money, undergoes the prescribed purification rites, shaves his head, and finally receives his second initiation. A short time later (11.29.1 *post pauculum tempus*) comes both a new dream and the order to submit to yet another initiation. Lucius suspects that this new divine intimation is due to some deficiency in the rites he has performed before: perhaps the priests did not initiate him properly the last time? But another dream soon reveals that this will actually be a further advance into the mysteries; and moreover, the sacred garments Lucius was wearing in Corinth are still in that city, so Lucius needs to get new clothes anyway. This time Lucius does not lament his poverty, but he says he has organized everything in accordance with his deep devotion rather than his wealth. We are left with the impression that once more the rites require a large amount of money, perhaps more than Lucius can afford.

Indeed, Isiac religion pays attention to worldly matters, too, and the adept's life is certainly not inexpensive. Apuleius' novel is not the only ancient source to yield this impression: the mercenary aspect of foreign cults offered an easy target to Juvenal and Persius, who considered them a sign of

---

with this exception the picture of the Egyptian cult is suffused with holy awe and admiration."

54. But this does not seem to be an expense required by the cult; I do not think we are obliged to conclude, with Van Mal-Maeder 1997a, 102 n. 56, that "Lucius is obliged to rent a seat in the temple."

the moral decline of Rome.⁵⁵ Lucius' enthusiasm in submitting himself to as many as three expensive initiations might very well reflect Apuleius' veiled skepticism and give the account of those rites a satirical tone.

It is certainly easy to take an ironic view of such a mix of spiritual and worldly interests, and moralizing literature often censured religious practices on the grounds that they were overly wordly. However, it is also clear that the interpretation of episodes such as Lucius' expensive initiations depends to a large degree on the perspective of the interpreter. A Christian might find no trace of irony, or any note of sarcasm, in the story of the poor widow who offers all her savings at the temple,⁵⁶ but others might regard that as a paradigm of foolish and overly-devout behavior. This is exactly Winkler's position: Apuleius' text does not push its readers towards either faith or irony—instead, it can suggest both attitudes simultaneously. It is up to the reader to choose if he prefers to identify himself with Lucius' religious enthusiasm, trusting in the probity of the priests of Isis, or to carry out an ironic/satirical reading of their conduct, as well as of Lucius' faith. What we need to check, therefore, is whether the text is really open to both these interpretations.

First of all, it is useful to recall a passage of text found in the *De deo Socratis* (chapter 14), in which Apuleius describes the existence of demons (*daimones*). According to this passage, the *daimones* act as intermediaries between gods and men, a scheme that, in Apuleius' view, explains the structure of religious rites and sacrifices. The *daimones* are responsible for the "solemn processions," "silences of the mystery cults," "the ceremonies officiated over by priests," and the "sacrificial rites." Later in the text (chapter 22), he criticizes those who spend large amounts of money every day for many different reasons, but do not spend anything for themselves or for the cult of their own *daemon*, "a cult that is nothing else but an initiation into philosophy." This does not necessarily mean that the rituals described in the last book of the novel are to be interpreted as a sort of metaphor for philosophical initiation, but it certainly prevents us from ascribing to Apuleius a generally disillusioned or overly critical view of religious practices.

I think it is telling that each time Lucius' expenses are mentioned in the novel, something happens to mitigate his losses. Before the first initiation, Lucius is informed in a dream that he is going to regain some of the possessions he had lost in Thessaly, as well as a slave named Candidus. The next

---

55. Juvenal 6.539 ff.; Persius 2.68 f. Cf. Van Mal-Maeder 1997a, 103. There is also an episode in Josephus (*AJ* 18.65 ff.; cf. Nock 1933, 153) where a group of Isiac priests are hired to assist in the seduction of a woman who would believe anything they said.
56. Mark 12.41–43; Luke 21.1–4.

morning, his slaves and his white horse (the "Candidus" of the dream) actually arrive. It is not properly an income, but Lucius interprets this occurrence as a good sign for his future (11.21.1) and is encouraged by his dream to attend the sacred rituals. At 11.23.4 the crowd gives him a great number of presents, so that Lucius receives yet another material benefit before his first initiation. But in the case of the next two initiations, Lucius emphasizes the material benefits he receives to cover his losses.

At this point in the novel, Lucius has had to sell his wardrobe to pay for the second initiation. His habitual visits to the temple

> afforded the greatest comfort for my stay abroad in Rome, and furthermore it even provided a richer livelihood—not surprisingly, since my profits from pleading at law in the Roman language were nourished by the breeze of favoring Success. (11.28.6)[57]

Before the third initiation, Lucius confesses that he has spent more than he could afford, but he also immediately adds:

> Yet, by Hercules, I felt no regret for my toil and expense: after all, through the bountiful care of heaven I was comfortably provided for by the income I earned as a lawyer. (11.30.2)[58]

The god encourages him in a dream to go on with his *gloriosa patrocinia* and not to be worried by the slander spread by those who envy him. The god even grants him a high position in the temple hierarchy, appointing him pastophor and quinquennial decurion.[59] Consequently, we can say that Lucius' social and economic status at the end of the novel seems to be somewhat favorable. This material emphasis certainly might discourage an overly spiritual and mystical reading of Book 11, but it is impossible to claim that the Egyptian priests reduce Lucius to poverty. On the contrary, it would be more to the point to say that, according to Book 11, Lucius fares well as a result of this deal.[60]

---

57. *Quae res summum peregrinationi meae tribuebat solacium nec minus etiam victum uberiorem subministrabat, quidni? spiritu faventis Eventus quaesticulo forensi nutrito per patrocinia sermonis Romani.* Some commentators interpret *patrocinia* as a reference to the profession of rhetor rather than lawyer: see Griffiths 1975, 336 *ad loc.*, with further references.

58. *Nec hercules laborum me sumptuumque quidquam tamen paenituit, quidni? liberali deum providentia iam stipendiis forensibus bellule fotum.*

59. The position of *decurio quinquennalis* is not attested elsewhere in connection with Isiac cults (except perhaps in a dubious Pompeian inscription): cf. Griffiths 1975, 342 f. *ad loc.*

60. So Gianotti 1986, 51 n. 51. For a different view see e.g. Harrison 2000, 240: "we find Lucius

In fact, at the end of the novel, Lucius does not appear to be poorer than when he began his adventures. He starts as a young man of good family (see e.g. the *clarissimae nuptiae* of his mother Salvia, referred to by his aunt Byrrhena at 2.3.2), but he is also only a *scholasticus* (2.10.2), an ex-schoolboy who has yet to succeed in life. When we meet him for the first time, he is going to Thessaly "on business" (*ex negotio*: 1.2.1). We may infer that his business is similar to those ascribed to his fellow travelers at the beginning of the novel, Aristomenes and Socrates. Aristomenes travels all over Thessaly, Aetolia, and Boeotia dealing in cheese and honey (1.5.3); Socrates, the main character of Aristomenes' tale, is also going to Macedonia on business (1.7.6).[61] Lucius travels with a horse and at least a couple of slaves,[62] nothing like the luxury in which Thiasus lives and travels at 10.18.3. At 1.24.3 Lucius goes to the market to buy a fish for dinner; there he meets an old schoolmate who is an aedile and is rather patronizing to Lucius—or at least he makes a show of his importance in front of him. Finally, at the end of the novel, Lucius practices *gloriosa patrocinia*[63] in the Roman Forum, leads a comfortable life, and has an important position in the hierarchy of the Isiac cult. I would say that there is no diminution at all of his economic and social status—quite the contrary, perhaps.

Even if Lucius' conversion is expensive, this does not necessarily mean that the priests are greedy sharks who want to exploit Lucius' gullibility and steal part of his profits. Against this view we might mention that when Lucius wants fervently to be initiated at 11.21.3, it is none other than the priest who curbs his impatience. But it bothers many scholars that there are three episodes of initiation with large expenditures, not one. Lucius himself expresses some suspicion after the gods press him towards the third initiation:

---

at the end of the novel as a shaven-headed official of the Osiris-cult in Rome, having gullibly surrendered his social status, career ambitions, and financial resources to an exploitative religious organization."

61. See also Keulen 2007b, 95 on the parallelism between Lucius and Socrates, and on some possible implicit meanings of the words *ex negotio* at 1.2.1.

62. The text refers to Lucius' slaves both in the plural (2.15.5; 11.20.6) and in the singular (2.31.4; 3.8.7; 3.27.4; 7.2.2). This is not necessarily a contradiction or a slip: Apuleius often mentions minor characters only when it is necessary, and it is likely that Lucius' slaves, who always remain anonymous, appear in the narrative according to the needs of the moment, either individually or in small groups (cf. Van Mal-Maeder 2001, 242).

63. 11.30.4. This is not explicitly stated in the text, but it is difficult to think that Lucius' success in his forensic activity is not to be connected somehow to his Isiac fellowship: after all, he was just a stranger at Rome, and the circle of Isiac adepts could offer him a springboard to enter Roman society.

> I was troubled with serious concern and extremely perplexed, as I anxiously pondered these questions in my mind. What was the aim of this new and unheard-of design of the gods? What element remained to make my initiation complete, despite its already having been performed twice? "Doubtless," I thought, "both priests calculated wrongly, or at least incompletely, in my case." And, by Hercules, I even began to have misgivings about their good faith. (11.29.2–3)

It may be relevant that, in the penultimate chapter of the book, Apuleius describes Lucius' perplexity at some length. However, this is absolutely not his last word on the subject: another dream immediately (11.29.4–5) drives away any suspicion on his part about this new initiation, as well as any doubts he had had regarding the fairness of the priests involved in his two previous initiations. We must also note that what really bothers Lucius in the passage above is not the need for a further initiation *per se*, but the possibility that Mithras and Asinius Marcellus could have made some mistake in the rites they had previously celebrated. In fact, this chapter, if we look at it in its entirety, seems to have been conceived to prevent and dispel any possible doubt by the reader as to whether Lucius is overly fatuous, rather than to provoke any suspicion to that effect.

In regard to the problem of multiple initiations, Ellen Finkelpearl[64] has argued that the last four chapters of the novel constitute an epilogue, which functions to inform the reader about what has happened after the conclusion of Lucius' adventures.[65] Its exact purpose would be to confirm that after one year Lucius still perseveres in his religious devotion. The amount of time that passes between the first and second initiation—one full year[66]—reinforces the idea that these last chapters are a *Nachgeschichte;* in adding this epilogue, Apuleius is following the pattern of the Greek novels, many of which briefly inform their readers on the aftermaths of the adventures just concluded.[67] To sum up,

---

64. Finkelpearl 2004.

65. At 11.26.3 Lucius is leading a peaceful and serene life; in the Isiac cult he even finds a sort of new home away from home (*fani quidem advena, religionis autem indigena*). The hero, therefore, finally comes back home, and his adventures are concluded. On this and other features that suggest that the passage is a "closure," see Finkelpearl 2004, 320 f.

66. 11.26.4: *ecce transcurso signifero circulo Sol magnus annum compleverat, et quietem meam rursus interpellat numinis benefici cura pervigilis et rursus teletae, rursus sacrorum commonet.*

67. Finkelpearl 2004, 323 ff. mentions Xenophon's *Ephesiaka* and Longus' *Daphnis and Chloe*. In addition, she points out that *Cupid and Psyche* also has a very short epilogue, which narrates the birth of a child to the two main characters (a birth that had to take place some time after the marriage: 6.24.4). I would add that Achilles Tatius' novel does not end, as one would expect, with the

Recognizing that the events described in this last section do not follow immediately upon that apparent resolution of 11.26.4, but occur a year later gives the reader less a sense of comic repetition and more of an impression that the continued initiations testify to Lucius' long-term commitment.[68]

The mingling of religious practices and financial concerns, quite understandably, does not appeal to all readers, ancient or modern. But if we take into account the passage from the *De deo Socratis* I have quoted above, it seems unlikely that Apuleius advocated a complete separation between religious faith and worldly concerns. The *Metamorphoses* certainly does not pass over this potentially unpleasant aspect of the Isiac cult in silence, but neither does it seem to do anything to prompt a detached and ironic reading, or to provoke an interpretation of the last book as a satire of religious fatuousness.

2.4 Isis and her sisters

Those scholars who argue that the last book reveals a serious commitment to religion usually point out that the first ten "Milesian" books need to be reinterpreted in the light of the speech of Mithras at 11.15. Mithras summarizes Lucius' adventures as a story of his fall—caused by *curiositas, serviles voluptates* and *Fortuna caeca*—and final redemption thanks to Isis. His speech can be read as providing an intentional contrast between the first ten books and the last one. Isis therefore stands out distinctly against other characters endowed with supernatural powers, such as the witches Meroe,

---

marriage of Leucippe and Clitophon but continues by mentioning a voyage to Byzantium that the newlywed couple plans for the following year. This is a rather problematic conclusion, on which see e.g. Rabau 1996. But the conclusion of the *Metamorphoses* also raises some problems, and Van Mal-Maeder 1997a, 110–117 actually suggests that the "real" conclusion became lost in the manuscript tradition (see Graverini 2003b, 181–183 for a skeptical view on this hypothesis; in this volume, I will always take for granted that the novel really ends at 11.30.5). On the endings of the ancient novels, see Fusillo 1997. Plato's *Symposium,* which represents a sort of proto-novel for some scholars, also has a sort of narrative coda: the banquet goes on even when some of the guests begin to go away, and Aristodemus' recollection begins to be more blurred; even when Socrates himself has already left Agathon's house, the narration goes on, and we are told how Socrates spends the following day. Whether it is a proto-novel or not, the *Symposium* remains a text with which the *Metamorphoses* is deeply involved (see esp. pp. 123 ff.).

68. Finkelpearl 2004, 326. Some confirmation that the last four chapters are a sort of coda can be found in the comparison between the narrative structures of the novel and of the *Odyssey:* see § 4.1 p. 168 n. 10. Egelhaaf-Gaiser 2000 concludes that "The text offers no ground to think that the behavior of Isis' ministers implies a criticism of religion and resorts to the traditional topos of the greedy and corrupt priests. Rather, the multiple mentions of Lucius' expenses realistically suggest that the activities of a sanctuary and the celebration of religious rituals were associated with significant costs" (p. 89).

Panthia, and Pamphile (as well as her maidservant Photis); or the soothsayer Diophanes the Chaldean; or, finally, the Egyptian priest or the Dea Syria. In my opinion, this kind of reading has much to recommend it, though I should point out that it can be taken too far. Danielle Van Mal-Maeder,[69] for example, rightly points out that many of the textual hints that are supposed to build an opposition between Photis and Isis can be easily explained away as literary commonplaces, and therefore offer no proof of the authorial intention to set the two figures in competition with each other.[70]

As we shall see, we should not infer that the novel places Isiac religion on the same level as witchcraft or the corrupt cults of Books 8 and 9.[71] In fact, it would have been easy for Apuleius to suggest substantial analogies between Isis and the witches of the first books, had he wanted to do so. Winkler himself notes that, "in popular culture Isis had a fairly close connection with magic—which is *not* what Apuleius presents in Book 11."[72] Winkler also makes the dubious suggestion that Isis is described as powerless against magic, since the goddess must depend upon roses to save Lucius and restore him to human form: she should have been able to simply cancel the effects of Photis' ointment.[73] This is indeed a curious idea: the connection between roses and salvation is a *Leitmotiv* revisited throughout the novel,[74] and it would have been a slip on Apuleius' part to abandon it at the end,

---

69. Van Mal-Maeder 2001, 409–411.

70. Heine 1978, 34 notices that there are several parallels, both verbal and thematic, in which the text seems to make no semantic investment: however, Heine himself admits that the repertoire of words, expressions, and narrative topoi an author can use is necessarily limited, and therefore it is inevitable to find such instances. All of this cannot be used to rule out that there are *some* unifying themes in the novel—for example, *curiositas*.

71. See e.g. Harrison 2000, 248 f.: "It might be argued that as such it [*sc.* the description of the cult of the Dea Syria] forms a narrative precursor to the genuine and climactic cult of Isis, praising the latter by providing an inferior and repulsive lower form of the cult which is surpassed by the true religious experience of the novel's end. However, continuity could be the point just as much as difference. The suggestion could equally be that all cult-officials are at bottom corrupt and venal, something which is at least hinted at in Book XI." According to Van Mal-Maeder 2001, 410–411 "the book of Isis should not be read as a systematic opposition to the previous ten books, but as a continuation of them . . . Isis and her cult do not play, in the *Metamorphoses,* a different role from Photis, the magicians or the fortune-tellers we meet in the first ten books"; see also Van Mal-Maeder 1997a, 97 f. On hair as an element of thematic continuity between Photis and Isis, erotic passion, and religious experience, see Van Mal-Maeder 2001, 22 and Schmeling-Montiglio 2006, 38 f. On witches and witchcraft in Apuleius' novel, see now also Frangoulidis 2008.

72. Winkler 1985, 214 n. 17, with several examples (among which is the priest of Memphis who learns the secrets of magic from Isis in Lucian, *Philops.* 34) and further bibliographical references; and Van Mal-Maeder 1997a, 97 n. 38.

73. Winkler 1985, 214. See also Penwill 1990, 22 n. 51: "it is as if Christ had effected the miracle cures recorded in the Gospels by use of antibiotics."

74. See above, p. 63.

merely in order to extol Isis' powers. In fact, the *Metamorphoses* never establishes an explicit comparison, much less a competition, between the powers of the witches and of Isis. They are both omnipotent, but their powers are opposite. This is how the beggar Socrates describes Meroe's powers:

> A witch . . . with supernatural power: she can lower the sky and suspend the earth, solidify fountains and dissolve mountains, raise up ghosts and bring down gods, darken the stars and light up Tartarus itself. (1.8.4)

Lucius gives a contrasting description of Isis' omnipotence:

> The spirits above revere you, the spirits below pay you homage. You rotate the earth, light the sun, rule the universe, and tread Tartarus beneath your heel. The stars obey you, the seasons return at your will, deities rejoice in you, and the elements are your slaves. At your nod breezes breathe, clouds give nourishment, seeds sprout, and seedlings grow. Your majesty awes the birds travelling in the sky, the beasts wandering upon the mountains, the snakes lurking in the ground, and the monsters that swim in the deep. (11.25.3–4)

There is clearly some degree of analogy between the two passages. Both Meroe and Isis possess unlimited powers; there are other verbal similarities between the passages as well. But speaking about verbal coincidences is hazardous, since both passages are constructed primarily with commonplaces of the literary tradition that are often used in such contexts.[75] Most of all, these words and phrases cannot be correctly evaluated without sufficient regard for their context. If we read the two passages side by side, we can see a distinct difference between the powers of Meroe and Isis. Meroe's magic is paradoxical and destructive (heaven is lowered, earth is raised, stars die out, the underworld lights up); Isis' powers are productive and generate life, making the Universe what it is. The relationship between the two passages cannot be explained away as a simple "continuation thématique."[76]

---

75. Useful parallels in Keulen 2007b, 205 f. *ad loc.;* Van Mal-Maeder 2001, 122 (*ad* 2.5.4, where Byrrhena describes Pamphile's powers to Lucius).

76. Van Mal-Maeder 2001, 17; cf. also 1997a, 97 f. For an opposite view, see e.g. Schmidt 1982, 272 ff. Van Mal-Maeder 1997a, 98 f. suggests that there is another parallel between the secrecy that surrounds both Pamphile's powers and Isis' mysteries (3.15.3–5 ~ 11.23.5–7). But while Photis hesitates to reveal Pamphile's secrets because she fears the revenge of the powerful witch, Lucius has no fear, even if he is still bound by a sense of respect (*licet . . . liceret*), and mentions the possibility of *noxam contrahere*. Lucius and Photis clearly have very different attitudes towards the secrecy required by magic and Isiac religion. I would also add that Lucius in the end says something about the myster-

The same can be said of the effects that Meroe and Isis have on those whom they encounter. There is indeed an analogy, and an alarming one: they both seem to reduce their followers to poverty. But this is only a false impression. While it is true that Socrates is ruined as a consequence of his misadventures, Meroe is to blame for the fact that he is reduced to the point of having nothing to wear:

> I was done immediately, as soon as I slept with her; that one sexual act affected me with a lengthy, disastrous relationship. I even gave her the clothes the good robbers had left me to cover myself with, and even the scant wages I earned as a sack-carrier while I was still vigorous. (1.7.9–10)

Similarly, at the beginning of the novel, Lucius was already willing to pay a high price (2.6.1 *ampla cum mercede*) to know the secrets of magic. As he performs the Egyptian rites, he ends up penniless and almost naked like Socrates, by order of the god Osiris himself:

> I was being pressed again and again by the god's insistence. After I had been, to my great discomfort, frequently goaded, and finally commanded, I sold my clothing, little as it was, and scraped together a sufficient sum. This had been my specific instruction: "Surely," he said, "if you were intent on some object for the production of pleasure, you would not spare your rags; now when you are on the verge of such important ceremonies, do you hesitate to entrust yourself to a poverty which you will have no cause to regret?" (11.28.3–4)

In this case, too, the similarity of the situation cannot eclipse a deeper difference. Lucius' poverty is only temporary, and the god himself will be praised for Lucius' regained prosperity, while Socrates, in spite of Aristomenes' intervention, will not be able to escape the destructive power of Meroe. While Socrates is certainly a victim of witchcraft, there is no hint that Lucius is a victim of the Egyptian gods.

Magical powers in the novel are treated with timid respect (with the exception of the skeptical comments made by Aristomenes' unnamed fellow traveler at 1.3.1 and 1.20.1, and by Aristomenes himself at 1.8.3–5).[77] This

---

ies of Isis, but it is only a very partial and reticent account; the mysteries of magic, on the contrary, are described in minute detail in the novel. This represents an important difference in how Lucius and Photis obey their respective prohibitions.

77. The scene that describes Lucius preparing to change into a bird by flapping his arms has naturally an almost breathtakingly comic effect (3.24.3–6), but at this point the attention of the reader is focused not on magic, but on Lucius and his destiny.

narrative strategy might reflect the fact that the novel depends on magic for the metamorphosis of its main character into an ass. However, in encounters with the supernatural thoughout the first ten books, Apuleius' narrator is inclined to use parody and satire—calling even more attention to the lack of either in the final book. I therefore think that we should ask ourselves a question. Why should we leave open to interpretation what is so obvious on earlier occasions in the novel? Consider for example the impious miller's wife, who

> scorned and spurned all the gods in heaven, and, instead of holding a definite faith, she used the false sacrilegious presumption of a god, whom she would call "one and only," to invent meaningless rites to cheat everyone and deceive her wretched husband, having sold her body to drink from dawn and to debauchery the whole day. (9.14.5)

This text clearly has "a satirical agenda, for this religious devotee is characterized as a hypocritical sink of all the vices."[78] The same is true in the chapters that describe Lucius' service with the depraved priests of the Dea Syria. The old cinaedus that comes on stage at 8.24.2 is bald, like Lucius at the end of the novel, but once more this potential analogy serves only to highlight their differences. Philebus (this is his name: cf. 8.25.6) in fact is

> a pervert, and an old one at that; bald on top but with grey ringlets of hair dangling round his head; one of those common people from the dregs of society who walk through the city streets and towns banging their cymbals and rattles, carrying the Syrian goddess round with them and forcing her to beg. (8.24.2)

Philebus' baldness is therefore not a symbol of purity, like the Isiac priests' shaven head, but rather a simple lack of hair due to old age, which he tries to remedy by arranging his few remaining hairs in effeminate and disgusting curls.[79]

Lucius clearly displays, from the very beginning, an aversion to Philebus and his comrades (8.25.5). He spells out the religious aberration of that

---

78. Harrison 2000, 249. On the issue, not relevant here, of the woman's possible Christian faith, see Griffiths 1975, 359; Schmidt 1997 and 2003. More notes on Apuleius and Christianity in Hunink 2000. See also pp. 191 n. 82.

79. Cf. *GCA* 1985, 288 f.; the Dutch commentators point out also that at 8.25.4 "mockingly the narrator has the priest speak of his loose-hanging hair" (n. 9). On Lucius' and Philebus' bald heads, see § 2.5.

cult,⁸⁰ the greed of its priests,⁸¹ and the deceitfulness of their oracles.⁸² His account of their actions is by no means neutral. A rational and theological criticism is found at 8.27.8, but it is especially worth noting that here the narrator is indulging in irony. Such is the case also at 9.8.1, where the narrator describes Philebus and the other soothsaying profiteers as "those chaste and holy priests." Lucius is not the only one to speak with irony and contempt about these priests; many others who deal with them speak in similar terms. Hence at 8.29.6 a crowd mocks their "pure chastity": they are "odious and detestable in everyone's eye" (8.30.1) because of their licentiousness.⁸³ As we can see, neither the narrator nor the other characters spare moralizing or ironical comments, and this presents an important distinction (in degree, if not in essence) from the text of the pseudo-Lucianic *Onos*.⁸⁴

A detailed comparison of Egyptian religious practices with those of the Dea Syria's priests is certainly possible,⁸⁵ but a clear difference in the nar-

---

80. 8.27.8: "one of them . . . simulated a fit of madness—as if, indeed, the god's presence was not supposed to make men better than themselves, but rather weak or sick."

81. 8.28.6 "they greedily raked it all in"; and then repeatedly up to the theft in the temple of the Mother of the Gods at 9.9–10.

82. 8.29.2 "by constructing a false prophecy they demand from one of the farmers his fattest ram for a sacrifice"; and then especially 9.8.1–6.

83. The fact that the ass carries the image of the goddess can already suggest a form of exploitation: the proverbial saying "I am the ass that carries the sacred objects" (applied to those who toil for someone else's gain) is attested as early as Aristophanes (*Frogs* 159). In Apuleius, the ass Lucius shows a certain inclination to embody proverbs: cf. 9.42.4 *de prospectu et umbra asini*. See below, p. 110 n. 178 for more information on this subject.

84. *Onos* 35–41. Pseudo-Lucian is implicitly critical of the corrupt priests, but an explicit criticism appears in chapter 38, where the ass tries to voice his disgust for what Philebus and the others are doing to the farmer. As in Apuleius, his hee-haw attracts a crowd who start scoffing at the priests, and the priests themselves feel embarrassed at being caught in the act. More criticisms emerge in the episode of the theft in the temple at chapter 41. The Groningen commentators (*GCA* 1985, 289) suggest that Apuleius might be harsher than pseudo-Lucian in his disapproval precisely in order to avoid confusions and elicit parallels with the Isiac faith (of course, the author of the *Onos* had no such problem). It must also be noted that Apuleius' disparagement is directed only at the priests, and it never touches the crowd as they make donations and believe in the false prophecies. This applies to the rich man who gives them hospitality, too; the narrator seems almost to be trying to portray him in a good light and explains he is a man "who besides a general religious disposition showed a special reverence for the Goddess" (8.30.5: nothing like that in *Onos* 39, where it is simply said that the priests arrive εἰς ἀγρὸν πλουτοῦντος ἀνθρώπου). His respect (evidently ill-advised) for the charlatan priests is then pictured in a context of true religiosity and devotion.

85. See *GCA* 1985, 287–298. Not all the parallels are convincing, and it is possible that some verbal echoes are due to the inevitable occurrence of topoi and standard phraseology (as is the case with the relationship between Photis and Isis, on which see above, p. 76 with n. 70). For example, the Groningen commentators compare the music that accompanies Isis' procession at 11.9.4 *symphoniae dehinc suaves, fistulae tibiaeque modulis dulcissimis personabant* with the description of the corrupted priests who roam *per plateas et oppida cymbalis et crotalis personantes* (8.24.2); but (leaving aside the rather obvious use of the verb *persono*) there are no real reasons to think that the first passage echoes

rator's attitude suggests that their relationship is one of opposition rather than continuity. For the opposite case to be true (namely, a relationship of continuity), it would be necessary for the text to disavow, explicitly or implicitly, Lucius' judgment in the last book, and for the narrator to distance himself from the main character, laughing at him together with the reader.

This is exactly what happens in other parts of the novel, when Lucius proves to be a bad interpreter of what is happening around him. At 7.10.3–4 the ass sees Charite making sheep's eyes at the brigand Haemus, who is actually her husband Tlepolemus in disguise. Charite, of course, recognizes him, but Lucius cannot; therefore, he is deeply disconcerted and outraged by what he considers a demonstration of the girl's immorality. At this point, Lucius' voice becomes double: the retrospective narrator, who knows the true identity of Haemus, ironically exposes the rashness of the judgment of Lucius-actor: "and indeed, at that moment the character and principles of all womankind depended on an ass's verdict."[86] Nothing of this nature happens in Book 11; if Lucius is still somehow asinine, there are no remarks by the retrospective narrator that can reveal it to the reader. If such were the case, we would have expected that the narrator would emphasize with clarity any enduring asininity on Lucius' part, especially after the momentous changes of his retransformation and his affiliation with the Egyptian cults.[87]

Nevertheless, a novel can certainly discredit a character implicitly, without any ironical intervention by its narrator; and, at least in theory, it is possible that for some reason Apuleius assumes a different narrative stance in the last book. If what I have been saying so far is true, there is nothing that allows us to think that Lucius, after his retransformation, is a gullible character exploited by a rapacious cult; however, we do not see a complete and unconditioned abandon to mysticism, either. Before I try to reach a conclusion that can explain this ambivalence, I will consider one last element that has profound significance as a symbol, and that could question

---

the second. We could also compare 11.9.4 with 8.30.5 *tinnitu cymbalorum et sonu tympanorum cantusque Phrygii mulcentibus modulis excitus procurrit*, but again this trait (the psychagogic sweetness of music—as we have seen in chapter 1, a feature of the whole novel) is so common that its appearance here is insignificant.

86. Cf. also the clearly ironic words *prudenti asino* at 7.12.1. On the interplay of the two narrating voices at 7.10 as a satiric feature, see M. Zimmerman 2006, 96 f.

87. It is not important, in my opinion, that Lucius never says explicitly (either as auctor or as actor) that he accepts Mithras' religious and teleological reading of his adventures at 11.15 (*pace* e.g. Van Mal-Maeder 2001, 410). Lucius makes it very clear, both with his actions and his words, that he adheres totally to the Isiac religion; in this context, an expression of Lucius' doubt regarding Mithras' interpretation would need to be explicitly stated in the text, and not the contrary.

the seriousness of Lucius' Isiac faith, as well as the integrity of the Egyptian cults described in the novel.

2.5 Lucius' shaven head

Satirical readings of Book 11 find a potent symbol in Lucius' shaven head, which he so proudly parades in the last sentence of the novel (11.30.5):

> Rursus denique quaqua raso capillo collegii vetustissimi et sub illis Sullae temporibus conditi munia, non obumbrato vel obtecto calvitio, sed quoquoversus obvio, gaudens obibam.

> Then, once more shaving my head completely, neither covering up nor hiding my baldness, but displaying it wherever I went, I joyfully carried out the duties of that ancient priesthood, founded in the days of Sulla.

Winkler asks himself why this detail is given such a relevant position at the end of the novel.[88] In fact, Lucius had already shaved his head for his second initiation (11.28.5), and this is only mentioned in passing, without any particular emphasis. In this case, the position of the image at the very end of the novel does provide such emphasis, and must be significant. But what is its meaning?

A shaven head could have a wide variety of connotations.[89] It was, of course, one of the external signs of Isiac faith, and at 11.10.1 the initiates go in procession with their "heads completely shaven and their skulls gleaming brightly." As with any external sign, a shaven head attracts the attention of supporters, detractors, and simple onlookers. At the top of a long list of paradoxical customs of the Egyptians, Herodotus 2.36.1 includes the priests' habit of shaving their heads, and at 2.37.2 explains it as a purification ritual. Plutarch moralistically points out that "having a beard and wearing a coarse cloak does not make philosophers, nor does dressing in linen and shaving the hair make votaries of Isis" (*de Iside et Osiride* 352c). And it is precisely the adept's shaven head that attracts the attention of Juvenal and Martial

---

88. Winkler 1985, 225.

89. On what follows, more sources and bibliographic references can be found in Griffiths 1975, 192 f. (*ad* 11,10,1); *GCA* 1985, 288–289; Winkler 1985, 225–227; Van Mal-Maeder 1997a, 106–108 and 1997b, 199 n. 98. On the connection between baldness and sexuality see Jensson 2004, 240 ff. Schmeling-Montiglio 2006, 39 suggest that Lucius' shaven head is a sort of figure for the novel itself, whose end is "as luxuriant and undulating as the hair which Lucius so much admires."

as they satirize religious practices.⁹⁰ Shaving the head could also have a religious significance outside Egyptian cult: it can be an act of devotion or of thanksgiving, offered by a freed slave or a survivor from a shipwreck.⁹¹

If it is not the result of a religious practice, a bald head is not usually a source of pride. For example, in the *Metamorphoses*, at 5.30.6 Venus threatens to chastise Cupid by having his head shaven, and at 5.9.8 one of Psyche's sisters regrets having married a man who is older than her, shorter than a kid, and balder than a pumpkin.⁹² Other shaven-headed characters appear in Achilles Tatius 5.17.3 (Leukippe), and in Xenophon of Ephesus 5.5.4 (Anthia): for both women baldness is a shameful mark that reflects their servile condition. In Petronius, the freedman Trimalchio has a shaven head (32.2); at 103.1–2 Encolpius and Giton have their heads shaven to look like slaves and go unnoticed by Lichas and Tryphaena, but another passenger aboard their ship takes this as an ill omen, since shipwreck survivors usually shave their heads.⁹³ Furthermore, as many scholars point out, a shaven head recalls the bald characters of comedies and mime: often the butt of jokes and tricks, they are usually not particularly bright, have an abnormal sexual proclivity, and come from servile origins (cf. e.g. Plautus, *Amph.* 462).⁹⁴

At this point, we must introduce a few qualifications. The first stipulation concerns the selection of sources: bald men certainly were not usually admired, but not all the passages often quoted by scholars actually support this notion. For example, Martial 5.7 mocks a bald man not because he is bald, but because he hides his baldness under a wig; and at 10.83 the poet derides a person who combs his hair to cover a bald patch. In these cases, we have more a criticism of excessive delicacy and deceptive appearances than a mockery of baldness *per se* (the same is true at 1.72.8, in a metapoetical context; at 3.74, with a witty inversion, Martial laments the poor bald head of one Gargilianus, who plucks it obsessively). A wig also comes into play in

---

90. Juvenal 6.532 ff.; Martial 12.28.19. Elegiac poets had a different focus, and they often attacked religious prohibitions against sex during specified periods: see Propertius 2.28.61 f. and 2.33.1 f.; and cf. Ovid, *Am.* 1.8.74; 3.10.1.

91. Cf. Winkler 1985, 225.

92. Apuleius himself, in *Apol.* 74, considers baldness as a *deformitas*. The *ianitor* at 1.15.2 has a *cucurbitae caput* (or, better, claims he does not have one); on the connection of this character with the *mimus calvus*, see Keulen 2007b, 295 *ad loc.* and 339.

93. Cf. Juvenal 12.81 f.; Lucianus, *Merc. cond.* 1 and *Herm.* 86; Artemidorus of Daldi 1.22; *AG* 6.164. In Petronius, the debate about the shaving of Encolpius and Giton's heads goes on at 107.6 ff., and at 109.9–10 Eumolpus even composes an elegy on that subject; in the following chapter, the two characters put on wigs.

94. The *cocio* in Petronius 15.4 is bald, too; he takes part in a farcical scene for Panayotakis 1995, 141 with n. 14.

a fable by Aesop: the comic aspect of the story is that the wind blows a wig off the head of a bald man, but the target of the satiric attack is the crowd who laughs at him and not the bald man himself.[95]

It is also useful to make a distinction between a shaven head and natural baldness.[96] As we have seen above in our consideration of Philebus, the priest of the Dea Syria, there is a great difference between the shaven head of an Egyptian priest and the partially bald head of a repulsive old man. The first loathsome bald man of Greek literature, Thersites, had a "pointed head, and a scant stubble grew on it" (*Il.* 2.219). Most of the bald men who appear in Martial's epigrams are "naturally" bald, too, with some remaining hair. In such characters, baldness is not their only negative aspect, and they have more physical and/or moral blemishes. Thersites demonstrates this, but we can also mention the "little bald-headed tinker who has made money and just been freed from bonds" in Plato, *Resp.* 6.495e; and, finally, the "bald-pate with that pot-belly sticking out a foot and a half" in Persius 1.56–57. In some cases, baldness alone can offer a motive for mockery. One very famous and susceptible bald man was Julius Caesar (Suetonius, *Iul.* 45—indeed, a rather gossipy source). Since he could not bear to be scoffed at for his receding hairline, he used to comb his remaining hair to cover the bald patch; and, among the many honors the people and the Senate of Rome accorded to him, he appreciated especially the right of wearing the laurel wreath, which was very useful for covering his naked scalp.

With regard to the distinction between a shaven and a naturally bald head, it is not completely clear what we should make of the bald characters in comedies and mimes. Their heads can be shaven, as we learn from Juvenal 5.171 and Arnobius *Nat.* 7.33; however, in Pollux 4.144 ff. the "brothel-keeper" is ἀναφαλαντίας . . . ἢ φαλακρός, "has a receding hairline or is completely bald."[97] There is some ambiguity in the iconographic sources as well. Many of them portray actors whose heads are not shaven, or completely bald, but simply show a deeply receding hairline.[98] The resemblance,

---

95. Aesop, 282 Hausrath.

96. Only a few scholars make this distinction: see e.g. *GCA* 1985, 206, commenting on Philebus at 8.24.2.

97. Also the *Hermonios* is ἀναφαλαντίας; the "second *Hermonios*" instead is "shaven and with a pointed beard" (4.145). The so-called κάτω τριχίας is a slave with a receding hairline and red hairs; the "curly slave" is similar to him, while the cook and the "cicada slave" are φαλακροί (but the latter still has a few curls: 4.149–150).

98. Winkler quotes Nicoll 1931, 43–49, 88–89 and Richter 1913. However, many of the comic and mimic actors portrayed in the iconographic material collected by Nicoll are not bald but simply have deeply receding hairlines. Furthermore, the bronze figurine described by Richter represents an actor who is not really bald: "he has whiskers and short, straight hair, which leaves the temples bald. On the crown of the head is a round, shallow depression, of which the most probable explanation is

therefore, between Lucius and a comic actor is oblique. We should note also that the baldness of comic actors is usually associated with other grotesque features, such as oblong and almost animal-like faces, large noses, and large (or even enormous) ears. With just a bit of exaggeration, we could say that Lucius more closely resembles a comic buffoon when he has changed into an ass than when, having returned to his human shape, he shaves his head. For example, at 6.39.15 f. Martial suggests that "long ears that move like an ass's" are the most revealing sign that one of Cinna's sons is actually the son of the buffoon (*morio*) Cyrta.

I am not saying that it would be absurd to compare Lucius to a comic actor. On the contrary, Lucius is in a sense a comic actor from beginning to end. The prologue to the novel shares some features with comic prologues;[99] in the theater of Hypata, Lucius is the unintentional and unwitting main character of a farce in the god Risus' honor. As an ass, he is also a story-teller who shows some inclination to present his account as a scenic performance (cf. § 3.4). In Book 10 he seems to be destined to end his life in another theater, at Corinth. At the end of the novel, his shaven head adds another detail to this kind of characterization, but it is certainly not the most ridiculous and disruptive one of them—nor the most obvious. His baldness is something we must take into account, but not something that undermines any possible "serious" message in the novel.

To evaluate this feature, we need to complete our reconstruction of the novel's literary and cultural background, leading us to a better comprehension of the portrayal of Lucius at the end of the novel. Since, as we have seen, the adjective *calvus* refers to both kinds of baldness, it would be wise to point out that Thersites-like characters are not really a direct and immediate parallel for Lucius' shaven head, and to point out that there is also some significant ambiguity in his connection to comic actors. But most of all, if we want to take natural baldness into account, we need to bear in mind several texts that describe it in a favorable light, as one of the features of the wise man. Thersites was bald, but so was Odysseus—at least for a short time. Athena "destroyed the flaxen hair from off Odysseus' head" to disguise him as an old beggar (*Od.* 13.431; cf. 13.399). This disguise, of course, does not contribute to Odysseus' respectability, and Penelope's suitors make fun of his bald head: Eurymachus insults him by saying "there is a glare of torches

---

that it was originally inlaid, perhaps with silver, to indicate a shiny bald spot" (p. 149). More iconographical sources in Bernabò Brea 1981 (theatrical masks from Lipari, dated fourth to third century B.C.E.). Reich 1903, 116 and Cicu 1988, 170 f. make no distinction between total or partial baldness of the *stupidus*.

99. See Smith 1972, 513–520; Dowden 2001, 134–136.

from him—from his head, for there is no hair on it, no, not a trace!" (*Od.* 18.354 f.). It is clear, however, that this scene suggests a contrast between external appearance and reality, and Eurymachus makes the mistake of judging by appearances. Synesius, with some taste for paradox, points out that the suitors—who were large in number, but were no more than "dissolute longhairs"—were killed by Odysseus, who was completely bald (ἅπαντα φαλακρός), and whose head shone so brightly that it lit up the whole room (*Calv.* 11).[100]

Socrates, too, was bald-headed—according to Varro he was even the paradigm of baldness itself.[101] The Athenian philosopher, certainly not a handsome man, was for Synesius in good company: "You can go and admire the pictures in the Museum, I mean, those that depict Diogenes, Socrates and all those you want among the wisest men of the ages: you will think it's a show of bald men" (*Calv.* 6.3). Paul Zanker points out that between the second and third centuries the number of images of bald people, previously quite rare, shows a surprising increase: the new fashion considers baldness favorably, as a typical feature of the wise and learned man. The bald man has a spiritual look that recalls the classical portrayals of wise men, Socrates in particular.[102] In fact, there is other evidence that suggests a shaven head could carry a positive connotation. For example Persius, although he uses *calve* as an insult at 1.56, shows a liking for the "sleepless and shaven youths" at 3.54 who stay up late studying Stoic philosophical teachings. They provide a sort of counterpoint to the addressee of the satire, a young man who is rich and lazy.

It would be possible to list many more examples like these, but there is no reason to go on: a bald head can invite several different interpretations, and it would be impossible to restrict its allusiveness. For the moment, it will suffice to have shown that baldness has an ambiguous meaning, even outside of religious contexts. The binary classification Winkler suggests, placing baldness as a religious practice on one side, and comic and ridiculous on the other, is therefore somewhat artificial.[103] We also need to take into

---

100. On Odysseus' baldness see Arnould 1989.

101. *Men.* 490 *tam glaber quam Socrates*.

102. Zanker 1997, 252 ff. It was a very common style, but not, of course, without exception: Zanker himself (p. 191) notes for example that according to Philostratus, Apollonius of Tyana does not approve of haircuts (*VA* 8.7: "let every sage be careful that the iron knife does not touch his hair"). Following Zanker, see now also James-O'Brien 2006, 248 ff.

103. "In addition to being an extreme religious practice, baldness is simply funny to many" (Winkler 1985, 225). The four categories into which he divides depictions of baldness (Isiac shaving, generically religious shaving, ridiculous baldness, theatrical baldness) can be easily reduced to two. Of course, in Winkler's perspective, it is important that religious shaving is often mocked in literary texts.

account "philosophical" baldness, whose icon—a paradoxical, but very common one—is Socrates.[104] Even more importantly, in none of the passages I have quoted does baldness have a definite meaning *per se:* it is the context that makes baldness significant in one way or another.

Consequently I have no difficulty in admitting that Lucius' flaunted baldness can give the ending of the novel a nuance of pleasant and perhaps paradoxical comedy, highlighting what was exotic and strange for a Roman reader in the portrayal of an Isiac initiate.[105] Moreover, this effect is evidently intentional. The atmosphere would have been much different if, for example, the novel had ended at its "natural" conclusion—namely, before the last four chapters (which Ellen Finkelpearl has defined as "epilogue"[106]) and after the inspired aretalogy Lucius delivers at 11.25. But to consider Lucius' baldness as the final seal of a comic-satirical treatment of his affiliation to the Egyptian mysteries, we would need an appropriate context, as is present in all the texts I have listed above, where baldness is a sign of foolishness. If what I have been saying so far is true, Apuleius' novel does not provide any such context.

On the contrary, if we read the last lines of the novel carefully, the text seems to anticipate potential misinterpretations, and tries to prevent them. At 11.20.3–4 Osiris appears to Lucius in a dream and encourages him to practice his *gloriosa patrocinia* in the Forum with no fear for his enemies' slander—*disseminationes*—due to their envy of his *laboriosa doctrina*. But who exactly is enviously trying to discredit Lucius? Gwyn Griffiths thinks that the slander comes from inside the Isiac circle: he thinks it strange that Lucius, in addition to performing his religious duties, applies himself to forensic activity, so he suggests that the true reason why Lucius is envied is that the god granted him permission to practice a "secular" profession.[107] It is impossible for us to say whether Lucius' situation was exceptional, since there are no ancient sources attesting Isiac pastophors who also practice

---

104. It is interesting that Socrates' paradoxically ugly appearance is rather asinine in Xenophon, *Symp.* 5.7 and that the philosopher is very often compared to the asinine image of a Silenus. On this see below, § 2.8 pp. 122 with n. 213. See also the interesting pages devoted by Zanker to a figurine representing Diogenes completely naked, with all the ugly and awkward features of a very old man; his head, however, is the solemn head of a philosopher, bald, with a long beard and a thoughtful expression. Indeed, a paradoxical representation, in "Socratic" style (Zanker 1997, 199 ff.).

105. It is likely that Osiris' priests themselves used to wear a wig during their daily life, when they were not involved in ritual activities: see James-O'Brien 2006, 246 and n. 17, with further references. Takács 1995, 129 clearly follows Winkler and points out that "a description of an Isiac with a shaven head is supposed to stress the grotesque, the uncivilized, i.e un-Roman."

106. Finkelpearl 2004; see above, p. 74.

107. Griffiths 1975, 336 *ad* 11.28.6 *patrocinia sermonis Romani;* and 342 *ad* 11.30.4 *disseminationes.*

forensic or other forms of rhetoric, or attesting the existence of prohibitions or customs to the contrary. But, in any case, the hypothesis that the slander originated from inside the Isiac circles seems to be contradicted by the adverb *ibidem*. It is more likely that these *disseminationes* arose in the Forum, among Lucius' colleagues. Osiris says that the true reason of such slander was Lucius' *studiorum . . . laboriosa doctrina* (11.30.4), but obviously that could not possibly be the direct object of gossip and defamation. Of course we can imagine that Lucius' asinine past could offer a good subject for slander,[108] but the text suggests that the cause was rather his Isiac affiliation, whose most obvious symbol (and, as we have seen, also the one most easily ridiculed) was his shaven head. Lucius' enthusiasm in shaving his head immediately after his dream, and in parading his baldness through the streets of Rome, appears to be a direct response to Osiris' encouragement.

Lucius' shaven head clearly does not perfectly match the Socratic, or more generally philosophical, iconography that was becoming fashionable in Apuleius' day. My point is that the portrayal of the Isiac devotee shows the same paradoxical features that are typical of the "Silenic" portrayals of Socrates (on which see more thoroughly § 2.8). Lucius' description is charged with puzzling and "alien" features, but also symbolizes a deep religious commitment, and can be considered an adaptation of that iconographical type to the cultural climate of the second century, as well as to Apuleius' religious-philosophical interests.

In fact, Apuleius was attentive to the ideological values of iconography, and he did not hesitate to take advantage of them, particularly when he had to describe himself. He does so in *Apol.* 4, when he must defend himself from the preposterous accusation of being a *philosophus formonsus*. The portrait he gives of himself is indeed paradoxical:

> It is not just that I am gifted with only mediocre looks, but incessant literary activity wipes out my bodily charm, makes me perceptibly meagre, consumes my vital life-sap, effaces my healthy color, disables my strength. Just look at my hair! With an outright lie they said I wear it long "to make my beauty alluring." Well, you see how pleasant and elegant it is: it is all entwined and stuck together, much like flax for stuffing cushions, irregularly shaggy, bunched, and piled up, a terrible tangled mess. That is because for a long time I have not taken the trouble of unravelling and parting it, let alone arranging it.

---

108. This asinine past is also subtly referred to by the words *laboriosa doctrina*: see below, § 3.3 p. 152.

Unkempt hair, just as much as baldness, was one of the typical iconographical traits of the philosopher who is devoted to his studies and averse to worldly goods (such as the inheritance of a rich widow, for example). However, it is very difficult to imagine Apuleius going around every day with disheveled and knotted hair. The witty rhetorician is evidently creating a literary *persona*, and when he describes it here, he is clearly paying more attention to the literary and procedural needs of the moment than to the reality of his biography.[109]

Both Apuleius' self-portrait and his portrait of Lucius present strange and "funny" features, but I do not believe that in Lucius' shaven and gleaming head we can catch a glimpse of a narrator who is laughing at his main character behind his back. This does not necessarily mean we have to abandon ourselves to a thoroughly mystical reading of Book 11, obliterating the ambiguous and bizarre nature of the portrait of the "bald sage" or the exotic shine of an Isiac devotee's shaven head. Lucius, a shaven-headed lawyer or rhetorician, is suspended between two hardly compatible worlds: the Forum and the temple. His baldness is, as it was for Socrates, an essential feature of a paradoxical portrait, urging the reader towards both laughter and meditation.

These two elements are inextricably connected in the *Metamorphoses*. If we do not want to consider this novel as a senseless patchwork (Perry) or a detective story without a solution (Winkler), we need to approach it in a way that can fully take into account the paradoxical nature of Lucius' shaven head.

2.6 Horizons of expectation

We have seen that Apuleius' novel has some difficulty placing itself unambiguously on one side or the other of the borderline dividing satire from philosophical/religious propaganda (as if, so to speak, these interpretive strategies were engaged in a battle). Winkler's aporetic reading gives this ambiguous juxtaposition a fundamental significance. He considers the novel a *roman à clef*, but in a highly original way: the key to the novel is not a philosophical or religious belief, but rather the hermeneutic game in which the reader finds himself involved. Each reader has to choose his own approach, be it satirical or committed, but the choice itself is not as important as the interpretive

---

109. Cf. Zanker 1997, 263 ff, which contains several other iconographical examples of "unkempt philosophers."

activity leading up to it. However, it is not easy to reach a perfect equilibrium between (or, better, indifference to) satirical detachment and involved commitment, and Winkler himself does not seem able to balance both pans of the scale. After presenting several analogies between the *Metamophoses* and the *Life of Aesop*, he wishes to avoid giving the impression of having abandoned his aporetic stance:

> But lest this chapter's treatment seem to play favorites in Apuleius's mock trial of issues, secretly advocating the bald clown over the bald deacon, I shall now give an example of another, contrary intricacy that can be traced in this closely tatted [*sic*] text. (p. 291)

He then initiates a complex argument to support his choice of a title in Varronian and Menippean style for the novel, that includes both the titles attested in the direct and indirect traditions: *Asinus aureus*, περὶ μεταμορφώσεων (*Asinus aureus*, since Augustine and Fulgentius both refer to the novel with that phrase; and *Metamorphoseon libri* or *Metamorphoseis* from the *subscriptiones* in the codex Laurentianus). The first part of such a title could conjure up several associations for a learned second century reader, but the most important meaning would be hidden, according to Winkler, in the adjective *aureus*. In Egyptian mythology, Seth was the golden one, the god who was an enemy to Isis and Osiris, and usually associated with an ass.[110] However, Apuleius never suggests any explicit association of Lucius in asinine form with Seth,[111] and this fact can be explained for Winkler only if the allusion in the title represents "an intention more satiric than evangelical. If the novel were simple propaganda for Isis, the Seth-formula would undoubtedly be explained for those readers willing to be converted."[112] I fully agree with this statement, particularly its second part. But it certainly does not serve Winkler's purpose, namely to balance the impression of partiality that might have been left from the previous chapter, "secretly advocating the bald clown over the bald deacon." I think that this difficulty in keeping a perfect balance between satire and religious commitment can explain why many scholars today incline toward the comic-satiric interpretation, relying on the same arguments already offered by Winkler.

A completely aporetic novel would also be difficult to place in the context of the literary culture of the second century. It is certainly obvious that

---

110. Winkler 1985, 306 ff.; Winkler elaborates a proposal by Martin 1970, and reworked by Hani 1973.

111. At least until 11.6.2, when Isis defines the ass as *pessima mihique iam dudum detestabilis belua*.

112. Winkler 1985, 316.

"religious knowledge as such has this comedic aspect, that one person's saving system is another person's joke,"[113] but it is definitely not easy to find an ancient text that clearly adopts this ambiguity. The *Metamorphoses*, if interpreted this way, would be the brilliant product of an isolated author, who would anticipate (somewhat remarkably) a mentality that is mostly modern and contemporary. In fact, we can find several other texts, contemporary to or earlier than Apuleius' novel, that treat religious subjects with serious commitment, or with a satiric intent against excessive credulity.[114] But Winkler encounters difficulty when he tries to reconstruct a credible cultural background for the *Metamorphoses* as he reads it—that is, as a text that can be *both* serious *and* satirical at the same time. In my opinion, his reading does not really fit the "horizon of expectations" of a learned reader in Apuleius' day.

In particular, the texts dealing with the topic of the "quest of wisdom," discussed by Winkler at some length, do not seem to reveal this kind of background, even though they can provide an instructive comparison for the narrative structure of the *Metamorphoses*. Photius, as is well known, stated that the difference between the *Onos* (which he attributed to Lucian) and the lost *Metamorphoses* by Lucius of Patrae is that "Lucian, as in all his other writings, ridicules and scoffs at heathenish superstitions, whereas Lucius, taking quite seriously and believing the transformations of men into other men and brutes, and of brutes into men, and all the idle talk and nonsense of ancient fables, set them down in writing and worked them up into a story" (129.96b). Of course, there is no need for us to believe what Photius says about the lost *Metamorphoses*, a work that he considers both sincere and naive;[115] but, leaving aside this lost Greek novel, it is clear enough that the general structure of the story of the ass has something to do with the topos of the "quest for truth," and that the *Onos* in particular can be considered as an extended parody of that theme.[116] In fact, the story of a man who, being curious about magic, ends up transformed into an ass and suffers many vicissitudes before regaining human shape can be fruitfully compared, from a structural point of view, to several other

---

113. Winkler 1985, 275.
114. Of course, analogies and parallels between the *Metamorphoses* and other kinds of texts can tell us nothing about the nature of the *Metamorphoses* itself: the *Hieroi logoi* by Aelius Aristides can be both a parallel (though "sanctimonious and ethereal," according to Winkler 1985, 286), and the target of a parodical attack. For the various analogies see the thorough analysis by Harrison 2000–2001, who supports the second hypothesis; my point is that we can interpret such analogies one way or the other only if we have already taken a stance about the general "meaning" of the novel.
115. Cf. below, p. 176 n. 34.
116. Winkler 1985, 257.

texts. Among them Winkler selects the following: 1) the autobiographical account that is included in Thessalus of Tralles' botanical treatise (first century C.E.);[117] 2) a hypothetical text (probably by Bolus of Mendes and apparently narrated in the first person) which relates Democritus' travels in Phoenicia and Egypt in search of arcane knowledge;[118] 3) Harpokration of Alexandria's epistle to his daughter, which narrates his journey to Babylon in search of wisdom;[119] finally, he notes that the narrative structure of the "quest for wisdom" is also adopted in the novels by 4) Iamblichus and 5) Antonius Diogenes.[120]

The relationship that links Apuleius' novel to this narrative structure, according to Winkler, is not simply parody, as in the *Onos,* nor simply imitation, as in the two other Greek novels mentioned above. The *Metamorphoses* would rather imply *both* parody (in the first ten books, where Lucius' quest for wisdom leads him to an animal metamorphosis) *and* imitation of that topic (in the last book, where Lucius actually obtains salvation and wisdom). Again, it is up to the reader to decide if the "key" to the novel is to be found in the first ten books or in the last; that is, if the last book urges us to a religious reinterpretation of the previous ten, or if the first ten books demand that the last be read in a comical vein. Apuleius himself seems to offer no textual help for making such a decision, and abstains from sharing his opinion directly. In this regard, he shows the same attitude as Plutarch, who clearly shows he does not believe in some forms of arcane knowledge that are applied to medicine; nevertheless, he does not refrain from discussing them as entertaining subjects.[121]

Plutarch offers us an example of an aporetic—or, better, tolerant—reception of texts that contain elements of arcane knowledge, but we still have no other text that expresses this aporia thoroughly and directly, as Winkler believes the *Metamorphoses* does. Thessalus, pseudo-Democritus and Harpokration clearly offer sincere accounts of their travels and adventures, and, as far as I can see, there is no hint in them of ambiguity or self-irony. Most of all, I wish to point out that Winkler's idea that the first ten books of the *Metamorphoses* are a parody of this kind of text, and the last one an imitation of them, is highly artificial. In fact, mistakes, setbacks, and even

---

117. Winkler 1985, 258–260. Text in Friedrich 1968; translation and notes in Festugière 1991, 153–159.

118. Winkler 1985, 260–262; the existence of this text is deduced especially from references in Pliny, *Nat.* 30.9–10.

119. Winkler 1985, 262–265.

120. Winkler 1985, 265–270.

121. *Quaest. conv.* 2.7.641b; see Winkler 1985, 264 f.

ridicule fully belong to the topos he maintains is parodied in the first ten books of our novel. Thessalus, for example, finds an ancient text by the Pharaoh Nechepsos that explains how to cure any part of the human body with twelve plants and twelve minerals. He believes he has found a treasure of wisdom, and he announces a glorious and triumphant return home. But when he realizes that Nechepsos' remedies are fake and that he has made a fool of himself, he is ashamed of going back home defeated and ridiculed. He leaves Alexandria and undertakes a long journey in search of wisdom, until the god Asclepius reveals to him what he yearns for, and predicts that he will finally find glory. Thessalus' story, therefore, is structurally similar to the story of Lucius in Apuleius' version (that is, a divine revelation follows an experience of error and ridicule). And it is not easy, when we compare Apuleius with Thessalus, to draw a sharp line of demarcation between parody and imitation.[122] Moreover, I would say that the correlation itself between parody and imitation is partially misleading, and that in the *Metamorphoses* these two attitudes coexist and interact. Apuleius' novel clearly has the structure of a "quest for truth," and draws from this kind of narrative both the serious pursuit of knowledge and the comic element of failure and ridicule. His novel amplifies this last element and draws it out at great length. In this context, then, Lucius' metamorphosis into an ass corresponds to the temporary "fall" of the character who goes in pursuit of knowledge, and certainly does not represent a parodic reversal of the topic of the "quest for wisdom" itself.[123]

The *Life of Aesop* also displays an elusive affinity to the *Metamorphoses*.[124] Aesop is described as a plebeian Socrates: he is of servile origins and vulgar manners, even more ugly and unattractive than Socrates, but, like him, bright and intelligent; in debates and riddle-solving contests he regularly overcomes other characters who represent "institutional" wisdom and polite society, but he has no comprehensive philosophical system to promote. His wisdom is, in Winkler's words, "aporetic and skeptical."[125]

---

122. We cannot say much about pseudo-Democritus, since we do not have his text; but Pliny (*Nat.* 30.9) claims that, like Pythagoras, Empedocles, and Plato, he obtained knowledge *exiliis verius quam peregrinationibus susceptis*. Winkler neglects the "fall" of the main character and his being ridiculed when he lists the common features of the "quest for wisdom" narratives (these are the difficulty of deciphering foreign and arcane languages, the detailed description of the writing materials themselves, the secrecy of the knowledge contained in them, the joy and salvation that derive from this knowledge, and their exotic character: see Winkler 1985, 272).

123. If there is parody, it is more the result of intensification than of reversal; this is, in general, a common practice in Apuleius, on which see § 3, passim.

124. See also above, § 1.3.1 pp. 16 f.

125. Winkler 1985, 283.

We can highlight several useful parallels between the *Metamorphoses* and the *Life of Aesop*,[126] even though doubts about the chronology and origin of the latter warrant caution if we want to suggest a direct connection between them. In fact, the pervasive influence of popular and folkloric narrative must be taken into account as a possible reason for several of the analogies between the two texts. More generally, as Winkler says, a common feature of both texts is that they view the world from a "low" and grotesque perspective (in one case the perspective of the ugly but wise Aesop, and in the other, of Lucius as an ass). This perspective allows the use of a wealth of realistic and even vulgar content that was also typical of the popular theater of the day. We cannot forget, however, that there are also differences between the texts. The *Metamorphoses,* for example, never exploits the theme of opposition either to the established truth or to conventions of social life, both constant features in the *Life of Aesop*. This text, it must be noted, is certainly not completely aporetic, lacking any intellectual or moral program:[127] Niklas Holzberg, for example, rightly points out that "criticism of moral defects by means of satire was . . . most probably one of the primary objectives of the *Life*."[128]

To conclude, a comparison with these kinds of texts cannot effectively support an aporetic reading of Apuleius' novel. Its affinity to the *Life of Aesop,* however, offers some particularly useful hints that can lead us toward a more convincing contextualization of the *Metamorphoses* within the ancient literary system, and I will develop them in the next few pages. The satirical program of the *Life of Aesop* is embodied in a character with an ugly appearance and servile origins, and its contents are communicated through dialogue and narration rather than through direct teaching. All this is part of a narrative strategy that, in my opinion, also plays a very important role in Apuleius' novel, and offers an explanation for its peculiar mixture of serious and comic elements. In the next part of this chapter I will discuss the history and features of this narrative strategy. We will see that the literary program of the *Metamorphoses* is indeed "satirical," even though this fact will not lead us to interpret the novel as a satire of religious credulity—an interpretation that, as I hope I have demonstrated, is extremely unlikely.

---

126. See Winkler 1985, 283–285 and especially Finkelpearl 2003.

127. Winkler himself acknowledges that the reader of the *Life* is not tempted to "glamorize or mystify the author/actor"—a temptation that, on the contrary, is extremely important in his reading of the *Metamorphoses* (Winkler 1985, 286).

128. Holzberg 1996, 639.

2.7 An old wives' tale (*anilis fabula*)

The old maidservant's introduction to the tale of *Cupid and Psyche* provides a good place to begin. The central tale of the novel is, according to this old narrator, an "old wives' tale."[129] In the following pages, I will try to clarify the meaning of this definition, which is all the more significant since *Cupid and Psyche* is a sort of *mise en abyme* of the *Metamorphoses* as a whole; therefore, it might be appropriate to apply to the novel itself the same definition the old woman applies to this tale.[130]

Since this story is actually told by an old woman, from a "realistic" point of view it is not strange at all that she calls it an *anilis fabula*. However, we must not forget that expressions like *anilis fabula* have a remarkable literary history as generic designations; surprisingly, this history could compel us to consider these words as a rather derogatory definition of the central tale of the novel. In fact, all narrative literature whose only goal was to offer entertainment, and which had no "higher" or "deeper" meaning, was commonly defined as "old wives' tales"—a label for tales of no importance, which were addressed to a non-committed audience, and consequently could not be held in high regard. How could this definition be compatible with a tale like *Cupid and Psyche*, which holds a very important place in the narrative structure of the novel, and clearly has some literary and even philosophical ambitions (at least for many interpreters)? Before trying to answer this question, it is important to note that this derogatory definition has not at all mitigated the success that the tale of *Cupid and Psyche* has enjoyed in all eras, a success that has often been independent of the novel containing it.[131] Significantly, stand-alone editions of *Cupid and Psyche* usually exclude its framing passages, perhaps because they put the tale and its narrator in a bad light (4.27.8 *anilibus . . . fabulis;* 6.25.1 *delira et temulenta illa narrabat anicula*).[132]

---

129. 4.27.8: *sed ego te narrationibus lepidis anilibusque fabulis protinus avocabo.*

130. After all, as we will see shortly, this is exactly what Septimius Severus (in the *Historia Augusta*) and Macrobius do. On the thematic links of *Cupid and Psyche* to the novel as a whole, see especially Smith 1998. I have already pointed out (see above, pp. 4–6 and n. 30) the parallelism between the prologue and the old woman's introduction to her tale.

131. On the success of *Cupid and Psyche,* see the introductory essay in Moreschini 1994a. On the influence of the myth in Renaissance art, see J. L. de Jong 1998, and Guerrini-Olivetti-Sani 2000.

132. This is also true of the recent *GCA* 2004.

2.7.1 LITERARY POLEMICS, PHILOSOPHICAL POLEMICS

In the 1970s, the term *anilis fabula* was thoroughly researched in a paper by Matteo Massaro. Since his primary aim was to interpret the phrase in a passage of Horace, his work has gone unnoticed by Apuleian scholars.[133] In this section, I will discuss just a few of the passages he has carefully assembled and add a few others to the dicussion. I will conclude by shifting the focus from Horace and satire back to narrative literature, and finally to Apuleius. I begin with two passages that I have already discussed on several other occasions, and that are well known to Apuleianists, even though they eluded Massaro's attentive eye. The first is from a letter addressed to the Senate by Septimius Severus, quoted in the *Historia Augusta*:

> maior fuit dolor, quod illum pro litterato laudandum plerique duxistis, cum ille neniis quibusdam anilibus occupatus inter Milesias Punicas Apulei sui et ludicra litteraria consenesceret. (*Alb.* 12.12)

> It is even a greater source of chagrin, that some of you thought he should be praised for his knowledge of letters, when in fact he is busied with old wives' songs, and grows senile amid the Milesian stories from Carthage that his friend Apuleius wrote and such other learned nonsense.

A similarly prejudiced view of Apuleius and of most kinds of fiction is expressed by Macrobius in his commentary on Cicero's *Somnium Scipionis*:

> Fabulae, quarum nomen indicat falsi professionem, aut tantum conciliandae auribus voluptatis aut adhortationis quoque in bonam frugem gratia repertae sunt. Auditum mulcent vel comoediae, quales Menander eiusve imitatores agendas dederunt, vel argumenta fictis casibus amatorum referta, quibus vel multum se Arbiter exercuit vel Apuleium non numquam lusisse miramur. Hoc totum fabularum genus quod solas aurium delicias profitetur e sacrario suo in nutricum cunas sapientiae tractatus eliminat. (1.2.8)

> Fables—this very name acknowledges their falsity—serve either merely to gratify the ear or to encourage good works. Our ears are charmed by the comedies of Menander and his imitators, or by the narratives full of imaginary vicissitudes of lovers in which Petronius Arbiter so freely indulged and

---

133. Massaro 1977; see his n. 1 at p. 205 for a thorough overview of previous bibliography.

with which Apuleius, astonishingly,[134] often amused himself. A philosophical treatise expels this whole category of fables that promises only to gratify the ear from its shrine and relegates them to nurses' cradles.

The passages in the *Historia Augusta* and Macrobius[135] are two late examples of an age-old literary tradition that uses (or alludes to) the definition of "old wives' tales"[136] as a weapon in literary polemic. The phrase was used to identify a lower and contemptible kind of narrative, which has nothing to teach superior minds in search of philosophical truths: it was, as we would say, "pure fiction."

Philosophy itself plays a major role in this story. It appears that Plato (who, of course, was an indisputable model for our *philosophus Platonicus*) was the first author to frequently adopt expressions such as γραῶν ὕθλος and μῦθος,[137] thereby granting them some literary pedigree. In the Athenian philosopher's works, an old wives' tale is often a false myth, a story that has no rational ground and that should have no place in the philosopher's utopia. At *Resp.* 2.377a–378d Socrates explains that all the myths that mothers, nurses, and elderly people tell children should be carefully evaluated and selected, to rule out all those which could have deleterious effects on their education (the majority of myths fall into this category). At *Tht.* 176b Socrates has nothing good to say about the common idea that one must

---

134. Regali 1983, 220 f. (followed by Keulen 2007a, 115 n. 25) gives *miramur* a positive meaning (interpreting it as an appreciative remark on Apuleius' literary versatility) rather than the negative one suggested and defended by Stahl 1952, 84 n. 5. In spite of the fact that Apuleius in *Apol.* 9 defends his own literary *lusus* (and we would certainly not expect anything else from their author), I think it unlikely that Macrobius shares Apuleius' view. Macrobius is trying to demonstrate that there is a sharp distinction between purely hedonistic *fabulae* and those tales that have a moral or philosophical value. The narratives by Menander, Petronius, and Apuleius belong for him to the former group: hence his astonishment—I would say his outrage—that a *philosophus Platonicus* like Apuleius engaged in such trifles. Of course, there is no need for us to agree with Macrobius, but it would be a strained interpretation to say he admires Apuleius for the fertility of his imagination, shown by writing in a wide variety of literary genres (i.e. narrative, in addition to his more "committed" works). On the other hand, I also believe it is a strained interpretation to use Macrobius' statement as an argument (if a secondary one) to support a satiric interpretation of the *Metamorphoses*, by arguing that Macrobius does not detect any "serious" meaning in the novel (see Van Mal-Maeder 1997a, 92): if Macrobius lists the novel among pointless and worthless literary works, it is clear, I think, that he does not detect any "satiric" commitment in it either.
135. On which see e.g. Harrison 2002a, 144 f.; Graverini 2005b, 193.
136. Here, and in the rest of this chapter, I will assume that there is no difference between old women, nurses, and midwives, at least in regard to their narrative skills. Their tales are almost always dismissed as children's talk, as the various passages quoted in the text show.
137. See Massaro 1977, 106–108 (and see p. 106 n. 1 on the possibility that the poet Corinna wrote books of Γεροῖα = *aniles fabulae*). Massaro quotes *Tht.* 176b, *Ly.* 205d, *Resp.* 1.350e, *Grg.* 527a and *Hp. ma.* 285e–286a; add also *Lg.* 10.887c–e, *Resp.* 2.377a, and *Ti.* 26b–c.

pursue virtue merely in order to enjoy a good reputation: to him, the idea is nothing more than a γραῶν ὕθλος. Plato does mention a few examples of old wives' tales that are at least partially good and useful. At *Lg.* 10.887c–e the Athenian rails against those who do not believe in the existence of the gods, despite all the myths they heard from their mothers, and took in along with the breastmilk of their nurses; and at *Ti.* 26b–c Critias refers to an instructive tale he has heard from his old father.

Indeed, Plato's view of myths and tales fluctuates, and for good reason: he sees that the stories narrated by poets can confuse and mislead those who hear them, but he is also aware of a good story's potential to transmit useful ideas in an agreeable and effective manner. Socrates himself explicitly points out this ambivalence at the end of the *Gorgias*. He tells Callicles a μάλα καλὸς λόγος, a "very beautiful story," about the judgement that awaits the soul after a man's death (523a–526d); he is afraid that Callicles might consider this tale merely a μῦθος ... γραός, an "old wives' tale" (527a), and therefore he insists that the story is both true and useful. He concludes:

> Let us therefore take as our guide the doctrine now disclosed, which indicates to us that this way of life is best—to live and die in the practice alike of justice and of all other virtue. This then let us follow, and to this invite every one else; not that to which you trust yourself and invite me, for it is worth nothing, Callicles. (527e)

So, at the end of the *Gorgias,* a tale that is truthful and is (or should be) of the greatest importance for its audience is disguised as a μῦθος ... γραός: it is up to the reader to grasp its true meaning and not to appreciate (or despise) it solely for its "mythical" qualities. Nevertheless, this same text confirms for us that an old wives' tale is, strictly speaking, useless. When Plato indicates any positive quality in myths (such as in the passages from the *Laws* and the *Timaeus* mentioned above), he normally avoids expressions like μῦθος γραός, adopting wider turns of phrases like "the tales which they have heard as babies and sucklings from their mothers and nurses" (*Lg.* 10.887d), as if to avoid the contempt that was usually connected to such definitions.

This contempt has a long literary history after Plato. I will not go over all the passages examined by Massaro now, but rather will produce a new one that will lead us closer to Apuleius' era. In Philostratus' *Vita Apollonii* 5.14.1, Menippus dismissively defines the Aesopic tales as "frogs, ... asses, and nonsense only fit to be swallowed by old women and children."[138] It is clear that

---

138. 5.14 βάτραχοι ... καὶ ὄνοι καὶ λῆροι γραυσὶν οἷοι μασᾶσθαι καὶ παιδίοις. Apollonius does not agree with Menippus: see below, p. 108.

nurses could also have a more sophisticated repertoire, since at *Eikones* 1.15 Philostratus considers the possibility that they might have taught the reader the tale of Ariadne's abandonment by Theseus on the shores of Naxos. But, whether sophisticated or not, nurses' tales are always false, or at least require careful scrutiny before being credible. Their primary quality is well described by a Phoenician in *Heroikos* 7.10:

> When I was still a child I believed these things, and my nurse cleverly amused me with these tales, singing and even weeping over some of them.

Of course, the musicality and seductive charm[139] that make such tales agreeable and believable to children are off-putting to many adults, especially when serious education is at issue. An essential step on the path toward moral and intellectual improvement, it seems, was jettisoning childlike narrative illusions—at least the worst of them.

Quintilian, for example, uses "old wives' tales" when referring to the idle pedantry of excessive and superfluous commentary on the poets. *Enarratio historiarum* ("the explanation of stories") is, for him, a part of the *grammaticus'* job. However, a *grammaticus* should not dwell on minute details or obscure authors: whoever concerns himself with these things, he says, could just as well devote himself to *aniles fabulae*.[140] In this passage, the distinction between *historiae* and *fabulae* is not the same as the distinction between historiography and fiction.[141] According to *Inst.* 2.4.2 the *grammaticus* should treat only poetic *fabulae*, leaving historiography exclusively to the *rhetor*. In his treatment of the *grammaticus'* task, Quintilian is therefore tracing a boundary that is completely restricted to the realm of fiction (*fabulae*): what should remain outside the classroom are only those *fabulae* that are trivial, ludicrous or morally repugnant, and that are not part of the normally agreed upon corpus of myths treated by renowned authors.[142] Cicero, in *N.D.* 3.12, does not show the same interest in tracing boundaries, but it is clear that for

---

139. Two typical features of myths and fiction: see pp. 40 f.

140. Cf. Quint. *Inst.* 1.8.19 *nam qui omnis etiam indignas lectione scidas excutit, anilibus quoque fabulis accommodare operam potest* ("for anyone who goes carefully through every page, whether worth reading or not, may just as well deploy his energy on old wives' tales").

141. *Pace* Massaro 1977, 122, who catalogues this passage by Quintilian under the heading of "historiographical polemic."

142. 1.8.21 *Quod evenit praecipue in fabulosis usque ad deridicula quaedam, quaedam etiam pudenda, unde improbissimo cuique pleraque fingendi licentia est, adeo ut de libris totis et auctoribus, ut succurrit, mentiantur tuto, quia inveniri qui numquam fuere non possunt* ("This happens especially in mythology, and sometimes reaches ludicrous or even scandalous extremes, so that the most unscrupulous writer has plenty of scope for invention, and can even lie in any way that occurs to him about whole books or authorities—all quite safely, because what never existed cannot be found").

him *aniles fabellas* are myths that convey an overly human and base image of the gods.[143]

Seneca[144] is harsher and more drastic—and, for our purposes, more interesting. In the *De beneficiis* the philosopher maintains that, for the subject he has chosen, it would be pointless to discuss the three Graces and their iconography:[145] these topics are typically adopted by Chrysippus and more generally by the Greeks (1.3.8), but they are detrimental to clarity in his exposition. Seneca thinks it is better to come directly to the point:

> As for those absurdities, let them be left to the poets, whose purpose it is to charm the ear and to weave a pleasing tale (*aures oblectare . . . et dulcem fabulam nectere*). But those who wish to heal the human soul, to maintain faith in the dealings of men, and to engrave upon their minds the memory of services—let these speak with earnestness and plead with all their power; unless, perchance, you think that by light talk and fables and old wives' reasonings (*levi ac fabuloso sermone et anilibus argumentis*) it is possible to prevent a most disastrous thing—the abolishment of benefits. (Sen. *Ben.* 1.4.5–6)

Here we are well beyond Plato's stern caution: what is at stake in this passage is the very notion that a myth or a story could possibly be useful in support of moral and philosophical reasoning. All the *fabulae* are relegated to the realm of poetry, of what is *dulce* and not *utile*[146] and of what is merely devoted to *aures oblectare*. This inevitably reminds us of Apuleius' prologue and its promise to *aures permulcere*.

2.7.2 THE TRADITION OF SATIRE

In view of this, when we read Apuleius' prologues in the *Metamorphoses* from a Senecan perspective (both the prologue to the novel as a whole, voiced by

---

143. Other relevant passages by Cicero are listed in Massaro 1977, 108–109.

144. See Massaro 1977, 114.

145. But this is only a *praeteritio,* and Seneca actually offers a short essay on allegoresis: "Their faces are cheerful, as are ordinarily the faces of those who bestow or receive benefits. They are young because the memory of benefits ought not to grow old. They are maidens because benefits are pure and undefiled and holy in the eyes of all; and it is fitting that there should be nothing to bind or restrict them, and so the maidens wear flowing robes, and these too are transparent because benefits desire to be seen" (1.3.5). Even for Seneca, it seems, old wives' tales are not totally meaningless.

146. On the standard connection between "sweetness" and fictional character of a tale, see above, pp. 40 f.

the *ego,* and the prologue to *Cupid and Psyche,* voiced by the sub-narrator, the *anus*[147]), we are forced to consider the possibility that these narrators are deliberately adopting the discredited *persona* of a brilliant entertainer, who addresses his public merely to amuse and entertain it without any "higher" purpose. But it is still too early to reach such a conclusion, since not all ancient authors shared Seneca's harsh judgment about the utter uselessness of *mythoi* and *aniles fabulae.* Plato did not recommend their complete elimination, as we have seen, even if he advised the rulers of his utopian city to carefully select such tales, and to purge them of anything that could be dangerous to the good health of the state and its citizens. After all, in Plato's dialogues Socrates frequently employs myths in philosophical discussions.

As a matter of fact, expressions like *anilis fabula* are not always polemical; this is especially true when the author applies such an expression to his own work, often with fairly evident self-irony (either directly or, as is often the case in narrative texts, through the voice of a fictional character). Socrates, as we have seen, nearly adopts such a self-ironic pose at the end of the *Gorgias.* Horace's *Satire* 2.6 takes a step further. Here are the verses 77–79 that introduce the well-known Aesopic story of the two mice:

> Now and then our neighbor Cervius rattles off old wives' tales that fit the case (*garrit anilis / ex re fabellas*). Thus, if anyone, blind to its anxieties, praises the wealth of Arellius, he thus begins . . . [148]

The tale is told during a country banquet, where the food is simple but the table conversation is worthy of the platonic *Symposium* ("we discuss what has more relevance to us and what is an evil not to know," 72 f.).[149] This story serves as a narratological counterpart to a discussion about happiness, friendship, and the nature of the Good (73–76). Of course it contains a moral teaching—do not all Aesopic fables have a moral?—but we must con-

---

147. On the identity of the speaking *ego,* see above, p. 52 n. 1; on the parallelism between the two prologues, see §§ 1.1 and 1.3.2.

148. This passage is the main focus of Massaro 1977: he links Horace's verses especially with Plato's usage of self-ironic expressions like γραῶν μῦθος in the *Gorgias* and states that "The attitude in which the Socratic spirit seems revived more faithfully in Horace than in Cicero is that of a preference for thoughtful irony, which leads them both to present formally and substantially their truth as if it had been heard as an *anilis fabella*" (p.110). At p. 112 he points out a similar attitude in Apuleius.

149. Bond 1985, 85 even sees this fable as the equivalent of a Platonic myth. On the connection between Horace's country dinner and Plato's *Symposium,* see e.g. Muecke 1993, 205 *ad* 2.6.67 ff. and *passim.* According to West 1974, 74, the City Mouse's dislike for the country is similar to the feelings Socrates expresses at *Phdr.* 230d; and the City Mouse "is a philosopher, not however a Myo-Platonist, but a fashionable Pseudo-Epicurean." More generally, on the relationship between Greek philosophy and Roman satire, see Mayer 2005.

sider the destabilization provoked by an introduction that uses deprecatory terminology (*garrit; anilis . . . fabella*), and more generally by specific traits of the satirical genre itself, such as self-irony and the use of a satiric persona. As a result, the reader feels compelled to draw a moral teaching from this *fabula*, but this task turns out to be more difficult than it seemed at first. It is also difficult to decide to what extent Horace himself directly espouses this lesson, and even to whom it is addressed. These interpretive pitfalls are well described by Susanna Morton Braund:

> It seems as if the moral of the fable—that a simple, safe and independent life is preferable to a luxurious and dangerous life of dependency—is designed to stand as the moral for the satire as a whole. But, we might ask, who is actually responsible for the telling of this fable—and, by extension, endorsing its moral? Horace the author? "Horace" the character within the poem? The neighbour Cervius? Or even Aesop? And which of the audiences is the target of the fable? The original group of neighbours, including "Horace," at the dinner-party in the country? The implied audience in the poem as a whole, that is those inside Maecenas' coterie and those outside who envy those inside? Or the original Roman audience when Horace the poet first produced this poem? Or any audience since then? Us? This small example highlights the wide range of potential relationships between author and audience in the genre of satire. Satire is always a tricky and slippery type of discourse to interpret. The author tends to play games with us by creating a mask or voice, a satirist who is persuasively and seductively authoritative, and then by undermining that authority. This he does by writing into the mask some equivocation, inconsistency or ambivalence which creates uncertainty for us about the relationship between author and mask, between poet and *persona*.[150]

Both Platonic dialogue and satire are dialogic-narrative literary genres in which the author does not (necessarily) speak directly to his audience, but lets his characters speak in his place: in fact, the author can even be part of the audience, as is the case in Horace's *Satire* 2.6.[151] For many ancient authors, dialogue and narrative provide a privileged means of conveying moral and philosophical ideas, but they also present a hindrance to those readers who, like modern scholars, try to reconstruct with some degree of accuracy the thoughts of an ancient author. Socrates narrates the final myth

---

150. Braund 1996, 59.
151. Probably in Aristides' *Milesiaka* as well: see pp. 45 f.

of the *Gorgias,* and the text offers no explicit hint about Plato's attitude towards Socrates' words. Of course we can make reasonable hypotheses, but ultimately the exact degree of correspondence between Plato's thought and Socrates' words is a matter of speculation,[152] just as is the degree of historicity in Plato's portrait of Socrates. Dialogue and *mythos,* in short, are useful tools for transmitting moral and philosophical ideas in an agreeable form, but they are also obstacles that prevent us from directly accessing Socrates' or Plato's thoughts, and from effectively distinguishing between them. Something similar is afoot in Horace's *Satire* 2.6. The tale of the two mice indeed tells us something, namely that wealth has its drawbacks (cf. the *sollicitas opes* of v. 79, where, in a less intrusive and pedantic form, Horace's introductory verses play the role of Aesop's ὁ μῦθος δηλοῖ ὅτι, "the story shows"). But if we want to gather more information or more definite lessons from this text, all we can do is to try to read between the lines and make educated guesses. To what extent did Horace (and the question can be asked both of the "real" Horace and his poetic persona) really yearn for a poor and rustic life? How many hardships must one suffer to be *tutus ab insidiis?*[153]

More than the exact answer to these questions, my chief concern here is the deprecatory terminology adopted in Horace's introductory verses. Despite all the hermeneutic uncertainty that surrounds this text, I think it is fairly clear that the irony conveyed by the words *garrit anilis . . . fabellas* is directed not against any moral teaching that the story may convey (however indirectly), but rather against its being merely a tale, serving as table-talk: morally relevant, perhaps, but certainly not the highest possible exercise in literary or philosophical discourse. More precisely, what we have here is self-irony, since in these verses Horace is explicitly placing his own satire at a literary level well below that of Plato's *Symposium*—an inescapable literary model for any serious dinner conversation. That Horace does so by adopting terminology most probably derived from Plato only imbues the passage with more irony.

---

152. The "division of roles" between the author Plato and his character Socrates is exploited by Sedley 2004, 8 in his interpretation of the *Theaetetus:* "The *Theaetetus* does indeed contain a Platonic message, but that message is not articulated by the speaker Socrates. Socrates fails to see the Platonic implications, and instead it is we, as seasoned readers of Plato, who are expected to recognize and exploit them."

153. Oliensis 1998, for example, states that "the 'country mouse' costume does not quite suit the poet of the Sabine farm" (p. 50, with further bibliographical references at n. 38). *Satire* 2.2—and, in broader terms, the satiric genre as a whole—poses a similar problem. Freudenburg 2001 points out that at 2.21 Horace promises to teach us *quae virtus et quanta . . . sit vivere parvo,* but it is the peasant Ofellus who is entrusted with this teaching: and "the relationship of Horace to his invented (or really remembered?) Ofellus is every bit as problematic and inscrutable as that of Socrates to the Wise Diotima, or of Plato to Socrates" (p. 112). See also W. S. Anderson 1982, 48.

This kind of self-irony seems to be particularly well-suited to satire, since that genre often prompts the author to meditate upon himself and his own work, and to emphasize its merits even as he recognizes the low status satire holds in comparison to "higher" poetry.[154] It is not by chance, I think, that we find such self-irony applied to the introduction of a tale. A tale can be, after all, a perfect tool for the satirist, allowing him to hint at serious ideas in an intermediate register and without seeming pedantic.[155] And as we have seen, it also serves to keep a safe distance between the poet and his satiric *persona* (a particularly useful feature in the second book of Horaces' *Sermones*). I would further suggest that tales provide a good opportunity for blending the *utile* and *dulce*, recommended by Horace at Ars Poetica 333 ff.:[156] such a blend, as we will see shortly, was often advertised as a quality of tales and fables. But first, it will prove useful (and also pleasant, I hope) to follow the history of *aniles fabulae* thoughout the genre of Latin *Satura*. This requires us to incorporate a much broader timeframe into the discussion.

Martianus Capella's *De nuptiis Philologiae et Mercurii*, while much later than Apuleius' novel, nevertheless forms an ideal bridge between satire[157] and narrative, our primary concern here. In regard to both style and subject matter, Martianus is indeed highly indebted to his renowned fellow-countryman Apuleius.[158] In fact, it is unclear, at least to me, whether the model for the passage we are going to read was Horace, Apuleius, or both of them at the

---

154. At *Sat.* 1.4.34 ff. for example Horace reports several critical statements made by those who do not like his choice of genre (*quos genus hoc minime iuvat,* 24): they describe his verses as something similar to old wives' tales (*et quodcumque semel chartis illeverit, omnis / gestiet a furno redeuntis scire lacuque, / et pueros et anus*). Horace replies by confessing that he does not even consider himself a poet (*primum ego me illorum dederim quibus esse poetas / excerpam numero*).

155. The first poem in Horace's collection contains sketches of as many as four different tales: the fable of the ant (1.1.33 ff.), the anecdote of the Athenian (64 ff.), Tantalus' myth (68 f.), and Ummidius' *fabula* (95 ff.). On the importance of tales in ancient satire, see e.g. Beck 1982, 210 f.: for him, Petronius' narrative technique is founded on the satiric and elegiac poets' experimentation with tales and poetic personae (an extremely useful analysis, even though it pays insufficient attention to the *Satyricon*'s links with the Greek narrative tradition). For more on fables in Horace's *Satires,* see Cucchiarelli 2001, 158 ff.

156. This passage is also concerned with fiction: cf. 1.338 *ficta voluptatis causa sint proxima veris.* The correct mix of *utile* and *dulce* was of course the subject of a larger debate in ancient literary criticism (see below in the text, and § 1.3.2); Horace even seems to make a joke about this oppostiion at *Epist.* 1.16.14 f., where he describes the beautiful landscape of his country house (*infirmo capiti fluit utilis, utilis alvo. / hae latebrae dulces . . .*).

157. On the satiric and Menippean qualities of the *De nuptiis,* see Cristante 1978, 685 and n. 14; Shanzer 1986, 29–44; Pabst 1994, 105–133; Grebe 1999, 848–857; Kenaan 2000, 373–378.

158. See e.g. Grebe 1999, 28 and *passim;* however, see also the remarks by Lenaz 1975, 96 n. 389, who is unwilling to consider Martianus as a "singe d'Apulée" with regard to language and style. Shanzer 1986, 44 brings the crucial point into focus very well: "there is an important lesson about Martianus to be learnt through Apuleius—to keep both the mystery-mongers and the Milesians in sight simultaneously."

same time. The *De nuptiis* ends with a dialogic *sphragis* that functions to dramatize an uncertain relationship between the satiric poet, his work, and the *personae* who populate it. In these final verses "the work is described as a *fabula* told by a personified *Satura;* however, she denies having inspired it, and claims that Martianus is solely responsible."[159] The first line is particularly interesting in this context, where we find the phrase *habes anilem, Martiane, fabulam* (p. 997,1 Kopp; 384,19 Willis). Here, the author again attaches the definition of "old wives' tale" to a work that, though bizarre, certainly has some didactic aim, and provokes allegorical interpretation. It should be noted that in this passage *anilem* is the reading offered by James Willis.[160] In light of the fact that the phrase *anilis fabula* is a frequent occurrence, while *senilis fabula* is unprecedented, I think that Lucio Cristante is right in recommending *senilem*, which is both better attested and clearly the *lectio difficilior*.[161] In other words, Martianus is humorously elaborating on a well-known topos, taking a definition commonly used in literary and philosophical polemic, and adapting it to himself as an old man (*senilis*). In my opinion, however, the debate about whether the adjective applies to *Satura* or Martianus (a subject discussed at some length by Cristante) is not relevant to the choice of *senilis:* a tale can be *anilis* even if its narrator is not an *anus* like the old housekeeper in the brigands' lair. Socrates and Cervius were not old women, of course,[162] and a similar example is offered by another late text that was probably influenced by both Apuleius and Martianus.

Fulgentius defines his own *Mitologiae* as a *rugosa sulcis anilibus fabula* (*Myth.* 1, p. 3.13 ff. Helm: "a story furrowed with an old woman's wrinkles"); just like Martianus' *senilis fabula*, it has been conceived at night by the light of a lamp (*nocturna praesule lucerna* in Fulgentius; *lucernis flamine* in Martianus).[163] Fulgentius places himself not far from the realm of *satura:* he

---

159. Cristante 1978, 683.

160. Willis 1983; cf. 1975, 133. He accepts a variant found in codex E; D1 and R1 have *sanilem,* C1 *sinilem,* all the others *senilem.*

161. Cf. Cristante 1978, 689 f. Of course, old men occasionally tell stories (e.g. Critias' father in *Ti.* 26b–c;). In fact, as we will see shortly, it seems that the longest and most elaborate "old wives' tales" are usually told by men; and in this regard, *Cupid and Psyche* is an exception to the rule. However, I am unaware of any occurences in Greek or Latin of phraseology such as *senilis fabula* or πρεσβύτου μῦθος. In any case, whatever solution to this textual problem we choose, it is obvious that "in tota hac narratione componenda ante oculos habuisse Martianum festivam illam Apuleii de Cupidine Psycheque fabulam, quae et ab anicula narretur et anilis fabula ab auctore vocitetur" (Willis 1975, 133; but note that in Apuleius the tale is defined as an *anilis fabula* not by the *auctor,* but by the old woman).

162. Even though, as is well known, in the *Theaetetus* Socrates repeatedly defines himself as an old midwife (149a ff. and *passim*).

163. On Fulgentius' passage and its relationship with Martianus and Apuleius, see Pabst 1994, 137; Kenaan 2000, 384–387; Mattiacci 2003, 232–234.

says that his master, to whom the work is dedicated, always appreciates his *cachinnantes ... nenias lepore satyrico litas,* "ridiculous lullabies peppered with satiric charm." He also distinguishes his work from that of a *poeta furens,* and puts it on a lower level: he is merely an interpreter of dream-like and trivial stories, *onirocreta soporis nugas ariolans.*[164] His witty lullabies and old wives' stories, however, are meant to be taken seriously, and Fulgentius stresses this point with some literary and mythological examples: he is not curious like Psyche nor shameless like Sulpicia; he is not interested in Phaedra's turbid passions; nor is he unsteady like Hero, who let her torch die out, and allowed her beloved Leander to drown in the sea without its guidance. His model will instead be Cicero, the Platonic rhetor, and his philosophical use of myth in the *Somnium Scipionis* (1.3–5 p. 3.16–4.7 Helm). In spite of some explicit textual references, Fulgentius' perspective is rather different from Macrobius' in the passage I quoted earlier (*Somn.* 1.2.8), even if both writers focus on the serious interpretation of fictional tales. Macrobius' aim was to differentiate the *Somnium Scipionis* from those *fabulae* that are only intended to titillate the ears of their audience and offer no philosophical teaching,[165] while Fulgentius instead implies that all, or at least most, myths can be read with the purpose of obtaining philosophical instruction. Fulgentius condemns Psyche's curiosity and Phaedra's passions, but he will not refrain from telling their stories and extracting a meaning from them (*quid sibi illorum falsitas sentire uoluerit:* 3.117 p. 69.3–4 Helm). Thus, while Macrobius rejects Apuleius' novel and all similar *fabulae,* confining them *in nutricum cunas,* Fulgentius can exploit a wider tradition of myths and tales and bend them to his philosophical purposes. His attitude is less stern than Macrobius', and he can even indulge in some self-irony about his own work, defined as a *rugosa sulcis anilibus fabula.*[166] With these words, Fulgentius likens himself to the old narrator of *Cupid and Psyche.*[167]

---

164. Note that (*h*)*ariolor* means "to speak by divine inspiration or with second sight, prophesy," but it can also be used (esp. in comedy) in a facetious or pejorative sense (see *OLD* s.v.); the *ThLL* (VI 2534.7) offers a meaning of "absurda loqui, nugari."

165. Cf. above, pp. 96–97 and n. 134.

166. Kenaan 2000, 384 ff. is right in emphasizing that, in his allegorical reading of *Cupid and Psyche,* Fulgentius banishes from his own text Apuleius' original, lengthy, and ingenuous story, and concentrates instead on a censored and paraphrased version in order to provide a skeleton that can serve as the basis for an allegorical reading. Above all, Fulgentius obliterates the narrative situation that provides the context for the tale in Apuleius, and "completely disregards the story's female narrator and female audience" (p. 387). In so doing, he eliminates its attributes as an *anilis fabula,* and thereby makes it similar to the *fabulae* that Macrobius also found acceptable. Nevertheless, both in his prologue and in the discussion proper, Fulgentius is clearly less censorious than Macrobius in his selection of myths that are fit for serious interpretation.

167. I think it is noteworthy that the activity of Apuleius' old woman could also be well defined

2.7.3 The tradition of narrative

Fulgentius is by no means an isolated example. After all, it was nearly a requirement of the narrative genre to cross the frontiers of purely childish entertainment and to approach the realm of education and instruction. Phaedrus is very well aware that he is working within a minor literary genre, but nevertheless points out repeatedly that his stories contain useful moral precepts. Consider, for example, the verses with which he introduces a tale *de mustela et muribus:*

> I seem to you to be fooling, and I do indeed wield the pen lightheartedly, so long as I have no very important theme. But take a careful look into these trifles (*neniae*): what a lot of practical instruction (*utilitas*) you will find in tiny affairs! They are not always just what they seem to be. Many people are deceived by the façade of a structure; it is the unusual mind that perceives what the artist took pains to tuck away in some inner nook.[168]

Phaedrus' stories are, in the author's words, only a literary *lusus*, and nothing more than *neniae*, trivial tales[169]—a definition not unlike *anilis fabula* that, as we have seen, Septimius Severus attached to Apuleius' "Milesian" work in his letter to the Senate. These *neniae* will, however, if carefully interpreted, offer their reader great *utilitas*. We find ourselves, therefore, in a literary space that is between *dulce* and *utile*, and includes them both. Even in antiquity the term σπουδογέλοιον was occasionally used to describe this ambiguous literary space,[170] and Phaedrus' prologue makes reference to it:

> A double dowry comes with this, my little book: it moves to laughter, and by wise counsels guides the conduct of life (*duplex libelli dos est: quod risum movet / et quod prudentis vitam consilio monet:* 1 pr. 3–4).

---

using an *onirocreta soporis nugas ariolans* (as opposed to *poeta furens*, as in Fulgentius) as paradigm. As we have seen (p. 30 with n. 93), she is described by Apuleius as a sort of vulgarized epic poet. She also begins her tale as a reaction to a bad dream that has scared Charite: she interprets it, and then she offers the girl a comforting prophecy. Therefore Fulgentius, in spite of his claim to be unlike the curious Psyche, seems to suggest he is a reincarnation of the old narrator—nobler than the original, true, but still prone to belittling himself.

168. 4.2.1–7. Cf. also 3 pr. 10 *legesne quaeso potius viles nenias.*
169. See also Petronius 46.4, where *nenia* is used with the meaning of "toy, plaything, pastime for kids." J. L. Heller 1943, 215 notes that "the central meaning of the word [*sc. nenia*] was . . . 'plaything,' 'play' in general . . . in this sense it was applied, at an early date, to the burlesque song-and-dance performances of amateur actors at funeral processions."
170. For more on this see below §§ 2.7.4 and 2.8.

But the coexistence of *utile* and *dulce* is a typical feature of the literature of fables from the beginning, and Phaedrus is most probably following a tradition already established by Aesop. Gellius says about the latter:

> Aesop, the well-known fabulist from Phrygia, has justly been regarded as a wise man (*sapiens*), since he taught what it was salutary (*utilia*) to call to mind and to recommend, not in an austere and dictatorial manner, as is the way of philosophers, but by inventing witty and entertaining fables (*festivos delectabilesque apologos*) he put into men's minds and hearts ideas that were wholesome and carefully considered, while at the same time he enticed their attention (*cum audiendi quadam inlecebra*). (2.29.1)

As we have seen in Philostratus, *VA* 5.14.1, Menippus claims that Aesop's tales are nothing more than "frogs, . . . asses, and nonsense (λῆροι) for old women and children to chew on." Apollonius, however, replies that he considers Aesop's tales "more conducive to philosophy" than the myths told by poets. One of the reasons he adduces is that Aesop "uses humble subjects to teach great lessons" (ἀπὸ σμικρῶν πραγμάτων διδάσκει μεγάλα: 5.14.2). Another reason is the attitude towards truth he displays in telling stories. The poets tell their myths pretending they are real, but Aesop,

> by promising a story that everyone knows to be untrue, tells the truth precisely in not undertaking to tell the truth . . . someone who tells an untrue tale while adding instruction, as Aesop does, makes plain that he uses falsehood for the benefit of the listener. It is also a charming trait to make dumb animals nicer and deserving respect from humans. (5.14.5)

As we see in this passage, Philostratus' *Life of Apollonius* represents Aesopic fables as tantalizingly close to the novel. The claim that Aesop "tells the truth precisely in not undertaking to tell the truth" inevitably reminds us of Lucian's programmatic statement in *True Stories* 1.4.[171] Menippus' dismissive definition contains the same tone, and practically the same words, as the passages from the *Historia Augusta* and Macrobius' *Commentary* I have already quoted several times. The interaction of τὸ χρήσιμον and τὸ ἡδύ, both connected to the idea of fiction and falsity, τὸ ψεῦδος, is an important feature of both the Aesopic tale and the novel.[172]

---

171. "I did not wish to be the only one to make no use of this liberty in yarn spinning—for I had no true story to relate, since nothing worth mentioning had ever happened to me; and consequently I turned to romancing myself. But I am much more sensible about it than others are, for I will say one thing that is true, and that is that I am a liar."

172. Cf. above, pp. 40 f.

Even though a novel can very well be an old wives' tale about an ass, there is also a great difference between the novel and Aesopic fables: apart from any consideration regarding the extent and complexity of its narrative structure, the ending of a typical novel lacks an explicit moral, such as we find in Aesop's formula ὁ λόγος δηλοῖ ὅτι, "the tale shows . . . "[173] The novel is also remarkably different from satire (be it after the manner of Menippus,[174] Horace, or Martianus Capella) and from philosophical dialogue. However, all these genres share an inclination to understatement and self-irony that hints at their lower position in comparison with the nobler genres (such as moral and philosophical treatises, or poetic treatments of myth in epic and drama). Paradoxically, it is through this very understatement that these texts reassert their ambition to achieve the same edifying goals as the higher genres, though by means of a different and lower literary form, one which is open to entertainment and narrative illusion, as well as to teaching and truth.[175] This intention is clear enough in the way the old narrator introduces the tale of *Cupid and Psyche:* it would be easy, she says, to offer solace drawing from the oneirocritic tradition, but she prefers to obtain the same result by telling a pleasing *anilis fabula* (4.27.5–8). I think that this way of characterizing the central tale of the novel—and, as we will see, the novel itself as a whole—could be listed among the "Systemreferenzen" that, according to Maaike Zimmerman, associate the novel with satiric poetry[176] (in addition, of course, to the other literary genres I have mentioned above).

---

173. Mithras' and Sisimithres' speeches in Apuleius 11.15 and Heliodorus 10.39 are closest to what could be called an explicit moral in ancient novels; however, they are views expressed by characters inside the narrative, not direct authorial interventions.

174. As regards Apuleius in particular, a connection of the *Metamorphoses* with Menippean satire has been accepted by some scholars and rejected by others. As we have seen above, p. 90, Winkler suggests that the original title of the novel was in Varronian and Menippean style; on the contrary, Weinbrot 2005 shares the opinion of some seventeenth- and eighteenth-century translators and readers, according to whom the *Metamorphoses* would be "too raunchy to be taken seriously, as Menippean satire requires" (p. 8). Even though his conclusions are questionable, Weinbrot offers a good overview of the difficulty of offering a clear definition of the borderlines of the Menippean genre.

175. In satire, satiric personae and self-irony are features that prevent the poet from fashioning himself as a superior, authoritative, and reliable model; however, they do not absolutely prejudice the protreptic value of his poetry. See e.g. Freudenburg 1993, 21: "Horace understands that the scoffer cannot exempt himself from the degradation he metes out, for his own humiliation is central to his mission of leveling and exposure, a festival mission that concerns the dying nature of all men, the instability of their beliefs and their institutions. Anything that has pretensions to stability in a world where the wheels of life and death are constantly in motion the satirist unsettles, his own self included. In so doing he teaches the pretentious fool how to live, how to join the larger party of the dying, helpless fools who know that wealth is to be spent, wine is to be drunk, and authority mocked because tomorrow brings death. His mockery, despite all appearances, is deeply felt and moral in nature. He preaches the one true, unalterable fact of human behavior, that all must die, and in so doing he teaches us how to live."

176. M. Zimmerman 2006; cf. below, § 2.8 pp. 121 ff.

In conclusion, *neniae* and *aniles fabulae* are often used as disparaging definitions in literary polemic,[177] but when an author adopts such definitions self-ironically and in reference to his own work, he is in fact applying to it a sort of trademark that discloses its seriocomic nature.

2.7.4 CUPID AND PSYCHE

In my opinion, this is exactly the case in Apuleius. There is no doubt that the old maidservant of the robbers, defining her tale as an *anilis fabula*, underscores it as a mere diversion, a means of soothing the young Charite's desperate grief. It is worth noting that this *anilis fabula* is actually told by an old woman;[178] to my knowledge, this is the only example of this, while all the other major *aniles fabulae* are told by men (Socrates, Cervius, Martianus Capella, Fulgentius and so on). It could even be said that this is a case of a verbal expression being converted into fictional reality.[179] At the end of the tale (6.25.1), the ass defines the old woman as a *delira et temulenta . . . anicula*, and his words do indeed contribute to the negative characterization of her as a narrator. However, as I have shown elsewhere,[180] Lucius' comment should be read also as a subtle way of showing that the tale is a sort of degraded epic. Indeed, drunkenness and madness were traditionally considered ideal conditions for an epic poet to receive inspiration. After all, this is only a confirmation of the well-known fact that the central tale of the *Metamorphoses* shares several structural and thematic features with epic poetry.[181]

---

177. This disparaging meaning is almost constant in the Christian tradition, which is influenced by Saint Paul's exhortation to avoid βεβήλους καὶ γραώδεις μύθους (*1 Tim* 4.7; *ineptas . . . et aniles fabulas* in the *Vulgate*) to devote ourselves to the exercise of εὐσέβεια/*pietas*. See again Massaro 1977, 115 ff.

178. Again, I think that Kenaan 2000 is right in emphasizing that both the old narrator and her intended audience, Charite, are female: this underscores even more the "feminine" qualities of this particular *anilis fabula*. However, I cannot see how Lucius' definition of *bella fabella* at 6.25.1 can strip *Cupid and Psyche* of its *fabula anilis* qualities and be "a first step in transforming this text into . . . a philosophical allegory" (Kenaan 2000, 383). While I clearly agree that philosophy and allegory play a role in *Cupid and Psyche,* and that the tale has different "layers of meaning" (p. 384), Lucius' words at 6.25.1 resonate for me on the very same level as the old narrator's introduction at 4.27.8. Both passages can be read as plain statements made by ingenuous characters in the tale *and* as forms of self-ironic winking by a skilled author that skilled readers can recognize; as such, they allude to the different kinds of reception invited by this tale.

179. There are other instances of this process in the *Metamorphoses:* see Keulen 2003b, 167 f.; Plaza 2006; McCreight 2006, 125 and *passim*. For a similar treatment of poetic similes, see Graverini 2003a, 211 with n. 10. See also above, p. 80 n. 83 on the transformation of proverbs into narrative.

180. Graverini 2003a, 214 f.; cf. also above, p. 30 with n. 93.

181. See e.g. Harrison 1998b. This is true even though, as Danielle van Mal-Maeder and Maaike Zimmerman rightly point out (1998, 86), her being an alcoholic explains the fact that wine-drinking

Thus, before the beginning of *Cupid and Psyche,* the old woman introduces her tale as an *anilis fabula;* after the end of the tale, the narrator herself is described as a *delira et temulenta anicula.* Both collocations, if we consider their literary history, are useful clues to lead the reader towards a well-defined reading practice. These seemingly disparaging definitions are infused with self-irony: they make an implicit reference to a more ambitious and "useful" kind of literary discourse, and in so doing they highlight both the "lower" status of *Cupid and Psyche* as a literary product, and Apuleius' "higher" models. Horace, Phaedrus, Martianus Capella, and Fulgentius all show a similar self-irony. These authors place themselves in an ambiguous position: they have a message they want to transmit, but they transmit it indirectly and surreptitiously, by narrating a pleasant tale and leaving to the reader the task of extracting a meaning out of it, if he is so inclined.[182]

Each author, of course, has his own way of balancing serious and comic elements, as well as distancing himself from his poetic persona or the character-narrator. Horace's *Satires,* as we have seen, appropriate the narrative devices of Platonic dialogue, including—or even enhancing—those which allow him to create a distance between the author and the "meaning" of the narration. Apuleius, in the tale of *Cupid and Psyche,* goes even further. As in Horace's *Satire* 2.6, the narrator is not the author himself or his poetic persona, but another character. Moreover, she is a character whom it would be very difficult to consider as a credible teacher of moral or philosophical values: the old drunken maidservant is undoubtedly much less reliable and authoritative than the "rustic sages" of Horace—not to speak of Plato's Socrates. From the point of view of reliability, it is useful to consider not only the narrator of *Cupid and Psyche,* but also the chain of transmission through which the tale reaches the reader. The narrator is old, and the audience contains Lucius while still in asinine form—and we have already seen that an ass was traditionally a very bad listener.[183] And since the *Metamorphoses* is the first-person account of Lucius' adventures, the reader must ultimately depend upon the recollections and words of an ass. Moreover, Lucius'

---

is repeatedly highlighted in the tale. The old and drunken woman is a character typical of comedy: cf. Plautus, *Cist.* 149 *et multiloqua et multibiba est anus; Curc.* 76–77 *anus . . . multibiba atque merobiba.*

182. There are clearly individual variations (needless to say, Fulgentius shows a more pedantic attitude than Horace), but self-irony is an important common feature in all these authors. As for the expression *anilis fabula,* Apuleius uses it in a more decidedly disparaging sense in other circumstances. At 9.16.1 the ass relates an *aniculae sermo* that has come to his ears: an old servant induces the miller's wife to commit adultery, and for that purpose she tells her the story of the successful adultery of Barbarus' wife (9.17–21). The old woman's story has a protreptic value in this case too, but its moral is wicked. Apuleius seems to be playing with the conventions he himself has adopted.

183. See above p. 24, on King Midas' asinine ears.

account attracts some suspicion on the part of the reader: he admits explicitly that, for obvious reasons, he could not write down the *bella fabella* as he was listening to it.[184] The comic belittlement of *Cupid and Psyche* involves both its narrator and its primary audience.

But if, together with this self-irony, we also take into account the philosophical and religious interpretations that the tale came to inspire, the status of *Cupid and Psyche* becomes ambiguous—akin to the tales of Aesop and Phaedrus, the story of the two mice in Horace, and the final myth in Plato's *Gorgias*. On one hand, it is clear enough that religious or Platonizing interpretations are often contradictory, and seem to be more acceptable when they are general and lack detail;[185] on the other, there are several reasons why it is also unsatisfactory to categorically deny any allegorical reading, as Rudolf Helm did when reacting to the excesses shown by previous criticism.[186] The symbolism in the names of the two characters, for example, is patently evident, even though those names are frequently used in Hellenistic erotic poetry;[187] and it is difficult to deny that the story has something to teach, despite the fact that it is difficult to define the details of its teaching. Certainly it could have taught something to Lucius: if nothing else, the ass could have been induced to realize that the real cause of his miserable condition was not so much "Photis' mistake" (9.15.5), as it was his own morbid and reckless curiosity about magic. He could also have been encouraged to hope for some kind of divine salvation: a reader who knows Plato's *Phaedrus*[188] cannot avoid a sense of *déjà vu* when Psyche sees Cupid flying away from her and clings to his ankle until, exhausted, she falls down to the

---

184. Cf. 6.25.1 *astans ego non procul dolebam mehercules quod pugillares et stilum non habebam qui tam bellam fabellam praenotarem*: it is therefore a case of oral transmission. See below, § 3.4, on the "fictional orality" of the *Metamorphoses*, that privileges an oral/aural relationship between author and audience; hearing is traditionally discredited as a reliable channel for the transmission of information, but it is better suited to excite passions and to urge the reader to identify himself with the characters.

185. See e.g. Griffiths 1978, 148 on the theories of Kerényi and Merkelbach: "It is the degree of intellectual complication assumed by these equivalences that is the primary objection. The trouble is most manifest when the equivalences themselves are multiple, as when Merkelbach tells us (p. 32), "Psyche-Io-Isis betet zu Iuno-Isis." That Apuleius himself was thinking on these lines is incredible. If he has a deeper purpose than is evident on the surface, then it is one attached to a moral and thematic aim rather than to a sophisticated theological syncretism."

186. Helm 1914, 190 ff. On the story of the interpretations of *Cupid and Psyche*, see the thorough overview by Moreschini 1994a, 48 ff.

187. See *AG* 5.57; 5.179; 12.80; 12.91; 12.98; 12.132. However, in these epigrams "Love" and "Soul" are mostly abstractions, while in the novel they are truly humanized characters.

188. See Trapp 1990 on the importance of the *Phaedrus* in the culture of the second century C.E.

ground (5.24.1).[189] Narrative elements like this are certainly enough to connect Apuleius' tale to Plato's myth of the fall of the soul (*Phdr.* 248a ff.). But if the road towards a philosophical interpretation is open, it is very difficult to find more detailed parallels to Plato's teachings: in the *Metamorphoses,* for example, Psyche has no wings, either before her fall or after her apotheosis; and the *Phaedrus* never mentions the soul's *curiositas*—on the contrary, while in Apuleius Psyche is punished for having seen too much, in Plato the soul falls to earth because she could *not* see the "Plain of truth" (this is Adrasteia's law, 248c).[190]

More than with all the possible detailed analogies between Apuleius' tale and the Platonic and Middle-Platonic theories on the soul, I am concerned here with a more general issue: does *Cupid and Psyche* actually prompt the reader towards an allegorical reading, or is it simply a pleasing and entertaining tale with no "hidden" meaning?[191] What I have been saying so far seems to encourage a complex reading, one that includes both hedonism and intellectual commitment, and does not consider them as separate or incompatible reading practices. The question now is whether we find in *Cupid and Psyche* (and in the *Metamorphoses* as a whole) more corroboration of the satirical or, more generally, seriocomic character I have highlighted in the definition of *anilis fabula*.

In a way, there can be no final answer to such very general interpretive issues, especially in the field of narrative literature. When reading a novel, the reader enjoys an almost complete hermeneutic freedom—much more so than when he reads other kinds of texts, such as philosophical treatises or historiographical works. From this point of view, *any* interpretation is permissible, since the hermeneutic stance of the reader is its ultimate source; here, Winkler's aporetic interpretation cannot be easily dismissed. However, I also think that textual clues and cultural contexts can, and indeed should, contribute to defining and directing a philologically conscious reading, even in the case of a novel. In the following pages, we will see how the *Metamorphoses* tries, in a very subtle manner, to control and direct its audience's reading, and we will reconsider what models of reception were available in the ancient and late-antique sources.

---

189. On this passage and its interpretations, see *GCA* 2004, 294 *ad loc.;* Walsh 1970, 206 f., with further references.

190. These and other details could be seen as a reflection of second-century Middle Platonism, which was open to Gnostic influences: see Moreschini 1978, 1–42 and *passim;* Dowden 1982 and 1998.

191. For a short overview of this subject, see e.g. Walsh 1970, 218 ff.

2.7.5 MODELS OF RECEPTION

The novel suggests two different interpretive approaches to the tale of *Cupid and Psyche*. At first Lucius makes no attempt whatsoever to find any meaning in the tale. He limits himself to enjoying a pleasant tale and remains deaf to any possible moral. His attitude is consistent until the beginning of Book 11, where he does resolve to seek salvation through divine intercession (but there is no explicit mention of any reflection on the tale at this point in the text). Lucius' approach to *Cupid and Psyche* is more or less tantamount to the one suggested by Helm in the early twentieth century; in antiquity, Septimius Severus (in the *Historia Augusta*) and Macrobius seem to have taken a similar approach to the novel in its entirety. We can even say that Lucius' attitude justifies their approach, and inscribes it into the text itself. Readers like Helm, Septimius Severus and Macrobius consider the *Metamorphoses* as nothing more than an entertaining story, void of meaning, offering the reader nothing beyond pleasure.

These readers take the definition of *anilis fabula* at face value; yet there is no need to think of them as unskilled—I would even postulate that they would agree with the reading of the prologue I have offered in the first chapter of this book. However, I would also suggest that they appear to be single-minded readers. Perhaps we should not forget that, in the novel, this kind of reading is described as typical of an ass, and before that, as typical of the young and inexperienced *scholasticus* Lucius;[192] and we will see shortly that Lucius does not have the last word in this interpretive debate. Furthermore, Septimius Severus and Macrobius do not present paradigms of unbiased interpretation: both have their own agenda, and a "true" interpretation of Apuleius' novel is clearly not their main goal. Septimius Severus' aim is to discredit a rival in front of the Senate by highlighting his low culture; Macrobius needs to demonstrate that Cicero's *somnium Scipionis* is a narrative worthy of interpretation, a philosophical and "useful" tale, and to do so he has to show that it is different from and better than other tales (ultimately, he does what Plato had already done, defining all the stories that were not useful to his philosophical intents as "old wives' tales"). Both Septimius Severus and Macrobius need to find a credible culprit, and Apuleius' novel provides an easy and well-known target for their allegations.

But besides the ass, who else could provide us with a different interpretive model? The tiny audience of *Cupid and Psyche* in fact includes another lis-

---

[192]. In fact, Lucius is an asinine reader (or, better, an asinine listener) even before becoming an ass. At 1.20.5 he says he has enjoyed Aristomenes' tale, but he does not draw any conclusions from it about the dangers of magic. Thelyphron's tale provides a second missed opportunity.

tener, Charite—indeed, she is not a casual listener like Lucius, but the "true" and "intended" audience of the tale. Nevertheless, the novel does not record her reactions, but only those of Lucius, and perhaps with good reason. It is easy to imagine that the old maidservant's tale did console Charite's distress, and that, unlike Lucius, she could apply what she had been told to her own situation. Perhaps at this early stage in the novel Apuleius preferred not to present a model of a careful reading (since an explicit reference to the ending of the novel would be immature); or, on the contrary, perhaps he does not want to discredit Charite by attributing to her the same obtuseness as he does to Lucius.[193] But perhaps the most important reason Apuleius might have elided Charite's reaction is that the significance of *Cupid and Psyche* is far more relevant to Lucius than to the young kidnapped maiden.

In any case, there are some traces of a more committed and less hedonistic reading of the central tale of the novel. In a sense, we could say that the priest Mithras is a "reader" of *Cupid and Psyche*, too. Obviously, he had no chance to hear the tale, but a dream has informed him of what was going to happen at the procession (11.13.1) and has provided him with the necessary knowledge to resume and reinterpret Lucius' vicissitudes at 11.15.[194] Therefore, *Cupid and Psyche* can be read as a reflection of Lucius' vicissitudes, just as (thanks to Mithras' interpretation) Lucius' vicissitudes can be read as a reflection of *Cupid and Psyche*. Mithras' sermon has always been the keystone of "unitarian" readings of the novel; we will see that it also strengthens a reading of the central tale as a *mise en abyme*.

In Mithras' sermon, Lucius' youthful inexperience is responsible for the fact that he has sunken into servile pleasures (*ad serviles delapsus voluptates*, 11.15.1). Certainly it would be going too far to say that *delapsus* echoes the use of the verb *dilabitur* at 5.24.1, where Psyche falls to the ground; in any case, it is more important to point out that the words *serviles voluptates* connect Mithras' speech to a Platonic text—and, more precisely, to a context strictly related to the myth of the fall of the soul. Now, expressions such as *servire voluptatibus* or δουλεύειν ταῖς ἡδοναῖς are rather common both in Latin and Greek, but such expressions in the form of noun plus adjective are far more rare, and show direct parallels in Plato. At 11.15.1–2 Mithras makes a distinction betwen Lucius' *serviles voluptates*, to which he had aban-

---

193. For example, Sandy 1999b, 131 claims that "Charite does not realize that the tale of Cupid and Psyche has special relevance to her own situation, that it is a *fabula de se*." However, at the end of the story, Charite's apprehension seems to have been placated, since there is no further mention of it; and when Charite comes back on stage, she exhibits a *virilis constantia* in her attempt to escape (6.27.5–6).

194. This is obviously a narrative stratagem to justify the fact that Mithras has a broad (if generic) knowledge of Lucius' adventures, even though he could not have witnessed them in person.

doned himself, and *religiosa beatitudo,* which he is about to receive from Isis. The language in Mithras' speech closely resembles several passages in Plato where Socrates distinguishes different kinds of pleasures:[195] in *Resp.* 9.587c, for example, the philosopher explains that there are three different kinds of ἡδονή, one of which is legitimate, and two illegitimate. The tyrant, who avoids both law and reason, devotes himself to the lowest kind of pleasure, and he lives among "servile pleasures" (δούλαις . . . ἡδοναῖς). Even more important here is a passage that occurs almost in the middle of the *Phaedrus,* where the central theme of the dialogue is introduced:[196]

> SOCRATES—What, then, is the method of writing well or badly? Do we want to question Lysias about this, and anyone else who ever has written or will write anything, whether a public or private document, in verse or in prose, be he a poet or ordinary man?
> PHAEDRUS—You ask if we want to question them? What else should one live for, so to speak, but for such pleasures? Certainly not for those which cannot be enjoyed without previous pain, which is the case with nearly all bodily pleasures and causes them to be justly called slavish (ἡδοναὶ . . . ἀνδραποδώδεις, 258d–e).

As an interlocutor who is also an enthusiastic lover of any kind of λόγοι, Phaedrus sometimes presents a challenge to Socrates, who is instead trying to direct his friend's attention toward what is good and truthful. To accomplish this, Socrates must make a distinction between the different kinds of

---

195. In Latin, the only parallel seems to be Seneca, *De vita beata* 7.7.3 *Altum quiddam est virtus, excelsum et regale, invictum infatigabile: voluptas humile servile, inbecillum caducum, cuius statio ac domicilium fornices et popinae sunt.* Seneca opposes *virtus* to *voluptas* and is not interested in defining different kinds of *voluptas*. But such a differentiation is precisely what connects Apuleius' passage to Plato, rather than the vague notion that a certain kind of pleasure is somehow "servile." As far as I know, these parallels with Plato have so far escaped the attention of commentators. Only the first is briefly mentioned by Keulen 1997, 225 and n. 99, and then by Harrison 2000, 253 n. 205. If, as I believe, these Platonic passages are highly significant to an interpretation of the novel, then it is not entirely true that "nothing like an integrated picture of any . . . Platonic-Isiac synthesis emerges from the *Metamorphoses*" (Kenney 2003, 183). Religious paraenesis appropriates the language and ideas of philosophy; and, in turn, Plato adopts religious metaphors to describe the soul's progress towards the world of the ideas (cf. Riedweg 1987; in *Phdr.* 250e, for example, the knowledge of Beauty is implicitly compared to a religious initiation; see also Diotima's description at *Symp.* 209e f.).

196. Nehamas 1999, 341 suggests on good grounds that the central subject of the *Phaedrus* is not Eros, as is often assumed, but "rhetoric—its nature, the proper way of pursuing it, if any, and its relation to philosophy." The idea of "servile pleasures" was recurrent in Plato and can be found elsewhere: see e.g. *Symp.* 210d βλέπων πρὸς πολὺ ἤδη τὸ καλὸν μηκέτι τὸ παρ' ἑνί, ὥσπερ οἰκέτης, ἀγαπῶν παιδαρίου κάλλος ἢ ἀνθρώπου τινὸς ἢ ἐπιτηδεύματος ἑνός, δουλεύων φαῦλος ᾖ καὶ σμικρολόγος . . .

pleasures that are derived from different experiences and place them in a hierarchy. In fact, at 250e Phaedrus repeats, practically verbatim, Socrates' description of a man who is not newly initiated (ὁ . . . μὴ νεοτελής) to the contemplation of beauty.

> He does not quickly rise from this world to that other world and to absolute beauty when he sees its namesake here, and so he does not revere it when he looks upon it, but gives himself up to pleasure (ἡδονή) and like a beast (τετράποδος νόμον) proceeds to lust and begetting; he makes licence his companion and is not afraid or ashamed to pursue pleasure in violation of nature (παρὰ φύσιν ἡδονήν).

On the contrary, Socrates says, at first the man who has been recently initiated feels a sort of pain (with a "Sapphic" symptomatology) when he sees a face closely imitating beauty. But this is a productive pain, such as when a child is teething: the soul is growing her wings. After this initial pain, the soul

> is bathed with the waters of yearning . . . and this pleasure which it enjoys is the sweetest of pleasures (ἡδονὴ . . . γλυκυτάτη: 251e).

Thus, Socrates differentiates between two different kinds of ἡδονή: one sort is the pleasure of those who, like the beasts, only aspire to "lust and begetting"; the other is a sweet pleasure resulting from the contemplation of beauty. Phaedrus' words imply precisely the same difference—despite the fact that Phaedrus himself seems to be more excited at the prospect of examining the speeches by Lysias (and others) with Socrates than he seems to anticipate any contemplative pleasure. Indeed, Phaedrus might appear to be curious and asinine like Lucius; but it is most important to recognize this "beastly" quality in Lucius, and the ease with which he neglects the contemplation of divine beauty to devote itself to "servile" and "unnatural" pleasures.[197]

In this way, the central myth of the *Phaedrus* shows an influence not only on *Cupid and Psyche,* but also on Mithras' sermon. His sermon authorizes and suggests, to some extent, a Platonic reading of Lucius' story, and by extension, of *Cupid and Psyche.* Once again, this parallel cannot be pushed to the level of minute detail, and we must apply to Mithras' words the same

---

197. This, of course, does not prevent us from seeing in the words *serviles voluptates* a reference to the erotic relationship of Lucius with Photis (which in any case can hardly be the only explanation for the priest's choice of words: cf. e.g. Sandy 1974 and 1999a, 97; Griffiths 1975, 247 f. *ad loc.*). It is pointless, I think, to ask ourselves if Mithras could consciously make the connection or not; it must be more than clear to the *auctor* Apuleius.

caution that is necessary for any philosophical or religious reading of the *Metamorphoses*. However, there are at least two conclusions we can safely draw in connection with this speech:

- It is offered to the reader as a model not only for a religious reinterpretation of Lucius' adventures, but more generally for the possibility of a committed reading of a story that presents itself as a simple narrative diversion, and that is received (at first) precisely as such;
- The possibility of a committed reading, both of *Cupid and Psyche* and of the whole novel, is not only a consequence of Mithras' interpretation, but was suggested earlier to the "attentive reader," who could understand the significance of the phrase *anilis fabula* and other metaliterary signs.

In my opinion, this is a forceful argument against the idea supported especially by Winkler, namely that there is a discontinuity between the comic tone of the first ten books and the religious inspiration of the last, to such a degree that "nothing in the ancient world authorizes us to infer from jokes or entertaining tales (Books 1–10) the imminent presence of a goddess."[198] The interaction between comic and serious is not a sort of "vinaigrette":[199] the two elements are not simply placed side by side, but combine and blend in the novel as a whole to produce a literary form that has a close relationship to other literary genres, such as philosophical dialogue and satire. This is true of Apuleius' work to a greater degree than most of the other texts we usually include in the list of "ancient novels." In order to fully understand this novel, then, we will have to take into account the paradoxical nature of satire and philosophical dialogue.

2.8 Paradox, satire, and levels of reading

At this point in the book, I believe there is sufficient reason to claim that a seriocomic reading does not necessarily require accepting Winker's aporetic approach, which would grant the reader complete freedom to choose between a religious/philosophical interpretation and a comic/satiric one. Such an opposition appears distinctly artificial and does not accurately rep-

---

198. Winkler 1985, 233.
199. Winkler 1985, 228 uses this image to describe an interpretive model that sees in the novel a free and chaotic hodgepodge of comic and serious: see e.g. Walsh 1970, according to whom "there is in fact a central ambivalence in the romance, a tension between Milesian ribaldry and Platonist mysticism, which reflects the complexity of the author's personality" (p. 143).

resent the range of interpretations appropriate to the text. From what I have been saying so far, it should be clear that we have two options: one is to allow the text to suggest moral, philosophical or religious ideas,[200] but the other is rather different from what Winkler suggested. In the first four sections of this chapter I have tried to demonstrate that there are only a few elements that could support a comic/satiric interpretation (at least as Winkler and others meant it), and these are uncertain. The "lighter" alternative to a religiously or philosophically committed reading is to view Lucius' vicissitudes not as a satire of his naivety, but rather to consider the novel as merely a hedonistic and entertaining text—just as Lucius listened to both the *bella fabella* of *Cupid and Psyche* and the tale of Aristomenes without considering what he might learn. As I have argued above, this is the kind of approach that the prologue suggests to the reader; it is also a sort of generic feature that we find in several other narrative texts.

Most importantly, we need to realize that both these interpretations are mutually dependent; each is incomplete when taken individually. The "hedonistic" reading is certainly effective and well-suited to the text in many ways. The *Metamorphoses* is a fascinating text, varied and literarily sophisticated; it can offer the average reader relaxation and an opportunity to escape into a fantasy world, while more learned readers will also find much to satisfy their cultural interests in it. Yet this approach leads the reader to neglect a layer of meaning that some sections of the novel (for example, the tale of *Cupid and Psyche* and the last book) seem to demand with particular clarity; in the end, this would amount to preferring Lucius over Mithras as a hermeneutic model. But even if some passages (and at least one prominent character) support a committed reading, we must consider the fact that many passages of the novel do not contribute at all to the construction of a symbolic meaning.[201] Moreover, any moral/religious/philosophical system we could infer from the novel must be somewhat general and undetailed. Mithras himself, in his speech at 11.15, offers only a general description: the reader is only

---

200. Religion and philosophy are not always set apart from each other. It is well known that Apuleius had both religious and philosophical interests: see e.g. Hijmans 1987 and Moreschini 1978 (who, *pace* Hijmans 1987, 397 n. 2, does not seem to suggest that there is a sharp distinction between the two). Plato frequently adopts religious language to describe the philosophical initiation: see above, p. 117 n. 187.

201. It is true that symbolic readings are sometimes convincingly practiced on portions of the text, which seemed impervious to symbolism at first glance, such as the scene of Pythias trampling the fish at the market (1.25: cf. Derchain-Hubaux 1958). Yet it is impossible to extend such symbolic interpretations to the whole novel. As far as I can see, no symbolic reading is possible for the robbers' tales in Book 4; and, if the *anilis fabula* of *Cupid and Psyche* is open to committed interpretations, the same is not true for the *aniculae sermo* at 9.16.1.

told that unbridled curiosity and youthful inexperience can put one on the wrong path, and that Isis can grant salvation even in the most desperate situations. The reader can venture forward, of course, and attempt to interpret Mithras' speech by looking for hidden meanings and correspondences with religious and philosophical texts; but since he would be exploring a text that was designed to evoke and suggest ideas, more than to define them accurately, he would soon find himself in unmapped territory without a reliable guide.

So, as it happens, almost all the clues that urge the reader toward a committed reading are rather vague, and they do not allow him to forget that a more hedonistic approach is also possible. This also serves as a narrative device. The text seems to do its best to put the reader in the same (asinine) conditions as Lucius: what Lucius could learn from *Cupid and Psyche* is also presented to the reader, who enjoys Lucius' adventures and even identifies with him on a personal level. Yet, as we have seen, the tale is discredited in every possible way: it is put into the mouth of an unreliable narrator and reaches the reader through an untrustworthy channel; it is introduced as a mere "old wives' tale," told to console a young girl; and, last but not least, it is implicitly qualified as a *fabula Milesia* at 4.32.5. This is an aspect of a deliberate narrative strategy (on which see § 3.3), which allows the reader to identify with the main character: in a sense, what Lucius does not understand is also hidden from the reader, so that their perspectives show a high degree of continuity.

We must also take into account the generic features of the novel. Compared to satire, and even more to Platonic dialogue, the novel shows an inverted order of priorities: narratives and tales are mainly self-sufficient, and are not only intended to carry moral, religious, or philosophical meanings, which would be inevitably somewhat blurred and vague.[202] We should apply the same caution to narrative literature that modern scholars usually observe in the hazardous business of reconstructing a satiric poet's biography and his beliefs from his poetry. In satire, the author's personality and opinions are veiled by the use of a satiric persona; in narrative literature, the author is always hidden behind the words and the actions of his characters, and these characters certainly have a weaker claim on reality and reliability than the satiric *ego*.[203]

---

202. This does not mean, of course, that a novel cannot be committed, but only that narrative does not lend itself very easily to conveying clear and precise ideas. For example, Michael Crichton's novel *State of Fear* (New York: 2004) has something to say about science, progress, and ecology; but the author, to articulate his thought unambiguously, has added a long appendix, which we can consider as a modern reincarnation of the Aesopic ὁ λόγος δηλοῖ ὅτι.

203. Beck 1982, 206 points out that, while in the case of most Latin satirical texts it is not difficult

The tendency to discredit narration and narrators is common in Apuleius' novel, surfacing sometimes even more explicitly than in the case of *Cupid and Psyche*. At 7.10.3–4, for example, the *auctor* is ironical about the *actor*—the ass who misinterprets the show of affection between Charite and Haemus/Tlepolemus, and launches into a completely out-of-place invective against women. Another self-ironical invective is addressed to corrupt judges (10.33). When his tirade is over, the narrator expresses fear that his *indignatio* is misguided, and that his audience will wonder why they "have to stand an ass lecturing us on philosophy." Thus, the narrator and/or the author tends to disassociate himself from the main character, who would otherwise naturally present an *alter ego*, since he speaks in the first person. This pattern has been persuasively compared to the satiric poet's custom of assuming the "persona" of a moralizer and simultaneously discrediting that persona.[204] To a certain extent, this is also true of *Cupid and Psyche*, a story with great potential for symbolic interpretation. It is explicitly reduced to the rank of *anilis fabula*, and then related by a dubious narrator, just as in Horace's tale of the two mice. This satirical vein of disparagement, therefore, involves both narration and narrator; ultimately, it discredits the novel itself by characterizing it in the prologue as a story of little account that seeks only to entertain its audience—just as we find with the tale of *Cupid and Psyche*.

There are several traits that link the novel to satiric poetry and, to a lesser extent, philosophical dialogue. These are the oscillation between identification and ironic distancing of the narrator/author from his characters;[205] the disparagement thrown on the narration of the story; and the tendency towards self-irony and understatement.[206] Another similarity is the realistic program of satire, which often describes everyday life, sometimes to the point that we can sense a distance from public *negotia*.[207] This separation is only partially redeemed by the poet's moral commitment, and establishes a bridge

---

to understand who is satirizing whom, in the case of Petronius' *Satyricon* "the author has abdicated his role as satirist to a narrator who shows himself so implicated in the action . . . that the author's standpoint and hence the whole satiric thrust of the work have become quite elusive."

204. M. Zimmerman 2006, 95 ff.; cf. also, more generally, Keulen 2003c, 131.

205. That happens also at 11.27.9 *Madaurensem sed admodum pauperem:* see § 4.4.1, p. 187.

206. § 2.7.2 p. 104. Besides the already-quoted study by M. Zimmerman 2006, other recent contributions to the relationship between *Metamorphoses* and satire are found in Smith 1996, Plaza 2003, and Keulen 2004a, 2004b (esp. 262–264, 269–270), and 2006; see also Dowden 2006, 42 ff. on the dialogic form of Apuleius' prologue. This approach has been more widely practiced for Petronius' *Satyricon:* see now Rimell 2005.

207. Cf. La Penna 1968, xlix: "In a well-known passage of the first satire of Book 2 (71 ff.) Horace clearly borrows an important aspect of Lucilius' work: that is, he considers satire as a kind of *relaxatio animi*. After the toils of public *negotia*, the friends of Scipio's circle get together in a private place, far away from the eyes of the *vulgus*, where they can dedicate themselves to clever and facetious conversation."

between the literary spaces occupied by satire and the novel. The dialogic form is another important feature of satire that also establishes a connection between the poem's characters, the poet, and his audience. For example, at *Sat.* 1.10.81 ff. Horace creates a setting of an intimate dialogue with a few friends. This situation closely resembles the atmosphere of a confidential and relaxed conversation that was created by *at ego tibi* in the prologue, as well as the narrative frame of many Platonic dialogues.[208] According to Cicero, *De Or.* 2.25 (and cf. Pliny the Elder, *pr.* 7), Lucilius claimed to address an audience that was neither too learned nor too ignorant, a statement that is, at least in part, provocative, and that fits both satire and the novel very well.[209] As regards the relationship of satire to the other literary genres, Alessandro Barchiesi and Andrea Cucchiarelli, for example, point out that the satiric genre "does not present itself as a fixed and separate literary form. Rather, it thrives on producing analogies with other literary forms, such as with the grand texts of epic and tragedy . . . it can mimic the text it stands alongside, or parody it";[210] again, this is also true for the novel.

In this web of analogies, the satirical disparagement of the narrator, perhaps more than any other feature, is what makes the Latin novel distinct, and it can help us to gauge the distance between Petronius and Apuleius on the one hand, and Greek narrative tradition on the other.[211] (This statement, of course, must allow for the fact that we have access to only a fraction of the Greek narrative tradition, since it was in fact the Byzantines who selected the texts which we can still read).[212] Satirical disparagement does not necessarily render a character's words and beliefs completely degraded—paradoxically, it can even contribute to making them more convincing. Again, the prototype of such a paradoxical character is Socrates; he has, in the literary tradition, the same ambiguous features we have already noticed in his iconography at § 2.4. For example, we know from Cicero that Zeno used to call him "the Athenian buffoon,"[213] but his most lively portrayal is offered by Alcibiades

---

208. Cf. Tatum 1979, 26; I. J. F. de Jong 2001, 202; Keulen 2003a, 25 ff. and 2007b, 27 ff.; Dowden 2006, 43.

209. On the readers of the ancient novels, see below, § 4.5.

210. Barchiesi–Cucchiarelli 2005, 208. Epic models are important for both satire and novel: see Connors 2005.

211. See esp. Smith 1996.

212. This difference between Greek and Latin novels is even more blurred if we take into account the fact that for some Greek novels we know of some reading practices (in late antiquity) that highlight the presence of religious or philosophical meanings in a "low" literary form, apparently intended only for entertainment: see below, pp. 129 ff. However, I do not think that we can speak of a satiric treatment of narrators or characters in the case of these texts.

213. *N.D.* 1.34.93 *Zeno . . . Socraten ipsum . . . scurram Atticum fuisse dicebat.* On Socrates described as a buffoon and a Silenus, see Lanza 1997.

at the end of Plato's *Symposium*.[214] Socrates and his speeches are similar to a figurine of a Silenus (215a), which can be opened and contains another statuette:

> If you choose to listen to Socrates' discourses you would feel them at first to be quite ridiculous (γελοῖοι); on the outside they are clothed with such absurd words and phrases—all, of course, the hide of a mocking satyr. His talk is of pack-asses, smiths, cobblers, and tanners, and he seems always to be using the same terms for the same things; so that anyone inexpert and thoughtless (ἄπειρος καὶ ἀνόητος ἄνθρωπος) might laugh at his speeches for scorn. But when these are opened, and you obtain a fresh view of them by getting inside, first of all you will discover that they are the only speeches which have any sense in them; and secondly, that none are so divine, so rich in images of virtue, so largely—nay, so completely—intent on all things proper for the study of such as would attain both grace and worth. (221e–222a)

Socrates' irony is, first of all, self-irony. He constantly asserts his ignorance and makes a show of his ugliness, challenging the Greek ideal of καλοκἀγαθία; his speeches usually take inspiration from everyday life and are crowded by "pack-asses, smiths, cobblers, and tanners."[215] Through these self-ironic and comic features, he presents himself not as an idealized character, but as a pleasant and receptive conversationalist. This allows him to engage his interlocutors in dialogue and lead them towards contemplation of the Beautiful and the Good, by zealously identifying their contradictions and mistakes. One of Socrates' self-ironic *personae* is the old midwife (cf. *Tht.* 149a ff., and *passim*); in a sense, then, all of Socrates' speeches are "old wives' tales," and we could say that he bears a resemblance to the old narrator of *Cupid and Psyche*.[216]

---

214. Alcibiades also has some ambiguous traits: he speaks very seriously of Socrates and says important things in the economy of the dialogue, but he is also in a clear state of alcoholic excitement (σφόδρα μεθύων: 212d).

215. Alcibiades' speech in the *Symposium* is used as a model to highlight the seriocomic character of Apuleius' novel by Gianotti 1986, 97, who suggests that the word *cantherium* (a word found frequently in the *Metamorphoses*) echoes the *Symposium* passage I have cited above. In this passage Alcibiades makes reference to the fact that Socrates frequently speaks about κανθήλιοι.

216. In a study of the satirical critique of intellectuals contained in Apuleius and Gellius, Keulen 2004a, 226 f. points out that, according to Gellius, Plato could use non-paradigmatic characters in his dialogues (at 10.22.1 he defines Callicles in the *Gorgias* as a *persona . . . non gravis neque idonea*); such characters nevertheless "feature as the mouthpiece of authorial ideas and opinions." In the *Metamorphoses* Lucius is clearly the object of satirical irony, but "Apuleius' intended reader . . . would be able to see through an ambiguous *persona* like Lucius, who is a morally dubious character, but at the same time *alter ego* and mouthpiece of the author Apuleius." Cf. also Keulen 2003b, 169 f.

This provocative ambivalence on the part of Socrates and other characters prompted Mikhail Bakhtin to view both satire and Socratic dialogue as the "authentic predecessors of the novel."[217] In fact, Bakhtin considers the distinguishing features of Socratic dialogue to be laughter, Socratic irony, and "the entire system of Socratic degradations combined with a serious, lofty and for the first time truly free investigation of the world, of man and of human thought."[218] Although Bakhtin astutely links the novel to Socratic dialogue and Menippean satire, he overemphasizes the substance of these connections, and defines the novel itself in terms that do not show an adequate concern for historical context. His theory can generate unexpected and undesirable conclusions: for example, some scholars have used it to define Plato's *Symposium* as "the first novel in human history."[219] The boundaries of the novelistic genre are of course rather vague, but they are not infinite. If the *Symposium* is situated clearly beyond these borders, as I believe, this means that Bakhtin's theory might require some revision—an endeavor, however, that would be well beyond the purview of this study.

While it is certainly important to highlight the seriocomic character of the novel in general (and of Apuleius' *Metamorphoses* in particular), this characteristic does not present us with a master key to defining a literary genre. The term σπουδογέλοιον is not commonly used by ancient authors: it is found in Strabo 16.2.29 (applied to Menippus of Gadara), and in Diogenes Laertius 9.17 (in reference to an Heracleitus);[220] finally, the late grammarian Stephanus of Byzantium mentions a poet Blaesus who wrote σπουδογελοῖα.[221] Naturally enough, the notion "seriocomic" is far more widespread than the word, but it describes a literary posture more

---

217. Bakhtin 1981, 25.
218. Bakhtin 1981, 22.
219. Corrigan–Glazov-Corrigan 2005, 38. Bakhtin himself (1981, 29) regarded Xenophon's *Cyropaedia* as a novel (the statement is not completely baseless, if certainly extreme; for some bibliography on the subject, see Graverini-Keulen-Barchiesi 2006, 59).
220. In both cases, the term is masculine and is applied to the author and not to his work—much less to a literary genre (but Diogenes' text suggests that it is an εἶδος, a writing style or a particular manner of performance); the same is true of an inscription at Imbrus, *IG* 12.8.87. On the σπουδογέλοιον in antiquity the only general overview is Giangrande 1972, a collection of material that remains useful, even though Wallach 1975 presents several valid criticisms of Giangrande's work. A good introduction can be found in Branham 1989, 11–63; see also Camerotto 1998, 120–130 (as well as the more detailed *Prosimetrum e spoudogeloion* 1982); Ercolani 2002. For the σπουδογέλοιον in Plato's *Symposium,* see Hunter 2004, 9–13. Bakhtin's studies repeatedly point out the close connection between novel and σπουδογέλοιον; on this point, see the collection of studies edited by Branham 2005a, among which see especially Branham 2005b, 9 ff.
221. *Ethnika* p. 357.3 Meineke, a passage usually neglected by scholars; see also p. 193.6, where Stephanus echoes Strabo's testimony on Menippus. On the possibility that Blaesus wrote something similar to Menippean satires, see Kaibel 1897.

than a literary genre. In fact, a great many texts could be said to combine the comic with the serious. In Aristophanes' *Frogs*, for example, the Chorus beseeches Demeter to bestow on them both laughable and serious things, γελοῖα and σπουδαῖα (389–90). More generally, we can say that all ancient comedy offers its audience reasons to laugh and to think. Even in *Odyssey* Book 8 we find the close juxtaposition of a sorrowful story (the fall of Troy) and a comic narration (Hephaestus catching Ares and Aphrodite in the act of adultery).[222] Scholars have tried to circumscribe what is properly σπουδογέλοιον by limiting it to those texts in which seriousness and comedy are not only placed side by side, but also interact, so that the comic element itself becomes instructive.[223] But I doubt that this is really the difference between, for example, the *Frogs* and the *Odyssey* on one hand, and the Platonic dialogues or Cynic diatribes on the other. Readers of the *Odyssey* certainly drew from the poem not only literary instruction and narrative pleasure, but also edification and models of conduct (in some cases, negative models);[224] moreover, the transmission to the audience of moral and civic values was hardly foreign to ancient Greek and Latin comedy.[225] The ancient use of the term σπουδογέλοιον does not provide a narrow or exact meaning. The term occurs rarely, and describes a heterogenous collec-

---

222. Note, however, that even this tale was read as if it had an educational or moralistic intent; see e.g. Athenaeus, *Deipn.* 1.24: "Demodocus at the Phaeacian court sings of the amours of Ares and Aphrodite, not in approval of such passion, but to deter his hearers from illicit desires." Similarly, Phemius sang the Achaeans' *nostoi* to the suitors of Penelope to warn them about what was in store for them. Cf. also Plutarch, *De aud. poet.* 19e ff.

223. See e.g. Roca Ferrer 1974, whom I quote from Camerotto 1998, 125 n. 209: "It is not enough that a single literary work contains serious and comic elements to define it as an instance of *spoudogeloion*: laughter can simply be intended as a relaxing element (as in epic poetry); or it can be a form of abuse (as in iambic poetry); or, indeed, it can be the main purpose of that work (as in comedy). Only when the comic element has an educational purpose—either to make men better, or to prove or disprove a thesis—do we have *spoudogeloion* proper. In this case, laughter is a means to transmit a valuable message." For a slightly different emphasis, see Branham 1989, 235–236 n. 81, who claims that in Aristophanes (as in Apuleius, Petronius, Plato, and others) "there is an interaction between contrasting elements such that their combined effect is different in kind from the sum of its parts."

224. Nikeratos, in Xenophon's *Symposium* (4.6–7), claims that the σοφώτατος Homer included in his poems all human knowledge, from economics to oratory to the art of war. Ajax, Nestor, Odysseus, and Agamemnon are presented as models. He also thinks that Homer's poems offer useful instruction for everyday life: they show how the charioteer has to swerve at the end of the track, and that onions go well together with wine. On the contrary, Seneca has a very skeptical outlook on Homer as a source for philosophical teachings—but nevertheless, his *Epist.* 88.5 gives further evidence of the diffusion of such readings. See also above, n. 222; and pp. 130 ff.

225. Cf. e.g. Adriani 2005, who discusses the "image of the comedic writer as master and moral guide for the audience, a role traditionally assumed by theatrical poets, and particularly by Aritsophanes." For the Latin theater see Beare 1964, 132: "The dramaturge was an artist, not a teacher; nevertheless, many of the *Adelphoe*'s spectators would have perceived that the text held some message for them"; see also p. 182 on the moral precepts contained in the mimes of Publilius Syrus.

tion of figures: a Cynic philosopher, a former citharode (who had switched to a different poetic or performative genre), and the otherwise unknown poet Blaesus. "Seriocomic" appears to have a loosely defined meaning, despite the fact that it effectively describes the features of several literary genres (among them the novel). We can certainly draw distinctions about the relative proportions of comedy and seriousness, and about the degree of effective interaction between them, but I think it is impossible to define a "proper" seriocomic genre.

It is important to stress that the text of the *Metamorphoses* simultaneously provokes both serious and comic hermenutic approaches. This interaction has a similar and explicit functional significance in Plato's *Symposium*, where Socrates himself is a kind of symbol for a perfect, if paradoxical, blend of seriousness and comedy.[226] Apuleius' novel might be read, both in general terms and in several passges of text, as a seriocomic reaction to or reflection on ideas and images offered by Plato's dialogue. The story of the ass provided Apuleius with a plot and a character who could easily absorb the paradoxical traits that Alcibiades attributes to Socrates: the philosopher looks like a Satyr and a Silenus, but he also has a profundity of thought that is totally unexpected at first sight.[227] Comparing Socrates to the partially theriomorphic divinities seems to have been something of a tradition: for example, in Xenophon's *Symposium,* Critoboulos claims he is much more handsome

---

226. Socrates is a seriocomic character in Xenophon's *Symposium* too. In the short prologue (1.1), the author explains that "to my mind it is worthwhile to relate not only the serious acts of great and good men but also what they do in their lighter moods (οὐ μόνον τὰ μετὰ σπουδῆς πραττόμενα ... ἀλλὰ καὶ τὰ ἐν ταῖς παιδιαῖς)." Socrates is the object of laughter at 2.17 (for his desire to devote himself to dance), and at 3.10 (when he says he is proud of his attitudes as a panderer); at 4.29 some of his table companions laugh at his words, others take them seriously; at 6.6 Socrates defines himself as ἀφρόντιστος; his grotesque appearance is pointed out at 4.19 and 5.5–7. Yet, among those who take part in the banquet, Philippus and not Socrates is the true γελωτοποιός (1.11); in addition to his comic features, Socrates clearly displays a didactic and moralistic attitude.

227. Alcibiades' speech itself presents all the features of σπουδογέλοιον. He introduces his praise of Socrates with these words: "The way I shall take, gentlemen, in my praise of Socrates, is by similitudes. Probably he will think I do this for derision; but I choose my similitude for the sake of truth, not of ridicule" (*Symp.* 215a). The end of his speech meets with the general laughter of all the guests (222c); Socrates himself insinuates that Alcibiades' praise might be due only to his jealousy of Socrates' friendship with Agathon. Yet Alcibiades' speech urges us to conclude that "to love Socrates is to be a philosopher." This very serious point is made through the broad comedy that characterizes the whole episode of Alcibiades: so Nehamas 1999, 313 points out that the mixture of serious and comic elements provides the keynote of the dialogue. At 223d, when many guests are clouded with sleep and wine, Socrates claims that "the same man could have the knowledge required for writing comedy and tragedy—that the fully skilled tragedian could be a comedian as well." For a useful comparison between Plato's *Symposium* and the *Metamorphoses*, see now Hunter 2004, 128–129 and Dowden 2006. Keulen 2003a, 25 ff. and 2007b, 27 ff. provides parallels with Plutarch's *Quaestiones convivales* and some satiric "Symposia."

than Socrates, "otherwise I should be the ugliest of all the Satyrs ever on the stage" (4.19). At 5.5, we read a more detailed description of the philosopher: Socrates' eyes are bulging at the sides, like those of the crab; he has a snub-nose, and his lips are swollen. Socrates is again compared to a Silenus at 5.7. We need not rely on our imagination to recognize some asinine traits in this portrait.[228] One of the theriomorphic features of Satyrs and Sileni is the length of their ears, not dissimilar to the long ears of an ass. In fact, according to Artemidorus (2.12), dreaming of an ass is a good omen, since this animal is sacred to the "dearest daemon Silenus."[229] In Xenophon, the philosopher's prominent lips are explicitly compared to the lips of an ass by his interlocutor: Critoboulos laments that, if one says that Socrates' lips are prettier than his, "it would seem that I have a mouth more ugly even than an ass's" (5.7).[230] When Lucius is being transformed into an ass (3.24.5–6), his physical traits are described in detail: his ears "grow immoderately long," his lips become "pendulous" (*labiae pendulae;* cf. παχέα ... χείλη in Xenophon, *Symp.* 5.7), and his nostrils open wide (*nares hiantes;* in Xenophon, *Symp.* 5.6, Socrates says οἱ ἐμοὶ [*sc.* μυκτῆρες] ἀναπέπτανται). Last but not least, Lucius' only consolation is the increase in the size of his penis, clearly a satyr-like feature.[231] The ass, in a sense, can be considered nothing more than an exaggeration of Socrates' portrait, which was already grotesque.[232] Does the ass, too, hide a god, like the statuettes of the Sileni mentioned by Alcibiades? At 6.29.5 Charite voices exactly the same doubt: "if Jupiter truly bellowed in a bull, perhaps in this ass I am riding lurks the face of a man or

---

228. Socrates' asinine features are thoroughly highlighted by Pinotti 2003 (and cf. Lanza 1997, 26–33 and *passim*); however, I do not believe Pinotti is right when she claims (p. 74) that Socrates' asininity is explicit in Plato or Xenophon (leaving aside Xenophon, *Symp.* 5.7, quoted below in the text).

229. On the Sileni's asinine traits see e.g. Krappe 1947, 227; Lanza 1997, 26.

230. At the beginning of the *Phaedrus,* Socrates compares himself to an animal (and perhaps even to an ass): the philosopher admits that Phaedrus is luring him outside the city "as people lead hungry animals by shaking in front of them a branch of leaves or some fruit" (230d).

231. Keulen 2003c, 114 f. excellently points out that the description of the Socrates who appears in Aristomenes' tale seems to take into account the comic and cynic tradition regarding the philosopher, which emphasized his shamelessness and sexual exuberance. The two Socrateses—both the philosopher and the novelistic character—are for Keulen "a reflection of Lucius' paradoxical identity as a narrator, both the author of an entertaining Milesian narrative and an initiate of a religious cult" (p. 109). However, when he proceeds to offer a general interpretation of the novel, Keulen seems to forget this paradoxical identity and adopts the typical post-Winklerian critical stance, so that "Lucius' Milesian narrative turns out to be the public confession of a professional superstitious charlatan" (p. 130).

232. All the more so if we consider that our ass, like the "Silenic" Socrates, obtains some renown as a consequence of his taking part in a "Symposium": see *Met.* 10.16–17. Cf. above, p. 85, on some traits the ass shares with the typical comic actor; and § 3, *passim* on the parodic extremization Apuleius often applies to his literary models.

the likeness of a god." In fact, only the maiden's first hypothesis is true; but like Socrates' outward aspect, the ass and his story (in a sense, the ass *is* his story[233]) hide a treasure of wisdom that can be revealed only if one does not judge by appearances. With Socrates and with the ass the σπουδογέλοιον works at its best: comic and grotesque features are by no means ornamental qualities, but a part of the "hidden message" itself, which necessitates going beyond appearances, conventions, and material reality.

Alcibiades says that it is necessary to "open up" Socrates' speeches to get to their inner meaning. The philosopher's intentions might not be manifest to those who do not know him: Alcibiades himself, at the beginning of his friendship with Socrates, was persuaded that the philosopher was attracted to him only by his physical beauty (217a ff.), but he had to revise his assumptions when Socrates proved utterly indifferent to the handsome young man's sexual advances. Socrates fascinates those who listen to him with his words, as does the satyr Marsyas with his flute (215b–c) and the Sirens with their songs (216a). Alcibiades is aware of the danger and the pain that those who are near Socrates have to suffer: the philosopher's words confront him with the unpleasant necessity of changing his ways, forcing him to be ashamed of his own demeanor. He is still irresistibly attracted to him, and cannot escape. Xenophon pushes this characterization of Socrates as an enchanting Siren even further. In the *Memorabilia,* he discusses more than once the relationship between Socrates and the young men who follow him, and the mysterious force that binds them. At 2.6.9–10 Socrates says that to make friends one needs to use magic (ἐπῳδαί and φίλτρα); a good example of such magical words, he says, is the song that the Sirens sang to Odysseus, tickling his desire for virtue and glory (the Sirens are also a positive model at a 2.6.31). At 3.11.16–17 Theodotes asks Socrates if he is really an expert in the use of φίλτρα and ἐπῳδαί, and Socrates answers:

> Why, what is the reason that master Apollodorus and Antisthenes never leave me, do you suppose? And why do Cebes and Simmias come to me from Thebes? I assure you these things don't happen without the help of many potions and spells and magic wheels (οὐκ ἄνευ πολλῶν φίλτρων τε καὶ ἐπῳδῶν καὶ ἰύγγων).

---

233. A story that has precisely the title *Asinus*. This identification between the ass and the story that contains his adventures has some possible ironic undertones: at 2.12.5, according to the Chaldaean Diophanes' prophecy, Lucius' destiny is to become the books that narrate his story, and therefore to become *Asinus*—both with and without the capital initial. The idea is suggested by Winkler 1985, 158; cf. also Graverini 2005a, 241 ff.

Socrates then has the power to charm anyone he wants to attract. His ability is almost magical, Siren-like, and easy to misinterpret:

> Observe how Socrates is amorously inclined to handsome persons; with these he is always busy and enraptured. Again, he is utterly stupid and ignorant, as he affects. Is not this like a Silenus? Exactly. It is an outward casing he wears, similarly to the sculptured Silenus. But if you opened his inside, you cannot imagine how full he is, good cup-companions, of wisdom. (Plato, *Symp.* 216d)

Translated into Apuleian terms, we could say that Socrates is a master of the art of *permulcere aures*. As we have seen in the first chapter, Apuleius' novel assumes the Athenian philosopher's Silenus- and Satyr-like appearance: it attracts its reader with a rhetoric that is sweet and enchanting, almost magical, and comparable to the singing of the Sirens. The reader is absorbed in a captivating story of adventures, magic and love, but if he "opens the statuette" he can also discover a deeper wisdom hidden inside. The last book of the novel, therefore, is not at all a palinode that revises the prologue's hedonism. Socrates and the Sirens are not incompatible, but represent different sides of a literary program that combines entertainment with moral and philosophical education (at least on some occasions: in the *Phaedrus*, as we have seen, Sirens and cicadas are temptations to resist). Alcibiades and others like him need to pass through the knowledge of the Silenic Socrates in order to know the "hidden" and wise Socrates, and this is not always an easy or painless experience.[234] At the end of the novel, Osiris states that Lucius has obtained a knowledge connected with his literary and rhetorical studies (*studiorum . . . laboriosa doctrina*); but also that his *labores*, or Odyssean adventures, have ultimately made him wiser.[235] The reader of the *Metamorphoses* travels the same route: he must surrender to the Sirens in the prologue, and abandon himself to the narrative. In so doing the reader places himself in the same risky position as Lucius, and risks suffering the consequences of his dangerous curiosity; in the end, however, he will be able to see, instead of a deadly reef, the statuette of a god—or, in this case, of a goddess.

This hermeneutic approach to the novel is usually attributed to Fulgentius, and therefore confined to late antiquity and discredited. I am certainly not inclined to support an overly detailed allegorical interpretation like the one we find in Fulgentius; however, it is very likely, in my opinion, that

---

234. Cf. 218a for the analogy between philosophy and a viper's bite; and 222b contains a saying about the boy who learns through suffering.
235. Cf. below, p. 152.

Apuleius expected his novel to be received as a text possessing aims greater than entertainment and escape. We have no direct testimonies by ancient readers of the *Metamorphoses,* and it is therefore not easy to prove such a statement beyond all doubt. To show that Fulgentius' reading is respectable and far from absurd (albeit partial and insufficient *per se*), I will need to resort to analogies with miscellaneous and heterogeneous evidence. For example, a codex of Heliodorus' *Aithiopika* contains the beginning of an essay by an otherwise unknown "Philip the philosopher," who may have lived in Constantinople in the fifth century. In it he interprets the *Aithiopika* from Platonic and Christian points of view.[236] Heliodorus' novel is certainly easy to read "seriously," but in the *Greek Anthology* we find an epigram (ascribed to Photius or to a "philosopher Leo") that urges those who aspire to wisdom to go beyond a superficial and frivolous reading of the lubricious novel by Achilles Tatius.[237] Richard Hunter points out that this has always been a common approach to Homeric poetry, from which moral and philosophical meanings were usually drawn:[238] it could be defined as a "second-level" approach, since it relied on a "first" hermeneutic level that was practiced in the schools of rhetoric, and was represented by linguistic and textual analysis. Such a reading practice, developed for epic poetry, could be all too naturally applied to prose narrative. Novelists themselves were well aware of the contiguity between novelistic and epic traditions;[239] and, in spite of the disrepute into which novelistic literature usually fell, there is some ancient evidence that depicts an erudite and didactic use of the novel. This allows us to discern a tradition of textual studies from which more thorough studies could stem.[240]

---

236. The manuscript is the Venetus Marcianus gr. 410. The dating of "Philip" and his geographic location has generated much debate: for arguments that support the choice of Constantinople in the fifth century, see Acconcia Longo 1991. Further bibliography can be found in Hunter 2005.

237. *AG* 9.203.7–10: εἴπερ δὲ καὶ σὺ σωφρονεῖν θέλῃς, φίλος, / μὴ τὴν πάρεργον τῆς γραφῆς σκόπει θέαν, / τὴν τοῦ λόγου δὲ πρῶτα συνδρομὴν μάθε· / νυμφοστολεῖ γὰρ τοὺς ποθοῦντας ἐμφρόνως ("if, my friend, you wish to be wise, do not pay attention to the adventitious beauty of the style, but first learn the conclusion of the discourse; for it joins in wedlock lovers who loved wisely").

238. Hunter 2005, 123. Cf. also above, n. 222. More generally, on the allegorical exegesis of Homer, see Lamberton 1986; Dawson 1992, esp. 38–52; Barnouw 2004, esp. 121 ff.; Pontani 2005, 69–71 and *passim.*

239. For Apuleius see below, § 3.3; a more general treatment of the subject can be found in the introductory chapter of Graverini-Keulen-Barchiesi 2006, with further bibliographical references.

240. Hunter 2005, 123 claims that the tradition of prose narrative studies was very different from that of the Homeric texts. This difference "allows us to see how paradoxical might be the very idea of 'interpretation of the novel,' given that there were no 'lower' exegetical foundations upon which to build; as far as we know, novels never permeated into the educational system in which such exegesis was rooted, at least before the Byzantine period." It is true that novels never became "classical" texts, but it seems likely all the same that they were occasionally used in school teaching: see the thorough

Hunter also observes that "Philip" seems to develop hermeneutic clues that were first offered by the text of *Aithiopika*.[241]

As for Apuleius in particular, Fulgentius provides a good example of the close connection between linguistic and philosophical interests (he draws linguistic material from the *Metamorphoses* in his *Expositio sermonum antiquorum*, and offers an allegorical interpretation of the tale of *Cupid and Psyche* in the *Mitologiae*),[242] while Sallustius' *subscriptio*[243] preserved by the manuscript tradition bears witness to the existence of a tradition of philological studies of Apuleian texts. Unfortunately, since no reaction by contemporary readers of the *Metamorphoses* survives, it is impossible to come to a definite conclusion, but it seems unlikely that the contempt shown in the *Historia Augusta* and Macrobius' *Commentary* presents a full or accurate account of the novel's early reception. In my opinion, it is more likely that "Fulgentius-like" interpretations were in fashion much earlier than the fifth century.[244]

2.9 Lucius, before and after

To conclude, let us return for a moment to the problem of the great difference between the brilliant entertainer of the prologue (who is to be identified, at least partially, with the main character of the novel)[245] and the silent

---

research by Stramaglia 1996a (especially on Greek narrative; a short but useful treatment of the Latin "Milesian" tradition can be found at pp. 145–146). Fronto, *Epist.* 4.3.2 p. 57.1–4 VdH² offers perhaps the most intriguing evidence: the rhetor provides a list of authors that offer the best examples of archaic style, a sort of "recommended reading" list for his disciple Marcus Aurelius; Sisenna is listed as a model *in lasciviis*.

241. Hunter 2005, 131.

242. Stramaglia 1996b, 123 f. notes that "[Apuleius'] narrative production was perceived as an integral but marginal part of his various activities as a *philosophus Platonicus*, versatile writer, and magician."

243. On Sallustius' *subscriptio* see the studies by Oronzo Pecere and Antonio Stramaglia, now collected in Pecere-Stramaglia 2003.

244. Obviously, allegorical interpretations of the *Metamorphoses* (and not only of *Cupid and Psyche*) were also popular after Fulgentius. We could even say that they are at the root of the modern philological activity regarding Apuleius, since they were adopted by the first Apuleian commentator, Beroaldus. In his Bologna edition of 1500, he claimed that *Apuleium quidem nostrum . . . sub hoc transmutationis involucro naturam mortalium et mores humanos quasi transeunter designare voluisse, ut admoneremur ex hominibus Asinos fieri: quando voluptatibus belluinis immersi Asinali stoliditate brutescimus nec ulla rationis virtutisque scintilla elucescit.* He then adds *lectio Asini Apuleiani . . . speculum est rerum humanarum istoque involucro efficti nostri mores expressaque imago vitae quotidianae conspicitur, cuius finis et summa beatitas est religio cultusque divinae maiestatis una cum eruditione copulata connexaque* (quotations from Heine 1978, 32). On Beroaldus' Apuleian commentary see now Gaisser 2003.

245. On this complex identity see above, pp. 152 n. 1 and 174 n. 26.

and reverent Lucius of 11.14.1—a passage that resembles a new and different prologue, and is paradoxically placed in the middle of the last book.

This "second prologue" is separated from the "real" prologue by as many as eleven books and one year, a remarkable narrative distance: this, combined with the intensity of Lucius' transformation back to human shape after the intervention of Isis, could explain some of the difference between the two prologues, and make that difference less surprising. However, we must also take into account the fact that the novel is Lucius' retrospective narration in the first person: from this perspective, the silent Lucius of 11.14.1 is very close to the brilliant entertainer of 1.1. In fact, we should recall that the voice of the "first" prologue is not in fact that of the naive and curious Lucius we met at the beginning of the novel, but rather belongs to the Isiac devotee of the last book, who has learned a lesson from his experiences. Nevertheless, at the beginning of the novel we are not offered a sermon or a moral lecture in the style of Seneca, who argued in the *De beneficiis* that a good philosopher should not titillate the ears of his audience with stories and old wives' tales—things that are better left to poets.[246] Lucius, like Socrates, does not hesitate to wear the mask of the buffoon and become, momentarily, his old curious and credulous self. Just like Aesop, his tale concerns "asses and nonsense for old women and children to chew on"[247] but, just as Aesop's fables carried a moral, his tale contains a deeper meaning, which those who wish to go beyond simple literary entertainment can find reasonably easily.

This meaning is more sophisticated than what one could derive from the Aesopic fables, and at the same time much less specific than what is explored in the Platonic dialogues. This fact helps us to gauge the distance that divides the novel from the other seriocomic genres and explains why we have such difficulty interpreting it. Indeed, the very idea of "interpreting a novel" needs to be carefully considered: inevitably, the object of the interpretation affects the goals and methods of the interpretation we apply to it.[248]

---

246. Seneca, *Ben.* 1.4.5–6; see above, p. 000.

247. Philostratus, *VA* 5.14; see above, p. 000. Asses appear frequently in Socrates' speeches: in addition to Alcibiades' speech at *Symp.* 221e ("his talk is of pack-asses, smiths, cobblers, and tanners"), cf. e.g. *Phdr.* 260b–c, *Tht.* 146a, *Apol.* 27e, and *Resp.* 8.563c. As it seems, the ass is a constant presence in seriocomic literature.

248. I have also discussed the seriocomic character of the novel as a literary genre in Graverini 2012.

3

Metamorphoses of Genres

AS WE HAVE SEEN, Socratic dialogue and the tradition of Greek and Roman satire offer a good frame of reference for illustrating the seriocomic character of the *Metamorphoses*. Though they share several similarities, of course, we cannot ignore the pronounced differences between literary genres—for example, the narrative structure of the novel is usually longer and far more complex than the narrative structure of a philosophical dialogue or satire. Similar genre-related differences and similarities will be explored in greater detail in the four sections of this chapter, devoted to philosophical dialogue, historiography, epic, and drama.

As such, the novel (both ancient and modern) is involved in a continuous dialogue with other literary forms. This interaction makes a vital contribution to the complexity and appeal of the *Metamorphoses,* a text that, while maintaining a delicate balance between comic and serious elements, appears to have been primarily designed as a sophisticated form of literary *divertissement.* In this chapter, we will see that this interaction constructs an identity for the novel as a "polyphonic" text,[1] one that lives and thrives by absorbing and synthesizing a wide variety of literary experiences for its own purposes.

---

1. On this definition see e.g. Fusillo 1989.

3.1 Philosophers on the road

One of the distinguishing marks of any narrative text is, of course, the manner in which characters are portrayed. Similarities in character descriptions reveal a close connection between Apuleius' novel and the Socratic dialogues. In chapter 2.8, I called attention to the physical portrayals of Lucius and Socrates, which shared two common elements: these were 1) the asinine traits assumed by Apuleius' main character after his metamorphosis, which may recall the typical portrayal of Socrates as a Silenus and a Satyr; and 2) Lucius' baldness, appearing at the end of the novel, a trait that would link him to the Athenian philosopher. Admittedly, in one case this baldness is natural, while in the other it is the result of shaving—but in both cases baldness provides the basis for a paradoxical portrayal of the wise man. At first glance, the validity of this parallel might seem limited to the sections of the novel that precede Lucius' metamorphosis. In Book 2, for example, Byrrhena points out the well-balanced harmony of Lucius' physical appearance, which is in no way grotesque or ridiculous:

> He inherited that well-bred behavior . . . from his pure and virtuous mother Salvia. And his physical appearance is a damnably precise fit too: he is tall but not abnormal, slim but with sap in him, and of a rosy complexion; he has blond hair worn without affectation, wide-awake light-blue eyes with a flashing glance just like an eagle's, a face with a bloom in every part, and an attractive and unaffected walk. (2.2.8–9)[2]

Even though there is no physical resemblance between them, we will see shortly that Lucius is, in fact, already linked to Plato's Socrates at the beginning of the novel. But in Book 1, we meet a character who even has the same name as the Athenian philosopher. The close relationship between the two "Socrateses" is further emphasized by their similar posture and physical appearance. When Aristomenes encounters his old friend Socrates in the novel, Socrates is sitting on the ground, dressed in rags, and begging for money. This Socrates is clearly embarrassed by his friend's persistent questions, and signals his embarrassment with a specific gesture:

---

2. Van Mal-Maeder 2001, 75 *ad loc.* correctly places this description in the context of the portrayals of the heroes in the Greek novels: the physiognomical features are those typical of "un jeune homme cultivé." Several scholars (see Van Mal-Maeder 2001, 74–75 for references) consider this to be a portrayal of Apuleius, but this is without a really solid basis; I would rather point out that, when Apuleius describes himself at *Apol.* 4, his self-portrayal (which of course is also conditioned by its rhetorical context, and is not necessarily realistic) exhibits the paradoxical features of the man who is wise, but not handsome: see above, p. 88.

he covered his face, which had long since begun to redden from shame, with his patched cloak. (*centunculus:* 1.6.4)

This gesture of embarrassment has a noble literary ancestry. See, for example, *Odyssey* 8.83 ff., where Odysseus tries to hide his tears from the view of the Phaeacians; and Plato's *Phaedrus* 237a, where Socrates is deeply embarrassed just before starting a speech on love.[3] In the *Metamorphoses*, Socrates' pose is far less dignified: he blushes out of embarrassment for less lofty concerns (he is reduced to poverty as a consequence of his insane passion for a powerful witch); and his ragged cloak is not long enough to cover both his head and his genitals at the same time. The unlucky man thus only succeeds in embarrassing himself even more. The scene is intrinsically comical, all the more so because *centunculi* and phallic displays are typical elements found in performances by mimes.[4]

This is only the first, subtle link to Plato's *Phaedrus* in Aristomenes' tale. The shade of a plane-tree is chosen as the backdrop for the end of his story (1.18.8), most clearly evoking the *Phaedrus*, since in the literary tradition that species of tree is inexorably linked to the Platonic dialogue.[5] Warren Smith and Baynard Woods have considered these and other parallels in a recent study;[6] here, I will try to adopt a broader perspective, and show how this link to the *Phaedrus* is prefigured as early as the first chapters of the novel, which serve as an introduction to Aristomenes' tale.

We can say that Lucius is a sort of Socrates, though in a more subtle way than the main character of Aristomenes' tale—he is a Socrates enticed by and trapped in his own intellectual games. One of his most distinctive traits is an unquenchable thirst for knowledge. His first significant action, at the very beginning of the *Metamorphoses*, is to eavesdrop on the conversation of two passers-by (1.2.6), an exchange that introduces the first inserted tale of the novel. This tale (1.5–19) satisfies Lucius' curiosity, exposed here for the first time; Lucius, however, is clearly ashamed to acknowledge his *curiositas* and to call it by its proper name. At 1.2.6 he claims not to be "inquisitive (*curiosus*)," but only "the sort who wants to know everything, or at least

---

3. See Graverini 2003a, 217 with n. 21 for the first passage; Smith-Woods 2002, 190 for the second.

4. See Keulen 2003c, 119 for the *centunculus*, and *passim* for more comical and theatrical features in Socrates. On the *centunculus* as theatrical garment, and on the phallic display of mimic actors, see Beare 1964², 176.

5. See above, p. 18 n. 50.

6. Smith-Woods 2002; see also Thibau 1965; Münstermann 1995, 8–22; Keulen 2007b, 28 ff. and 338 f. (*ad* 1.18.8); Keulen 2003c and 2004a. For further parallels with Plato's *Symposium*, see above, p. 126 n. 227.

most things." Lucius disguises this curiosity as a desire to alleviate the toil of the journey with pleasant conversation. At 1.2.6 he expresses the hope that "the charming delight of some stories will smooth out the ruggedness of the hill we are climbing." Indeed, Lucius receives the delight he had hoped for, even if he overlooks the ominous implications of Aristomenes' tale and all the dangerous consequences of involvement with magic he describes. Hence Lucius responds to his fellow travelers:

> I am . . . extremely grateful to him for diverting us with a charming and delightful story. I have come out of this rough long stretch of road without either toil or boredom. I think my conveyor is happy over that favor too: without tiring him I have ridden all the way to this city gate here, not on his back, but on my own ears. (1.20.5)

As it seems, Lucius' ears (that will become asinine at 3.24.5) can already do the duty of a horse, at least metaphorically speaking. Beyond Lucius' innate curiosity, the truthfulness and credibility of the tale provide the main points of debate among the fellow travelers, and this debate frames Aristomenes' story.[7] Aristomenes is the narrator, but also a character in his story and an eyewittness, and so declares that he is going to offer an absolutely true account of what has happened (1.5.1 "I shall swear to you by the Sun, this seeing god, that I am narrating events which I know at first hand to be true").[8] His fellow traveler believes instead that he is an outrageous liar (1.3.1; 1.20.1), while Lucius is easily taken in (1.3.2 "you . . . with your thick ears (*crassis auribus*) and stubborn mind, are rejecting what may be a true report"; cf. 1.4.6, and 1.20.3 "I consider nothing to be impossible"). It has already been noted that the discussion between Lucius and his fellow travelers "has the overtones of a philosophical debate";[9] I will now explore several parallels that suggest a more precise connection to philosophy.

It is a familiar notion in ancient literature that a good tale or a delightful song has the power to lighten one's toil: e.g. Virgil, *Ecl.* 9.64 "let us go singing on our way: it makes the road less irksome"; Theocritus 7.35–36; *Aen.* 8.309 ("alleviating the journey with varied talk"); and finally Heliodorus

---

7. Cf. Winkler 1985, 82 ff. This subject is treated inside Aristomenes' tale, too, and is a sort of *leitmotif* in Book 1: see Keulen 2007b, 327 f. and 339 on *Met.* 1.18.1–8.

8. But immediately after this statement, Aristomenes adds *nec vos ulterius dubitabitis si Thessaliae proximam civitatem perveneritis, quod ibidem passim per ora populi sermo iactetur quae palam gesta sunt.* Keulen (2007b, 149 *ad loc.*) correctly comments that "while apparently intended to underline the truth of the following account, the reference to hearsay simultaneously functions to expose the story's fictionality." On the criteria for truth in storytelling, see below, § 3.2.

9. Keulen 2007b, 114; cf. also James 2001, 263.

6.2.2, where Kalasiris says to Knemon "now it is the time for you to tell it [sc. "your story"], and in so doing you will not only be granting the request of Nausikles here but also making our journey less arduous."[10] It is, after all, an implicit acknowledgment of the charming power of poetry and narrative that, by absorbing a listener in an imaginary world, can allow him to forget the harshness of life. The same function is found in the tale of *Cupid and Psyche*, which is told in order to distract and comfort (4.27.8 *avocabo*) the disconsolate young Charite.[11] But even if we are dealing with a common topos, Plato's *Phaedrus* itself offers the most useful background to describe Lucius' attitude towards hearing tales. At the beginning of the dialogue, Socrates says to his friend Phaedrus, "I am so determined to hear you, that I will not leave you, even if you extend your walk to Megara, and, as Herodicus says, go to the wall and back again" (227d). At 230d, Socrates declares that he does not like to go out of the city, but Phaedrus, who is exciting his passion for λόγοι, has found a way entice him past the city limits. In fact, "eagerness" is too bland an expression for defining Socrates' passion for hearing λόγοι, and very soon the philosopher adopts vivid metaphors of illness and love (228b τῷ νοσοῦντι περὶ λόγων ἀκοήν; 228c τοῦ τῶν λόγων ἐραστοῦ).

A detail that in passing might seem trivial in fact confirms the intertextual relationship between the beginning of the *Metamorphoses* and the beginning of the *Phaedrus*. A few lines before Lucius mentions the power of a good tale to alleviate the toil of a hard walk, we are informed that Lucius is saddle-sore. He therefore dismounts and stretches his legs, to get rid of his "sedentary exhaustion" with a walk (1.2.3 *ut ipse etiam fatigationem sedentariam incessus vegetatione discuterem in pedes desilio*). This quasi-medical practice would be otherwise insignificant, but for the fact that it is mentioned at the very beginning of the *Phaedrus* (227a 1–8). In this passage, Phaedrus says that he sat for too long listening to Lysias' speeches and, following the physician Acumenus' advice, is now taking a stroll to relieve his fatigue (*kopos*). The presence of two such similarities in the introductory sections of these works is surely significant and demands further consideration.

---

10. At 4.4.2 Kalasiris' account has exactly the same effect on Knemon, who is not sleepy at all in spite of the late hour. In Ovid, *Met.* 14.121 Aeneas is very tired when he exits the Underworld, and he relieves his exhaustion by talking with the Sibyl (*cum duce Cumaea mollit sermone laborem*), who tells him her own story. In Plato, the *Symposium* is constructed as a single narration, told by Apollodorus to recount the banquet and its speeches to Glaucon; at 173b Glaucon says that "the road up to town is indeed well suited for telling and hearing."

11. In Ovid, *Met.* 15.487 ff. Virbius/Hyppolitus tells a tale to comfort Egeria, his audience, who is in despair because of her husband's death (a narrative frame markedly similar to that of *Cupid and Psyche*).

Needless to say, there are also marked differences between the *Metamorphoses* and the *Phaedrus*. It is to be noted that Socrates' fondness for λόγοι is connected to a deep concern for truth. At 242e–243a he realizes that his first speech about love is false and gives offense to the true divine nature of Eros, so much so that a palinode is needed; the necessity of knowing and telling the truth is pointed out at 245c and 247c and is finally reasserted in the dialogue's conclusion (277b). The problem of ἀλήθεια arises for the first time very early in the dialogue, when Phaedrus asks the philosopher if he believes that the myth of Boreas is true (229c). Socrates' answer is ambiguous and rather dismissive: he says that, while "wise men" are skeptical about the matter, he believes in the myth. But he also thinks that it would be nonsensical to look for a rationalistic and credible interpretation of this and other myths, and has no time (σχολή) to waste on such absurdities. At 230a Socrates claims, "Consequently, I don't bother about such things, but accept the current beliefs about them, and direct my inquiries . . . rather to myself."

At the beginning of the *Metamorphoses*, just as at the beginning of Plato's *Phaedrus*, we find a discussion about truth and falsehood in storytelling, underlining the protagonist's great desire to hear conversations and speeches made by other people. Another specific point of contact can be found in the *topos* that a good story can help the listener forget the weariness of his long journey. Thus, the narrative frame of Aristomenes' tale is fully coherent with the tale itself, and provokes us to draw a parallel between its main character and Lucius. Aristomenes is a Socrates dressed in rags, a slave to his own passions; he eats cheese under a plane-tree instead of discussing philosophy—perhaps a vulgarized form of abandoning oneself to the song of the cicadas. As for Lucius, he is introduced from the very beginning as a character who is like Socrates in curiosity, but completely lacking in the self-control that allowed the Athenian philosopher to see the difference between truth and falsehood, and between what deserves one's attention and what is better left aside. If we compare him to the "real" Socrates, Lucius seems to enact a subtle but telling semantic shift. Socrates is extremely fond of λόγοι, such as the speech of Lysias repeated to him by Phaedrus; but he does not waste his time with μῦθοι such as the myth of Boreas. Lucius, in his free adaptation of the Platonic model, seems to give to λόγος the meaning of *fabula*: at 1.20.5 he declares, in fact, that he has greatly appreciated Aristomenes' *fabula*, is grateful to the narrator, and completely believes him. In fact, Lucius here demonstrates that he is completely enamored of precisely the same sort of μῦθοι that Socrates considered fundamentally pointless.

I would say that, in this case, we do not have a truly parodic contrast between two literary figures. Rather, the text reinterprets and exaggerates several paradoxical features (certainly with some parodic elements) that were already present in traditional depictions of Socrates.[12] It would be too facile to reduce the relationship between Lucius and Socrates to a simple opposition between, e.g., *curiositas* and true philosophy; this would lead us to disregard the fact that not only a "healthy" intellectual curiosity, but also an addiction to any kind of *logoi*, were inescapable features of the complex portrait of the Athenian philosopher. If we consider Lucius as a sort of a literary reincarnation of Plato's Socrates in the first books of the *Metamorphoses*, we can see that Apuleius undoubtedly amplifies and exaggerates Socrates' features, but he also finds fertile material for elaboration in his Platonic model.

Moreover, it has been recently noted that there is a fundamentally analogous relationship between Plato's Socrates and the protagonist of Aristomenes' story. When Aristomenes meets his friend, now reduced to poverty and dressed in rags, he describes the man as *paene alius lurore* (1.6.1: "almost unrecognizable in his pallor"). Indeed, this could be interpreted as an ironic allusion to the great distance that divides the "original" Socrates from this beggar, "almost another man." Thibau[13] made this very point, but Warren Smith and Baynard Woods correctly add that "one hesitates . . . to conclude that Apuleius intended the two 'Socrateses' to be opposites of one another, since the philosopher Socrates was also sometimes lampooned as pale, unkempt, and dirty, and the fictional character evidently embodies these memorably humorous physical characteristics of his namesake."[14] Just like the protagonist of Aristomenes' tale, Lucius is certainly different from the Athenian philosopher; but he is not diametrically opposed to Plato's Socrates. He shows and exaggerates some of Socrates' paradoxical traits, but at the same time does retain a portion of Socrates' thoughtfulness, and shares in Socrates' inclination to seek a truth that is higher and more significant than the mere appearances of the material world.

Indeed, Lucius' quest proceeds along a tortuous path, and the first books, which prepare the way for his metamorphosis into an ass, seem to be dominated by errors and delusions. Lucius' reckless behavior is caused by his *curi-*

---

12. For similar remarks about Lucius' asinine traits, and his shaven head at the end of the novel, see above, §§ 2.5 and 2.8.
13. Thibau 1965, 106.
14. Smith-Woods 2002, 189. See also Keulen 2003c, 110: "It is . . . possible to speak in terms of correspondences instead of contrasts" between the two Socrateses, since "Socrates' reputation as a satirist can be traced back to Plato."

ositas, which has a disastrous influence on the way he understands what he hears: the great attention and credulity with which he listens to Aristomenes' tale will have terrible consequences for him. After his first night in Hypata, Lucius is still deeply affected by this credulous zeal. He wakes up and realizes that he is in the middle of Thessaly, a land of magic and witchcraft, in the very city where the events narrated by his fellow traveler had taken place. Lucius begins to superimpose an imaginary world onto reality:

> Nothing I looked at in that city seemed to me to be what it was; but I believed that absolutely everything had been transformed into another shape by some deadly mumbo-jumbo: the rocks I hit upon were petrified human beings, the birds I heard were feathered humans . . . Soon the statues and pictures would begin to walk, the walls to speak, the oxen and other animals of that sort to prophesy; and from the sky itself and the sun's orb there would suddenly come an oracle. (2.1.3–5)

Lucius, then, turns out to be a completely gullible listener; the stories he hears utterly consume him and transport him away from the real world. This young man of good family, who introduces himself as an intellectual with good credentials,[15] actually shows himself to be worthy of novelistic heroes such as Don Quixote or Lewis Carroll's Alice: Lucius will become an object of derision by abandoning himself totally and recklessly to the illusion of the narrative. This is precisely the result that Socrates anticipated, had he and Phaedrus abandoned themselves to the musical fascination of the cicadas when they rested under the plane-tree.[16]

---

15. Cf. 1.2.1 *Thessaliam—nam et illic originis maternae nostrae fundamenta a Plutarcho illo inclito ac mox Sexto philosopho nepote eius prodita gloriam nobis faciunt—eam Thessaliam ex negotio petebam.* Keulen 2007b, 94 comments that "with his Plutarchan credentials Lucius poses as an intellectual, but he turns out to embody various vices satirised by Plutarch." See also below, p. 191. I would also point out that the closure of Lucius' speech, *eam Thessaliam ex negotio petebam*, sounds like an abrupt return to a reality that is rather far from the atmosphere of intellectual refinement that the solemn and self-important opening seemed to announce: the self-irony I have spoken about at such length in the previous chapter is already working in this first chapter of the novel. I think it is extremely unlikely that "from the words *nam* and *ex negotio* a reader . . . might be led to infer that this visit might have some connexion with philosophical enquiry" (so Kenney 2003, 165).

16. Plato, *Phdr.* 259a: "Now if they [*sc.* the cicadas] should see us not conversing at mid-day, but, like most people, dozing, lulled to sleep by their song because of our mental indolence, they would quite justly laugh at us." In Plato, those who do not practice philosophy (or who practice it badly) are constantly at risk of being ridiculed: see e.g. *Tht.* 147a ff.; 153a; 154b; 158e; 161e; etc. As for Lucius, he is publicly ridiculed at Hypata, during the Risus festival; and he serves as the object of laughter in several other passages, such as 8.23.5, 9.12.1, 9.42.4, and 10.15.5. See Slater 2003 on Lucius as an unwitting and oblivious protagonist in a variety of spectacles throughout the novel.

3.2 Eyes and ears as criteria for truth

Obviously, it is a crucial skill to be able to distinguish between illusion and reality, and to make thoughtful decisions after a careful assessment of all the available information. Unfortunately, despite all his education and his Plutarchean ancestry, this is a skill that Lucius does not possess. For example, he fights with three wineskins after mistaking them for bandits (2.32); and at 3.24, Lucius blindly puts his trust in Photis, and uses an ointment that transforms him into a donkey, though he had thought he would become a bird. His recklessness is a direct consequence of the unquenchable *curiositas* that dominates him: Lucius' thirst for knowledge is matched only by his haste in making decisions.

The metamorphosis into a donkey does not ameliorate these tendencies—on the contrary, it even reinforces them. When he ponders his miserable asinine life, Lucius goes so far as to declare that his one consolation is that everyone near him acts and speaks freely, as if they were alone (*et agunt et loquuntur:* 9.13.3). This allows Lucius (now in the form of an ass) to satisfy his *ingenita curiositas,* more so than if he were in human form. What really interests our hero is the opportunity to hear and relate amazing stories to his readers.

But it is inevitable that—in light of the intellectual ambitions of Lucius, and the tendency toward literary disguise typical of the ancient novels—Lucius' gossipy *curiositas* will ultimately be sublimated into a more respectable thirst for knowledge:

> That divine inventor of ancient poetry among the Greeks, desiring to portray a hero of the highest intelligence (*summae prudentiae virum monstrare cupiens*), was quite right to sing of a man who acquired the highest excellence by visiting many cities and learning to know various peoples. In fact, I now remember the ass that I was with thankful gratitude because, while I was concealed under his cover and schooled in a variety of fortunes, he made me better-informed, if less wise (*etsi minus prudentem, multiscium reddidit:* 9.13.4–5).[17]

This Odyssean reference is not surprising, since the ancient novels commonly associate their characters with Homer's wandering hero in one way or another. In Heliodorus' *Aithiopika,* for example, Kalasiris says that his

---

17. This passage has attracted the attention of many scholars: see Winkler 1985, 165–168 and 289 with n. 24; Harrison 1990a, 193 ff.; James 1991, 164 ff.; Kenney 2003; Graverini 2005a, 191 ff.

guest Nausikles "is a merchant . . . and . . . leads a nomadic existence; he has visited many cities and seen into the hearts and minds of many men" (2.22.3); in Xenophon of Ephesus 1.10.3, Habrocomes and Anthia leave "to see some other land and other cities." In Heliodorus and Xenophon, then, as well as in Apuleius, the allusion to the first lines of the *Odyssey* is transparent; but these lines have been echoed many times by many authors. Odysseus' exemplarity goes well beyond narrative literature; for writers in many periods, he became the model of the wise and experienced man, guided by reason and the thirst for knowledge.[18] Our first exploration into Apuleius' passage, therefore, will lead us to historiography, rather than epic poetry or narrative literature.

Apuleius introduces this Homeric allusion by saying that the divine poet described Odysseus as a hero who obtained experience and wisdom thanks to his long travels (*summae sapientiae virum monstrare cupiens*, 9.13.4). This phrase closely recalls a passage in Polybius, quoted below, in which the historian quotes the first lines of the *Odyssey* in support of Heraclitus' dictum that eyes make better witnesses than ears. According to Polybius, the good historian should relate not things he has only learned from books, but rather events known to him through direct inquiry or, even better, through personal experience. This opposition between direct experience and bookish information roughly corresponds to the difference between sight and hearing, since reading aloud was the prevalent practice; as a result, hearing provides the means through which one consults books and written documents.[19] Timaeus, who chose to use his ears instead of his eyes, took the easiest and most pleasing way, but also the worst one (ἡδίω μέν, ἥττω δὲ: 12.27.2).[20] Direct experience is always to be preferred, and Homer himself gives evidence for this claim:

> Wishing to show us what qualities one should possess in order to be a man of action (βουλόμενος ὑποδεικνύειν ἡμῖν οἷον δεῖ τὸν ἄνδρα τὸν πραγματικὸν εἶναι), he [i.e. Homer] says: "The man for wisdom's various arts renowned / long exercised in woes, O muse, resound / wandering from clime to clime." (Polybius 12.27.10)

---

18. On this see more below, p. 147 and n. 32.

19. In fact, Polybius specifies (12.27.3) that one can also gain knowledge through hearing in two ways, by reading books (ὑπομνήματα) and by direct inquiry (ἀνάκρισις). Timaeus used his ears instead of his eyes and did it in the worst way, resorting more to ὑπομνήματα than to ἀνάκρισις. At *Tht.* 201b–c Plato connects hearsay with ἀληθῆ δόξα, and personal experience (seeing) with ἐπιστήμη.

20. We need to remember that "sweet" is a typical attribute of fiction (see pp. 40 ff.): Polybius is strongly criticizing Timaeus' reliability.

There is a striking similarity between Polybius' phrase βουλόμενος ὑποδεικνύειν ἡμῖν οἷον δεῖ τὸν ἄνδρα τὸν πραγματικὸν εἶναι, and Apuleius' *summae prudentiae virum monstrare cupiens*. Indeed, Apuleius' phrase almost seems to be a translation of Polybius. Furthermore, both phrases introduce an allusion to or quotation of the beginning of the *Odyssey*. Indeed, Apuleius frequently exploits historiographical literature for his own purposes, but it is perhaps more prudent not to consider this case to be a direct allusion to Polybius.[21] In this passage, we must take a broader context into account, since ancient historians seem to have been particularly fond of the hero's common depiction as a man of experience. Like Polybius, Diodorus also programmatically refers to the beginning of the *Odyssey* in his prologue:

> ... although the learning which is acquired by experience in each separate case, with all the attendant toils and dangers, does indeed enable a man to discern in each instance where utility lies—and this is the reason why the most widely experienced of our heroes suffered great misfortunes before he "of many men the cities saw and learned / their thoughts"—yet the understanding of the failures and successes of other men, which is acquired by the study of history, affords a schooling that is free from actual experience of ills. (1.1.2)

Polybius and Diodorus have different agendas. Polybius' position is that personal research and experience, as opposed to hearsay, should form the basis of the historian's work, and that the best historian is a man of action like Odysseus.[22] Diodorus, who has no interest in demonstrating that only a man of action can be a good historian, maintains that history is superior to personal experience (cf. also 1.1.4).[23] Nonetheless he agrees that first-hand examination of the subject (αὐτοψία) is necessary for writing hsitory, so much so that he traveled extensively through Asia and Europe to avoid the errors made by less accurate writers (1.4.1). At 1.83.9, after relating an anecdote, Diodorus points out that he knows the story not by hearsay (ἐξ ἀκοῆς), but because he was an eyewitness to the events.

---

21. Cf. Graverini 1997b; McCreight 1998.
22. 12.28.1: "it appears to me that the dignity of history also demands such a man."
23. 1.1.4: "Certainly all men prefer in their counsels the oldest men to those who are younger, because of the experience which has accrued to the former through the lapse of time; but it is a fact that such experience is in so far surpassed by the understanding which is gained from history, as history excels, we know, in the multitude of facts at its disposals. For this reason one may hold that the acquisition of a knowledge of history is of the greatest utility for every conceivable circumstance of life."

Sight and hearing, ὄψις and ἀκοή, are the metaphorical poles of the typical conflict between personal experience and indirect knowledge. Historians (and philosophers), of course, usually sided with the former, and censured those writers who relied on the latter.[24] Lucian was even harsher: according to him, Ctesias of Cnidos wrote "things that he did not see in person, nor heard from others" (*VH* 1.3).[25] Here Homer comes once again into play. With his typical wit, Lucian claims that Odysseus (who served as a model for the perfect historian in Polybius), was the progenitor of mendacious historians (such as Ctesias, and, ultimately, Lucian himself):

> The founder of this school of literary horseplay is Homer's Odysseus, with his stories at Alcinous's court . . . he spun many such fanciful stories to the Phaeacians, who knew no better. (*VH* 1.3)

Odysseus here is the perfect liar; his narrations have nothing to do with real life and personal experience, but are sheer fiction.[26] Indeed, Homer's

---

24. On this topic see Walbank 1967, 408 (who also quotes a paradoxical reversal of this topos by Isocrates, *Panath.* 150); Schepens 1970; further bibliography in Mazza 1999, 144 n. 71. More extensive treatments of the subject, not limited to historians, can be found in Solimano 1991 and Napolitano Valditara 1994; on the same topic in the speeches of tragic and comic messengers see Oniga 1985, 123 f. and I. J. F. de Jong 1991, 9–12. Wille 2001 also provides a wealth of information. With reference to Heliodorus, see also Liviabella Furiani 2003. The contrast of sight and hearing also recurs at the beginning of Philostratus' *Heroikos* (7.9): the Phoenician declares that he is distrustful of myths (τὰ μυθώδη), because nobody has ever seen the events they narrate personally, but everyone has heard them told by others; the vine-dresser is instead reliable because he is an eyewitness. Keulen 2004a, 239 f. convincingly points out that "such a confirmation of autopsy had become commonplace in paradoxography, and could therefore be interpreted as a marker of fiction." Some irony, for example, is to be understood in Gellius' exploitation of the *topos* at 9.4.13 (Pliny wrote in the seventh book of his *Natural History* about "things he did not hear or read, but only things he knew and had seen in person"; cf. also 5.14.4). Philostratus, then, is probably pointing out the fictive nature of the vine-dresser's account by qualifying him as an eyewitness. If what I will claim in the following pages is correct, Apuleius does the same in a more traditional (though still ironic) manner, by emphasizing Lucius' dependence on his own ears. I cannot agree with May 2007, who believes in a completely inverted hierarchy of sight and hearing; May concedes, however, that Apuleius' text repeatedly emphasizes its own fictionality.

25. Lucian is probably criticizing Ctesias by adopting his vocabulary. According to Photius, *Bibl.* 72.36a, Ctesias "claims to have been an eyewitness (αὐτόπτην) to most of the events he narrates; and that, when this was not possible, he has heard them directly (αὐτήκοον) from the Persians themselves." The conventional character of such statements is confirmed by Lucian, who in *Hist. conscr.* 29.3 teases a historian who never left Corinth, but who nevertheless said that ὦτα ὀφθαλμῶν ἀπιστότερα. γράφω τοίνυν ἃ εἶδον, οὐχ ἃ ἤκουσα.

26. A similar view can be found in Philostratus' *Heroikos* 25.13 and *passim*: most of Odysseus' adventures are forgeries by Homer, and Palamedes refuses to acknowledge Odysseus as a wise man at 33.8. But already in Sophocles' *Philoctetes* "Odysseus represents one of the worst products of the fifth-century sophistic movement—the quibbling, unscrupulous, corrupt, ambitious, self-seeking sophist, rejoicing to make the worse argument appear the better, delighting to corrupt the youth of Athens

hero has an extremely flexible image, especially in the hands of a clever and witty author like Lucian: the contrast between Polybius' ἀνὴρ πραγματικός and Lucian's charlatan could not be any sharper.

Apuleius joins in the same game and plays by its rules. In fact, Lucius' statement at 9.13.4 makes a great deal more sense when interpreted in the context of the historiographical debate mentioned above, which concerned the usefulness of sight and hearing as criteria for truth. Apuleius' narrator, in accordance with the general trend of many ancient novels, occasionally poses as an historian,[27] and before sharing his stories, explains to the reader how and why he has come to know them. In comparison to Polybius or Lucian, Apuleius' narrator takes on a more complex stance regarding the fiction and veracity of his tale. Apuleius' asinine version of Odysseus is neither the prototypical historian portrayed by Polybius, nor the hardened liar found in Lucian; he embodies a mixture of both characterizations. Lucius' personal experience is clearly the (pretended) basis of his knowledge; but at the same time, his personal experience has been acquired primarily through ἀκοή, rather than through ὄψις. In this instance, the historian's hierarchy of values has been turned on its head.

Significantly, shortly after our hero has compared himself to Odysseus, Apuleius alludes to Lucius' reliance on his ears again at 9.15.6:

> ... although I was deeply angry at Photis' mistake in making me an ass when she was trying to produce a bird, nevertheless I was at least heartened by this one consolation in my painful deformity: namely, with my enormous ears I could hear everything very easily, even at a considerable distance.[28]

These two images—one of the experienced Odysseus, and the other of a long-eared ass—are closely juxtaposed, but they remain irreconcilable. The result is comic and parodic: even though he is a sort of long eared-Odysseus,

---

with insidious arts" (Stanford 1954, 110). See above, § 1.3.3, esp. p. 26 on his "whispering" and deceitful voice.

27. Also see Gianotti 1986, 102, who suggests that "here we have a singular and humorous application of *autopsia* and *akoe*, namely, the same criteria for truth that the ancient historigraphical tradition considered crucial in order to provide a trustworthy account of the facts; everyday reality has finally found its own historian!" For an overview on the relationship between ancient novel and historiography, see my treatment in Graverini-Keulen-Barchiesi 2006, 44 ff. (with notes at p. 59).

28. See also 6.32.3 on the *magnae aures* of the donkey. In *Socr.* 19 Apuleius criticizes the ancient practice of kledomancy, which consisted of interpreting scraps of other people's conversations as prophetic utterances in their own right; according to Apuleius, they think *non animo sed auribus*. In that same chapter, as in the preceding one, Odysseus and Socrates are defined as judicious interpreters of omens and oracles.

and despite the extent of his experiences as an ass, Lucius falls short of both the hero's wisdom and the historian's accuracy.[29]

Passages like this tell us something important not only about the character Lucius, but also about his narrative—that is, more generally, about the novel itself. Apuleius fits in the tradition of the ancient novel by making his narrator wear the mask of the historian, but he is also a crafty man of letters, who likes to expose the artifice of that disguise. The narration pretends to be truthful, and the narrator explains how he came to know the events he reports. But his claim to be telling the truth is based on a deceptive epistemology: his criteria for truth are the very opposite of any that an ancient historian would defend.

The prologue of the *Metamorphoses*, as we will consider more thoroughly at § 3.4, describes the novel as an oral account related by the main character himself, which will appeal to the listener's ear. Several other passages in the novel also make reference to the oral (and aural) qualities of the narrative. We have just considered Lucius' remarks on his asinine ears, found in the introduction to the story of Barbarus and Philesiterus (9.16–21). This story provides a perfect example of a tale that Lucius has learned only though hearsay, from an old woman (9.16.1 *denique die quadam timidae illius aniculae sermo talis meas adfertur auris*). Lucius repeats the story to his audience at 9.14.1 (*fabulam denique bonam prae ceteris . . . ad auris vestras adferre decrevi*), inserting it into another tale about adultery, and introducing it with a Homeric simile at 9.3.4 (quoted at the beginning of this section). Tradition emphasized the unreliability of information relayed ear-to-ear, a fact that further highlights the fictionality of Lucius' narrative—it is nothing more, after all, than an *aniculae sermo*.

3.3 Lucius and his Sirens

Of course, the passages we have read in the previous section also tell us something important about the relationship between the *Metamorphoses* and the epic tradition. Lucius is like Odysseus, but an Odysseus for whom curiosity takes the place of the thirst for knowledge; and if he does attain any wisdom from his experience, it takes him a long time to do so. But here again we must remember that, in point of fact, the distinction between a thirst for knowledge and unbridled curiosity is somewhat artificial. For this reason,

---

29. He is not *prudens* like Odysseus, but only *multiscius*: I will pursue this important distinction immediately below. Of course, Lucius' long ears are not enough to explain his knowledge of several details of the story he narrates; the historian's mask does not completely eclipse the novelist behind it.

it should come as no surprise that Odysseus symbolized both attitudes in ancient culture. The image of an asinine and long-eared Odysseus (such as would be suggested by Apuleius' comparison) might seem bizarre, but it is not without precedent: according to Ptolemy Chennos,[30] Odysseus' original name was Οὖτις, "Nobody," because he had long ears, διότι ὦτα μεγάλα εἶχεν, a verbal pun that is clearly connected to the hero's traditional desire for knowledge, and that might date back to Middle Comedy.[31]

Among Odysseus' adventures, the episode of the Sirens was certainly the one that best represented his uncontrollable desire to know even the most strange, incredibile, and dangerous things.[32] Cicero felt the need to justify the hero's actions and explained that Odysseus had risked his own life for a more noble purpose than listening to beautiful songs:

> So great is our innate love of learning and of knowledge that no one can doubt that man's nature is strongly attracted to these things even without the lure of any profit.... For my part I believe Homer had something of this sort in view in his imaginary account of the songs of the Sirens. Apparently it was not the sweetness of their voices or the novelty and diversity of their songs, but their profession of knowledge that used to attract the passing voyagers; it was the passion for learning that kept men rooted to the Sirens' rocky shores. This is their invitation to Ulysses (for I have translated this among other passages of Homer):
>
> Ulysses, pride of Argos, turn thy bark
> and listen to our music. Never yet
> did voyager sail these waters blue, but stayed
> his course, enchanted by our voices sweet (*vocum dulcedine captus*),

---

30. In Photius 190, 147a. On Chennos see Chatzis 1914; Bowersock 1994, 24–27; Mazza 1999, 84–95; Pontani 2005, 72 f. I was unable to obtain a copy of Tomberg 1968.

31. Chatzis 1914, LXXX; on Odysseus' curiosity see Barnouw 2004, 75 ff. Chennos (or his source) is humorously elaborating on a verbal pun already exploited in the *Odyssey*: Polyphemus, after Odysseus revealed his true name to him, says he has been blinded by "a man of naught and a weakling," ὀλίγος τε καὶ οὐτιδανός (*Od.* 9.515). Perhaps, it should be noted that the pun Ptolemy Chennos makes on Odysseus' name also fits the title (or one of the titles) of Apuleius' novel: *Asinus aureus* because it has big *aures?* (A similar pun is perhaps exploited at 5.8.1 *sic allocuta opes domus aureae vocumque servientium populosam familiam demonstrat auribus earum*). James 1991 suggested with some irony that the novel's true title should be *Asinus auritus*: on James's "mischievous" proposal, and on the pun *aureus/aures*, see Bitel 2000–2001, 218 f.

32. See Stanford 1954, 75 ff., 124, and *passim;* Barnouw 2004, 75 ff.; Susanetti 2005, 59–80. On later instances of the topos, it is worth quoting at least Dante, *Inferno* 26.94 ff.: "The zeal I had to explore the world / and know the evil and the good in men / overcame my longing for my sweet son, / and my duty to see my old father, / and even my love for Penelope /—a love that was meant to make her happy."

> and having filled his soul with harmony,
> went on his homeward way a wiser man (*doctior*).
> We know the direful strife and clash of war
> that Greece by Heaven's mandate bore to Troy,
> and whatsoe'er on the wide earth befalls.
>
> Homer was aware that his story would not sound plausible if the magic that held his hero immeshed was merely an idle song! It is knowledge that the Sirens offer, and it was no marvel if a lover of wisdom held this dearer than his home. (*Fin.* 5.48–49)

Cicero's translation of *Od.* 12.184–191 is hardly biased; rather, it is in his remarks that the philosopher deliberately plays down the importance of the τέρψις promised to Odysseus by the Sirens. Atheneus takes the same position when he says that "the Sirens sing Odysseus the songs they know will please him most, by discussing matters that appeal to his ambition and love of learning" (*Deipn.*1.24). In any case, it was a well-established tradition that Odysseus sought *sapientia* or *prudentia*.[33] In fact, one might have thought he possessed these virtues before being "taught" by the Sirens, since he needed them to escape the Sirens' dangerous incantations. Apuleius himself makes a similar claim, in a passage that is probably related to Cicero's *De finibus*:[34]

> Homer . . . presented wisdom (which he in the manner of the poets named Minerva) as that hero's constant companion. It was with this comrade that Odysseus underwent all his terrible dangers, and conquered all adversity. It was with this helper that he entered the cave of the Cyclops, and emerged . . . that he drank Circe's potion and was not metamorphosed . . . that he heard the Sirens and did not go to them. (*Socr.* 24.177–178)

It would be difficult to say such a thing about Lucius: we know very well, if nothing else, that he toyed with magic ointments (if not potions); and unlike Odysseus, he could not avoid being transformed into an animal. But the parallel between these two characters is not a matter of speculation: the novel itself suggests an interesting approach to this similarity.

---

33. In *Socr.* 18 Odysseus and Diomedes symbolize respectively *consilium et auxilium, mens et manus, animus et gladius*. A few lines later, Odysseus and Nestor are defined as *sapientiae Graiae summa cacumina*.

34. Note that Apuleius, like Cicero, also quotes a poetic passage (from Accius' *Philoctetes*, frg. 520 Ribbeck) to support his reasoning.

Lucius states that he is like Odysseus, since he had many adventures and vicissitudes of various kinds; but despite his Odyssean adventures, he can only claim to be "better-informed, if less wise" (*etsi minus prudentem, multiscium* 9.13.5). We know that *prudentia* is Odysseus' typical virtue, and in fact, just a few lines above, the hero is defined as *summae prudentiae vir*. This definition is usually (and rightly) connected to the *incipit* of the *Odyssey*, ἄνδρα . . . πολύτροπον.³⁵ But what meaning should we derive from the fact Lucius' adventures make him not *prudens*/πολύτροπος, but only *multiscius*?

I think that the Groningen commentators are right in saying that "Lucius . . . simply admits that he does not quite dare to aspire to Odysseus' virtue of *prudentia*, which would make him *sapiens* in the philosophical sense of the word."³⁶ In other words, if Lucius were really *prudens* like Odysseus, he would not now have asinine ears. What would have happened to Odysseus if he had not been *prudens*? Horace was also intrigued by this question. He answers it after offering the Homeric hero as an *utile exemplar* of *virtus* and *sapientia*:

> You know the Sirens' songs and Circe's cups; if, along with his comrades, he had drunk of these in folly and greed, he would have become the shapeless and witless vassal of a harlot mistress—would have lived as an unclean dog or a sow that loves the mire. (*Epist.* 1.2.23–26)

Xenophon argued that both Hermes' advice and Odysseus' moderation in eating and drinking allowed him to avoid being transformed by Circe (*Mem.* 1.3.7–8). This idea is ascribed to Socrates, who suggested it in a seriocomic tone (τοιαῦτα . . . ἔπαιζεν ἅμα σπουδάζων). It is taken up again more seriously in Pseudo-Plutarch, *De Homero* 126, where Circe's magical power symbolizes the cycle of bodily transformation: Odysseus' wisdom (he is an ἔμφρων ἀνήρ) makes him immune to the process of metamorphosis.³⁷ It seems, then, that Lucius had to undergo a metamor-

---

35. See e.g. Mattiacci 1996, 140 *ad loc*. It might be useful to point out that, like Homer, Apuleius uses the accusative (*summae prudentiae virum*). In spite of the parallelism between *summae prudentiae virum* and ἄνδρα . . . πολύτροπον, Kenney 2003, 174 suggests instead that πολύτροπον is echoed by *multiscium* in Apuleius. I will offer a more likely explanation for the origin of the Latin adjective below in the text, but it is convenient to point out, with Kenney, that compound epithets beginning with πολυ- are typical of Odysseus: in Apuleius, the prefix *multi*- has in any case an "Odyssean" flavor.

36. *GCA* 1995 *ad loc*.

37. Cf. Lamberton 1986, 42.

phosis into an animal precisely because he lacked Odysseus' *prudentia*.³⁸ At least he is not *excors*, "witless," as Horace imagines Odysseus could have become; under his thick skin, Lucius still possesses a human intellect (this was true also of Odysseus' comrades, after they were transformed into pigs: cf. *Od.* 10.240).

Above all, Lucius' adventures make him *multiscius*. This is an unusual adjective, with a total of five occurrences, all in Apuleius. In all likelihood, it is a translation of a Greek word, perhaps one of the new coinages of which Apuleius is proud (cf. *Apol.* 38.3).³⁹ I think that the Sirens' promise to Odysseus can explain the origins of this adjective very well: they will make him πλείονα εἰδώς, "more knowledgeable," precisely the meaning of *multiscius* (Cicero had translated it more simply as *doctior*). Lucius is curious and craves knowledge like Odysseus, but while the wise (*prudens*, πολύτροπος) Odysseus could resist the Sirens' song, Lucius abandons himself, totally and without restraint, to his desire to experience more. Lucius is thus a degraded—or, better, we could say (again) exaggerated—version of Homer's Odysseus; he is like an Odysseus who drank Circe's potion without taking an antidote, or who listened to the Sirens' songs without tying himself to the mast of his ship.⁴⁰

---

38. Naturally, Lucius is also *stultus* (10.13.7 *neque tam stultus eram tamque vere asinus* . . .) and *cupidus* (e.g. 2.1.1 *nimis cupidus cognoscendi*), like Odysseus' comrades, according to Horace. Regarding the literary tradition about the hero's wisdom, his thirst for knowledge, and his curiosity, see above, p. 147 n. 32.

39. Cf. Stramaglia 1996b, 138. At *Apol.* 31.5 the adjective is connected to Homer: and according to the Groningen commentators "it suggests a comparison not just between Lucius and Ulysses, but between the narrator and Homer, and hence raises the further question as to the conflation of author and narrator" (*GCA* 1995, 132). Also, in the *Florida*, the word has a very positive sense, lacking all those doubtful nuances I think it has in the novel (see *Fl.* 3.9, of Apollo; 9.24, of Hippias; 18.19, of Protagoras); but it always points to a manifold competence or polymathy, and it is never used as a synonym for *sapiens* or *prudens*. Therefore, I cannot agree with A. La Rocca 2005, 42, according to whom Apuleius defines himself as *multiscius* in the *Florida* to give his audience a philosophical image of himself. Actually, Apuleius *never* defines himself as *multiscius* explicitly: La Rocca's statement is grounded on the possible identification of Apuleius with Apollo in fragment 3 (cf. his commentary at pp. 145 f.; Hunink 2001, 76). On *multiscientia* as an essential element of Lucius' (and Apuleius') characterization as a "sophist," see Kenney 2003, 162 (p. 168 on the difference between πολυμαθίη and πολυνοίη, and the opposition between *multiscius* and *prudens*); Keulen 2004a, 237 f.

40. I think that the passage from Apuleius' *Apology* quoted in the previous note corroborates to some degree the hypothesis that Apuleius created the adjective *multiscius* with Homer as his model. It was easy to attach to Homer an epithet (πλείονα εἰδώς / *multiscius*) originally attached to the Sirens, who are after all a sort of a substitute for an epic poet. It is unlikely, I think, that *etsi minus prudentem, multiscium* is a "deliberate echo" of Heraclitus' saying "much learning does not teach understanding" (πολυμαθίη νόον ἔχειν οὐ διδάσκει, frg. 16 M., suggested by S. Heller 1983, 331 n. 34). The relationship between polymathy and wisdom or philosophy is a widely debated subject among philosophers and men of letters: see e.g. Pseudo-Plato, *Amat.* 133c–139a; for an opposite view, see Strabo 1.1.1.

This is not an isolated example. Elsewhere Lucius is described as an Odysseus who does not "long for his return and for his wife" (*Od.* 1.13), but instead gives himself up to forgetfulness in the arms of an extremely erotic Calypso. This is clearly implied at 3.19.6, when our hero confesses his infatuation for the beautiful Photis:[41]

> You, with your flashing eyes and reddening cheeks and glistening hair and parted lips and fragrant breasts, have taken possession of me, bought and bound over like a slave, and a willing one. In fact I do not miss my home any more and I am not preparing to return there (*nec domuitionem paro*).[42]

There is an obvious thematic connection with the *Odyssey* in this passage. But besides that, the term *domuitio*—a rare, archaic, and poetic word, though not infrequent in Apuleius—is characteristically used in Latin literature in association with the return of the Greek heroes from Troy.[43] Furthermore, the expression *domuitionem parare* corresponds closely to the short prologue of the poem, where ἀρνύμενος . . . νόστον is listed among the essential qualities of Odysseus (*Od.* 1.5). The memory of his homeland and the desire to return there are two of his most typical identifiers: to lose them would be to lose his identity, something similar to the fate of the lotus-eaters, and those who fell under Circe's spells.[44]

This comparison is by no means unjustified. Like Calypso[45] and Circe, Photis is beautiful and voluptuous; nor is Lucius entirely unlike Odysseus.

---

41. This infatuation, of course, is also instrumental to Lucius' ultimate goal—that is, to learn the secrets of magic.

42. The Homeric model had been already used previously to describe an erotic and unhealthy relationship between two novelistic characters: the witch Meroe, from whom Socrates is trying to escape, ironically compares herself to Calypso, abandoned by Odysseus, and doomed to suffer eternal solitude.

43. In Apuleius, see *Met.* 1.7.7 (Socrates tells Meroe of his desire to go back home); 2.31.4 (Lucius goes back home after the banquet at Byrrhena's house); 4.35.2 (everybody returns home after leaving Psyche on the rock); 10.18.2 (Thyasus goes back to Corinth after his preparations for the *munus gladiatorium*); 11.24.6 (Lucius prepares his return home after his first initiation); *frg.* 8 (a short quotation by Fulgentius). Cf. also Pacuvius, *Trag.* 173, in Nonius 96M.; Accius, *Trag.* 173, in Nonius 357M.; *Rhet. Her.* 3.21.34; Hyginus, *Fab.* 125.2; Dictys Cretensis 1.20. In the *Onos*, Lucius forgets his business trip to Larissa because of amorous nights with Palaestra (11). Needless to say, there is no sense of homecoming here; the Odyssean connection has to be an Apuleian innovation—or, if it was in the lost Greek original, it has been neglected by pseudo-Lucian.

44. *Od.* 9.96–7 βουλόντο . . . νόστου . . . λαθέσθαι (the Lotus-eaters); *Od.* 10.236 ἵνα πάγχυ λαθοίατο πατρίδος αἴης (Circe). On the loss of identity of the hero who "forgets his return home," see also Bettini 1991, 31 ff.

45. If the parallel between *Met.* 3.19.6 and the beginning of the *Odyssey* is valid, then Apuleius is also probably exploiting a humorous contrast between the names of Calypso, "she who conceals," and Photis, "she who enlightens" (even though there are some ambiguities in the beautiful maidservant's name: see Van Mal-Maeder 2001, 138; Graverini 2001a, 428 n. 9).

Both characters enjoy the company of their enchanting temptresses, and I would say that an equal distance separates Lucius from both Odyseus and Socrates (as we have seen at § 3.1). The metamorphosis from epic hero into novelistic character, after all, is easy. If the moral and philosophical background for the text is deemphasized, *sapientia* quickly becomes unbridled curiosity, and Eros grows into an irresistible temptation. For readers like Cicero, this moral and philosophical background was the determining factor behind the hero's actions and choices. Lucius' easy metamorphosis brings bitter results—but luckily enough, they are mitigated by the hope of a return. Both Lucius and Odysseus' comrades can at least hope for some miraculous salvation from their bestial and sorrowful condition.

In fact, the gap between Odysseus and Lucius seems to narrow as we approach the end of the novel. In the last divine epiphany of Book 11, the god Osiris advises Lucius not to be afraid of those who envy his *studiorum . . . laboriosa doctrina* (11.30.4). At first glance, this expression is nothing more than a confirmation of the main character's successful career as a rhetor, already predicted in Asinius Marcellus' dream (11.27.9 *studiorum gloria*); and of course we can also connect it with the intellectual labors mentioned in the prologue (1.1.4 *advena studiorum Quiritium indigenam sermonem aerumnabili labore . . . aggressus excolui*). However, the adjective *laboriosus* suggests other possibilities that are not connected to studying texts. Odysseus was *laboriosus* in Horace, *Epod.* 17.16, where the Homeric epithet πολύτλας is clearly echoed;[46] and his comrades, too, were described as *laboriosi* in *Epod.* 16.60. *Labores* are, traditionally, the vicissitudes (πάθη) of any epic hero. This is true of Aeneas (see e.g. *Aen.* 8.380), but also of secondary characters such as the Trojan women in *Aen.* 5.769, or Macareus in Ovid, *Met.* 14.158. Our hero's *laboriosa doctrina*, therefore, is not solely the fruit of long nights spent studying books (an activity that, in fact, is never mentioned in the novel). At the end of his adventures, Lucius has finally come to know the world, as Dante says of Odysseus ("del mondo esperto," *Inferno* 26.98). His *doctrina* is very similar to the *sapientia* Odysseus acquired through his adventures and sufferings.[47]

---

46. See e.g. Massaro 1978, 181; Watson 2003, 551 *ad loc.*

47. We can also apply this interpretation to the *studia* that, according to Osiris, are the foundation of Lucius' *doctrina*. These *studia* might certainly be an intellectual activity, as at 1.1.4 and 11.27.9. However, the same noun is used to define Thrasyllus' unruly passion for Charite (8.2.1; 8.7.3; 8.8.4) and the erotic excitement provoked by Venus' promise of *septem savia suavia* (6.8.4). At 2.1.2 *studium* is the unbridled *curiositas* of Lucius, who is drawn to the irresistible mysteries of magic (*suspensus alioquin et voto simul et studio, curiose singula considerabam*); and the same temptation affects the *studiosus lector* at 11.23.5, who would like to know everything about the secret initiation rites of the Isiac cult. In these contexts, Lucius' *studia* are exactly what has caused his *labores*: unbridled curios-

Lucius' similarity to Odysseus—an Odysseus who cannot resist the Sirens' songs, and abandons himself to Circe's love—opens up other interesting perspectives. There is, in fact, a well-known precedent: in Petronius' *Satyricon*, Encolpius takes on the name *Polyaenos*—that is, the same epithet given to Odysseus by the Sirens at *Od.* 12.184—when he meets a beautiful woman named Circe, who, as chance would have it, sings with a sweet voice as melodious as the Sirens' (127.5–7).[48] Encolpius and Lucius, then, are both novelistic heroes who give in to the temptations of their Circes and Sirens. This might be pure coincidence, merely two independent literary applications of an obvious topos for characters involved in erotic adventures; but it is also possible that Apuleius was writing with Petronius in mind. Be that as it may, it is interesting to consider how differently the two authors make reference to Homer. Both Petronius and Apuleius make their characters meet with failure, but while Encolpius cannot match the sexual prowess of Odysseus (a virtue that we can only glimpse in Homer, when the hero "went up to the beautiful bed of Circe" at 10.347), Lucius cannot match the moral and intellectual virtues that Homer attributes to Odysseus (or that were attributed to him by the subsequent tradition of Homer's readers and interpreters). According to Hermes, Circe could have made Odysseus "no longer a man," ἀνήνορα (*Od.* 10.301; cf. 10.341). One could say that Encolpius and Lucius fulfill this prophecy, each in his own way: the former loses his manly strength, the latter his human shape.[49]

Once more, we can see a broad parallel between the novel and its main character. Lucius is a failed Odysseus, and the *Metamorphoses* could be considered a sort of an unauthorized revision of the *Odyssey*. In this regard the novel resembles the fascinating and dangerous song promised by the Sirens at *Od.* 12.189 f., which represents the possibility of an alternate version of the *Iliad:* "We know all the toils that in wide Troy the Argives and Trojans endured through the will of the gods."[50]

---

ity, youthful exuberance, and the *serviles voluptates* for which Mithras reproaches him (see above, pp. 115 ff.). Again, his *doctrina* is a learning acquired through mistakes and sufferings. To this Odyssean model we might add the proverb πάθει μάθος, which is used at Plato, *Symp.* 222b to describe the painful process of being scrutinized by Socrates' dialogue (cf. above, p. 129).

48. 127.5 *haec ipsa cum diceret, tanta gratia conciliabat vocem loquentis, tam dulcis sonus pertemptatum mulcebat aëra, ut putares inter auras canere Sirenum concordiam.* The comparison is prompted by the fact that at *Od.* 10.254 Circe λίγ' ἄειδεν: her voice is thus λιγύς, as the voice of the Sirens is λιγυρή at 12.44 and 183. See Barchiesi 1984, 170–173 for more on this episode of the *Satyricon* (particularly on the connection between the name Polyaenus, Encolpius' impotence, and Hermes' advice to Odysseus in Homer); also cf. above, pp. 34 f.

49. In Apuleius, the loss of human shape is paradoxically accompanied by a growing "virility": 3.24.6 *nec ullum miserae reformationis video solacium, nisi quod mihi . . . natura crescebat.*

50. Cf. above, p. 35.

As it seems, the Homeric poems already toyed with the idea of telling stories that could have dangerous consequences. But in Homer this possibility is marginalized, and becomes a concrete reality only in the musical performance of secondary and wicked characters such as the Sirens, whose song is not fully described, but only suggested. (When the reader of the *Odyssey* arrives at the Sirens' rock, we do not hear what Odysseus heard from the Sirens; as if our ears were plugged with wax, just like Odysseus' comrades, we are privy only to an indirect account of their song.) In Apuleius' novel, however, Lucius is determined to make a profession out of facing such narrative dangers. The *Metamorphoses*, as we have seen, presents itself as something sweet, fascinating, and potentially dangerous to read—especially for those who adopt Lucius' naive and credulous attitude towards fantastic stories.

3.4 Readers, listeners, and spectators

The *Metamorphoses* employs several strategies to allay the reader's suspicions, encouraging them to trust in the veracity of the narrative. We have seen that Lucius' neglect of the epistemological distinction between hearing and seeing renders him an incompetent historian. Lucius' ability to stimulate both the sight and the hearing of his audience does, however, make him an effective narrator. He can fascinate his listeners, luring them into a narrative world that has been created for them, and then convince them that this fiction is a reality. As I said above, the audience must undergo the same fate as Don Quixote, Alice, and many other famous novelistic characters. Alice enters the narrative world through a dream, and Don Quixote makes the same journey thanks to his visionary and bookish insanity; an ancient author, to obtain the same effect on his audience, often invited his audience to imagine that they were spectators in a theater. Sight and the hearing, of course, are paramount to the theatrical experience: as Seneca writes to Lucilius, "the arts of amusement (*ludicrae*) are those which aim to please the eye and the ear" (*Epist.* 88.22). Shadi Bartsch has clearly shown that in Achilles Tatius and Heliodorus "the readers of detailed descriptions of spectacles are invited to be 'spectators' of the spectacle themselves, sharing this with the characters in the text." As she shows, this literary habit is to be linked to the common rhetorical exercise of practicing *ekphrasis*.[51] In Apuleius, these elements of

---

51. Bartsch 1989, 111; for the rhetorical precepts see e.g. Nicolaus, *Prog.* 3.491 Spengel: [ἔκφρασις] δὲ πειρᾶται θεατὰς τοὺς ἀκούοντας ἐργάζεσθαι, "descriptions try to transform the listener into a viewer." On the five "canonical" Greek novels, see now also Bowie 2006. On the ambiguities of Aristotle's treatment of *opsis* in the *Poetics,* see Di Marco 1989 and Bonanno 1999.

"multimedia" are not limited to descriptions, but are involved throughout the novel; we could even say that narrative itself becomes a sort of *ekphrasis,* with a strong "theatrical" character.

The *Metamorphoses* prologue presents the novel simultaneously as both a written text and as an oral account—one of its many peculiarities. The prologue urges the reader to "look at" (*inspicere*) an Egyptian papyrus, but also promises to titillate his ears with a sweet whisper (*susurrus*). After such a preamble, the prologue's final incitement, *lector intende,* can only be ambiguous: *intende aures* and *intende oculos* are equally acceptable interpretations.[52] This ambiguity has intrigued many a scholar: Don Fowler, for example, points out the "disjunction . . . between an assumed orality and an actual written reception," and Ahuvia Kahane discusses "the paradoxes of written voices."[53]

It bears mentioning that the common ancient practice of having a written text read by an ἀναγνώστης would make the idea of "listening to a book" slightly less surprising. Nonetheless, the ambiguity is still provocative, and several authors—not only Apuleius—exploit it. In Virgil's *Eclogues,* for example, Pollio is a *lector* of Damoetas' poetry (3.85), even though the shepherd is obviously singing and not writing. This ambiguity is almost unavoidable in "performative" texts such as the *Eclogues,*[54] or Petronius' *Satyricon* (according to Gottschálk Jensson's interpretation of Petronius).[55] A written

---

52. As long as we do not prefer to understand *intende animum.* Keulen 2007a considers instead *intende* as an address to the reader-interpreter, who from that point onwards should modulate the pitch of his voice: "in rhetorical contexts, *intendere uocem* and *intentio uocis* are used for 'raising' the voice, or 'pitching' the voice to a certain tone."

53. Fowler 2001, 225; Kahane 2001, 238.

54. The phrase *nostris cantata libellis,* found in the Appendix Vergiliana *(Dirae* 26) presents a similar paradox. The "performative" nature of the *Eclogues* facilitated their adaptation for the stage; on theatrical performances of Virgil's *Eclogues,* see Tacitus, *Dial.* 13.2; Donatus, *Vita Vergilii* 26–27; Servius, *Buc.* 6.11; Gianotti 1991, 123 ff. On some instances of exchange between narrative literature and theater, see below, p. 163 n. 85. See La Penna 1992 for a broader treatment of the poet's tendency to represent himself as a writer. The notion of "listening to a book" can be interpreted as an instance of synaesthesis and is found elsewhere in ancient poetry. For example, it was possible even to "see" a sound (see e.g. Valerius Flaccus 6.201 *sibila respicit;* several other examples are offered by Fucecchi 2006 *ad loc.*).

55. See Jensson 2004, 44 f. about a "dichotomy of the written and the spoken" in Petronius; the *Satyricon* "seeks to hide its own textuality, leaving the impression of a living voice telling the story." On the theatrical elements in the *Satyricon,* see the thorough study by Panayotakis 1995. While performance is indeed a useful interpretive category for our understanding of the ancient novel, its importance should not be overemphasized; a balanced assessment is offered by Nimis 2004, 181: "The ancient novels are an important transitional moment in that trajectory [*sc.* the 'transformation from performance into reading']: still beholden for the most part to the protocols of performance, but with an emerging sense of a discourse no longer centered around the activity of a performer." Plato's *Phaedrus* exposes the same paradox: not only is it a written dialogue; it also points out the philosophi-

voice, and the ambiguity of a text that can be both "looked at" and "listened to," are elements typically found in any narrative that aims at transcending its own "textuality," in order to obtain the immediacy typical of spoken communication and theatrical performances.

True performativity, of course, is out of the reach of a written text, but viable alternatives exist. A text, as Wytse Keulen has pointed out,[56] actually *becomes* performance when it is read aloud, and we can certainly say that at least a part of the audience of the novel received it this way, having an experience not unlike listening to a public rhetorical declamation. But a text can also *suggest* performance, without necessarily entrusting all decisions regarding style and the mode of delivery to an ἀναγνώστης. By appealing to both the eyes and the ears of its audience, the text itself can evoke the multi-sensorial immersion typical of theater. Even before he begins, a reader must clearly have a surplus of imagination, and be willing to be deceived by the narrating voice; but this is true also of ancient theatrical performances, which employed a limited range of theatrical effects. A stage, a wall with three doors, and a small altar were normally the only scenery available to tragic and comic performances. It was up to the audience to imagine all the rest from a few hints embedded in the text.[57]

If we leave Apuleius aside for a moment, we can find in Heliodorus' *Aithiopika* an excellent example of how narration can conjure up a theatrical play. At 3.1.1 Knemon asks Kalasiris, who is updating him about what had happened previously to Theagenes and Charikleia, to make sure his account includes an accurate description of a procession (which the Egyptian priest had only mentioned in passing). Knemon is eager to *hear* the whole narration (εἰς πᾶσαν ὑπερβολὴν ἡττημένον τῆς ἀκροάσεως), but even that is not enough for him: he wants to *see* it with his own eyes (3.1.1 αὐτοπτῆσαι). Shortly after, he asks Kalasiris to sing the hymn that a choir of maidens had sung on that occasion, since he wants to be both "viewer"

---

cal excellence of orality over writing. "Writing performance," of course, was an important topic in the sections of rhetorical handbooks devoted to *actio:* see Gunderson 2000, 29–57.

56. Keulen 2007a.

57. The absence of artificial light, for example, forced the audience to imagine the nocturnal setting of some scenes that were necessarily staged in full daylight, such as the beginning of Plautus' *Amphitruo;* the play itself guided his audience's imagination, offering implicit staging directions and visual details, such as the lantern Sosia holds in his hand (149 *illic nunc cum lanterna advenit;* 154 *qui hoc noctis solus ambulem*). Of course, these were precious hints also for those who (like Apuleius) read Plautus' plays (or listened to somebody else who read them) instead of watching them staged in a theater. In Imperial times, pantomime could employ more elaborate sets, as Apuleius himself attests in his famous description of the Judgment of Paris at 10.29.4–10.34.2. It is clear, however, that *any* staging leaves ample space to the imagination of the audience. On ancient Roman scenography see e.g. Beare 1964², 204 ff.

(θεατής) and "listener" (ἀκροατής).⁵⁸ Kalasiris' description is so effective that it induces a quasi-hallucinatory state: "your description [*sc.* of Theagenes and Charikleia] portrayed them so vividly, so exactly . . . that they seemed to be before my eyes" (3.4.7).⁵⁹ Knemon, who "enjoys listening and has an insatiable appetite for good stories" (3.4.11),⁶⁰ is similar to Lucius, and can be considered both a model for and a parody of the "ideal" reader/listener of the novel.⁶¹ When the narration conforms to Knemon's tastes and satisfies his eagerness to see and listen, we can see the close relationship between narrative and theater, the only other literary genre that offers its audience a similar experience. It is not by chance that Knemon adopts a theatrical metaphor: when Kalasiris only mentions the procession without really describing it for Knemon, he says that the Egyptian priest is "raising the curtain and bringing it down again all in one phrase" (3.1.1).⁶²

In this passage from Heliodorus, the identification between narration and theatrical play is facilitated by the fact that the subject of the narration is a procession—not properly a theatrical play, but a form of performance nonetheless. After all, every narration could easily be presented as a theatrical performance: in my opinion, the self-fashioning of Apuleius' novel as something "to look at and to listen to" is intended to have exactly this effect. This self-fashioning begins in the prologue and is reasserted in several

---

58. On the power of an *ekphrasis* to stimulate sight and hearing, see Bartsch 1989, 17–19, with an example from Philostratus, *Eikones* 1.17; cf. above, n. 51. On the dialogue between Knemon and Kalasiris, see Liviabella Furiani 2003, 434 ff.; Crismani 2003; Bowie 2006, 77–81.

59. Knemon cries out, "It's them! It's Charikleia and Theagenes!"; and this misleads Kalasiris, who asks his friend to tell him where the two young lovers are. A very similar scene is found in Philostratus. *Her.* 10.5. Winkler 1982, 335 points out that this is "an old comic gag" (cf. Plautus, *Pseud.* 35 f.); according to Hardie 1998, 29 this passage, like many others, is "symptomatic of the text's wider tendency to confuse art and reality."

60. He is, we could say, yet another incarnation of Plato's Socrates, who was νοσῶν περὶ λόγων ἀκοήν: see above, p. 137.

61. See Winkler 1982, 41 on how Heliodorus' readers both identify with and dissociate themselves from Knemon; cf. also Fusillo 1989, 176, for whom Knemon is "the kind of reader interested in this genre of popular literature, and hence not at all the ideal reader of Heliodorus' novel." Winkler's position has been challenged by Morgan 1991, who states that "Knemon presents an exact fit, cognitively and affectively, with the reader" (p. 99); further reassessment can be found in Hunter 1998b, 53.

62. In Knemon's case, the αὐτοψία so valued by ancient historians is reduced to a form of hypnosis, induced by hearing the tale. It should be noted that not only theater, but also rhetoric (to the degree that it partakes in thetricality) can stimulate such participation by the audience. According to Solimano 1991, 16, "The orator's *actio* . . . is comparable to a *mise-en-scène*, striving to make the listeners/spectators 'see' the action and to excite their emotions through the orator/actor's body movements and voice modulations." Cf. n. 77 at p. 28, with further bibliography and examples from Cicero and Quintilian; to these I would add Cleon's reproach of the Athenians in Thucydides 3.28.4–7: "it is your wont to be spectators of words and hearer of deeds . . . you are in thrall to the pleasures of the ear and are more like men who sit as spectators at exhibitions of sophists than men who take counsel for the welfare of the state."

158   CHAPTER 3

other passages, though it appears in a stylized and less animated form than in Heliodorus. At 6.29.3 Charite says that her adventure with Lucius (a story entitled "A royal maiden flees captivity riding an ass") will be painted on a votive tablet, and thus be visually admired (*visetur*); but it will also be heard as a tale (*in fabulis audietur*), and put in fine writing (*doctorumque stilis . . . perpetuabitur*). Elsewhere the narrator addresses his reader directly, saying that, had he been present, he could have seen the action with his own eyes: for example, the joyful procession at 7.13.2 (*pompam cerneres . . . et hercules memorandum spectamen*), or the pack of ferocious dogs assaulting runaway slaves at 8.17.3 (*cerneres non tam . . . memorandum quam miserandum etiam spectaculum*). Two terms used in these passages, *spectaculum* and the less common *spectamen,* are highly significant in this context, since both terms derive from the language of theater.[63]

These passages, together with the prologue and other passages I will mention below, suggest that reading Apuleius' novel is an act of great complexity, a multimedia experience that appeals both to the eyes and ears, to seeing and hearing. The corresponding act of writing is, predictably, equally complex; not even an explicit mention of the tangible materiality of the book can lessen its complexity. At 10.2.1 the story of the wicked stepmother is introduced with these words:

> A few days later, I recall, an outrageous and abominable crime was perpetrated there, which I am adding to my book so that you can read it too (*sed ut vos etiam legatis, ad librum profero*).

This story is described in terms that remind us of the stage,[64] but, oddly enough, we are called readers and not spectators; nor are we invited to see or listen to the account, but rather asked to read a written text. This particular kind of writing, however, calls for a particular kind of reading. The odd expression *ad librum profero*[65] suggests that, even in a book, theatricality is still an important feature. We can translate the phrase simply as "I am adding to my book," as I did above (provisionally following Hanson's Loeb edition). But this translation misses an unmistakable pun drawing on

---

63. Cf. also 8.28.1 *specta denique;* 8.28.3 *cerneres.* This technique is also adopted by secondary narrators: e.g. the robber at 4.14.3 *cerneres,* and Charite's slave at 8.3.3 *spectate denique.* In his descriptions, Apuleius commonly adopts ecphrastic elements that enhance the "effect of presence" for the reader, who is thus encouraged to become a spectator too, like Knemon; see the commentaries by Keulen 2007b, 140 f. *ad* 1.4.5 *diceres* and Van Mal-Maeder 2001 *ad* 2.4.3 *ecce,* with further references.

64. Cf. also below on 10.2.4; on its theatrical antecedents see especially Fiorencis-Gianotti 1990; M. Zimmerman 2000, 417–432.

65. Cf. also 10.7.4 *ad istas litteras proferam.*

the technical significance of *profero ad* and related expressions in theatrical language, where it means to "stage" or "produce": see for example Plautus (*Amphitruo* 118) *veterem atque antiquam rem novam ad vos proferam;* or Laberius (in Macrobius *Saturnalia* 2.7) *quid ad scaenam adfero?*[66] A more accurate (but overly paradoxical) translation would be something along the lines of "I stage in this book." Writing a novel is akin to staging it; and reading a novel is somehow a substitute for going to the theater. This is consistent with the theatrical culture of Apuleius' day. Even if the canon of classical plays was still alive and well in the libraries and in the bookish education of learned men, these dramas had not been staged for a long time, and had been almost completely replaced by more popular genres, such as the mime and pantomime.[67] If Apuleius' *Phaedra* aspired to join the better known *Phaedrae* and the more noble *Hippolyti* of the classical tradition, the play could only have taken the form of a book.[68]

The bookish nature of Lucius' story is clearly exhibited in several passages in the novel that I will discuss below: these are 1) Diophanes' prediction to Lucius in book 2; 2) Lucius' comment at the end of *Cupid and Psyche* in book 6; 3) the introduction to the narrative told by Charite's slave that gives an account of his mistress' death in book 8; and 4) Lucius' apostrophe to the reader in book 9.

> When I asked him about the outcome of this trip of mine, he gave several strange and quite contradictory responses: on the one hand my reputation will really flourish, but on the other I will become a long story, an unbe-

---

66. Cf. also Cicero, *Planc.* 29 *omitto illa quae, si minus in scaena sunt, at certe, cum sunt prolata, laudantur;* Valerius Maximus 8.10.2 *in scaenam referrent;* and also Seneca, *Ep.* 90.28, where *sapientia . . . protulit mentibus* the *spectaculum* of the universe's true nature. Other examples in ThLL vol. X 2, pp. 1682.31 ff. and 1686.40 ff. In Apuleius, *Fl.* 9.13 *ad vos protuli* probably refers to the public delivery of speeches (so A. La Rocca 2005, 182), even though Hunink 2001, 109 argues that it indicates rather the publication of written speeches (and note that the context has many other terms connected to theater: 9.8 *coturno;* 9.9 *palliata;* 9.10 *togatus;* more generally, all of the *praeco*'s performance at 9.10–12 has a theatrical flavor). We might also compare Photius' definition (86,66a) of Achilles Tatius' novel: ἔστι δὲ δραματικόν, ἔρωτάς τινας ἀτόπους ἐπεισάγον, where ἐπεισάγειν corresponds to our *profero*: on this kind of theatrical terminology, see Marini 1991, 240 and n. 49. M. Zimmerman 2000, 61 (who translates our passage "I will put it on record" at p. 59) points out that *profero* is suited to the presentation of a new literary creation dealing with "a theme that has been treated in literature in many different ways," but both her examples (Plautus, *Am.* 118 and Horace, *Ars* 129 f.) refer to the theater.

67. See e.g. Schouler 1987, 274; Questa-Raffaelli 1990, 175 ff.

68. The same is not true, of course, of the different and less "textualized" forms of performance we find in the *Metamorphoses*. For some examples of mime scenes in the novel, see Fick-Michel 1991, 115–117; *GCA* 1985, 214 *ad* 8.25; Keulen 2006b, 2007b, 45 and n. 144, 2007a. For pantomime, M. Zimmerman 2000, 366 ff. *ad* 10.30.1; *GCA* 2004, 550 f. *ad* 6.24.3; May 2008.

lievable tale, a book in several volumes (*historiam magnam et incredundam fabulam et libros:* (2.12.5).⁶⁹

So ran the story told to the captive girl by that crazy, drunken old woman. I was standing not far off, and by Hercules I was upset not to have tablets and a stilus to write down such a pretty tale (6.25.1).

I shall tell you what happened from the beginning—such events as could justly be written down on paper in the form of a history by persons better educated than I, whom Fortune provides with the gift of the pen (8.1.4).

But perhaps as a careful reader you will find fault with my story, reasoning as follows: "How did it happen, you clever little ass, that though you were shut up in the confines of the mill you were able to find out what the women were doing in secret, as you insist?" So let me tell you (*accipe*) how I, an inquisitive man (*homo curiosus*) under the guise of a beast of burden, discovered all they did (9.30.1).

It should be noted, however, that such a list would be misleading as a demonstration of the narrator's concern for emphasizing the written nature of his account; on the contrary, we can read these passages as evidence that the novel aims not only to include writing, but also transcend it. The second and the third passages seem to deny the written form of the story, while in the first (as at 6.29.3, already quoted) oral and written transmission (*fabula* and *libri*) seem to coexist.⁷⁰ The last passage is an apostrophe to the reader, and the imaginary dialogue with him is represented vividly. We receive the impression of a lively and realistic conversation (also enhanced by *accipe*, which recurs in the prologue and is typical of direct speech).⁷¹

Furthermore, it is obvious that all the inserted tales are narrated by secondary characters (Aristomenes, Thelyphron, the robbers and their old servant, and so on). These inserted tales are presented as oral accounts made directly to Lucius, or overheard by him: as readers we are supposed to listen to them through Lucius' ears, and are thus invited to identify ourselves with him. When addressing his audience, the narrator sometimes displays a

---

69. On this passage see Graverini 2005a.
70. See Van Mal-Maeder 2001, 215.
71. Cf. Fowler 2001, 228 f.: "the exposure of textuality is accompanied by gestures of pretended presence: the reader is taken aside and into the narrator's confidence, as if they were in the same room."

similar pretence of orality, ignoring the fact that he is primarily addressing an audience of readers. In addition to the prologue, two more passages are of great relevance here:

> And so here is a story, better than all the others and delightfully elegant,[72] which I have decided to bring to your ears (*ad auris vestras adferre decrevi*: 9.14.1).

> Perhaps, my zealous *reader,* you are eager to learn what was said and done next. I would tell (*dicerem*) if it were permitted to tell; you would learn if it were permitted to hear (*audire*). But both ears and tongue would incur equal guilt, the latter from its unholy talkativeness, the former from unbridled curiosity (*parem noxam contraherent et aures et lingua, <ista impiae loquacitatis,>*[73] *illae temerariae curiositatis*: 11.23.5–6).

The first passage introduces the tale of the miller's wife, in which the theme of overhearing and eavesdropping is central,[74] so much so that Lucius, as we have seen, actually stops to praise the size of his asinine ears at 9.15.6. The narrator explicitly declares how he has come to know certain details: 9.16.1 "one day . . . there came drifting to my ears the following remarks (*sermo talis meas adfertur auris*)." The closeness of *meas adfertur auris* to the phrase *ad auris vestras adferre* at 9.14.1 suggests that our narrator shares the reader's eagerness to hear tales.[75]

Lucius' apostrophe at 11.23.5–6 shows the same ambiguity: he addresses his *lector,* but also mentions speaking and hearing, and the eyes and ears (*dicere, audire, aures et lingua*). The pretence of oral dialogue, which immediately replaces the suggested image of a reader with a book in his hands, vividly represents a close connection between narrator and reader (or listener), who, in this case, shares a strong desire to satisfy curiosity by hearing stories. This dialogue with the narrator allows the reader to participate in Lucius' joys, sorrows and temptations more easily, and to become a part of his narrative world.[76] Compared to a reader, a listener has a more direct and intense relationship with the narrator, and can communicate with him;

---

72. For the text and interpretation of *suave comptam,* see Mattiacci 1996, 141 *ad loc.*
73. The emendation is by Van der Vliet, and is accepted by Robertson in his Budé edition.
74. Cf. e.g. 9.16.1; 9.22.4; 9.30.1.
75. On the reader's ass-like ears, see above, p. 24 and n. 69.
76. The distinction between readers and listeners is also relevant in Chariton's novel, where, according to Hunter 1994, 1070 f., it is connected with the debate about *utile* and *dulce* in historiography; *contra,* Laplace 1997, 70 and n. 71.

he finds it easier to be consumed by the narration, and to identify himself with its main character.[77]

This recurrent fictional orality differentiates the *Metamorphoses* from the Greek novels, which are more inclined to highlight their bookish nature.[78] Apuleius, introducing his novel as a conversation between narrator and audience, must be either adding innovation to the Greek narrative tradition, or imitating the *Milesian Tales* by Aristides (or Sisenna's translation).[79]

Apuleius combines the theatricality inherent in the novel with a narrative strategy of direct and oral communication with the reader, a pretense that is designed to draw in the reader and make them participate in the narrative. In this context, the apostrophe at 10.2.4 offers further food for thought:

> So now, excellent reader, know that you are reading a tragedy, and no light tale, and that you are rising from the lowly slipper to the lofty buskin (*iam ergo, lector optime, scito te tragoediam, non fabulam legere et a socco ad coturnum ascendere*).

The metaphorical change of genre (from the comic slipper to the tragic buskin) anticipates the tragic tone of the tale that is about to begin. It may also, however, suggest a surprising exchange of roles between narrator and reader. It is the narrator, not the reader, who would have to "change his shoes" to match the tone of the new tale.[80] Again, narrator and audience are put on the same level; the apostrophe quoted above suggests that they somehow cooperate in the production of narrative. The relationship between the internal narrator and his audience can easily be considered parallel to the

---

77. Heliodorus describes very well the great psychagogic power of auditory experiences, which can even eclipse visual sensations: "So exquisite were the harmonies of the singers . . . that one's ears charmed one's eyes to be blind to what they saw" (3.3.1). In Plutarch, *De recta ratione audiendi* 41d, Melanthius, when asked to give his opinion about a tragedy, says he could not watch it (κατιδεῖν), since it was obscured by too many words; and many sophists, says the author, use words and intonation to veil the lack of significance in their speeches. At 38a, Plutarch quotes Theophrastus (fr. 91 Wimmer), according to whom "the sense of hearing . . . is the most emotional (παθητικωτάτη) of all the senses."

78. Cf. Chariton 8.1.4 σύγγραμμα (but see also above, n. 68); Lucian, *VH* 1,4 γράφω; Longus, *pr.* 2 βίβλους; Heliodorus 10.41.4 σύνταγμα. The protagonist and narrator of the pseudo-Lucianic *Onos* says he is a ἱστοριῶν . . . συγγραφεύς (55); and it is only too natural to think that the *Onos* itself is also one of those *syngraphai*.

79. On the *Milesiaka* see the interesting prologue to the pseudo-Lucianic *Amores*, quoted above at p. 45. On the oral diffusion of ancient narrative, see below, p. 199 n. 109.

80. Cf. e.g. Martial 8.3.13. Keulen 2007a, 131 discusses this same passage by Apuleius and argues that "the activity of the reader is not only the mental activity of the *lector doctus*, to whose erudition the text appeals by means of numerous allusions to various literary models. It is also the physical activity of reading aloud this text." The reader becomes actor and interpreter from this point of view as well.

relationship between the external author and his audience. With this most striking "effect of presence," the audience of the novel is invited on stage together with Apuleius himself, who simultaneously plays the role of author, producer, and protagonist of a theatrical production.

The experience of reading a novel is thus implicitly compared to being in a theater, and the reader is asked not only to be a spectator in the audience, but even to play a role as an actor on the stage. The passage we have just read is perhaps the best and most explicit confirmation of the importance of theatricality in the *Metamorphoses*. The wicked stepmother's tale is introduced as a tragedy, but in doing so the narrator clearly points out the "comic" qualities of what precedes this tale, and virtually of the whole novel: *tragoediam, non fabulam* defines the characters of both the tale that is beginning (a *tragoedia*) and the narration that contains it—namely, the whole novel (which could well be described as a *fabula*).[81] Even though the word *fabula* recurs several other times in the novel with the more generic meaning of "story,"[82] in this passage its opposition with *tragoedia* and its parallelism with the expression *a socco ad coturnum* compel us to understand *fabula* in the strict sense of "comedy." Of course, we should not take the narrator's statement too literally: after all, the wicked stepmother's tale cannot, for obvious reasons, be strictly defined as a tragedy; and even though Macrobius could associate Menander, Petronius and Apuleius as writers of *fabulae*,[83] it would not be appropriate to describe the *Metamorphoses* as a comedy *tout court*. Apuleius' novel does, however, undoubtedly contain both comic and theatrical elements.[84] Defining it as a (theatrical) *fabula* is correct, at least to the extent that such a definition includes narrative material that could be easily adapted for the stage. Generally speaking, novel and comedy are closely related literary genres: consequently, it is no accident that the ambiguous term *fabula* is used to describe both prose narratives and theatrical plays.[85]

---

81. So Schlam 1992, 44 and Finkelpearl 1998, 151 f.; M. Zimmerman 2000, 69 favors a more limited interpretation: "*a socco* obviously refers back to the comedy in the description of the *miles gloriosus* in the preceding episode."

82. *Fabulae* are the story of Aristomenes (1.2.6; 1.4.6; 1.13.3; 1.20.2; 2.1.2) and that of Thelyphron (2.20.7; 2.31.1), *Cupid and Psyche* (4.27.8), Charite's flight from the brigand's cave (6.29.3), some adultery tales (9.4.4; 9.14.1; 9.17.2; 9.23.5), and the story of the heinous murderess (10.23.2). Last but not least, the whole novel is defined as a *fabula* at 2.12.5 and 11.20.6. For discussion of the meaning of the term in the *Metamorphoses*, see Van Mal-Maeder 2001, 56–57 and 214–217; a broader study can be found in Lazzarini 1984.

83. *Somn.* 1.2.8; cf. above, pp. 96 f.

84. See e.g. M. Zimmerman 2000, 417–432; Keulen 2007a; May 1998, 2006, and 2007; Frangoulidis 1997, 145 ff. and 2001; Fiorencis-Gianotti 1990. On Plautine language, Pasetti 2007.

85. On the relationship between the ancient novel and theatrical genres, see, among many others, Fusillo 1989, 33–55; Morales 2004, 60 ff. (on Achilles Tatius); May 2006; see also § 1.5 in

In the prologue, the semantic ambiguity of *fabula* takes center stage (an appropriate metaphor in this case), where it emphasizes the fluctuation between a written and oral representation of the novel. The *Metamorphoses* is described from the very first sentence as a web of *variae fabulae* (1.1.1), and here *fabula* clearly means "tale"; but theatricality assumes a prominent position at the end of the prologue with the words *fabulam Graecanicam incipimus* (1.1.6). As Don Fowler points out, "The 'we' of *incipimus* is on one level the 'we' of the imagined company of actors who are putting on the *fabula* for us, the performers we are to watch. On another level, the 'we' associates author and reader in the joint production . . . that is the act of reading."[86] The metamorphosis of writtenness (the Egyptian papyrus) into orality and performance—a transformation that, as we have seen, is echoed several times throughout Apuleius' novel—is thus already prefigured in the prologue, and is clearly connected to the close relationship, and even an identification, between narrator and listener. Like Horace, who let himself to be transported by the magic of theater "now to Thebes, now to Athens,"[87] Apuleius urges the listener to enter, almost in a physical sense, the narrative world of his *Metamorphoses*.

Graverini-Keulen-Barchiesi 2006. As is well known, there are some traces of osmosis between narrative literature and theatrical performances: for example Lucian mentions Ninus, Metiochus, and Parthenope as characters in mimes and pantomimes (*Pseudol.* 25; *Salt.* 2 and 54). See also Mignogna 1996 for a mimic Leucippe; and Reardon 1996, 315–317 for the *Callirhoe* of Persius 1.134.

86. Fowler 2001, 228. On the theatricality of Apuleius' prologue, see also Smith 1972; Dowden 1982, 428; Winkler 1985, 200–203; Harrison 1990b; Dowden 2001, 134–136.

87. *Epist.* 2.1.213; cf. above, pp. 31 f.

4

Greece, Rome, Africa

IN THE PRECEDING CHAPTERS I approached the problem of identity in the *Metamorphoses* from a literary and hermeneutic perspective, by analyzing specific genre-markers suggested in the text. I then looked at the problem of the cultural context for the novelistic genre. In my opinion, this context suggests that Apuleius intended his work to have far more meaning than merely to provide a pleasant form of entertainment. Finally, I approached the problem of the relationship between the *Metamorphoses* and other literary genres.

This last chapter is devoted to a study of the cultural identity that emerges from the novel. It is a problem that turns out to be complex and absorbing, if we consider that Apuleius was born in Africa and frequently boasts that he is culturally bilingual, in both Greek and Latin. We could even say, in the style of Ennius, that Apuleius had "three hearts" (*tria corda*)—one Latin, one Greek, and one African.[1] In fact, at various points in time, scholarship has emphasized the predominance of each one of these three cultural elements above the others. Here I will begin by considering the literary geography in which the plot of the novel is situated, and I will consider the factors that could have had an influence on how Apuleius chose to describe it. This will

---

1. Ennius (if we can rely on Gellius 17.17.1, who reports his statement) actually emphasizes what was more properly his own trilingualism (Greek, Oscan, and Latin); we can plausibly surmise that Apuleius' mother tongue was Punic (cf. Harrison 2000, 2); and yet he never makes mention of this fact, even though *Apology* 24.1 confirms that he was not ashamed of his status as *seminumidam et semigaetulum*. In fact, Punic did not enjoy any cultural prestige (cf. *Apology* 98.8). On Apuleius' Greek and Latin bilingualism, see below p. 175 and n. 29.

166   CHAPTER 4

provide an opportunity to discuss both the "Romanization" of the Greek ass-story and how the dialectic between Greek and Roman culture functions in the *Metamorphoses*. Lastly, we will have a chance to see what might have been the significance of Apuleius' "third heart," the African one.

The novel offers several ways of approaching this question, but it will be necessary to include the *Florida* and the *Apology* in our analysis. Given that the cultural identity of our author and his audience had to coincide, at least in part, it will also be necessary to form a hypothesis about the composition of the readership for whom the novel was intended.

4.1 On the road with Lucius

The pseudo-Lucianic *Onos,* even though its geographical references are not particularly detailed, allows the reader to follow the main character's travels with a certain degree of precision. Lucius is from Patrae, in Achaia; he arrives in Hypata and then, by traveling northwards in Thessaly and Macedonia, proceeds up to Thessalonica. In that city he is restored to human shape, and from there he sails back to his homeland.

In Apuleius' *Metamorphoses*, on the other hand, Lucius is from Corinth.[2] At the beginning of the novel, we find him on the road to Hypata (as in the *Onos*) but then, after his abduction by robbers, the geographical setting becomes indefinite, and it is clear only that he is wandering in Thessaly. We return to a recognizable, concrete world again only when the ass arrives in Corinth-Kenchreai (10.19.1 and 10.35.3),[3] where the final metamorphosis takes place. Here too, as in the *Onos*, the metamorphosis is followed by a sea voyage. But instead of traveling to his homeland, our hero is taken to Rome (11.26.1), where, in the final chapters of the novel, he undergoes two last initiations into the Egyptian cults.

Scholarship has suggested a variety of motivations that could explain the absence of precise geographical references throughout the voyages of the ass in Greece. It is possible to attribute this phenomenon to the novel's origins in folktale, a type of story that is often set in a world between the confines of reality and fantasy, in which geographical points of reference have lost their importance. Alternatively we could explain it as a concession to the "Romanocentrism" of Apuleius' readership, who would have had

---

2. He has a letter of presentation addressed to his guest Milo by Demeas of Corinth (1.22.4); his Corinthian origin is even more explicit at 2.12.3 *Corinthi . . . apud nos,* "at Corinth, my home." See Van Mal-Maeder 2001, 209 *ad loc.* for further references.

3. Cf. M. Zimmerman 2000, 11 and n. 18; Slater 2002, 173.

little interest in minute details concerning the geography and landscape of central Greece[4]—and presumably could not have understood such details completely, had they been offered.

I think that these are valid points, and I shall try to offer a more detailed analysis of the second of these later in this chapter; but I would also like to suggest that the novel's lack of geographical specificity is the result of other literary choices made by Apuleius, namely, his decision to have Lucius come from Corinth rather than Patrae, and the choice of Corinth for Lucius' transformation back into human shape. The *Onos* had staged this second event in Thessalonica, and so, presumably, had the Greek original, even if we can say little about it with justified confidence. After these locations had been modified, it was of course impossible for Apuleius to follow the plot of the Greek original without leaving Lucius' travels more or less unmapped.

At this point it becomes unavoidable to ask why Apuleius found it necessary to introduce such important changes to the original plot by placing Lucius' origins and his retransformation in Corinth instead of Patrae and Thessalonica, respectively. Scholars, of course, have already debated this issue,[5] and here are, briefly, the most important reasons that have been adduced so far:

- Corinth was better known to a Latin audience than Thessalonica (again, the idea of a Romanocentric readership).
- Corinth was also well known as a rich but corrupt and immoral city: therefore, it was, by contrast, a good setting for the chastity and purity of Lucius, once converted to the Isiac faith.
- Corinth was an important center of the cult of Isis (an argument which partially contradicts the preceding).[6]

Stephen Harrison points out that Lucius makes an Odyssean *nostos* ("homeward journey") by returning to Corinth at the end of his wanderings,[7]

---

4. Cf. Harrison 1998b, 64 f., who suggests this second hypothesis.

5. See in particular Mason 1971, 160–165; Veyne 1965, 241–251; Marangoni 1977–78; M. Zimmerman 2000, 18; Egelhaaf-Gaiser 2000, 64–68. On the wealth and moral corruption of Corinth, see Wiseman 1979, 508; on Corinth as an Isiac center, Engels 1990, 102 ff.

6. For example Marangoni 1977–78, 224 ff. exploits the contrast between these two characterizations of Corinth: "Corinth, a city both perverse and holy, the site of Lucius' birth and of his rebirth . . . constituted . . . the symbol of the fundamentally dualistic principle of the Isaic religion," according to which, "reality is the result of the continuous clash between opposing forces, necessary and indestructible: that of the good, Osiris (destined to win), and that of evil, the ass-god Seth-Typhon (who is destined to never be completely defeated)."

7. Harrison 2002b, 43.

and this is, of course, a point well worth noting if we consider the frequently Odyssean character of the *Metamorphoses*.[8] Nevertheless, if Lucius is a Roman citizen (this is clear in the *Onos*, though the point is not stressed in the *Metamorphoses*),[9] then perhaps the real *nostos* is his return to Rome: in effect, just as in the *Onos*, the protagonist returns home *after* his retransformation; and the sea voyage, the direction from East to West, and Rome as the final destination would all seem to intensify the Odyssean echo as it is mediated by Virgil's *Aeneid*.[10]

In my opinion, each of the arguments considered above has its own advantages and disadvantages. However, the first argument is the most important, and in a sense encapsulates all the others: Corinth was more familiar to the intended audience of a novel written in Latin, and the readers of the *Metamorphoses* were in a better position to derive some meaning—whatever that might have been—from the choice of Corinth as a setting. The problem at hand is to decide precisely what this meaning was; and in this regard, all the explanations offered up to this point prove to be insufficient. The wealth of Corinth was not *per se* a particularly salient trait, and such an association cannot explain why Apuleius chose that city. For example, Patrae was also very prosperous, even if it was not as wealthy as Corinth.[11] Egyptian cults are also well attested in Thessalonica.[12] Rome itself could even have been chosen: the metropolis was wealthy and had a notable abundance of temples and cults of Isis; moreover, in terms of its fame for moral cor-

---

8. See above, § 3.3. There is an extensive bibliography on this subject; see e.g. Harrison 1990a and 2000, 223.

9. In *Onos* 55, Lucius has the *tria nomina* of a Roman citizen: "my name is Lucius, and that of my brother [is] Gaius, and the other two names we share with our father." *Metamorphoses* 9.39.3 makes clear that Lucius can understand the Latin-speaking soldier, and Latin is obviously necessary for the forensic activity he will practice in Rome (11.28.6). Cf. also Bowersock 1965, 289; Mason 1983; 1994, 1681 f.; Harrison 2000, 215 f.; a different view in Walsh 1968.

10. The Odyssean model can make sense of Lucius' last voyage from Corinth to Rome even if we prefer to think of Lucius as a Greek. The *Odyssey* concludes with the return of the hero to Ithaca, but this is only one leg of his eventual journey: Odysseus will take to the sea again and will head east, a journey that is treated only indirectly, as it is prophesied by Tiresias. From this perspective, we can also consider Lucius' journey to Rome as a form of narrative denouement after the *nostos* to Corinth. For a similar reading, see Finkelpearl 2004, 82 ff. For Slater 2002, 175 Lucius' voyage is "not so much a promotion as an exile."

11. Corinth, Athens, and Patrae were "the three centers of commercial and banking activities in Greece" (Wiseman 1979, 507). Harrison (2002b, 45) reminds us that Thessalonica was also a large city and capital of the Roman province of Macedonia.

12. Sources in Griffiths 1975, 15 and n. 4, 330, 349 f. As a minor suggestion, it is also worth mentioning that Corinth was a center of the cult of Pegasus and Bellerophon: see Engels 1990, 99 ff. The mythical couple is alluded to at 6.30.5; 7.26.3; 8.16.3; and 11.8.4; the winged horse (a winged ass in the last passage) seems to be a paradoxical symbol for Lucius, who tried to become a bird and was turned into an ass.

ruption, the city was probably second to none. Why, then, did Apuleius set only the last part of the novel in Rome, instead of the entire plot, or at least the narrative from Lucius' retransformation onwards? Here it becomes clear that the Greek topography of Apuleius' *Metamorphoses* corresponds very closely to the lost Greek original, so much so that almost the whole plot is set in Greece. In this regard Corinth constitutes an important exception, and probably explains the lack of geographical specificity found in most of the novel. I hope that, by examining Corinth in a new light, I will be able to provide a more convincing explanation for Apuleius' choice.

4.2 The reputation of Corinth

Corinth was indeed well known for its wealth and moral corruption, as well as for the presence of Isiac cults. But as we have seen, these facts become meaningful only at the end of the *Metamorphoses,* where they provide a sharp contrast to the retransformation and, above all, the conversion of Lucius.[13] They have little point at the beginning: Corinth is simply introduced as the birthplace of the main character (unless we prefer to consider the Corinthian origins of the protagonist as a vague allusion to his final destiny). I also doubt that a reference to Corinth would necessarily have carried connotations of wealth, corruption, or the cult of Isis for the literate Latin reader. I would instead point to an obvious fact that has been overlooked in Apuleian studies: Corinth had been one of the most prosperous cities in Greece until 146 B.C.E., when it was razed by a Roman army under the command of Lucius Mummius. After that year, Corinth practically disappeared from the geography of Greece, until it was rebuilt and repopulated as a Roman colony, first by Caesar and then Augustus.[14] These events resonated throughout Greek and Roman culture for many years afterward; thus, it is eminently reasonable to hypothesize that they provide the basis for Corinth's importance in the economy of Apuleius' novel.

---

13. The corruption of Corinth provides a background for the events of the tenth book, beginning with chapter 19. It is worth repeating, however, that from this perspective Corinth did not at all represent an obligatory choice. M. Zimmerman 2005, 39 notes that "in the age when Paul wrote to the flourishing Christian community, the city was probably no more debauched or noble than any other port or important center of commerce." Apuleius' representation of Corinth evokes "a world of paper" (Zimmerman); there are no doubt historically accurate details, such as the mention of the *duumvir quinquennalis* at 10.18.1, but the perspective with which the city on the isthmus is rendered depends completely on the first-person narrator, Lucius.

14. On the archaeological history of Corinth, in addition to Wiseman 1979 and Engels 1990, see Gilman Romano 2000 and Rothaus 2000. On Cenchreae, Hohlfelder 1976. On the destruction of the city by Mummius' army, and on the figure of the Roman general, see Graverini 2001b.

The destruction of Corinth and of Carthage (which had occurred a few months earlier) marked a turning point in the Mediterranean politics of Rome. By that time, the city was confident in its dominant role and ready to defend its interests at any cost. According to Cicero, Corinth and Carthage were "the two jewels of the sea-coast," and the only two cities (along with Capua) that could "bear the weight and the name of an empire." Cicero adds that the cities were destroyed "so that they could never rise again,"[15] and expresses embarrassment as he explains the Roman policy behind the decision to raze them; evidently it was still a source of some chagrin for him. The orator himself acknowledges that "through a specious appearance of expediency, wrong is very often committed in transactions between state and state, as by our own country in the destruction of Corinth" (*De officiis* 3.46). Even more telling is Florus, *Epit.* 1.32.1:

> As though that age could only run its course by the destruction of cities, the ruin of Carthage was immediately followed by that of Corinth, the capital of Achaea, the glory of Greece . . . this city, by an act unworthy of the Romans, was overwhelmed before it could be counted in the number of their declared enemies.

Even if the Romans shed crocodile tears, we can easily imagine the universal mourning brought about in the Hellenistic world by the destruction of Corinth, "the bright star of Greece" (Diodorus Siculus 3.27.1). As far as I know, an epigram by the Egyptian Polystratus (*AG* 7.297) is the first to make reference to the destruction:[16]

> Lucius has smitten sore the great Achaean Acrocorinth, the star of Hellas . . . and the sons of Aeneas left unwept and unhallowed by funeral rites the Achaeans, who burnt the house of Priam.

The identity of the victorious general is partially concealed here, since only his praenomen Lucius is disclosed (the Greek version of his nomen, *Mommios,* could also have fit the meter). The result is a generic mention of a Roman destroyer. As these verses describe it, the descendants of Aeneas took vengeance on the Greeks for the destruction of Troy, and the destruction of Corinth is more the nemesis of history than a consequence of the acts of a single general. Yet it was an epic deed, and Virgil alludes to Mummius

---

15. The first quotation is from *De natura deorum* 3.91; the other two are from *De lege agraria* 2.87.

16. The epigram seems to have been composed not much later than 146 B.C.E.: see Peek 1952.

in the procession of heroes in the underworld.[17] At *Aen.* 1.283 ff., Virgil expresses a similar sentiment: "There shall come a day . . . when the house of Assaracus shall bring into bondage Phthia and famed Mycenae, and hold lordship over vanquished Argos." Servius glosses the mythological reference as follows: "House of Assaracus: that is, the Trojan family . . . Assaracus begot Capys, Capys begot Anchises, and he gave birth to Aeneas, progenitor of the Romans; from them came Mummius, who defeated the Achaeans."[18]

In other texts, a paternalistic attitude replaces the notion of retribution for the destruction of Troy. Titus Flamininus began this trend in an inscription at Delphi, quoted by Plutarch, in which he calls himself "Titus, descendant of Aeneas" and commits himself to liberty for all Greeks (*Flam.* 1.11: the Roman general is again identified only by his praenomen). Plutarch (*Quaest. conv.* 9.2.737a) also preserves an anecdote in which Mummius is moved to tears at the sight of a young Corinthian slave, who had written a verse of Homer in the sand (*Od.* 5.306, "Thrice, four times blest, the happy Greeks that fell"), likening his fate to that of the Greeks who had died in front of the walls of Troy.

Mourning for the loss of such an important city and for the countless great works of art that adorned it naturally recurs in Greek authors such as Polybius (39.2 = Strabo 8.6.28). Long after the end of the wars between Greece and Rome, however, it became more common (as well as politically expedient) to express, in addition to a sense of grief, a sense of relief for the relatively light yoke placed upon Greece by Rome after the war (Pausanias 7.16.10), and to express gratitude for the generosity of Julius Caesar, who brought the ruined city back to life (Diodorus Siculus 32.27.1).

Even though the full responsibility for the conflict was usually attributed to the thoughtlessness of the leaders of the Achaean League, the severity of the Roman response was hard for the Greeks to accept, even for those most loyal to Rome (like Polybius, who seems to consider the doom of Corinth a fair price to pay for what would ultimately be a better outcome). When Pausanias describes the monuments of Corinth, he also thinks back to the history of the city; and, although there is no explicit anti-Roman criticism, nevertheless "his detailed narrative reflects his own often expressed concern

---

17. *Aeneid* 6.836–7: "he . . . triumphant over Corinth, shall drive a victor's car to the lofty Capitol, famed for Achaeans he has slain."

18. According to Nenci 1978, 1016, these verses of Virgil, and their interpretation by Servius, are influenced by a propagandistic tradition started by the same L. Mummius. At any rate, this seems to be impossible, since the idea of vengeance for Troy is already found in the epigram by Polystratus quoted above, which could hardly have been influenced in any way by the Roman general. Even granting that Mummius played a role in the dissemination of this idea, it certainly did not originate with him. For a discussion of Nenci's point, see Graverini 2001b, 143 ff.

for Greece's freedom and dignity."[19] Crinagoras (*Greek Anthology* 9.284) laments in no uncertain terms the new population of Corinth: "What inhabitants, O luckless city, hast thou received, and in place of whom? Alas for the great calamity of Greece!"

The Corinthian war booty had a definite impact on Roman society, as a massive quantity of money and artwork poured into Rome. Pliny the Elder disapproves of the laxity of morals induced by the great Mediterranean victories in the second century B.C.E., claiming that "the victory over the Achaean League, from which statues and paintings came to Rome, had a great importance in the decline of morality."[20] Eutropius 4.14.2 describes for us the three great triumphs celebrated in Rome in 145 B.C.E. Africanus Minor and Metellus had, respectively, Hasdrubal and Andriscus marching before their chariots, but before the chariot of Mummius, who had no captured enemy generals to show, "bronze statues and paintings and other ornaments of that most celebrated city were carried." There is not room here to explore the link between this Corinthian booty and the unbridled enthusiasm of the Romans for Greek and Oriental art, or to discuss the distinctive and eclectic tastes induced by the continuous stream of works of art that flowed from every nation into public and private collections in Rome. Instead, it will suffice simply to mention the celebrated "Corinthian bronze." The ancients believed that this alloy had been created in the destruction of Corinth, when the immense heat of the fire melted and mixed bronze with noble metals. Modern scholars doubt the composition and even the existence of such an alloy. Nonetheless, the metal unquestionably had a long and glorious literary life, as is attested in Petronius, among other places.[21]

It was, therefore, almost inevitable that Corinth should become a sort of symbol for the relationship between Greece and Rome, but this was due to historical events, as well as to literary and cultural echoes of its destruction and reconstruction. It was in Corinth that Flamininus, and later the emperor Nero, announced the freedom and independence of Greece.[22] Historical events and literary sources, then, combined to create a coherent web of ideological references.

The Romans, thanks in part to the Corinthian spoils, intensified their

---

19. Swain 1996, 338; cf. also Bowie 1996a, 216 ff.

20. *Nat.* 33.149; cf. also Livy 34.4.4.

21. *Satyricon* 50.5. On the diffusion of Greek art through the distribution of war spoils, see Pape 1975; on Corinthian bronze, Jacobson-Weitzman 1995.

22. Even the excavation of a canal across the isthmus under Nero gave rise to disputes regarding the cultural identities of the Greeks and Romans: cf. Whitmarsh 1999. On the close ties between Corinth and Rome, the "informal and symbolic threads that bound the Greek city to the capital of the empire," see also Alcock 1993, 168 f.

Hellenization and developed a passion for Greek art and culture. The Greeks, however, were always reluctant to lay down the crown of their cultural excellence. It was in front of a Corinthian audience that Favorinus of Arles (an author who has been repeatedly described by scholars as a kindred spirit of Apuleius)[23] played upon this feeling of superiority, a feeling so deeply rooted in the genetic code of the Greeks that it could be powerfully felt even among the citizens of a Corinth which by then was a Roman colony:

> If someone who is a Roman, not one of the masses but of the equestrian order, one who has affected, not merely the language, but also the thought and manners and dress of the Greeks . . . —for while the best of the Greeks over there [i.e. *in Rome*] may be seen inclining toward Roman ways, he inclines toward the Greek, . . . not only to seem Greek but to be Greek too—taking all this into consideration, ought he not to have a bronze statue here in Corinth? Yes, . . . because, though Roman, he has become thoroughly Hellenized, even as your own city has.[24]

Favorinus praises Corinth as a Roman colony that by that time had become thoroughly Hellenized: and it is clear that for the orator, as well as for his audience, this was a remarkable improvement. Favorinus considered himself a fully Hellenized Roman, but pointed to other Romans as true specimens of ignorance. Thus, in addition to chastising Mummius as the destroyer of Corinth, Favorinus poignantly emphasizes his lack of cultural refinement. He reminds us that the general had written the names of Nestor and Priam (two heroes who were invariably represented as old men) beneath a group of two statues depicting young Arcadian men. But Mummius was not alone in misidentifying the two heroes: "all the Roman mob, looking at these two youths of Arcadia, thought they were looking at Nestor and Priam."[25]

All this tells us something about the ideas and emotions that Corinth could arouse for a literate reader of Apuleius' day, Greek or Roman. Not only was it a rich city, and immoral, and a center of the cult of Isis; it was, perhaps above all, a powerful symbol of cultural identity. Its expressive potential

---

23. Vallette 1908, 187; Sandy 1997, 93 ff.; Gamberale 1996, 80–84 (with a useful treatment of the bilingualism of Favorinus, and of his competence in dealing with Roman culture; these traits emerge also in Gellius' testimony, but become obscured in other sources, including the same discourse of Favorinus mentioned above).

24. Dio Chrysostom 37.25–26. On the construction of Greek identity in Favorinus' Corinthian oration, see Whitmarsh 2001, 295 ff.

25. Dio Chrysostom 37.42.

was multivalent: a Roman could use the symbol of Corinth to celebrate the greatness of his people and the vengeance of Aeneas' descendants over the destroyers of Troy. A Greek, on the other hand, could use it to lament his loss of freedom, and to express his bitterness for the injustices he had suffered; he could also use it to parade his cultural superiority over the *feri victores* of the west. To both Greeks and Romans, however, Corinth inevitably provided an example of and a quasi-metaphor for the relations between Greece and Rome.

In this context we can gain a fuller and clearer view of the role played by Corinth in the *Metamorphoses*. Corinth is not only the native town of the main character and the place where he regains human shape; it is also mentioned in the prologue—together with Athens and Sparta, the two other symbolic centers of Greek civilization—as the fatherland of the novel itself.[26] The connection between the novel and the symbolic geography of Greek culture is clearly literary and book-oriented: Athens, Corinth and Sparta are in fact *glebae felices aeternum libris felicioribus conditae*, "fruitful lands preserved forever in even more fruitful books." But Greece is only the point of departure: right away (*mox*) the unknown speaker, after introducing the novel, shifts to Rome, where, with assiduous and exhausting effort (*aerumnabilis labor*), he learns and perfects a new language. This geographical shift of the "speaking I" (be it a book, its protagonist, the author, a personified prologue, or an undefined *ego* that combines all these identities) can be taken as a symbol for the fact that the *Metamorphoses* is primarily a Latin reworking of a Greek original.

And so, from beginning to end, Corinth, a Greek city both destroyed and refounded by the Romans, accompanies and prefigures the narrative movement in the novel from Greece to Rome. The novel sees Greece through the eyes of a Latin author, and the eyes of a protagonist-narrator who recounts his various adventures in retrospect. These adventures occur primarily in Greece, but are recounted only *after* the narrator has settled in Rome.[27] Lucius, the protagonist, in fact comes from Corinth and concludes his adventures in Rome, thus following, in the full sense of the word, the same journey of Romanization completed by both the *ego* of the prologue and by the book itself.

---

26. This, naturally, is true to the extent that we entertain Harrison's hypothesis of 1990b, in which the elusive *ego* that narrates the prologue can be identified with the book itself. Compare also Harrison 2000, 227 ff., and Nicolai 1999, who adopts Harrison's hypothesis with some qualification. For other references to the speaker of the prologue (a well-debated subject), see above p. 52. On the elegant tricolon *Hymettos Attica et Isthmos Ephyrea et Taeneros Spartiatica*, which indicates by synecdoche all of Greece, see Keulen 2007b, 75 f., who provides several useful parallels.

27. On this point, see below p. 192 with n. 83.

The capital of the empire, as we have seen, was replete with artwork transported from Greece (and, especially, with artwork from Corinth) by both plunder and trade. The *Metamorphoses*—described as a *fabula graecanica* in the prologue[28]—could also be well defined as part of this Roman tendency towards cultural appropriation. The constant exploitation of earlier literature and the frequent practice of literary *furtum* are characteristic of the style and composition of the novel. Just like the Romans of the second century B.C.E., Apuleius could be defined, with a bit of exaggeration and fancy, as a plunderer of works of art, even if, without a doubt, he is far shrewder and wiser than Favorinus' portrayal of Mummius.

4.3 Romanization

At this point I should clarify that the presence of Corinth in the *Metamorphoses* does not convey the notion of opposition between Greece and Rome, which did emerge from some of the Greek and Latin texts cited above. The novel, I believe, ought to be read in terms of cultural mediation and appropriation more than in terms of conflict. This position, moreover, is consistent with the movement of the novel from Greece to Rome, implied by the origin and narrative structure of the tale. It is also consistent with the bilingual culture that Apuleius so often vaunts elsewhere in his works.[29] In the first two chapters of this book, I sought to demonstrate that Apuleius was highly conscious of literary categories and of the generic traits that define (more or less implicitly) the Greek novel. I tried to show that he adds to these generic traits a dynamic of self-irony and satire, both of which are distinctive features of the Latin narrative tradition, particularly when compared to the Greek one.[30] The definition of narrative space in the novel also suggests a process

---

28. *Met.* 1.1.6; on this phrase and its implications, see Keulen 2007b, 19 f. and 90 *ad loc.*, with his bibliography (here I cite only Mason 1978).

29. Cf. *Apology* 4.1, with Hunink 1997 *ad loc.* Harrison, in my opinion, has little ground for his suspicion that Apuleius' "claims of complete bilingualism are likely to be exaggerated for effect and self-promotion" (2000, 15). Lee 2005, 168 rightly points out that "the absence of Greek in the Florida may in fact tell us less about him [*sc.* Apuleius] than about the Greek (or lack thereof) of the excerptor."

30. This is an assertion that, naturally, must take into account the fact that—excluding the *Historia Apollonii* (which, in the version that has come down to us, is much later and pertains to a temporal context very different from the one at hand)—our knowledge of the "Roman novel" is based solely on the *Metamorphoses* and the highly fragmented *Satyricon* of Petronius: in effect, too little to speak of a genuine "tradition." It is likely, however, that this scarcity of texts finds its origins in the fact that, although Petronius and Apuleius both adopt the narrative conventions of the Greek novels, they also subject those conventions to significant cultural shifts. Barchiesi 2006, 217 notes that "the forms adopted by Petronius and Apuleius, as compared to the 'sophistic' Greek romance, appear to be more

of appropriation and Romanization. This is true of the novel as a whole, not only the last chapters of Book 11. In contrast to the tendencies of the Greek romances, which are usually set in a world where the Roman Empire and its capital have no place,[31] Apuleius, from beginning to end, adopts a different position: the primary literary persona of the novel is Greek, but he has a Roman name and comes from a city refounded by the Romans—an ideal cultural bridge between Greece and Rome.

It is possible that this represents an even greater divergence from the direct model for Apuleius' novel, the lost *Metamorphoses* of Lucius of Patrae. We cannot say anything about this work with any certainty; nevertheless, in regard to the other novel that has been modeled on it, the *Onos* of Pseudo-Lucian,[32] I can only imagine that the Greek author felt a certain sense of satisfaction when he had to describe the transformation into an ass of a protagonist named Lucius, clearly identified as a Roman citizen (a case unique in Greek narratives).[33] If this was the case, it is not impossible that the lost novel of Lucius of Patrae adopted a similar position.[34]

It would be an arduous task to define how and in what proportions the Latin and Greek components of Apuleius' bilingual culture were mixed, and the positions offered by critics have seen considerable oscillation. Eduard Norden provided an excellent frame of reference for the prose style of Apuleius and that of his contemporaries in the Greek Second Sophistic, and for a long time it was popular to emphasize the Greek roots of Apuleius'

---

experimental and more daring; they are less bound up in continuity with the past . . . this dynamic will guarantee the Latin novel a remarkable fortune in the altered and mutable social conditions of the first modern age in Europe; but in antiquity it was not enough to create around the Latin novel a sufficiently stable area of consensus . . . the Latin novel remained the work of exceptional personalities, and does not succeed in finding a stable space in the ever-more-rigid system of literary canons and genres."

31. Cf. Connors 2002, 12: "the ancient Greek novels tell their stories of young love and high adventure in a realm apart from the everyday world inhabited by their authors and audiences." As the author notes, however, this space is not entirely isolated from connections to the present: "the shared body of geographical and historical knowledge and lore available to educated audiences in antiquity ensured that novelistic travels did not in fact unfold in a space that was 'naked' and abstract" (p. 13). Cf. also Barchiesi 2006, 209 ff.

32. On the relationship between the three versions of the ass-story see below, note 34.

33. Cf. Perry 1967, 220: "Nothing could be more surprising or startling to an ancient reader of fiction, especially burlesque fiction, than to find the leading character in a story, he who was the butt of the farce, a Roman of high social standing"; his arguments are taken up and developed by Hall 1995, 51 ff.; *contra* Walsh 1968.

34. This might seem unlikely, given that Photius affirms that the work of Lucius of Patrae, in distinction from the *Onos*, did not have a satirical tone. Still, the judgment of Photius does not always prove completely reliable, and therefore it is difficult to determine how serious the tone of the lost *Metamorphoseis* was. Cf. Winkler 1985, 252–256; Mason 1994, 1675 ff.; later references can be found in Keulen 2003c, 131 n. 50.

language and cultural formation. This resulted in several scholarly excesses, such as that of Paratore, for whom "Apuleius always retained the mentality of a Greek."[35] Modern criticism, without a doubt, has become more balanced. The definition of "Latin sophist" seems to have gained ample consensus thanks to the monographs of Gerald Sandy and Stephen Harrison;[36] and the recent surge of critical studies on the rich intertextuality of the *Metamorphoses*[37] has continued to provide evidence of a systematic connection between Apuleius' novel and the Latin literary tradition. All of this justifies without ambiguity the representation of Apuleius as "fundamentally Roman in cultural identity."[38] After all, a close connection with Greek language and culture was inscribed into the genetic code of every educated Roman.

A short example should suffice to give an idea of the process of Romanization the ass-story undergoes in Apuleius' novel, and how he has significantly reworked many of its literary and intertextual features. Some passages of the *Onos* of pseudo-Lucian offer a text that is very similar to the *Metamorphoses*, and it is therefore plausible to suggest that the *Onos* resesmbles fairly closely the lost original with which Apuleius was working. In such cases, it is possible to come to an understanding of how the *Metamorphoses* endeavored to find room for innovation, while still maintaining a story that closely paralleled the model. In Chapter 6 of the *Onos*, Lucius enters the house of his host Hipparchus and catches sight of the slave Palaestra in front of the fire as she cooks dinner, sensuously wiggling her hips as she stirs dinner in the pot. This is exactly the opportunity Lucius was waiting for: in fact, he had just decided to make use of this beautiful slave as a means of gaining access to the secrets of sorcery, practiced in secret by Hipparchus' wife. Here is the text, which describes Lucius' approach and Palestra's witty response:

---

35. Paratore 1942², 71; cf. 79: "His works and his personality are permeated by Greek elements, seeing as they are clearly detached from the Latin tradition." This notion is repeated and amplified in Paratore 1948, 37: "Stylistic analysis and an examination of his technical procedures, of his sources, and of the spiritual climate of his time all show us that this author was one of the most genuine sons of Greek culture to have written in Latin." On Greek elements in Apuleius' language, cf. also Geisau 1916; Bernhard 1927, 143–147; Callebat 1968, 59–68 and 83–84.
36. Sandy 1997 and Harrison 2000, though they have different emphases: for Sandy the essential part of this definition is 'sophist' (by means of which Apuleius becomes essentially "a transmitter of the Greek intellectual achievements of the East to the Latin West," p. 9), while Harrison presents a more balanced view and locates Apuleius in the context of Latin culture (as well as Greek culture, naturally).
37. A review of the scholarship dedicated to this question would be too long to include here: see for example the surveys in Harrison 2000, 220–226 and Keulen 2006a, as well as chapter 3 of this book.
38. Harrison 2000, 3.

I immediately took it from there (ἔνθεν ἑλών) and said, "Palaestra, you beauty, how rhythmically you twist and tilt your buttocks in time with the saucepan, and your loins flow as they move. Happy the man who gets a dip in there." Said she—for she was a very pert little hussy and a bundle of charms: "You'd scamper, my lad, if you had any common sense and wanted to go on living, since it's full of hot fire and steam. If you were to as much as touch it, you'd be sitting here with a shocking burn, and no one can cure you, not even the God of Healing, except me who burned you."

Helmut van Thiel[39] noted that the words chosen to introduce Lucius' speech are a reference to *Odyssey* 8.500, in which Demodocus begins to weave his song, "taking up the tale" (ἔνθεν ἑλών) from the point where the Argives feign a departure from Troy and leave the horse behind on the Trojan shore. It seems certain to me that this is the correct source of the citation. The formula was clearly not in common use:[40] other occurrences of this Homeric *incipit* confirm how catchy this phrase would have sounded and indicate that it was used to introduce direct speech with a certain solemnity (as it turns out here, a parodic solemnity). It is found, for example, three times in Chariton (1.7.6; 5.7.10; and 8.7.9) and once in Heliodorus (5.16.5.).[41] But above all we should notice that the same pretentious stylistic register is adopted in Palestra's menacing response: her phrase "no one will be able to heal you, not even the god of medicine" (θεραπεῦσαι δέ σε οὐδεὶς ἀλλ' οὐδὲ θεὸς ἰατρός) in fact recalls the dialogue between Odysseus and Polyphemus in *Odyssey* 9.520–525, in which the Cyclops, blinded by the Greek hero, claims that his father Poseidon will heal him, "him, nor any other of the gods or mortal men" (αὐτὸς δ', αἴ κ' ἐθέλῃσ', ἰήσεται, οὐδέ τις ἄλλος / οὔτε θεῶν μακάρων οὔτε θνητῶν ἀνθρώπων). Odysseus hurries to add that the wound cannot be healed (ὡς οὐκ ὀφθαλμόν γ' ἰήσεται οὐδ' ἐνοσίχθων).[42]

---

39. Van Thiel 1972, 33.

40. The *iunctura* is not prosaic, as Russell 1964, 164 notes (ad Ps. Longinus *On the Sublime* 34.4): "The phrase . . . had a certain vogue in late Greek in the sense of 'thereupon' with verbs of saying." Russell also notes the Homeric origins of the expression in his commentary on this passage.

41. For an overview of poetic citations in Chariton and the other Greek romances, cf. Robiano 2000, though he does not consider the passages discussed here. A fuller discussion can be found in Fusillo 1989.

42. Van Thiel 1972, 33 notes the parallel. We should also point out that these literary subtleties have been placed in the mouth of a slave who will later confess to Lucius that she has never learned to read or write (chapter 11). This element is absent in Apuleius, who seems to want to further emphasize the irony of Photis' intellectual superiority; the beautiful slave girl therefore addresses Lucius somewhat condescendingly, not unlike a teacher to his student: 2.10.2 *heus tu, scholastice* (cf. for example Gellius 17.20.4 *heus . . . tu rhetorisce*, spoken to Gellius by his master Taurus).

If indeed this Homeric coloring was present in the lost Greek original, Apuleius seems to have competed with his model in a contest of playful and learned allusions. In the parallel passage of the *Metamorphoses,* Lucius' dumbfounded reaction to the sight of the beautiful Photis brings us completely into epic territory: the phrase at 2.7.4 *isto aspectu defixus obstupui et mirabundus steti, steterunt et membra quae iacebant ante* ("Frozen by this sight I stood amazed, and my limbs froze in place; a part of my body stood up amazed, too, that before had been resting") is a pastiche of several Virgilian expressions,[43] among which *Aeneid* 1.613 (*obstipuit primo aspectu Sidonia Dido*) is especially prominent. Lucius' stupor at the sight of Photis recalls Dido's shock at the appearance of Aeneas, after the divine mist concealing him suddenly disappears. In the case of the novel, however, the term is loaded with sexual tension, since the rigidity typically accompanying *stupor* in Virgil (cf. e.g. 1.495 *dum stupet obtutuque haeret defixus in uno;* and 2.774 *obstipuit steteruntque comae et vox faucibus haesit*) is here concentrated on one part of Lucius' anatomy. Apuleius, therefore, has recognized in his model the potential for an epic depiction of an erotic scene. He has taken part in the same joke, but has substituted Virgil for Homer.

4.4 Romanocentrism

Naturally, the substitution of Virgil for Homer as a paradigm of epic diction does not constitute a particularly surprising or arcane process: the *Aeneid* makes up part of the literary tradition universally available to anyone who had some education and a modest ability to read Latin. But the Romanization of the ass-story takes place not only on the level of literary interweaving: as has been convincingly shown in the recent work of Gianpiero Rosati, Romanization in the novel also occurs at the most basic cultural level, in the form of references to customs, dress, and *Realien* specific to the Roman world.[44] A study that pays attention to these narrative elements can, without a doubt, help to define the cultural identity of Apuleius, who has been accurately described as a "cultural mediator between the Greek world and the Latin world, to the benefit of the latter."[45]

---

43. A deeper analysis of the rich intertextuality of this Apuleian passage (which is not in fact limited to the Virgilian passage noted here) can be found in Graverini 2001a, which contains further bibliography. See also the excellent comment of Van Mal-Maeder 2001 *ad loc.*
44. Rosati 2003.
45. Rosati 2003, 282; cf. Sandy 1997, ix.

We should ask, however, whether it is possible to be more specific. Were the *Metamorphoses* written for a general public able to read Latin, or were they written for a smaller circle of readers, who can be identified by means of geographical, social and cultural criteria? The analysis of *Realien*, to which Apuleius refers in the novel, can be of great service in a study of this kind. In other words, if we were able to identify references to specific facts, events, or pieces of information that were probably known only to a specific group of people, such references would no doubt help us define the readership of the novel; in turn, we could better define the novel itself from the perspective of the reader's cultural identity.

4.4.1 THE *METAMORPHOSES* IN ROME?

For example, it is certainly true that at several junctures the text presupposes the involvement of a reader who has a definite familiarity with the city of Rome, as well as with Latin culture at large. But to what extent can this factual material be used to affirm that the *Metamorphoses* were written for an audience of Roman citizens above all others, rather than, say, for Carthaginian readers, or readers more generally from the provinces of the Empire? To respond to this question, and to begin confronting the problem of Apuleius' cultural identity, let us examine the two cases that seem to me most significant.[46]

Apuleius mentions a *forum cupidinis* in Hypata three times (1.24.3; 1.25.1; 2.2.1). Rather than a reference to a real place in the Thessalian city, this seems to be a very learned allusion to the ancient *forum cupidinis* that existed in Rome three centuries before Apuleius' time.[47] In other words, the allusion would be utterly obscure to a readership that had little familiarity with the ancient topography of Rome ("ancient" already by the second century C.E.). Nevertheless, given that by Apuleius' time only the name of this spot had survived, Apuleius himself could only have known of the *forum cupidinis* through ancient literary sources, not direct experience. These sources, of course, were available, and were read, not only in Rome. Residence in Rome, then, is not an absolutely necessary prerequisite in recognizing the significance of this Roman place name.

---

46. Many other elements of Romanization introduced by Apuleius in the ass-story (though of less significance to those who would prefer to hypothesize a metropolitan rather than provincial audience) are collected by Scivoletto 1963 and Rosati 2003.

47. See Scivoletto 1963, 236 ff.; cf. also Van Mal-Maeder 2001, 66 *ad loc.*, who puts special emphasis on the wordplay ("for Lucius, who searches for a full satisfaction of his desires . . . all roads lead to the *forum cupidinis*").

The second case, concerning the *metae Murtiae* in the Circus Maximus, is more interesting, since these structures still existed in Apuleius' day. At 6.8.2, Mercury announces that Venus will reward with eight kisses the informer who reveals the place where the fugitive Psyche has taken refuge: the place to meet her, and the payment in reward, are set for a spot behind the *metae Murtiae*, as the area surrounding an ancient shrine to *Venus Murtia* was called.[48] The sketch is even more humorous if one knows that inside the Circus Maximus, where the old shrine of *Venus Murtia* was located, was the area to which one would go in search of the most popular young prostitutes.[49] Consequently, Mercury's announcement assimilates the beautiful goddess to a prostitute by implication. Nevertheless, here too I think we have reasonable grounds for doubting that this reference to a location in the city was obscure or unintelligible to people not living in Rome. Mentions of the shrine of *Venus Murtia* are not absent from literature: close to Apuleius' day we find Plutarch (*Q. Rom.* 20.268e) and Tertullian (*Spect.* 8.6), who speak of the *metae Murtiae* or of Venus' shrine. These authors probably did not think of people living in Rome as their primary audience. Of course, their writings had certain didactic aims, while Mercury's speech in the *Metamorphoses* is more allusive, and difficult to understand. The point of the reference to the *metae Murtiae* in the novel would, no doubt, be lost on the modern reader without the aid of a learned commentary. But I do not think that either Plutarch or Tertullian would have dealt with such details, even *en passant*, had they been completely abstruse for the majority of their readers. The Circus was represented in a great number of coins, mosaics and reliefs, and its shape was familiar throughout the Empire, as were its restorations and reconstructions by various emperors. The shrine of *Venus Murtia* is sometimes clearly recognizable in these iconographic media.[50] Finally, it is worth quoting the *elogium* of M. Valerius Maximus (*CIL* I², 189 n. V), originally located in the Forum Augustum, that survives for us in a copy found in Arretium. The inscription says that the dictator obtained the honor of a curule seat *ad Murciae spectandi causa*, that is, in a privileged place in the Circus, near the

---

48. For information and the sources on *Venus Murtia*, cf. Humphrey 1986, 60 f. and 95 f.; Coarelli 1996 and 1999. On the spelling *Murtiae* (rather than *Murciae*) and the connection between the ancient divinity *Murcia* and *Venus Murtia*, see above all Marangoni 2000, 84–87. In both Harrison 1998b and Rosati 2003, 280 the mention of the *metae Murciae* is one of the elements that might cause us to believe that Apuleius addressed a specifically Roman audience (but see also Harrison 2002b, 49, which seems to welcome the thesis espoused here, already represented in Graverini 2002b, 70 ff.).

49. Marmorale 1958, 203.

50. The sources are collected in Humphrey 1986; see also Coarelli 1996 and 1999. Examples include, e.g., depictions found on a relief in Foligno, a mosaic in the Piazza Armerina, and several coins issued by Trajan.

shrine. The *elogia* of the Forum Augustum, as well as other monuments, were reproduced in Arretium and elsewhere in the empire. It is, therefore, through literature, inscriptions, iconography, and coins that the shape of the capital of the empire—specifically its monuments, topography, and toponyms—were made familiar even to those who had never visited it.[51] Even without having set foot in Rome, a well-informed provincial could have known of the *metae Murtiae* and of the activities taking place around it—just as one need not be from New York City to know what is meant by a reference to Harlem or to Soho, should a modern reader encounter a novel that locates a scene there.

But above all, I would emphasize that Apuleius' text, though it incorporates some allusions that can be considered literate and detailed, does not invest these allusions with a fundamental significance. The *lector scrupulosus* (the "careful reader," whom the narrator addresses at 9.30.1) might fully comprehend these subtleties with greater or lesser ease, but those readers who were not as shrewd would not have their pleasure in the text jeopardized, even if they failed to grasp the fullest meaning of the allusions and details. They could well ignore everything about the *forum cupidinis* or the *metae Murtiae*, taking them as simple toponyms without specific literary resonances, and still enjoy the sketches of the zealous *curator annonae* Pythias trampling the fish Lucius has just bought, or of Mercury advertising the voluptuous reward promised by Venus. In the end, I think that none of these specific references to the city requires an audience that was primarily or exclusively made up of Roman citizens, or that was intimately familiar with the topography of the city.

Beyond toponyms, there are also other arguments that might press us to adopt a Romanocentric perspective (in a narrow sense), and to identify the city of Rome as the primary "market" for which Apuleius wrote the *Metamorphoses*. In particular, Ken Dowden maintained that the *Metamorphoses* were written in Rome itself, where we know Apuleius spent some time (*Florida* 17.4), probably before his trial in Sabratha (158–159 C.E.). In Dowden's view, naturally, the idea that the people of the capital city were

---

51. In Carthage, we know of copies of the *Ara Pacis Augustae* and of the *elogium* of M. Claudius Marcellus: see Torelli 1975, 99–100 and Galinsky 1996, 150, with further bibliography. On the periphery of the Empire there were a great number of Roman citizens carrying out administrative functions or doing their own business, and local elites often traveled to Rome: cf. Noy 2000, 252 ff., in particular, for travelers going to Rome from North Africa; and Fantham 1996, 236 ff. on the traveling poet Annius Florus. Ann Kuttner suggested to me *per litteras* that "a shared knowledge of the city of Rome" contributed to the bonding of Roman elites abroad. Of course, poetry and iconography also made the whole empire familiar to the citizens of Rome. For a short but dense survey of geographical and iconographical themes in Imperial poetry, cf. Connors 2000, 508 ff.

the primary target and immediate audience obviously gains strength.[52] Let us examine the arguments proposed by Dowden:

1) Rome as the traditional "market" for literary production. Although one would think that the provinces of the Empire were considered a prime audience for authors who were from the provinces, in effect "there is little evidence of anything but literature for the elite of Rome and for the imperial circles."[53] Latin authors usually wrote and published at Rome; if Apuleius had been primarily addressing provincial audiences and the North African market, he would be practically unique. The *Florida* and *Apologia* themselves were written for the Roman market: the same Carthaginian audience that attended Apuleius' oratorical displays is painted in "Roman colors," and Carthage becomes a sort of "derivative Rome."[54]

Indeed, it seems difficult to find significant exceptions to the rule that normally one wrote in Rome and for a Roman public. The twelfth book of Martial (or, at least, a good portion of the epigrams contained therein) was written in his native Spain, where the poet decided to return, disgusted with the capital; but the introduction overflows with regret at the loss of the cultural and social life that the capital alone could afford, and that had now been replaced by *provincialis solitudo* in Bilbilis. The second epigram of the collection is an apostrophe to the "traveling book," that will go to Rome to be reunited with its "brothers," who have already made their way there. Martial's farewell is loaded with a sadness that leads us to identify him with Ovid, after he was exiled to desolate lands of Pontus.[55] In the case of Book 12, Martial imagines a movement from the provinces to Rome, but in his own earlier poetry Martial described a centrifugal movement that, he hoped, would bring his writings and his fame to the edge of the most distant provinces of the Empire.[56] If Rome, then, is the primary destina-

---

52. Dowden 1994. Hunink 2002, the most recent contributor to the dating of Apuleius' novel, does not find Dowden's arguments completely persuasive, though he finds attractive the hypothesis of locating the *Metamorphoses* in the milieu of Roman culture (and, naturally, at an early stage of Apuleius' literary career).
53. Dowden 1994, 422; cf. Hunink 2002, 226.
54. Dowden 1994, 422.
55. Cf. for example Martial 12.2.2 *ibis, io, Romam nunc peregrine liber* with Ovid *Tristia* 1.1.1 *parve—nec invideo—sine me, liber, ibis in urbem.* See Graverini 2005a, 230 for a fuller discussion and bibliography.
56. 12.2.1-2 *Ad populos mitti qui nuper ab urbe solebas, / ibis, io, Romam nunc peregrine liber.* The aspiration to universal fame is a constant feature in Martial, who often proudly affirms that his epigrams will be read all over the world: cf. for example 1.1.2; 7.88.1 ff.; 8.3.4; 8.61.3-5; and 11.3.3 ff.; and see Graverini 2005a, 243 ff. A useful collection of similar passages in other authors (but with

tion of the poet's writings, he also imagined a wider diffusion from the outset. Moreover, Roman Africa, and Carthage in particular, constituted a more stimulating atmosphere from a cultural point of view than Martial's Spain; and from reading the *Florida* one can see that, in Carthage, Apuleius found himself in front of a large audience that was able to understand the rhetorical and philosophical subtleties of his orations.[57] With regard to the *Florida* themselves, we can by no means take it as given that a Roman rather than a Carthaginian audience was the primary target for the production of the anthology: considering the connections of many of the *Florida* fragments with Carthage and Africa, it is entirely probable that "the anthologist (whether Apuleius himself, or more likely, someone else) did his work from a personal sense of national pride, or with his eyes set on a clearly marked audience, e.g. the urban elite of Carthage."[58]

If then, *a priori*, there are very well-founded reasons for locating the *Metamorphoses* in this more general trend, and for viewing the city of Rome as the center of interest for the production of Latin literature, we must not forget the fact that many authors explicitly state their desire to find readers in every corner of the Empire. In Apuleius' day, Roman Africa was characterized by a vivacious cultural atmosphere, and Carthage was indeed the most direct and immediate intended audience for at least a portion of Apuleius' literary production (as evidenced by the *Florida*). There are certainly marked differences between Apuleius' rhetorical anthology and his novel, and the two cannot be treated identically. Nevertheless, as we will see later, there are important points of contact between the *Metamorphoses* and *Florida*, which allow us to imagine an audience for both works that was ultimately analogous. This audience was diverse and heterogeneous in regard to cultural background and social status. Naturally we could imagine this kind of audience in Rome, but there is nothing to hinder us from imagining it in Car-

---

special regard to Ovid) can be found in Citroni 1975, 15 (on Martial 1.1.2); see also Nisbet-Hubbard 1978, 333 ff. (on Horace, *Carm.* 2.20), who conclude that "the ambition for world-wide fame is attested as early as Alcman . . . and becomes a commonplace with Hellenistic and Roman poets."

57. On the Carthaginian audience of the *Florida* and on the vivacity of the African cultural climate, see for example Fick 1987; Harris 1989, 287 (for whom "only Africa Proconsularis, Numidia, Dalmatia, and Narbonensis are likely, as provinces, to have reached Italian levels of literacy"); Gualandri 1989b, 521 ff.; Sandy 1997, 16–20; Vössing 1997, 444 ff.; Dewar 2000, 521; A. La Rocca 2005, 35–49. On the wealth and importance of Carthage during the second century c.e., see Hurst 1993, 327–337. More generally, for a conception of Latin literary production that is less "centripetal" than Dowden's, see Gualandri 1989a.

58. Hunink 2001, 13; for Lee 2005, 14 "the Florida could be correctly termed Carthaginian orations." See also Harrison 2000, 132–134, who is more prone than Hunink to think that Apuleius himself had edited the original collection in four books, from which our current collection seems to have been drawn.

thage also, or in other cities on the periphery of the Empire that sustained a lively culture.

2) The manuscript tradition. The *Apology, Florida* and *Metamorphoses* have survived only because they were read and copied in Rome, as demonstrated by the *subscriptio* of Sallustius, now preserved in the Laurentian codex.[59]

The survival of Apuleius' works was due to an historical process, and not necessarily to Apuleius' intention. Sallustius' subscription proves only that somebody in Rome read Apuleius, not necessarily that Apuleius himself intended his work to be read primarily in Rome—nor that his works were actually read more there than in Africa. To the contrary, St. Augustine (*Epist.* 138.19) suggests that Apuleius, as an African, was more familiar to the Africans;[60] and if we can trust the *Historia Augusta,* Septimius Severus hinted that the familiarity Clodius Albinus demonstrated with the *Milesiae* of Apuleius ("his" Apuleius) was also connected to their common African nationality.[61] Neither Augustine, nor the *Historia Augusta,* naturally, can provide conclusive proof affirming that Apuleius addressed himself above all to a Carthaginian audience; nevertheless, these texts certainly encourage us to be wary of setting his literary production in an exclusively Roman context.

3) The absence of Carthage in the novel. This absence is particularly surprising in a novel that contains a number of clear-cut autobiographical allusions; it can be interpreted as an *argumentum ex silentio* for locating the composition of the *Metamorphoses* in a period earlier than Apuleius' move to Carthage, more specifically, during his sojourn in Rome.[62]

Undoubtedly, Africa sees little mention in the novel. We might have expected a reference to Africa in the prologue, where much of the rest of the Mediterranean world receives some notice: Greece (1.1.3 *Hymettos Attica et Isthmos Ephyrea et Taenaros Spartiatica*), Rome (1.1.4 *in urbe Latia*), Egypt (1.1.1 *Papyrum Aegyptiam argutia Nilotici calami inscriptam*), and Asia Minor (1.1.1 *sermone . . . Milesio*). Nevertheless, there is a rationale behind

---

59. Dowden 1994, 423–424. On the *subscriptio* of Sallustius, see several essays collected in Pecere-Stramaglia 2003.

60. *Epist.* 138.19 *Apuleius . . . qui nobis Afris Afer est notior.* On Augustine and Apuleius see now Hunink 2003.

61. *Albinus* 12.12; the text cited here is found on pp. 96 ff. On the precocious diffusion of Apuleius' works in Africa, see Stramaglia 1996b, 139 ff.

62. Dowden 1994, 425.

such a broad selection. The *Metamorphoses* makes adjustments to a preexisting Greek original, and this fact makes it nearly inevitable that a good portion of the story would be set in Greece; it also explains why Greece should play a prominent role in the prologue. The mentions of Rome, Egypt, and Asia Minor allude to precise literary choices made by Apuleius: these are his connection with the "Milesian genre,"[63] the importance of Egyptian cults, and Lucius' final voyage to Rome. The absence of Africa in the prologue, then, reflects its absence in the plot of the novel at large, since Apuleius' plot adheres closely to the lost Greek original. Indeed, Apuleius did significantly alter the closing of the novel by adding a new ending that was set in Rome. The fact that Lucius ends up in Rome rather than Carthage, for example, could be considered significant and might (along with many other factors) prevent us from defining the *Metamorphoses* as truly "local" literature, but it cannot tell us more than that. Apuleius' decision to set the ending of the *Metamorphoses* in Rome does not express a sort of metropolitan parochialism; rather, it reflects the universal significance Rome held throughout the Empire.

Furthermore, Africa is not entirely absent from the novel. I will return later in this chapter to the *celsa Carthago* mentioned in 6.4.1 in connection with the cult of Juno. For the moment, we will focus on the famous—or infamous—term *Madaurensem,* which appears near the end of the novel (11.27.9). The context indicates clearly that the adjective refers to Lucius, who is from Corinth; Apuleius, however, comes from Madauros. Is this an error introduced by the manuscript tradition,[64] or did Apuleius deliberately exchange the hometown of the protagonist for his own? It is difficult to say with complete certainty, though modern criticism has always found the second hypothesis most intriguing.[65] Putting aside for the moment the intrinsically attractive hermeneutics that derive from the term *Madaurensem,* I think there are good reasons (both literary and intertextual) for maintaining the manuscript reading. At the end of the *Onos,* too, the reader is invited more or less explicitly to identify the protagonist as the author of the story. Since there are far too many Luciuses in this story, we can leave aside here the problem of the author's name;[66] still, as it seems to me, it is significant

---

63. For more on this term, see above, p. 5 n. 12.

64. Robertson's Budé (1971–72[4]) declines to note the possibility of a textual error, while Helm's Teubner (1955[4]) includes Goldbacher's conjecture *mane Doriensem*. There are useful notes in Fredouille 1975, 15–18 and *ad loc.;* Griffiths 1975 *ad loc;* and Harrison 2000, 228–231. Of these, Fredouille is the least reluctant to adopt a conjecture over the manuscript reading.

65. A slightly more detailed analysis of this text and more bibliographical references can be found in Graverini 2005a, 231–232.

66. On this question see Mason 1994, 1669 ff.

that after his transformation, Lucius describes himself as an author of stories and tales (55: ἱστοριῶν καὶ ἄλλων εἰμὶ συγγραφεύς). It is quite likely that the lost Greek original contained some declaration to this effect, and so probably contributed to the inexorable confusion surrounding the character Lucius and the names of the authors "Lucius of Patrae" and "Lucian." If the Greek original did include such a reference, the unexpected identification between author and character found at the end of the *Metamorphoses* merely reproduces a literary form of play that had characterized the ass-story from its beginning.[67] We seem to be dealing, in effect, with a touch of self-irony, a quality that is well adapted to the "satiric" characteristics of the *Metamorphoses,* as I discussed above (§ 2.7). Apuleius is clearly conscious that the reader will tend to identify the author with the protagonist in a first-person narrative, and anticipates that he might be perceived as having actually been transformed into an ass (as is well known, Augustine seems uncertain as to whether the events narrated in the novel were fictitious or autobiographical).[68] Apuleius repeats the joke made by his predecessors, but with significant alterations. He identifies himself more explicitly with the term *Madaurensem,* far more suggestive than simply being a "writer of tales," the claim made by the protagonist in the *Onos.* At the same time, Apuleius introduces an element of constraint by immediately adding the phrase *sed admodum pauperem.* This detail might discourage the reader from exaggerating the validity of an identification with Apuleius, since, as has been noted, Apuleius was certainly not poor.[69] But of greater interest here is the manner in which Apuleius chose to suggest an identification between author and

---

67. The term *Madaurensem* at 11.27.9 consequently represents, it seems to me, a small but significant exception to the common view, in which "the end of Book 10 is the point where the *Met.* and *Onos* diverge permanently" (M. Zimmermann 2000, 18).

68. See Augustine, *Civ.* 18.18. Cf. Carver 2001, 169: "To the narrator's question *quis ille,* the response of pre-modern readers was generally 'Lucius Apuleius Madaurensis.'" This was the case, despite the fact that the autobiographical details supplied by the speaking *ego* in the prologue (in particular, his Greek nativity) do not agree with Apuleius' personal history. The structure of the ass-story, narrated in the first person, lends itself well to literary play of this kind: the potential to freely mix irony and satire with autobiographical cues is well demonstrated by the *L'asino d'oro* of Agnolo Firenzuola (1523–1525).

69. This interpretation, naturally, emphasizes the adversative force of the conjunction *sed,* in contradistinction to Van der Paardt 1981, 242. On Apuleius' wealth see *Apology* 23: Apuleius and his brother inherited approximately two million sesterces from their father, even though a variety of expenditures, and largesse, had diminished the inheritance remaining at Apuleius' disposal. It is, however, prudent to take into account that an array of literary and procedural strategies are at work here, and that it is consequently difficult to consider his testimony as an entirely objective source. Hunink 1997, 97 *ad loc.* correctly notes that "we are left with a rather confusing impression: Apuleius was, in a way, both poor and rich." In any case, it seems entirely reasonable to assume that *admodum pauper* is a definition better suited to the protagonist of the novel.

protagonist: the mention of Madauros could be interpreted in several ways, but we cannot exclude the possibility that it is a subtle nod to an African audience, who have thereby been invited to sympathize with a protagonist/author who comes from their own province.[70]

4) The Metamorphoses *in the* Apology? In several instances, the *Apology* and *Metamorphoses* utilize similar phraseology. An example of almost literal correspondence occurs at *Apology* 64.1, where Mercury is described as *iste superum et inferum commeator* ("messenger of both heaven and the infernal regions"), just as Anubis is described in the *Metamorphoses* (*ille superum commeator et inferum,* 11.11.1). Later in the same chapter of the *Apology* (64.7), the supreme deity is defined as *totius rerum naturae causa et ratio et origo initialis, summus animi genitor* ("the cause, reason and origin of all nature, highest creator of the human spirit"); similar terminology is used to describe Venus in the novel (*rerum naturae prisca parens . . . elementorum origo initialis,* "ancient mother of nature, the origin and beginning of the elements," 4.30.1). For Dowden these sorts of expressions are "called into existence by theological concerns, not invented for occasional use in a speech," and for this reason, "the likely direction of transit of these terms is from the *Metamorphoses* to the *Apologia.*"[71]

Now there is certainly nothing strange about defining Mercury as a god who acts as a mediator between the celestial and infernal deities, since the phrase is found at Horace *Carm.* 1.10.19–20, where Mercury is referred to as *superis deorum / gratus et imis* ("welcome to the gods highest above and furthest below"). Naturally, it may not be the case that Apuleius consulted Horace's poem before constructing this description of Mercury; yet, if Horace was indeed Apuleius' source, a more extended echo of *Carm.* 1.10 might be identified in the *Apology* than in the *Metamorphoses.* Apuleius' self-defense includes a description of a miniature statue of Mercury as having a *facies . . . suci palaestrici plena* ("a look full of athletic vigor"); this connection between Mercury and athletes is also found in *Carm.* 1.10.3–4

---

70. Naturally, one could come to the opposite interpretation, that it is a sort of self-ironic confession (or *captatio benevolentiae*) addressed to a Roman audience. For Bradley 2005, 22 Apuleius' birth in Madauros is indicative of the "cultural as well as geographic distance he traveled in making himself a man of Greek and Latin letters." For an overview of the interpretive possibilities afforded by the term *Madaurensem,* see Harrison 2000, 228 ff.

71. Dowden 1994, 427, with other less important examples noted in n. 19. Further possible influences of the *Metamorphoses* on the *Apology* and vice versa are examined in Hunink 2002, 226–232; they are fairly general comparisons, however, and Hunink finds, based on the collection of evidence, that we cannot draw any definitive conclusions regarding the relative dating of the two works.

(*formasti . . . et decore / more palaestrae* "you have decorously molded [sc. *men*], too, in the habit of the palaestra").

Beyond the possibility of there being a Horatian intertext, the phrase *superum et inferum commeator* has nothing peculiar or decorative about it in the context of the *Apology*. Apuleius was refuting the accusation (described in *Apology* 63) of having commissioned "an eerie representation of a cadaver" for use in rites of black magic, a miniature statue made of wood that the accusers had described with the words *sceletus, larva,* and *daemonium.* As a means of self-defense, Apuleius explains that the object in fact represents not a *daimon,* but the god Mercury; he goes on to say that the figure has nothing ghostly about it, but rather displays, as we have seen, a "graceful face, full of athletic vigor." For greater effect, the object itself was displayed in court. If the same representation[72] could be described as both a *larva* (ghost) and as a Greek god of athletic appearance (perhaps with a bit of exaggeration by one or both sides of the dispute), it is likely that the figure possessed some ambiguous traits, which would not have passed unobserved when it was put on display. Its dark color (it was carved from ebony-wood, as we learn from *Apology* 61.7) might certainly have given rise to suspicion. The decision to display the statue in court made it necessary to address anything ambiguous about the figurine, and to present it favorably by bringing it into evidence. It would have been pointless, and even counterproductive, to pass such traits over in silence. Apuleius adopted the same rhetorical strategy when he spoke about his long hair: it could either be interpreted as proof of his vanity or indicate a lack of concern for his appearance, in an attitude typical of a philosopher.[73] It is well established that Mercury was both a heavenly and infernal deity. What matters is not the statue itself, but the eye of the observer: *hunc denique qui larvam putat, ipse est larvans* ("who sees in this image a ghost, is himself ghastly"). In this way, Apuleius can invoke the curse of Mercury as an infernal deity on Aemilianus and retain for himself, as well as for the *Platonica familia,* the knowledge of all that is "pleasing, happy, sacred, divine, and heavenly" (64.3).

The description *superum et inferum commeator,* then, has a *raison d'être* in the *Apology,* just as it does in the *Metamorphoses*. In general, the *Apol-*

---

72. It is hard for me to imagine that Apuleius could have exhibited in court a miniature statue different from the one described by his accusers (*sic* Hunink 1997, 167 *ad* 63.4). This would have been a risky gambit to try in front of his accusers (who were not entirely unprepared) and particularly in front of the sculptor himself, Saturninus, since they were all in court at the time (cf. 61.6). Hunink suggests it is possible that Saturninus could have fabricated more than one statue for Apuleius, but this idea seems to be totally unwarranted.

73. *Apology* 4; cf. above, pp. 88 f.

ogy is hardly lacking in theological concerns, given that Apuleius endeavors in every way to emphasize his devotion to both the gods and to philosophy. This double devotion, he claims, explains his complete unfamiliarity with magical practices. Consequently, the recurrence in this work of a certain kind of standard phraseology, used for epithets and descriptions of divinities,[74] should not be a great surprise to us.

5) Culture and current events in Rome around 150 C.E. In the second half of the second century C.E., the philosopher Sextus was still active in Athens and in Rome (though he was probably quite elderly); at the beginning of the novel, Lucius mentions him along with Plutarch as being his most illustrious ancestor.[75] The cult of the *Dea Syria*, which Lucius describes in the most unflattering terms,[76] was prominent in Rome, but not in Africa; therefore, "for Apuleius to attack the *Dea Syria* at all implies a Roman perspective."[77] Furthermore, the particular attitude displayed by Apuleius towards this cult seems to echo a passage of the *Epitome* of Florus (2.7), normally dated to around the end of the reign of Hadrian (138 C.E.), or perhaps a few years later. The martyrdoms of Saint Tolomeus and Saint Lucius take place in Rome under Antoninus Pius (Justin, *Apol.* 2.2), and their stories present several analogies to the story of the miller's wife in *Metamorphoses* Book 9. The virulence of the narrator's attacks on her monotheism corresponds closely to the anti-Christian polemics of the Roman elite of that period.[78] The fact that several narrative elements in the novel would appear far more lively and contemporary in such a setting would seem to suggest Rome around 150 C.E. as a plausible context for the writing of the *Metamorphoses*.

---

74. A phraseology, however, that is not singular to Apuleius but has a discernible literary tradition; for the Lucretian roots of Apuleius' description of the highest god in the *Apology*, and of Venus and Isis in the *Metamorphoses*, see *GCA* 2004 *ad* 4.30.1; see also Finkelpearl 1998, 201 ff. Less significant seem to me the analogies proposed by Dowden 1994, 427 f. between *Apology* 43 (on the divinatory capacities more easily possessed by the young) and the description of Psyche in the *Metamorphoses*. There are undoubtedly similarities in phraseology (43.3 *animum humanum . . . puerilem et simplicem;* cf. *Met.* 5.18.4 *Psyche . . . simplex et animi tenella*), but the passages in question are more helpful in delineating the connections between Apuleius and Middle Platonic thought (on which see the excellent studies by Dowden [1982 and 1998]) than they are helpful in stabilizing a chronology for the two works.

75. *Met.* 1.2.1 *originis maternae nostrae fundamenta a Plutarcho illo inclito ac mox Sexto philosopho nepote eius prodita gloriam nobis faciunt.*

76. See above, pp. 79 ff.

77. Dowden 1994, 431.

78. On this question see Dowden 1994, 428–431 with further references and more detailed argumentation.

Naturally, we are dealing with arguments that have a purely general and approximate validity. Their force rests not so much in precise verbal correspondences (such as those suggested above), but rather in a convergence of several clues, which could suggest a time and place. Nevertheless, a few specific considerations weaken the link between contemporary events and these elements of the novel (elements that, furthermore, play only a secondary role). First of all, in regard to the philosopher Sextus, even in the third century C.E. the Sophist Nicagoras boasted that he was "a descendant of the philosophers Plutarchus and Sextus,"[79] precisely as Lucius had many years before him. Secondly, despite the fact that Apuleius' language resembles the passage in Florus, the Pseudo-Lucianic *Onos* also contains a passage expressing contempt for the ritual practices of the priest of the *Dea Syria* cult, even if that contempt is less pronounced than in Apuleius' version.[80] The *Onos*, then, provides an easier and better explanation for Apuleius' passage than current events in Rome. Finally, while the martyrdoms of Saint Tolomeus and Saint Lucius present analogies to the tale of the miller's wife in the *Metamorphoses*, they also show significant divergences from it. Above all, there is a complete reversal of roles, given that in Apuleius it is the husband who repudiates his wife for her vices (9.28.4), while in Justin's narrative, the wife repudiates her husband. The depiction of a depraved Christian woman (or probably Christian in the case of Apuleius), found in both texts,[81] presents decidedly little cause for us to believe that Apuleius had direct or indirect knowledge of the trials of the two martyrs; and if we need a contemporary reference to explain the ferocity with which Lucius rails against the woman's monotheism, we need only to consider the rapid spread of Christianity in Africa itself, where the martyrdom of the Scillitani occurred in 180 C.E.[82]

---

79. *IG* 22.3814; this astute observation was noted by Keulen 2007b, 94. Perhaps one might object that, in a Latin novel, the reference to Sextus is less 'natural' than in the case of a Greek sophist; and hence it would be more significant, should we want to preserve the possibility of a closer chronological proximity between the writing of the *Metamorphoses* and the activity of the philosopher. It seems to me, however, that if we take into account how often Apuleius vaunted his Greek culture, this argument would be particularly weak. Note also that Millar 1981, 65 and n. 14 locates the date after 161 and not before 150, when Marcus Aurelius heard Sextus lecture (who in that case would have had to live well past the middle of the second century).

80. *Onos* 35–41. In particular, chapter 38 emphasizes the licentiousness, ἀσέλγεια, on the part of the priests, who are termed also "impious," δυσσεβεῖς, at 41; their cult practices are described with manifest disgust in chapter 37, though the ass characteristically makes it clear that he is chiefly worried that "the goddess might also need the blood of an ass." Cf. also above, pp. 79 ff.

81. In Justin, however, the woman is depraved until she becomes Christian, and with her conversion to the Christian faith she abandons her previously sinful life—which obviously is not the case in Apuleius.

82. Baldwin 1989 also explores the historical context of this passage; he was the first to reveal the correspondence between Apuleius and the hagiographies in Justin. The comparisons offered by

In sum, it seems to me that the arguments in favor of locating the composition of the *Metamorphoses* in Rome around 150 C.E. are fairly weak. This impression is confirmed if we take notice of two further factors. First, the *Metamorphoses* itself seems to implicitly suggest that Lucius narrated, or wrote, his story in Rome, the final destination of his journeys;[83] but here we should keep in mind that the character of Lucius cannot be superimposed entirely onto the life of the author, Apuleius. The second point to be made, following the study by Filippo Coarelli, is that archaeology offers several clues that would permit an identification of the names not only of Apuleius, but also of the Asinius Marcellus named at 11.27.7, and locate them in Ostia about 150 C.E. Nevertheless, there is not a firm scholarly consensus regarding the conclusions reached by Coarelli, and, at the risk of repeating myself, it is not necessary to assume that the mention of Asinius Marcellus is a reference to a contemporary historical personality.[84]

On the other hand, the arguments usually presented for a later date are not entirely persuasive, either. Such a later date would make it more likely that Apuleius had written the novel in Carthage, but this must remain purely hypothesis. There is no need to deal with a detailed analysis here;[85] suffice it to say that the strongest argument is in fact an *argumentum ex silentio* (even if it might have a fairly firm logical basis). This argument claims that if indeed the *Metamorphoses* had already been written by the time of the trial in Sabrata, it seems quite odd that Apuleius' accusers did not make use of the novel when they charged him with practicing magic. This would explain why Apuleius did not have to concern himself with refuting this "element of proof" in his *Apology*.[86] Augustine, in fact, shows that it was entirely natural

---

Schmidt 2003, who sees an allusion to the Christian Eucharist in Apuleius' story, would also return the date to 160–170 C.E. Hunink 2002, 226, however, suggests (without solid basis) that "writing an anti-Christian novel would be a more promising enterprise in Rome of the 150s than in provincial Africa, of, say, the 170s." The question of whether Apuleius would have known of any Christian texts or events concerning the diffusion of Christianity has been much debated: see Dowden 1994; Hijmans in *GCA* 1995, app. 4, pp. 380–382; Mattiacci 1996, 142; Hunink 2000. See also above, p. 79 n. 78.

83. Rosati 2003, 277 makes this point. It is true that no reference to the future travels of Lucius is made, and that at the end of the novel we leave him happily established in the capital of the Empire, but it seems excessive to maintain that future movements seem to be excluded according to divine will (*sic* Rosati, citing 11.29.5 and 11.30.4 for support of his argument).

84. We cannot exclude the possibility of an homage dedicated to a friend or a patron who had died long since, perhaps in honor of one of his descendants. Furthermore, although Coarelli 1989 maintains that it is unlikely, the same Asinius Marcellus in the novel could in fact be a different person than the one referred to in the Ostia inscription (whose death can be dated to around 148)—perhaps a son or parent. On this question see above, pp. 68 f.

85. For an overview of this argument and further bibliography, see Münstermann 1995, 125 ff.; Hunink 1997, 21–22; Harrison 2000, 9 ff.; Hunink 2002.

86. According to Hunink 2002, 233, too, this *argumentum ex silentio* is the main foothold (though it is anything but certain) for dating the novel: "it seems impossible to imagine Apuleius

to consider the novel partially biographical, since it is narrated in the first person,[87] and Apuleius' accusers made use of far weaker and more fantastic arguments to prove their case.

4.4.2 CENTRIFUGAL FORCES AND INTEGRATION

The argument that Apuleius composed the *Metamorphoses* in his maturity and after the *Apology*, when he was probably established in Carthage, is therefore nothing more than an hypothesis, however reasonable and well accepted it may be. To take it as the starting point for larger interpretations of the novel could turn out to be risky; and, in fact, several scholarly positions that have operated under this assumption turn out to be open to question. For example, the question of the so-called *Africitas* of Apuleius' language once received a great deal of attention, but now it is generally agreed that there are no visible traces of linguistic usages that can be ascribed to a local African dialect.[88] Taking a different approach, Richard Summers analyzed thematic elements in the novel in an attempt to discern traces of an "African" or "provincial" perspective, and came to the conclusion that Apuleius was a staunch opponent of the central powers of the Empire. In his view, the purpose of the farcical trial in Book 3 (and of several other episodes in which Lucius or other characters suffer or fear an abuse of power by the established authorities) is to demonstrate that "justice in the provinces and for provincials can only be obtained if Rome returns the administration of criminal justice to the hands of the responsible municipal citizens rather

---

denying in court features which he had described himself in a popular novel." Hunink chiefly refers to passages such as *Apology* 84.3–4, where Apuleius denies *tout court* the existence of magic: therefore, "the speech cannot be possibly imagined if the novel with all its magic had preceded." Naturally, it is also possible—though it seems to me very unlikely—that Apuleius had already written the *Metamorphoses* by the time of the trial, and that his accusers had no knowledge of the novel, or decided not to make use of it; or that in his *Apology*, for some reason, Apuleius decided to pass over this part of the accusation in silence. Hunink 2002, 233 f. suggests that Apuleius could have written the novel during his years in Rome but kept it in a drawer until after the events in Sabratha, and then published it "in Rome or Africa not too long after 160." While this is a possibility that should be retained in theory, again, there appears to be no way to verify it.

87. *Civ.* 18.18; see above, p. 187 with n. 68.

88. The question was closed more or less definitively by Norden 1898, 588 ff.; more recently, Griffiths 1975, 59 ff. (especially 61–63) made an attempt to revitalize the idea of a partial and limited Punic influence on Apuleius' Latin, with little success; Kenney 1990, 29 suggests in more general terms that Apuleius' linguistic creativity shows an "exploitation of an adopted tongue, as by an Ennius or a Nabokov." Further references can be found in Dowden 1994, 421; Harrison 2002a, 161–162. See now also the fine analysis by Nicolini 2011, 31–37. More contributions on the subject will be contained in Lee–Finkelpearl–Graverini 2013.

than insisting upon the primary role of the provincial governor backed by the central authority of the emperor."[89] According to Summers, precaution and opportunity were Apuleius' motives for using a Milesian novel to convey these ideas. The message would have been clear to any reader in the provinces, but if the "shadow of Roman anger"[90] had turned against Apuleius, he could have argued that he had merely translated entertaining tales, and nothing more.

The improbability of this sort of picture becomes evident as soon as we look at it in a larger context: for example, in the *Apology* and *Florida* we can discern a clear loyalty in Apuleius' dealings with Roman magistrates. He even held the office of *sacerdos provinciae* in Carthage, a post that rendered him the ideal representative of the Carthaginians to the proconsul and the Roman senate, and entrusted him with maintaining the Imperial cult.[91] In any case, if we did in fact want to put stock in the depiction of Apuleius as an opportunist in his rhetorical works and as a secret revolutionary in his novel, we would have to lock horns with interpretative dilemmas of no small magnitude. In his effort to evaluate the episodes of the novel in the context of canons and codes of contemporary Roman law, Summers tends to ignore the literary context behind those episodes; and yet literary context provides the best explanation for them. Thus, his affirmation that Lucius' self-defense in the theater of Hypata (3.5–6) "vacillates between sincere and objective testimony and fear"[92] has the effect of eliding the vast discrepancy between what "really" happened that night in front of Milo's house and Lucius' account of it. Lucius had stabbed not innocent citizens (as the accusation maintained), nor violent brigands (as he himself claimed), but merely animal skins that had been animated by sorcery.[93] Clearly then, Lucius relates what he thought he saw through the fumes of alcohol, and his testimony is anything but "objective." Nor does it make much sense to maintain that Lucius was unjustly accused of having violated the *lex Cornelia de sicariis*, which applied to premeditated homicide, rather than some local law:[94] he

---

89. Summers 1970, 530.
90. Summers 1970, 531.
91. Following the testimony of Augustine, *Epist.* 138.19. On Apuleius' holding of this office, and more generally on the problems connected with the reconstruction of his political career in Carthage, see now the well-informed treatment of A. La Rocca 2005, 20 ff.; Lee 2005, 145–146.
92. Summers 1970, 513.
93. On these discrepancies, see most recently May 2007.
94. Summers 1970, 517. Needless to say, the difference between the different sorts of homicide was not unknown outside Rome: in the Greek novel, cf. e.g. Chariton 1.5.4, where Chaereas "used none of the arguments he could reasonably have used in his defense—that he was a victim of malicious slander, that he was moved by jealousy, and that his action was involuntary."

was in fact unjustly accused, regardless of premeditation. The distinction, furthermore, between premeditated homicide and manslaughter would have been the prerogative of every non-primitive judicial system, not only Roman law—and, in any case, a Roman reader would have naturally viewed this as a universal legal distinction. It is true, then, that Lucius and his accusers address premeditation (3.4–5), but according to the accusation (a false and farcical accusation, it is worth repeating), this homicide—whether it was premeditated murder or manslaughter—violates a universal norm, not the Roman *lex Cornelia*. It could be argued that, here and in other scenes of the novel, the established authorities appear to be threatening and unjust. But, at the same time, it seems to be forcing the text to maintain that the purpose of the account is to emphasize the abuses of power evident in the Roman administration of justice.[95] Clearly, all ends well for Lucius not because the presiding magistrates are citizens of Hypata rather than Romans,[96] but because it was a mock trial from the very beginning.

There are other analogous instances of overinterpretation that vitiate Summers's conclusions, such as, for example, his claim that "it is because of his dealings with Roman private law that Thelyphron suffers mutilation and humiliation."[97] This argument completely elides what is most important, namely, that the humiliation and ridicule Thelyphron undergoes are the direct consequence of his unscrupulous attitude towards sorcery, an attitude that prefigures Lucius' fate. Doubtless, Apuleius is fond of displaying his judicial erudition, and this is an important component of the Romanization of the ass-story; but it would bring us into dangerous and uncertain territory to venture too far down this road of biographical or even political interpretation of the judicial aspects of the novel.[98]

All this notwithstanding, there are at least two instances in which there

---

95. No more for example than Sosia's fear of being arrested and unjustly beaten (*Amphitruo* 155 ff.) would press us to make Plautus into a proponent of the cause of slaves and an opponent of the Roman judicial system. In general, it seems to be a more fruitful line of interpretation to view the trial in Hypata in the context of the narrative economy of the novel; see most recently Frangoulidis 2002.

96. Summers 1970, 520. But he himself cannot help but observe on the next page that "the entire trail scene is in fact a fantasy, in which logic plays a secondary role."

97. Summers 1970, 522. That the working relationship assumed between Thelyphron and the widow is more or less regulated according to the norms of the *locatio conductio operarum* clearly does not influence the outcome of subsequent events.

98. Along these lines see also Millar 1981, who reaches conclusions that differ greatly from Summers: "what the novel represents is Apuleius' assumptions as to how the local justice worked in these cities . . . when the governor was not there. . . . The world we are looking at is one wholly without policing by any Imperial forces. . . . Justice is highly localized" (pp. 70–71). Cf. also Elster 1991. Maehler 1981 calls attention to the humorous use of legal terminology. For a perspective that takes due notice of these judicial elements and locates them in the literary and narrative economy of the novel, see Keulen 1997.

are good arguments for identifying a "provincial perspective" in the novel. The most important of these episodes is perhaps that of the Roman soldier at 9.39.3, who speaks Latin and abuses a poor gardener who cannot understand his words. The text seems to imply that the *insolentia* of this soldier is typical of any soldier—by which is probably meant any *Roman* soldier:

> A tall man—a legionary soldier, as we were led to believe by his manners and dress—called to him in an insolent and arrogant tone, asking where he was taking an ass without any load. But my master, . . . who did not speak Latin, kept on going without a response. The soldier was unable to restrain the insolence typical of his kind (*familiaris . . . insolentia*): offended by the other's silence, as if he had been insulted, the soldier struck him with the vine-staff (*vitis*) he was carrying, and knocked him off my back.

In this case, too, we find several elements that would hinder us from considering the passage as an accurate and direct description of real life: the soldier is described simply as "legionary," but carries the *vitis* typical of a centurion;[99] it is also strange that the narrator mentions a legion, given that none were officially stationed in the province of Achaea.[100] Nevertheless, we clearly find here a vivid representation of the arrogance and brutality with which the centralized power of the Empire occasionally manifested itself, regardless of the scant attention the novel gives to depicting a reality that is "true," or its tendency toward stock characters such as are found in comedy generally.[101]

The second case is more complex, and of greater interest. Ellen Finkelpearl, in one of the most stimulating chapters of her book,[102] begins by observing that the description of Charite in Apuleius echoes Virgil's Dido in many respects, but that Apuleius depicts Charite as much more loyal to the memory of her dead husband. While Dido yields to the lures of a new lover, Charite instead resists the advances of Thrasyllus, and avenges the murder of her husband by blinding the wrongdoer before she kills herself

---

99. On this contradiction see Millar 1981, 68 with n. 25; GCA 1995, 236 *ad loc.*

100. Millar 1981, 68 with n. 27: "Apuleius might in this case have been misled by the system in Africa, where the *legio III Augusta* provided the *beneficiarii* for the proconsul." Does this represent another instance of provincial perspective? Cf. also GCA 1995, 324 *ad loc.*

101. Cf. Summers 1970, 526: "this scene, which is found in the *asinus* (44–45), has been adapted by Apuleius to place in clear focus the resentment of provincials toward the system of requisitions by the imperial government." For Millar 1981, 68 "the soldiers were a privileged official class whose presence was feared by the ordinary people." See also GCA 1995, 325 (*ad* 9.39.2 *superbo atque adroganti sermone*) and 326 (*ad* 9.39.4 *Graece*). On the corresponding scene in the *Onos* and its implications from the perspective of social history, see Hall 1995, 52.

102. Finkelpearl 1998, 115–148 ("Charite, Dido, and the Widow of Ephesus").

at her husband's tomb. Apuleius calls attention to his epic model through a variety of verbal allusions, but his divergence from Virgil becomes more significant when read in the context of how later African (or probably African) authors reacted to Virgil's version of the Dido-myth. This reaction takes shape in the form of a preference for pre-Virgilian versions of the Dido-myth,[103] in which Aeneas plays no role and the African queen's fidelity to her husband is not diminished.[104] In Apuleius, as in other authors, it seems likely that such literary choices were influenced by a sense of national pride in Africa, which produced a tendency to protect the Carthaginian heroine from Virgil's "slander."

There appear, then, to be at least a few instances in which Apuleius aims to stir up the emotions of readers who did not possess a "Romanocentric" point of view, or who were Romanocentric only in the broadest sense of the word—that is, readers whose fundamentally Latin cultural identity did not obliterate all cultural traditions and political perspectives that could be labeled as "local" or "provincial." This kind of reader is no chimera. In North Africa, the process of Romanization had been formidable, and left a deep mark on the region's language, religion, and urban landscape. Carthage in this era was no longer the same as the ancient Carthage, the age-old nemesis of Rome, destroyed in 146 B.C.E.; it was a new colony, like Corinth reborn under the rule of Caesar and Augustus. Roman culture, however, did not completely eradicate Punic tradition, but rather interacted with it in an historical process that never found a stable equilibrium, and which was still developing in Apuleius' day. The Punic language survived, even if it did not enjoy any prestige for men of culture like Apuleius (cf. *Apology* 98.8). Local influences can be detected in architecture, in religion, and even in nomenclature, which shows how even the descendants of the original Italic colonizers ended up giving their sons *cognomina* with Punic elements. Naturally, the degree of assimilation to Roman culture varied in relation both to an individual's social standing and to his level of urbanization.[105]

---

103. Macrobius, *Sat.* 5.17.5–6; Tertullian, *Apol.* 50; *Mart.* 4; *Castit.* 13; Augustine, *Conf.* 1.13.33; and *AG* 16.151. Cf. Finkelpearl 1998, 131 ff.

104. The lament of Dido in *AG* 16.151.9 is particularly significant: "O muses, why have you armed dire Maro and set him against me?" Finkelpearl 1998, 111–112 also stresses that Apuleius' literary process should be considered (consciously) antithetical to the account of the *Widow of Ephesus* found in Petronius, in which the novelistic version of Dido accentuates, rather than dampens, the traits of moral frailty ascribed to the Virgilian heroine. Petronius and Apuleius, then, seem to be exploring, albeit in different directions, the novelistic potential for transforming epic characters: "when novel and epic (or drama) come head-to-head, the subtlety of the characterization in the 'higher' genre, epic, is sacrificed, and its characters must be translated into the cardboard black or white figures we find in the novel" (p. 146).

105. Clear and up-to-date synthesis can be found in Finkelpearl 1998, 136–143, and Bradley

4.5 The readership of the novel

By necessity, all this compels us to ask what kind of readership Apuleius had in mind when he wrote the *Metamorphoses*. Thanks to the impossibility of dating the novel with any certainty, an answer to this question cannot help but involve a substantial degree of doubt and subjectivity, but it would be unwise to evade the problem. Every investigation into the literary and sociohistorical implications of a specific text must be based (whether implicitly or explicitly) on an hypothesis regarding the author and his readership.[106]

The complex intertextuality woven into the novel, as well as the literary humor that characterizes it, would seem to suggest that the work was written for the cultural elite. Nonetheless, this is an unwarranted assumption. Consider, for example, Umberto Eco's *The Name of the Rose*, which has been enjoyed by many readers who were not experts in medieval culture and who could not decipher its learned allusions (let alone read Latin). The modern system of copyright protection and royalties implies some degree of planning by Eco, or at least by his publisher, for a widespread distribution of his novel. In the case of Apuleius' readership, of course, we cannot point to the evidence of royalties, or to industrial systems of production and distribution. What little we know about Apuleius reveals that he liked to address large audiences, and that he put a high value on his fame and celebrity. Perhaps the *saccarii*—workers who loaded grain and transported it on cargo ships headed for Italy—would not have rushed to hear any of his public speeches in Carthage;[107] but since the crowd of listeners could fill a theater with a capacity of several thousand spectators, we must imagine that only a small fraction of them would have been made up of persons of

---

2005, which can be consulted for further details and bibliography. See also the full overview in Mattingly-Hitchner 1995, especially 184–186 and 204–209. For a discussion of "Romanization" as a concept, see now Mattingly 2004, with more references. An ample and highly detailed (though controversial) analysis of the interaction between Roman and African culture can be found in Bénabou 1976, who takes a divergent approach. Certainly, if the scope of the investigation is limited to literary facts that reflect a social and cultural elite (among whom the process of Romanization was more intense and more pervasive), the picture seems far more homogenous: thus Gualandri 1989b, 521 explains that "*Africanitas* . . . hardly appears to be cultural resistance to Rome." On the limits of Romanization in North Africa and the areas to which it was confined, see Cherry 1998. See also the forthcoming collection of studies edited by Lee–Finkelpearl–Graverini 2013.

106. Naturally, to speak of "readers" may already imply a prejudiced and misguided assumption. On the possibility of a partially oral diffusion not only for the pre-sophistic Greek novels but also for the *Metamorphoses*, see below n. 109.

107. Bradley 2005, 8 and 21.

refined culture.¹⁰⁸ Apuleius makes an explicit reference to his audience at *Florida* 18.1–2:

> So great is the crowd that has gathered to listen to me, that I must congratulate Carthage for the great number of aficionados of culture that it counts among its citizens, rather than excuse myself—I who am a philosopher—for not having refused to speak. In fact the crowd that has gathered is in keeping with the dignity of the city, and this place was chosen in proportion to the size of the audience.

But should the *Metamorphoses* be likened to a *prolalia* heard in the theater, or rather to a philosophical treatise, which Apuleius himself maintains is poorly adapted to a large and heterogeneous audience? I think that there are good arguments for the first option, even if the novel's complex literary elaboration (and the clear influence of philosophy and religion) might tempt us to think of it as a philosophical treatise. One might also object that, though novels were read publicly, they would not have been read in a crowded theater.¹⁰⁹ The playful literary allusions typical of the *Metamorphoses* undoubtedly represent an intellectual provocation aimed at highly cultured readers, but, as I argued in chapter 2, this fact does not preclude the possibility that a less-educated audience could enjoy the novel. And with regard to the philosophical and religious aspects of the novel, these are rather vague, and are conveyed from a satirical stance. They are encapsulated in a "low" narrative literary form, which claims to have been designed for entertainment. There is nothing in the novel that would make it inaccessible to a wider audience; some readers would fully appreciate the literary and philosophical allusions, while others would read for pleasure and entertainment,

---

108. Cf. A. La Rocca 2005, 263–265 on *Florida* 18.1; Bradley 2005, 19–21. For an analogous case of the heterogeneity and size of the readership of Martial, whose epigrams display both literary refinement and the desire to entertain the reader (but also in other authors only apparently less available to a vast audience, such as Virgil, Ovid, and Statius), see for example Citroni 1990, 111 ff.; also 1995 (especially 475–482 on the early Imperial period). On the readers of ancient novels and their level of sophistication, see Wesseling 1988; Stephens 1994; Hägg 1994; Bowie 1994 and 1996b.

109. Cf. Keulen 2007a. For a useful discussion of the evidence for public *akroaseis* of both poetry and works in prose, as well as for the possible connection of these recitations to the development of the Greek novel, see Ruiz-Montero 2003, 55 ff. (particularly significant is the story of Chaereas and Callirhoe, which was recited in the theater of Syracuse in Chariton 8.7.9). As Hägg 1994, 58 suggests, "it is probable that the . . . dissemination of the novels down the social scale, as far as it did take place, was primarily by means of recitals within the household, among friends, or even publicly—i.e., the novel in such circumstances had an audience proper rather than a readership." Hägg makes reference mainly to the older, "pre-sophistic" Greek novels; but such a possibility is not absurd for the *Metamorphoses*. See also Stramaglia 1999, 82 ff. for the oral diffusion of different kinds of narrative.

though—more or less unexpectedly—they might also find that some parts of the text provoked reflection on their part. Recent scholarship views the *Florida* from a largely analogous perspective. Adolfo La Rocca, for example, emphasizes the "epideictic" character of the philosophy shown in many of the *Florida* fragments,[110] which were directed at a wide audience. He argues it was a protreptic form of philosophy, rather than complex or doctrinal in nature. As Keith Bradley has astutely observed, the *doctrina* found in Apuleius' rhetorical fragments often takes the form of anecdotes that feature historical and mythological personalities, presented in an accessible manner, and showing a "moralistic flavor."[111] It seems significant, then, that these two Apuleian works feature philosophical elements aimed at a wide audience, as well as the protreptic use of *fabulae*.

Naturally, we cannot simply ignore the differences of genre that make the *Metamorphoses* a completely different entity than the *Florida*, but we can assume that Apuleius' intended audience was essentially the same for both works. It is difficult to be more precise than this, but I would maintain that the readership of Apuleius' novel did not consist exclusively of a restricted circle of the elite, despite the fact that more highly educated readers were obviously included in that group.[112] And if it is true that the novel saw a wider diffusion by means of oral transmission and public readings,[113] we could consequently ascribe an even larger audience to the *Metamorphoses*.

4.6 Between Rome and the provinces

If in fact Apuleius had a wide audience (and one that was heterogeneous in respect to its social composition), it becomes more difficult to make fine distinctions regarding geography. As we have seen, there are no persuasive reasons to conclude that Apuleius wrote the *Metamorphoses* chiefly for an audience that lived in Rome. Furthermore, he affirms in the *Florida* that the Carthaginians read his works and held them in high regard:

---

110. A. La Rocca 2005, 36 ff.
111. Bradley 2005, 17–18.
112. On the broad and diverse audience of the novel, see for example Gianotti 1986, 107 ff.: "the amount of space allotted to comedy, horror, magic and entertainment, to erotic impulses, and to crime stories, is directly proportional to the force invested in communicating a core of serious and committed ideas to recipients that would otherwise hardly be within reach" (p. 111). Bradley 2005 adopts a similar perspective for the *Florida*, though in place of a diversity of sociocultural classes he substitutes a dynamic of center and periphery in the Empire: "Apuleius' speeches can be understood not only as vehicles of entertainment but as active transmitters of metropolitan culture to a provincial population under constant exposure to new forms of Roman influence" (p. 21).
113. Cf. above, n. 109.

I am no stranger to your homes, you often saw me in my youth; you know my masters, and my philosophical sect; you have heard me speak, and have read and appreciated my books . . . your ears have become attuned to my voice, in both languages, for six years now, and my books have received no greater praise than the approbation they have received from you. (*Florida* 18.14–16)

Needless to say, we have no way of knowing whether the books to which Apuleius refers would have included the *Metamorphoses,* but nothing would prevent us from reaching such a conclusion. Augustine's statement about the distribution of Apuleius' works (which I have cited several times now), "Apuleius, inasmuch as he is African, is better known to us, who are Africans,"[114] implies a wide distribution, perhaps intended for an African audience.

On the other hand, calling Apuleius' novel strictly Carthaginian or African does not make sense, since it has the effect of marginalizing the work; it has also proved unsatisfactory to read the novel as an expression of a local culture that resisted and opposed the colonial forces exerted by Rome. The poor vegetable gardener who falls victim to the abuse of a Roman soldier is not enough to render Apuleius a fierce opponent of the Roman regime;[115] moreover, Apuleius "correction" of Virgil, which retold the story of Dido by drawing on alternative traditions (and particularly ones highly regarded in Africa), does not intrinsically imply any anti-Roman sentiment.[116] I might also add that, though it is possible to consider Apuleius as the representative of a cultural area in which the process of Romanization saw a high degree of variation, and in which we can even identify examples of resistance and open opposition to Roman influence, he himself seems completely open to Roman cultural influences and appears to be well integrated into the apparatus of provincial administration.[117] It would be difficult to make him into a champion of cultural resistance to Rome; nor is it an accident that Marcel Bénabou, who is intently focused on valorizing all phenomena of this type, considers Apuleius (along with Tertullian and Saint Augustine) as a potential standard-bearer for all those who would like to demonstrate the success of Romanization in the province of Africa.[118]

---

114. *Epist.* 138.19.
115. Similarly, in Tacitus' *Agricola,* the historian's reflection on the connection between acculturation/assimilation and slavery (21.3 *humanitas vocabatur, cum pars servitutis esset*) does not oblige us to make Tacitus into an enemy of Roman imperialism: cf. for example Soverini 2004, 205 *ad loc.*
116. Finkelpearl 1998, 143 reaches a similar conclusion, though she sees a slightly more oppositional view of Apuleius' Romano-African identity than is proposed here.
117. On the Romanization of Africa, see above n. 105. On Apuleius' political career in Madauros and Carthage, see for example A. La Rocca 2005, 16–25.
118. Bénabou 1976, 582.

More than cultural conflict and resistance, Apuleius' works display a dynamic of integration, emulation, and even possibly competition that links the center and periphery of the Empire in the pursuit of a common cultural ideal. A good example of this can be found at the end of *Florida* 20, where Carthage is lauded as *Africae Musa caelestis . . . Camena togatorum*. The city is the celestial muse of Africa, but also the *Camena* of those who wear the toga: clearly a sort of encroachment on Rome's territory, by means of which Carthage evidently is able to compete for cultural prestige; and if, as it appears, *caelestis* refers to the *dea Caelestis* (the Punic deity identified with Juno),[119] the juxtaposition of this term with the ancient Italic *Camena* is all the more striking.

Something similar, also involving the term *caelestis,* can be found in the novel, the only time Carthage receives mention in the work. Psyche tearfully calls upon Juno to intercede on her behalf:

> magni Iovis germana et coniuga, sive tu Sami, quae sola partu vagituque et alimonia tua gloriatur, tenes vetusta delubra, sive celsae Carthaginis, quae te virginem vectura leonis caelo commeantem percolit, beatas sedes frequentas, seu prope ripas Inachi, qui te iam nuptam Tonantis et reginam deorum memorat, inclitis Argivorum praesides moenibus, quam cunctus oriens Zygiam veneratur et omnis occidens Lucinam appellat. . . . (6.4.1)

> O sister and consort of great Jove, whether you dwell in the ancient temples of Samos, which alone can glory in your birth, your infant wails, and your nursing; or whether you honor with your presence the blessed dwellings of lofty Carthage, who worships you as the virgin who rides through sky on the lion's back; or whether along the banks of the river Inachus you guard the famous walls of the Argives, who now honor you as the bride of the Thunderer and the queen of the gods; you whom the East worships as *Zygia* and all the West calls *Lucina*. . . .

As he had in the prologue, Apuleius offers us a broad panoramic of the ancient world. Juno is venerated at Samos, in Carthage, and in Argos; she is worshipped throughout the East with the epithet *Zygia,* clearly a Greek word,[120] and throughout the West with the epithet *Lucina,* clearly Latin. But, in contrast to the prologue, here Apuleius introduces a new element by mentioning Africa. In this passage, he is not required to set the stage for the

---

119. A. La Rocca 2005, 286 *ad loc.*

120. It is not attested elsewhere in Latin, as is pointed out by *GCA* 2004, 390 *ad loc.*; Festus and Servius mention instead the epithets *Iuga* and *Iugalis*.

narrative and thematic development of the novel, nor is he at all required to follow a direct model (whereas it is probable that the prologue preserved traces of the original prologue from the now lost Greek precursor).[121]

In this passage, Apuleius' models are of a different sort. The literary texture of these phrases, as the Dutch commentators[122] have aptly noted, points decidedly to Greek and Latin epic, especially the epithet *magni Iovis germana et coniuga*, which recalls analogous formulations in Virgil (*et soror et coniunx*, *Aen.* 1.47; *germana . . . atque . . . coniunx*, 10.607), as well as in Homer (*Il.* 16.432 κασιγνήτην ἄλοχόν τε). The opening of the *Aeneid* (1.12–16) appears to be the most direct model for Apuleius' description here, which links Juno closely with Carthage and Samos:

> Urbs antiqua fuit (Tyrii tenuere coloni)
> Karthago, Italiam contra Tiberinaque longe
> ostia, dives opum studiisque asperrima belli,
> quam Iuno fertur terris magis omnibus unam
> posthabita coluisse Samo.

> There was an ancient city, Carthage—held by colonists from Tyre—far from Italy, and far from the mouths of the Tiber, rich, powerful, fierce, and warlike; they say Juno cherished it before all other cities, even Samos.

In the beginning of the poem, Juno is hostile to the Trojans, and even before the events that will trigger Dido's resentment of Aeneas, the description of Carthage (*Italiam contra*) seems to prefigure an irreducible antagonism that will set her against Rome. This perspective of conflict will be superseded at the end of the *Aeneid*—at least in the case of Juno's wrath against the Trojans. In Ovid, however, this antagonism seems to be on the verge of resurfacing. He evokes Virgil as he describes Juno's resentment over the fact that she had no month named after her:

> paeniteat quod non foveo Carthaginis arces,
>   cum mea sint illo curros et arma loco;
> paeniteat Sparten Argosque measque Mycenas
>   et veterem Latio subposuisse Samon. (*Fasti* 6.45–49)

> I regret that I do not favor the citadel of Carthage,
> though I still have my chariot and weapons there.

---

121. On this subject see above, pp. 142 ff.
122. *GCA* 2004, 387 ff. *ad loc.*

I regret that I placed Sparta, Argos, my Mycenae,
and ancient Samos second to Latium.

But this is only a momentary outburst. Two lines later, Juno's statement shows that she will not become the same wrathful divinity seen in the opening of the *Aeneid:* "No, I do not regret it, and no people is dearer to me than this one; I want to be worshipped here, and here I want a temple next to my Jove" (6.51–52).

Apuleius looks to Virgil without forgetting Ovid, whose broader Mediterranean perspective he adopts by including Argos among the list of Juno's cults in addition to Samos (he also mentions Samos' *vetusta delubra:* cf. Ovid's *veterem . . . Samon*). A reference to Latium, which was already implied in the prayer's general reference to the West, is made explicit by the epithet *Lucina*.[123] The strategy of the passage is decidedly inclusive: no trace in Apuleius remains of the ancient hostility that had set Rome in opposition to Juno and to Carthage, and which took such a prominent place in the texts of Virgil and Ovid.

Even the contrast between Juno and Venus, which is of great importance in Virgil, becomes completely obliterated. Responding to Psyche, Juno affirms that she cannot offer any help, because to do so would force her to act contrary to the interests of her daughter-in-law Venus, whom she has "always" (*semper*) loved like a daughter (6.4.5). This adverb is a pointed allusion to a literary past of epic hostility that Juno (or Apuleius) is trying to conceal here. More than literary memory, this is a case of literary amnesia—a feigned amnesia, of course; and also a very provocative one, since at the beginning of the *Aeneid* Juno's wrath is a *memor ira* (1.4); her anger is programmatically eternal, and she is incapable of forgetting (cf. also 1.36 *aeternum servans sub pectore vulnus*). Carthage, more than being set opposite to Rome (as it was in Virgil's poem, where the city was described as looking from afar to the mouths of the Tiber, with uneasiness and hostility), here finds itself inserted with "full membership" into a circuit of divine cults that encompasses all the Mediterranean. Nevertheless, this integration does not make all of its terms homogeneous, and Carthage in particular retains its own distinct cultural identity (and identity of cult). Carthage's Juno is the Hera-Juno of Greek and Roman mythology, but also the *Iuno Caelestis* of local cult, identified through syncretism with the Punic god-

---

123. Cf. Varro, *Ling.* 5.10.69 *ab Latinis Iuno Lucina dicta*. Other allusions to Ovid are found in Apuleius' phrase *nuptam Tonantis* (with Ovid, *Fasti* 6.33 *matrona Tonantis*); cf. also *reginam deorum* with Ovid's line 37 *regina vocor princepsque dearum*.

dess Tanit, who is often depicted on the back of a lion.[124] The city itself receives a position of great distinction. The epithet *celsa* connotes not only the height of the hill of Byrsa,[125] but also finds precedents in epic poetry: the formula αἰπὺ πτολίεθρον recurs four times in Homer,[126] and Virgil speaks of "lofty Carthage" at *Aen.* 4.97 and 4.265. In this view, Apuleius' phrase *celsae Carthaginis . . . beatas sedes* can be read as a sort of "correction" to Virgil's *suspectas . . . domos Carthaginis altae,* set in Juno's mouth. This correction removes every trace of hostility found in Virgil's text between Juno and Venus, or between Carthage and Rome. Carthage thus becomes like the other great and 'lofty' cities of the epic tradition, resembling Rome above all. Just a few lines before his description of Carthage, Virgil refers to the Italian metropolis as *alta Roma* (*Aen.* 1.7). This perspective, in my view, closely mirrors the perspective of *Florida* fragment 20, in which Carthage becomes the *Camena togatorum*.

In the *Metamorphoses,* then, neither Corinth nor Carthage seem to preserve a memory of past suffering at Rome's hands, or of any ancient hostilities. The mention of these two cities does not require a strategy for reading the text that would take into account a putative cultural resistance to the power of the Empire. On the other hand, the geography of the novel does not in any way press us to place Rome (and Rome alone) at the heart of Apuleius' interests. Africa does, admittedly, play a less prominent role in the *Metamorphoses* than in the *Florida,* and receives mention only in passing; when Africa does appear, however, it is not the *inulta tellus* of Horace,[127] a conquered territory, bitter and peripheral, abandoned by its own inhabitants. Instead, Carthage is represented as an urban center that aspired to play a leading role in the Mediterranean world, refusing to be eclipsed even by the splendor of Rome—precisely as it is charatcerized in the *Florida*. Rome itself is the *sacrosancta civitas* that provides the setting for the last five chapters of the novel after *Metamorphoses* 11.26.2, but clearly it is not of interest *per se:* the novel passes in silence over Rome's monuments and riches, as well as

---

124. See E. La Rocca 1990, 817–839; *GCA* 2004, 389, though his comment identifying the goddess as "the Juno of Horace (*Carm.* 2.1.25) and Vergil" is somewhat misleading, inasmuch as Virgil and Ovid did not identify distinct cultural traits in Juno's cult—this despite her being the divine protector of Africa. On the cult of *Juno Caelestis* in Rome, see Cordischi 1993. Further references can be found in Frazer 1929; see Bömer 1958 on Ovid, *Fasti* 6.45. Nisbet-Hubbard 1978, 25 *ad* Horace, *Carm.* 2.1.26 are more skeptical than Cordischi about Servius' claim that Juno had been transferred with the rite of *evocatio* from Carthage to Rome before the destruction of the city.
125. Virgil describes this hill at *Aeneid* 1.419 as *qui plurimus urbi / imminet.*
126. *Iliad* 2.538; *Odyssey* 3.485, 10.81, and 15.193. Further references can be found in Pease 1935, 165 *ad* Virgil *Aen.* 4.97. Pease, however, maintains that in Apuleius the epithet *celsa* refers to the height of Carthage in a literal sense.
127. *Carmina* 2.2.26 ff.: in Horace and Virgil's day, the rebirth of Carthage had scarcely begun.

any reference to culture or politics. The few details that do receive mention are mainly connected to the cult of Isis.[128] The text offers far more detail, for example, about the relatively small city of Hypata; and at 2.19.5–6 Byrrhena delivers a lengthy encomium of the easy but active life in a provincial city, which, in her view, leaves nothing to be desired in comparison to Rome.

To conclude: there are clearly many factors—among them the manifest process of Romanization found in Apuleius' version of the Greek ass-story—that would lead us to locate the *Metamorphoses* in a more general trend of Latin literary history, and not to identify it as the marginal product of an African provincial subculture. At the same time, we should not be tempted to consider the novel as a work that had to be written in Rome for a Roman audience—what would essentially amount to another form of marginalization. This is the case not only because there are subtle traces of centrifugal forces and an attention to provincial affairs, but also, perhaps above all, because we cannot but locate the novel in a more general trend in Latin literary production. Imperial literature is often addressed to an audience in which the inhabitants of Rome certainly held a position of great significance, but not in a manner that obliterates all other possibilities: Horace, Ovid, and Martial all declare their ambition for a universal fame. In the case of Virgil, we have clear evidence of a wide and precocious diffusion of his poetry, which easily crossed over geographical, social, and cultural barriers.[129]

Apuleius addressed himself to a wide world, much of which he had visited in person.[130] To the extent that we can imagine the prologue of the *Metamorphoses* as being spoken by the book itself,[131] one can conclude that the novel explicitly shares the author's ambition for travel and for cultural

---

128. 11.26.2 makes mention of the Port of Augustus, and 11.26.3 refers to the Iseum in the Campus Martius; a reference to the Isiac college of *pastophoroi*, "instituted in Sulla's day," is included at 11.30.4–5. M. Zimmerman 2005, 40 emphasizes that "the reader will look in vain for descriptions of the marvels of the city and its famous buildings, such as Clitophon gives us of Ephesus and of Alexandria in Achilles Tatius' novel."

129. On the influence of Virgilian poetry in epigraphical texts, see Hoogma's classic study of 1959 and Gigante 1979, 163–194. On the progressive enlargement of the number of readers, also of "high" Augustan literature, see Citroni 1990 and 1995. The same period was attended by a "tumultuous development of book commerce," which is also evidence of the growing diffusion of works of literature throughout the provinces (Fedeli 1989, 357; on the papyrus of Cornelius Gallus discovered in Nubia, see for example Pecere 1990, 334 f.). On the basis of several epigrams of Martial, it seems that the army, too, could occasionally be a factor in the distribution of texts in the peripheral areas of the Empire (Fedeli 1989, 374 f.; on the literacy of Roman soldiers, see Best 1966; and see Bowman 1994, 91 f. on the Virgilian quotation found among the Vindolanda tablets); this was true also for "lighter" narrative, if we take account of the well-known anecdote from Plutarch, *Crassus* 32.4 concerning the Roman official who had with him a copy of the *Milesiae* of Aristides (perhaps in Sisenna's translation).

130. On the biography and travels of Apuleius, see Harrison 2000, 5 ff.; A. La Rocca 2005, 13 ff.

131. See above, p. 174 n. 26.

mediation. In any case, it is entirely probable that Apuleius, as a good sophist, hoped his fame and his works would enjoy as wide a distribution as possible. Naturally, we cannot be completely certain of this fact, but nothing hinders us from imagining that Apuleius looked to this great "market" from his own *celsa Carthago*.

bibliography

(N.B. Journal titles are abbreviated according to *L'Année Philologique*. Other abbreviations are listed in the bibliography itself.)

AAGA 1978 = B. L. Hijmans Jr.–R. Th. Van der Paardt, eds. *Aspects of Apuleius' Golden Ass.* Groningen.

AAGA 1998 = M. Zimmerman, V. Hunink, Th.D. McCreight, D. van Mal-Maeder, S. Panayotakis, V. Schmidt, and B. Wesseling, eds. *Aspects of Apuleius' Golden Ass.* Vol. II: *Cupid and Psyche.* Groningen.

AAGA 2012 = W. Keulen, U. Egelhaaf-Gaiser, eds. *Aspects of Apuleius' Golden Ass.* Vol. III: *The Isis Book.* Leiden-Boston.

Acconcia Longo, A. 1991. "Filippo il filosofo a Costantinopoli." *RSBN* 28: 3–21.

Adriani, E. 2005. *Storia del teatro antico.* Rome.

Alcock, S. 1993. *Graecia capta: The Landscapes of Roman Greece.* Cambridge.

Alpers, K. 1980. "Innere Beziehungen und Kontraste als hermeneutische Zeichen in den *Metamorphosen* des Apuleius von Madaura." *WJA* 6: 197–207.

Anderson, G. 1990. "The Second Sophistic: Some Problems of Perspective." In Russell 1990a, 91–110.

Anderson, W. S. 1982. *Essays on Roman Satire.* Princeton, N.J.

Aragosti, A. 2000. *I frammenti dai Milesiarum libri di L.C. Sisenna.* Bologna.

Arnould, D. 1989. "Le chauve et le glouton chez Homère: remarques sur le personnage d'Ulysse." *REG* 102: 510–514.

Bakhtin, M. 1981. "Epic and Novel: Toward a Methodology for the Study of the Novel." In *The Dialogic Imagination: Four Essays,* 3–40. Austin, Tex.

Baldini Moscadi, L. 2005. *Magica musa. La magia dei poeti latini. Figure e funzioni.* Bologna.

Baldwin, B. 1989. "Apuleius and the Christians." *LCM* 14: 55.

Barchiesi, A. 1984. "Il nome di Lica e la poetica dei nomi in Petronio." *MD* 12: 169–175.

———. 2006. "Romanzo greco, romanzo latino: problemi e prospettive." In Graverini–Keulen–Barchiesi 2006, 193–218.

Barchiesi, A.–Cucchiarelli, A. 2005. "Satire and the Poet: The Body as Self-Referential Symbol." In Freudenburg 2005, 207–223.
Barnes, T. D. 1981. *Constantine and Eusebius*. Cambridge, Mass.-London.
Barnouw, J. 2004. *Odysseus, Hero of Practical Intelligence: Deliberation and Signs in Homer's Odyssey*. Lanham, Md.
Bartsch, S. 1989. *Decoding the Ancient Novel*. Princeton, N.J.
Beard, M.–North, J.–Price, S. 1998. *Religions of Rome*. Vol. I: *A History*; vol. II: *A Sourcebook*. Cambridge.
Beare, W. 1964². *The Roman Stage*. London.
Beavis, I. C. 1988. *Insects and Other Invertebrates in Classical Antiquity*. Exeter, U.K..
Becatti, G. 1954. *I Mitrei*. Scavi di Ostia, vol. II. Rome.
Beck, R. 1979. "Sette sfere, sette porte, and the Spring Equinoxes of A.D. 172 and 173." In *Mysteria Mithrae*, ed. E. Bianchi, 515–530. Leiden.
———. 1982. "The *Satyricon*: Satire, Narrator, and Antecedents." *MH* 39: 206–214.
———. 1996. "Mystery Religions, Aretalogy, and the Ancient Novel." In Schmeling 1996, 131–150.
———. 2000. "Apuleius the Novelist, Apuleius the Ostian Householder, and the Mithraeum of the Seven Spheres: Further Explorations of an Hypothesis of Filippo Coarelli." In *Text and Artifact in the Religions of Mediterranean Antiquity: Essays in Honour of Peter Richardson*, ed. S. G. Wilson and M. Desjardins, 551–557. Waterloo, Ont.
Behr, C. A. 1981. *P. Aelius Aristides, The Complete Works*. Vol. 2. Leiden.
———. 1994. "Studies on the Biography of Aelius Aristides." In *ANRW* 2.34.2: 1140–1233.
Bénabou, M. 1976. *La résistance africaine à la romanisation*. Paris.
Bernabò Brea, L. 1981. *Menandro e il teatro greco nelle terracotte liparesi*. Genoa.
Bernhard, M. 1927. *Der Stil des Apuleius von Madaura*. Stuttgart.
Best, E. E. 1966. "The Literate Roman Soldier." *CJ* 62: 122–127.
Bettini, M. 1991. "Sosia e il suo sosia: pensare il 'doppio' a Roma." Introductory essay in *Tito Maccio Plauto: Anfitrione*, ed. R. Oniga, 9-51. Venice.
Bitel, A. 2000–2001. "*Quis ille Asinus aureus?* The *Metamorphoses* of Apuleius' Title." *Ancient Narrative* 1: 208–244.
Bömer, F. 1958. *P. Ovidius Naso, Die Fasten*. Heidelberg.
Bonanno, M. G. 1999. "Sull' *opsis* aristotelica: dalla Poetica al Tractatus Coislinianus e ritorno." In *Dalla lirica al teatro: nel ricordo di Mario Untersteiner (1899–1999)*, ed. L. Belloni, V. Citti, and L. De Finis, 252–278. Trento.
Bond, R. P. 1985. "Dialectic, Eclectic and Myth (?) in Horace, *Satires* 2.6." *Antichthon* 19: 68–86.
Borghini, A. 1991. "Il platano e la morte: a proposito di Apul. *Met*. I 19." *Aufidus* 15: 7–14.
Bowersock, G. W. 1965. "Zur Geschichte des römischen Thessaliens." *RhM* 108: 277–289.
———. 1994. *Fiction as History: Nero to Julian*. Berkeley, Los Angeles-London.
Bowie, E. L. 1994. "The Readership of the Greek Novels in the Ancient World." In Tatum 1994, 435–459.
———. 1996a. "Past and Present in Pausanias." In *Pausanias historien*, ed. J. Bingen, 207–230 and 231–239 (discussion). Geneva.
———. 1996b. "The Ancient Readers of the Greek Novels." In Schmeling 1996, 87–106.

———. 2006. "Viewing and Listening on the Novelist's Page." In *Authors, Authority, and Interpreters in the Ancient Novel: Essays in Honor of Gareth L. Schmeling*, ed. S. N. Byrne, E. P. Cueva, and J. Alvares, 60–82. Ancient Narrative suppl. 5. Groningen.
Bowman, A. K. 1994. *Life and Letters on the Roman Frontier.* London.
Bradley, K. 2005. "Apuleius and Carthage." *Ancient Narrative* 4: 1–29.
Branham, R. B. 1989. *Unruly Eloquence: Lucian and the Comedy of Traditions.* Cambridge, Mass.-London.
———, ed. 2005a. *The Bakhtin Circle and Ancient Narrative.* Ancient Narrative suppl. 3. Groningen.
———. 2005b. "The Poetics of Genre: Bakhtin, Menippus, Petronius." In Branham 2005a, 3–31.
Braund, S. M. 1996. *The Roman Satirists and Their Masks.* Bristol, U.K.
Brink, C. O. 1971. *Horace on Poetry: The 'Ars Poetica.'* Cambridge.
Callebat, L. 1968. *Sermo cotidianus dans les Métamorphoses d'Apulée.* Caen.
Cameron, A. 1995. *Callimachus and His Critics.* Princeton, N.J.
Camerotto, A. 1998. *Le metamorfosi della parola: studi sulla parodia in Luciano di Samosata.* Pisa, Rome.
Capra, A. 2000. "Il mito delle cicale e il motivo della bellezza sensibile nel Fedro." *Maia* 52: 225–247.
———. 2007. "Dialettica e poesia: Platone e il 'mesmerismo' di Socrate." In *La poesia filosofica*, ed. A. Costazza, 29–44. Milan.
Carver, R. H. F. 2001. "*Quis ille?* The Role of the Prologue in Apuleius' *Nachleben.*" In Kahane–Laird 2001, 163–174.
Cavallo, G.–Fedeli, P.–Giardina, A., eds. 1989–90. *Lo spazio letterario di Roma antica.* Vol. 2: *La circolazione del testo*, 1989; vol. 3: *La ricezione del testo*, 1990. Rome.
Chatzis, A. 1914. *Der Philosoph und Grammatiker Ptolemaios Chennos: Leben, Schriftstellerei und Fragmente.* Paderborn. Reprint, New York, 1967.
Cherry, D. 1998. *Frontier and Society in Roman North Africa.* Oxford.
Chini, P. 1996. "Iuppiter Dolichenus." In *LTUR* 3: 133–134.
Cicu, L. 1988. *Problemi e strutture del mimo a Roma.* Sassari.
Citroni, M. 1975. *M. Valerii Martialis Epigrammaton liber primus.* Florence.
———. 1990. "I destinatari contemporanei." In Cavallo–Fedeli–Giardina 1990, 53–116.
———. 1995. *Poesia e lettori in Roma antica: forme della comunicazione letteraria.* Rome, Bari.
Clausen, W. 1994. *A Commentary on Virgil, Eclogues.* Oxford.
Coarelli, F. 1989. "Apuleio a Ostia?" *DArch* 7: 27–42.
———. 1996. "Murcia." In *LTUR* 3: 289–290.
———. 1999. "Venus verticordia, aedes." In *LTUR* 5: 119–120.
Colonna, A. 1938. *Heliodori Aethiopica.* Rome.
Connors, C. 2000. "Imperial Space and Time: The Literature of Leisure." In Taplin 2000, 492–517.
———. 2002. "Chariton's Syracuse and Its Histories of Empire." In Paschalis–Frangoulidis 2002, 12–26.
———. 2005. "Epic Allusion in Roman Satire." In Freudenburg 2005, 123–145.
Cordischi, L. 1993. "Caelestis." In *LTUR* 1: 207.
Corrigan, K.–Glazov–Corrigan, E. 2005. "Plato's *Symposium* and Bakhtin's Theory of the Dialogical Character of Novelistic Discourse." In Branham 2005a, 32–50.

Crismani, D. 2003. "La donna velata e altri ricordi di scena tra le pagine del romanzo greco." In Guglielmo–Bona 2003, 235–241.
Cristante, L. 1978. "La Sphragis di Marziano Capella (*spoudogeloion*: autobiografia e autoironia)." *Latomus* 37: 679–704.
Cucchiarelli, A. 2001. *La satira e il poeta: Orazio tra Epodi e Sermones*. Pisa.
Cueva, E. 2004. *The Myths of Fiction: Studies in the Canonical Greek Novels*. Ann Arbor, Mich.
Cumont, F. 1896. *Textes et monuments figurés relatifs aux mystères de Mithra*. 2 vols. Brussels.
D'Alessio, G. B. 1996. *Callimaco. Inni, epigrammi, frammenti*. Milan.
D'Asdia, M. 2002. "Nuove riflessioni sulla domus di Apuleio a Ostia." *ArchClass* 53: 433–464.
Davies, M.–Kathirithamby, J. 1986. *Greek Insects*. London.
Dawson, D. 1992. *Allegorical Readers and Cultural Revision in Ancient Alexandria*. Berkeley-Los Angeles-Oxford.
de Jong, I. J. F. 1991. *Narrative in Drama. The Art of the Euripidean Messenger-Speech*. Leiden.
———. 2001. "*The Prologue as a Pseudo-Dialogue and the Identity of Its (Main) Speaker.*" In Kahane–Laird 2001, 201–212.
de Jong, J. L. 1998. "Il pittore a le volte è puro poeta: Cupid and Psyche in Italian Renaissance Painting." In *AAGA* 1998, 189–215.
De Romilly, J. 1975. *Magic and Rhetoric in Ancient Greece*. Cambridge.
De Sanctis, D. 2003. "I nomi delle sirene nel Catalogo di Esiodo." *SIFC* 96: 197–206.
De Smet, R. 1987. "The Erotic Adventure of Lucius and Photis in Apuleius' *Metamorphoses*." *Latomus* 46: 613–623.
DeFilippo, J. 1990. "*Curiositas* and the Platonism of Apuleius' *Golden Ass*." *AJPh* 111: 471–492 (later in Harrison 1999, 269–289).
Defosse, P., ed. 2002–3. *Hommages à Carl Deroux*. Vol. 2: *Prose et linguistique, médecine*, 2002; vol. 4: *Archéologie et histoire de l'art, religion*, 2003. Brussels.
Derchain, Ph.–Hubaux, J. 1958. "L'affaire du marché d'Hypata dans la '*Métamorphose*' d'Apulée." *AC* 27: 100–104.
Deremetz, A. 2002. "Les *Métamorphoses* d'Apulée: de l'aventure à l'oeuvre." In Defosse 2002, 128–141.
Dewar, M. 2000. "Culture Wars: Latin Literature from the Second Century to the End of the Classical Era." In Taplin 2000, 519–545.
Di Marco, M. 1989. "*Opsis* nella *Poetica* di Aristotele e nel *Tractatus Coislinianus*." In *Scena e spettacolo nell'antichità*, ed. L. De Finis, 129–148. Florence.
Doherty, L. 1995. "Sirens, Muses, and Female Narrators in the *Odyssey*." In *The Distaff Side: Representing the Female in Homer's Odyssey*, ed. B. Cohen, 123–136. New York, Oxford.
Dostálová, R. 1996. "La dissoluzione della storiografia: il 'romanzo storico.'" In Pecere-Stramaglia 1996, 167–188.
Dowden, K. 1982. "Psyche on the Rock." *Latomus* 41: 336–352.
———. 1994. "The Roman Audience of *The Golden Ass*." In Tatum 1994, 419–434.
———. 1996. "Heliodoros." *CQ* 46: 267–285.
———. 1998. "*Cupid & Psyche:* A Question of the Vision of Apuleius." In *AAGA* 1998, 1–22.

———. 2001. "Prologic, Predecessors, and Prohibitions." In Kahane–Laird 2001, 123–136.
———. 2006. "A Tale of Two Texts: Apuleius' *sermo Milesius* and Plato's *Symposium*." In Keulen–Nauta–Panayotakis 2006, 42–58.
Drews, F. 2006. "Der Sprecherwechsel zwischen Apuleius und Lucius im Prolog der *Metamorphosen*." *Mnemosyne* 59: 403–420.
Egelhaaf-Gaiser, U. 2000. *Kulträume im römischen Alltag. Das Isisbuch des Apuleius und der Ort von Religion im kaiserzeitlichen Rom*. Stuttgart.
Elster, M. 1991. "Römisches Strafrecht in den *Metamorphosen* des Apuleius." In *GCN* 4: 135–154.
Engels, D. 1990. *Roman Corinth*. Chicago-London.
Ercolani, A., ed. 2002. *Spoudaiogeloion: Form und Funktion der Verspottung in der aristophanischen Komödie*. Stuttgart-Weimar.
Ernout, A. 1922. *Pétrone, Le Satiricon*. Paris.
Fantham, E. 1996. *Roman Literary Culture from Cicero to Apuleius*. Baltimore.
Fantuzzi, M.–Hunter, R. 2004. *Tradition and Innovation in Hellenistic Poetry*. Cambridge.
Fedeli, P. 1989. "I sistemi di produzione e diffusione." In Cavallo–Fedeli–Giardina 1989, 343–378.
———. 2005. *Properzio. Elegie, Libro II: Introduzione, testo e commento*. Cambridge.
Ferrari, G. R. F. 1987. *Listening to the Cicadas: A Study of Plato's Phaedrus*. Cambridge.
Festugière, A. J. 1991. "L'esperienza religiosa del medico Tessalo." In *Ermetismo e mistica pagana*, 143–169. Genoa. (Published earlier in *Hermétisme et mystique païenne*, 141–167 [Paris, 1967] = "L'expérience religieuse du médecin Thessalos." *Rbi* 48 [1939]: 45–77.)
Fick, N. 1987. "Le milieu culturel africain à l'époque antonine et le témoignage d'Apulée." *BAGB*: 285–296.
Fick-Michel, N. 1991. *Art et mystique dans les Métamorphoses d'Apulée*. Paris.
Finkelpearl, E. D. 1998. *Metamorphosis of Language in Apuleius: A Study of Allusion in the Novel*. Ann Arbor, Mich.
———. 2003. "Lucius and Aesop Gain a Voice: Apuleius *met*.11,1–2 and *Vita Aesopi* 7." In Panayotakis–Zimmerman–Keulen 2003, 37–51.
———. 2004. "The Ends of the *Metamorphoses* (Apuleius *Metamorphoses* 11.26.4–11.30)." In *Metamorphic Reflections: Essays Presented to Ben Hijmans at His 75th Birthday*, ed. M. Zimmerman and R. van der Paardt, 319–342. Leuven-Dudley, Mass.
Fiorencis, G.–Gianotti, G. F. 1990. "Fedra e Ippolito in provincia." *MD* 25: 71–114 (later in Magnaldi–Gianotti 2000, 265–296).
Fo, A. 2002. *Apuleio, Le Metamorfosi o L'asino d'oro*. Milan.
Fowler, D. 2001. "Writing with Style: The Prologue to Apuleius' *Metamorphoses* between *Fingierte Mündlichkeit* and Textuality." In Kahane–Laird 2001, 225–230.
Frangoulidis, S. A. 1997. *Handlung und Nebenhandlung: Theater, Metatheater und Gattungsbewußstsein in der römischen Komödie*. Stuttgart, 1997.
———. 2001. *Roles and Performances in Apuleius' Metamorphoses*. Stuttgart-Weimar.
———. 2002. "The Laughter Festival as a Community Integration Rite in Apuleius' *Metamorphoses*." In Paschalis–Frangoulidis 2002, 177–188.
———. 2008. *Witches, Isis, and Narrative: Approaches to Magic in Apuleius' Metamorphoses*. Berlin-New York.
Frazer, J. G. 1929. *Publi Ovidii Nasonis Fastorum libri sex*. London. Reprint Hildesheim-New York, 1973.

Fredouille, J.-C. 1975. *Apulei Metamorphoseon Liber XI. Apulée, Métamorphoses Livre XI.* Paris.

Freudenburg, K. 1993. *The Walking Muse: Horace on the Theory of Satire.* Princeton, N.J.

———. 2001. *Satires of Rome: Threatening Poses from Lucilius to Juvenal.* Cambridge.

———, ed. 2005. *The Cambridge Companion to Roman Satire.* Cambridge.

Friedrich, H.-V., ed. 1968. *Thessalos von Tralles.* Meisenheim am Glan.

Fucecchi, M. 2006. *Una guerra in Colchide. Valerio Flacco, Argonautiche 6, 1–426.* Pisa.

Fusillo, M. 1989. *Il romanzo greco. Polifonia ed eros.* Venice.

———. 1997. "How Novels End: Some Patterns of Closure in Ancient Narrative." In *Classical Closure: Reading the End in Greek and Latin Literature,* ed. D. H. Roberts, F. M. Dunn, and D. Fowler, 209–227. Princeton, N.J.

———. 2002. "*Tra epica e romanzo.*" In G. Moretti 2002, 5–34.

Gaisser, J. 2003. "Reading Apuleius with Filippo Beroaldo." In *Being There Together: Essays in Honor of Michael C. J. Putnam,* ed. Ph. Thibodeau and H. Haskell, 24–42. Afton, Minn.

Galinsky, K. 1996. *Augustan Culture.* Princeton, N.J.

Gamberale, L. 1996. "Confronti e incontri di cultura nell'età degli Antonini." In *Filellenismo e tradizionalismo a Roma nei primi due secoli dell'impero,* 57–84. Rome.

GCA 1985 = B. L. Hijmans et al. *Apuleius Madaurensis. Metamorphoses, Book VIII.* Groningen.

GCA 1995 = B. L. Hijmans et al. *Apuleius Madaurensis. Metamorphoses, Book IX.* Groningen.

GCA 2000: see M. Zimmerman 2000.

GCA 2001: see Van Mal-Maeder 2001.

GCA 2004 = M. Zimmerman et al. *Apuleius Madaurensis. Metamorphoses, Books IV 28–35, V and VI 1–24: The Tale of Cupid and Psyche.* Groningen.

GCN = H. Hoffman and M. Zimmerman, eds. *Groningen Colloquia on the Novel.* Vols. 1–9. Groningen 1988–98.

Geisau, J. von. 1916. "Syntaktische Gräzismen bei Apuleius." *IF* 36: 71–98 and 242–287.

Georgiadou, A.–Larmour, D. H. J. 1998. *Lucian's Science Fiction Novel: True Histories.* Leiden-Boston-Cologne.

Giangrande, L. 1972. *The Use of Spoudaiogeloion in Greek and Roman Literature.* The Hague-Paris.

Gianotti, G. F. 1986. *'Romanzo' e ideologia. Studi sulle Metamorfosi di Apuleio.* Naples.

———. 1991. "Sulle tracce della pantomima tragica: Alcesti tra i danzatori?" *Dioniso* 61: 121–149.

Gibson, B. 2001. "*Argutia Nilotici Calami:* A Theocritean Reed?" In Kahane–Laird 2001, 67–76.

Gigante, M. 1979. *Civiltà delle forme letterarie nell' antica Pompei.* Naples.

Gilman Romano, D. 2000. "A Tale of Two Cities: Roman Colonies at Corinth." In *Romanization and the City: Creation, Transformations, and Failures (Proceedings of a Conference Held at the American Academy in Rome to Celebrate the 50th Anniversary of the Excavations at Cosa, 14–16 May 1998),* ed. E. Fentress, 83–104. Portsmouth, R.I.

Gleason, M. 1995. *Making Men: Sophists and Self-Presentation in Ancient Rome.* Princeton, N.J.

Goldhill, S. 1991. *The Poet's Voice.* Cambridge.

Gowers, E. 2001. "Apuleius and Persius." In Kahane–Laird 2001, 77–87.

Graverini, L. 1996. "Apuleio, Virgilio e la 'Peste di Atene'. note ad Apul. *Met.* IV 14." *Maia* 48: 171–187.
———. 1997a. "Un secolo di studi su Mecenate." *RSA* 27: 231–89.
———. 1997b. "*In historiae specimen*. Elementi della letteratura storiografica nelle *Metamorfosi* di Apuleio." *Prometheus* 23: 247–278.
———. 1998. "Memorie virgiliane nelle *Metamorfosi* di Apuleio. Il racconto di Telifrone (II 19–30) e l'assalto dei coloni ai servi fuggitivi (VIII 16–18)." *Maia* 50: 123–145.
———. 2001a. "L'incontro di Lucio e Fotide. Stratificazioni intertestuali in Apul. *Met.* II 6–7." *Athenaeum* 89: 425–446.
———. 2001b. "L. Mummio Acaico." *Maecenas* 1: 105–148.
———. 2002a. Recensione di Kahane–Laird 2001. *Ancient Narrative* 2: 251–262.
———. 2002b. "Corinth, Rome, and Africa: A Cultural Background for the Tale of the Ass." In Paschalis–Frangoulidis 2002, 58–77.
———. 2003a. "The Winged Ass. Intertextuality and Narration in Apuleius' *Metamorphoses*." In Panayotakis–Zimmerman–Keulen 2003, 207–218.
———. 2003b. "Note di aggiornamento." In Pecere–Stramaglia 2003, 179–202.
———. 2005a. "A Booklike Self: Ovid and Apuleius." In *Aetas Ovidiana?* ed. D. Nelis, 225–250. Dublin (= *Hermathena* 177–178).
———. 2005b. "Sweet and Dangerous? A Literary Metaphor (*aures permulcere*) in Apuleius' Prologue." In Harrison–Paschalis–Frangoulidis 2005, 177–196.
———. 2006a. "An Old Wife's Tale." In Keulen–Nauta–Panayotakis 2006, 86–110.
———. 2006b. "La scena raccontata: teatro e narrativa antica." In *La scena assente: Realtà e leggenda sul teatro nel Medioevo*, ed. F. Mosetti Casaretto, 1–24. Alessandria.
———. 2006c. "A *lepidus susurrus*. Apuleius and the Fascination of Poetry." In Nauta 2006b, 1–18.
———. 2007. "The Ass' Ears and the Novel's Voice: Orality and the Involvement of the Reader in Apuleius' *Metamorphoses*." In Rimell 2007, 138–167.
———. 2009. "Apuleio e Achille Tazio. Una scena di caccia e una 'regola aurea.'" In *Il romanzo latino: modelli e tradizione letteraria*, ed. F. Gasti, 61–95. Atti della VII Giornata Ghisleriana di Filologia Classica, Pavia, 11–12 ottobre 2007. Pavia.
———. 2010. "Amore, 'dolcezza,' stupore. Romanzo antico e filosofia." In *"Lector, intende, laetaberis". Il romanzo dei Greci e dei Romani*, ed. R. Uglione, 57–88. Atti del Convegno Nazionale di Studi Torino, 27–28 Aprile 2009. Alessandria.
———. 2012. "*Prudentia and Providentia*. Book XI in Context." In *AAGA* 2012, 86–106.
———. 2013a. "Amazing Stories." In *Festschrift B. Kytzler*, ed. M. Pachalska and B. D. MacQueen (forthcoming).
———. 2013b. "Crying for Patroclus: Achilles Tatius and Homer's *Iliad*." In *Proceedings of the IV International Conference on the Ancient Novel (Lisbon, July 21–26, 2008), Crossroads in the Ancient Novel: Spaces, Frontiers, Intersections* (forthcoming).
Graverini, L.–Keulen, W.–Barchiesi, A. 2006. *Il romanzo antico*. Rome.
Grebe, S. 1999. *Martianus Capella: 'De nuptiis Philologiae et Mercurii'. Darstellung der Sieben Freien Künste und ihrer Beziehungen zueinander*. Stuttgart-Leipzig.
Griffiths, J. G. 1975. *Apuleius of Madauros. The Isis-Book (Metamorphoses, Book XI)*. Leiden.
———. 1978. "Isis in the *Metamorphoses* of Apuleius." In *AAGA* 1978, 141–166.
Grimal, P. 1971. "Le calame égyptien d'Apulée." *REA* 73: 343–355.
Gualandri, I. 1989a. "Per una geografia della letteratura latina." In Cavallo–Fedeli–Giardina 1989, 469–505.

———. 1989b. "Persistenze e resistenze locali: un problema aperto." In Cavallo–Fedeli–Giardina 1989, 509–529.

Guerrini, R.–Olivetti, A.–Sani, B., eds. 2000. "Dal testo all'immagine. Amore e Psiche nell'arte del Rinascimento." *Fontes* 3 (monographic journal issue).

Guglielmo, M.–Bona, E., eds. 2003. *Forme di comunicazione nel mondo antico e metamorfosi del mito: dal teatro al romanzo*. Alessandria.

Gunderson, E. 2000. *Staging Masculinity: The Rhetoric of Performance in the Roman World*. Ann Arbor, Mich.

Gutzwiller, K. J. 1991. *Theocritus' Pastoral Analogies: The Formation of a Genre*. Madison, Wis.

———. 1998. *Poetic Garlands: Hellenistic Epigrams in Context*. Berkeley, Los Angeles.

Habinek, T. N. 1990. "Lucius' Rite of Passage." *MD* 25: 49–69.

Hägg, T. 1994. "Orality, Literacy, and the 'Readership' of the Early Greek Novel." In *Contexts of Pre-Novel Narrative*, ed. R. Eriksen, 47–81. Berlin, New York.

Hall, E. 1995. "The Ass with Double Vision: Politicising an Ancient Greek Novel." In *Heart of the Heartless World: Essays in Cultural Resistance in Memory of Margot Heinemann*, ed. D. Margolies and M. Joannou, 47–59. London-Boulder, Colo.

Hani, J. 1973. "*L'Âne d'Or* d'Apulée et l'Égypte." *RPh* 47: 274–280.

Hardie, Ph. 1998. "A Reading of Heliodorus, *Aithiopika* 3.4.1–3.5.2." In Hunter 1998a, 19–39.

Harris, W. V. 1989. *Ancient Literacy*. Cambridge, Mass.-London.

Harrison, S. J. 1990a. "Some Odyssean Scenes in Apuleius' *Metamorphoses*." *MD* 25: 193–210.

———. 1990b. "The Speaking Book: The Prologue to Apuleius' *Metamorphoses*." *CQ* 40: 507–513.

———. 1996. "Apuleius' *Metamorphoses*." In Schmeling 1996, 491–516.

———. 1997. "From Epic to Novel: Apuleius as a Reader of Vergil." *MD* 39: 53–74.

———. 1998a. "The Milesian Tales and the Roman Novel." In *GCN* 9: 63–73.

———. 1998b. "Some Epic Structures in *Cupid and Psyche*." In *AAGA* 1998, 51–68.

———, ed. 1999. *Oxford Readings in the Roman Novel*. Oxford.

———. 2000. *Apuleius: A Latin Sophist*. Oxford.

———. 2000–2001. "Apuleius, Aelius Aristides, and Religious Autobiography." *Ancient Narrative* 1: 245–259.

———. 2002a. "Constructing Apuleius: The Emergence of a Literary Artist." *Ancient Narrative* 2: 143–171.

———. 2002b. "Literary Topography in Apuleius' *Metamorphoses*." In Paschalis–Frangoulidis 2002, 40–57.

———. 2003. "Epic Extremities: The Openings and Closures of Books in Apuleius' *Metamorphoses*." In Panayotakis–Zimmerman–Keulen 2003, 239–254.

Harrison, S. J.–Hilton, J.–Hunink, V. 2001. *Apuleius: Rhetorical Works*. Oxford-New York.

Harrison, S. J.–Paschalis, M.–Frangoulidis, S., eds. 2005. *Metaphor and the Ancient Novel*. Ancient Narrative suppl. 4. Groningen.

Heine, R. 1978. "Picaresque Novel versus Allegory." In *AAGA* 1978, 25–42.

Heller, J. L. 1943. "*Nenia* 'παίγνιον.'" *TAPhA* 74: 215–268.

Heller, S. 1983. "Apuleius, Platonic Dualism, and Eleven." *AJPh* 104: 321–339.

Helm, R. 1914. "Das 'Märchen' von Amor und Psyche." *Neue Jahrb. f. d. Klass. Altertum* 33: 170–209 (later in *Amor und Psyche*, ed. G. Binder and R. Merkelbach [Darmstadt, 1968], 175–234 [the page numbers in the text refer to this edition]).

———. 1955⁴. *Apuleius Platonicus Madaurensis: Metamorphoseon libri XI*. Leipzig.
Hercher, R. 1869. "Fragmentum Marcianum." *Hermes* 3: 382–388.
Heseltine, M. 1956. "Petronius." In *Petronius, Seneca, Apocolocyntosis*, trans. M. Heseltine–W. H. D. Rouse. London, Cambridge, Mass.
Hijmans, B. L. 1978. "Significant Names and Their Function in Apuleius' *Metamorphoses*." In *AAGA* 1978, 107–122.
———. 1987. "Apuleius Philosophus Platonicus." In *ANRW* 2.36.1: 395–475.
Hinds, S. 1998. *Allusion and Intertext: Dynamics of Appropriation in Roman Poetry*. Cambridge.
Hofmann, H., ed. 1999. *Latin Fiction: The Latin Novel in Context*. London-New York.
Hohlfelder, R. L. 1976. "Kenchreai on the Saronic Gulf: Aspects of Its Imperial History." *CJ* 71: 217–226.
Holzberg, N. 1996. "Fable: Aesop; Life of Aesop." In Schmeling 1996, 633–639.
Hoogma, R. P. 1959. *Der Einfluss Vergils auf die Carmina Latina Epigraphica*. Amsterdam.
Hubbard, M. 1974. *Propertius*. London.
Humphrey, J. H. 1986. *Roman Circuses*. London.
Hunink, V. 1997. *Apuleius of Madauros, Pro se de magia (Apologia)*. Vol. I: *Introduction, Text, Bibliography, Indexes*; vol. II: *Commentary*. Amsterdam.
———. 2000. "Apuleius, Pudentilla, and Christianity." *VChr* 54: 80–94.
———. 2001. *Apuleius of Madauros, Florida*. Amsterdam.
———. 2002. "The Date of Apuleius' *Metamorphoses*." In Defosse 2002, 224–235.
———. 2003. "Apuleius, *qui nobis Afris Afer est notior*: Augustine's Polemic against Apuleius in *De Civitate Dei*." *Scholia* 12: 82–95.
Hunter, R. 1983. *A Study of Daphnis & Chloe*. Cambridge.
———. 1989. "Winged Callimachus." *ZPE* 76: 1–2.
———. 1994. "History and Historicity in the Romance of Chariton." In *ANRW* 2.34.2: 1055–1086.
———, ed. 1998a. *Studies in Heliodorus*. Cambridge.
———. 1998b. "The *Aithiopika* of Heliodorus: Beyond Interpretation?" In Hunter 1998a, 40–59.
———. 1999. *Theocritus: A Selection*. Cambridge, New York.
———. 2004. *Plato's Symposium*. Oxford, New York.
———. 2005. "'Philip the Philosopher' on the *Aithiopika* of Heliodorus." In Harrison–Paschalis–Frangoulidis 2005, 123–138.
Hurst, H. 1993. "Cartagine, la nuova Alessandria." In *Storia di Roma*, ed. A. Momigliano and A. Schiavone, vol. 3.2: *I luoghi e le culture*, 327–337. Turin.
Jacobson, D. M.–Weitzman, M. P. 1995. "Black Bronze and the 'Corinthian Alloy.'" *CQ* 45: 580–583.
James, P. 1987. *Unity in Diversity. A Study of Apuleius' Metamorphoses with Particular Reference to the Narrator's Art of Transformation and the Metamorphosis Motif in the Tale of Cupid and Psyche*. Hildesheim-Zurich-New York.
———. 1991. "Fool's Gold . . . Renaming the Ass." In *GCN* 4: 155–171.
———. 2001. "From Prologue to Story: Metaphor and Narrative Construction in the Opening of the *Metamorphoses*." In Kahane–Laird 2001, 256–266.
James, P.–O'Brien, M. 2006. "To Baldly Go: A Last Look at Lucius and His Counter-Humiliation Strategies." In Keulen–Nauta–Panayotakis 2006, 234–251.
Jensson, G. 2004. *The Recollections of Encolpius: The Satyrica of Petronius as Milesian Fiction*. Ancient Narrative suppl. 2. Groningen.

Kahane, A. 2001. "Antiquity's Future: Writing, Speech, and Representation in the Prologue to Apuleius' 'Metamorphoses.'" In Kahane–Laird 2001, 231–241.

Kahane, A.–Laird, A., eds. 2001. *A Companion to the Prologue to Apuleius' Metamorphoses.* Oxford.

Kaibel, H. 1897. "Blaesus, n. 4." In *RE* 5, col. 556.

Kenaan, V. L. 2000. "'Fabula anilis': The Literal as a Feminine Sense." In *Studies in Latin Literature and Roman History,* ed. C. Deroux, 10: 370–391. Brussels.

Kennedy, G. 1963. *The Art of Persuasion in Greece,* Princeton, N.J.

Kenney, E. J. 1990. *Apuleius, Cupid & Psyche.* Cambridge.

———. 2003. "In the Mill with Slaves: Lucius Looks Back in Gratitude." *TAPhA* 133: 159–192.

Keulen, W. 1997. "Some Legal Themes in Apuleian Context." In Picone–Zimmerman 1997, 203–229.

———. 2003a. *"Apuleius Madaurensis. Metamorphoses, Book I, 1–20: Introduction, Text, Commentary."* PhD diss., Rijksuniversiteit Groningen, Groningen.

———. 2003b. "Swordplay-Wordplay: Phraseology of Fiction in Apuleius' *Metamorphoses.*" In Panayotakis-Zimmerman-Keulen 2003, 161–170.

———. 2003c. "Comic Invention and Superstitious Frenzy in Apuleius' *Metamorphoses*: The Figure of Socrates as an Icon of Satirical Self-Exposure." *AJPh* 124: 107–135.

———. 2004a. "Gellius, Apuleius, and Satire on the Intellectual." In *The Worlds of Aulus Gellius,* ed. L. Holford-Strevens and A. Vardi, 223–245. Oxford.

———. 2004b. "Lucius' Kinship Diplomacy: Plutarchan Reflections in an Apuleian Character." In *The Statesman in Plutarch's Works: Proceedings of the Sixth International Conference of the International Plutarch Society, Nijmegen–Castle Hernen, May 1–5, 2002,* ed. L. De Blois et al., 261–273. Leiden.

———. 2006a. "Il romanzo latino." In Graverini–Keulen–Barchiesi 2006, 131–177.

———. 2006b. "The Wet Rituals of the Excluded Mistress: Meroe and the Mime." in Nauta 2006b, 43–61.

———. 2007a. *"Vocis immutatio:* The Apuleian Prologue and the Pleasures and Pitfalls of Vocal Versatility." In Rimell 2007, 106–137.

———. 2007b. *Apuleius Madaurensis, Metamorphoses, Book I.* Groningen.

Keulen, W.–Nauta, R. R.–Panayotakis, S., eds. 2006. *Lectiones Scrupulosae: Essays on the Text and Interpretation of Apuleius' Metamorphoses in Honour of Maaike Zimmerman.* Ancient Narrative suppl. 6. Groningen.

Krabbe, J. K. 1989. *The Metamorphoses of Apuleius.* New York.

Krappe, A. H. 1947. "Ἀπόλλων ῎Ονος." *CPh* 42: 223–234.

Kuch, H., ed. 1989. *Der antike Roman: Untersuchungen zur literarischen Kommunikation und Gattungsgeschichte.* Berlin.

La Penna, A. 1968. "Orazio e la morale mondana europea." Introductory essay in: *Quinto Orazio Flacco: tutte le opere,* ed. E. Cetrangolo, IX–CLXXIX. Florence (later in La Penna 1993, 1–237).

———. 1973. "Una polemica di Sallustio contro l'oratoria contemporanea?" *RFIC* 101: 88–91 (later in *Aspetti del pensiero storico latino* [Turin, 1978], 187–191).

———. 1992. "L'autorappresentazione e la rappresentazione del poeta come scrittore da Nevio a Ovidio." *Aevum (ant)* 5: 143–185 (later in *Da Lucrezio a Persio: Saggi, studi, note,* ed. M. Citroni and A. Perutelli [Milan, 1995], 110–160).

———. 1993. *Saggi e studi su Orazio,* Firenze.

La Rocca, A. 2005. *Il filosofo e la città. Commento storico ai Florida di Apuleio*. Rome.
La Rocca, E. 1990. "Iuno." In *LIMC* 5: 814–856
Lamberton, R. 1986. *Homer the Theologian*. Berkeley-Los Angeles-London.
Lanza, D. 1997. *Lo stolto: di Socrate, Eulenspiegel, Pinocchio e altri trasgressori del senso comune*. Turin.
Laplace, M. M. J. 1997. "Le roman de Chariton et la tradition de l'éloquence et de la rhétorique: constitution d'un discours panégyrique." *RhM* 140: 38–71.
Lazzarini, C. 1984. "*Historia / fabula*. Forme della costruzione poetica virgiliana nel commento di Servio all'*Eneide*." *MD* 12: 117–144.
Lee, B. T. 2005. *Apuleius' Florida: A Commentary*. Berlin, New York.
Lee, B. T.–Finkelpearl, E.–Graverini, L. 2013. *Apuleius and Africa*. Proceedings of the Apuleius and Africa Conference held at Oberlin, April 29th–May 2nd 2010. Forthcoming.
Lenaz, M. 1975. *Martiani Capellae De nuptiis Philologiae et Mercurii liber secundus*. Padua.
LIMC = *Lexicon Iconographicum Mythologiae Classicae*. Zurich-Munich, 1990.
Liuzzi, D. 1988. *Manilio, Astronomica, Libro III*. Lecce.
Liviabella Furiani, P. 2003. "L'occhio e l'orecchio nel romanzo greco d'amore: note sull'esperienza del bello nelle *Etiopiche* di Eliodoro." In *Studi di filologia e tradizione greca in memoria di Aristide Colonna*, ed. F. Benedetti and S. Grandolini, 417–441. Naples.
López, V. C. 1976. "Tratamiento del mito en las novelle de las *Metamorfosis* de Apuleyo." *CFC* 10: 309–373.
LTUR = *Lexicon Topographicum Urbis Romae*. Ed. E. M. Steinby. Vol. 1: 1993; vol. 2: 1995; vol. 3: 1996; vol. 4: 1999; vol. 5: 1999. Rome.
MacAlister, S. 1996. *Dreams and Suicides: The Greek Novel from Antiquity to the Byzantine Empire*. London-New York.
Maehler, H. 1981. "Lucius the Donkey and Roman Law." *MPhL* 4: 161–177.
Magnaldi, G. 2000. "L'edizione di Apuleio ad usum Delphini: *Metamorfosi, Apologia, Florida*." In Magnaldi–Gianotti 2000, 75–116.
Magnaldi, G.–Gianotti, G. F., eds. 2000. *Apuleio: Storia del testo e interpretazioni*. Alessandria.
Marangoni, C. 1977–78. "Corinto simbolo isiaco nelle 'Metamorfosi' di Apuleio." *AIV* 136: 221–226.
———. 2000. *Il mosaico della memoria. Studi sui Florida e sulle Metamorfosi di Apuleio*. Padua.
Marini, N. 1991. "Δρᾶμα: possibile denominazione per il romanzo greco d'amore." *SIFC* 84: 232–243.
Marmorale, E. V. 1958. "Un appuntamento al Circo Massimo." *GIF* 11: 61–65 (later in id., *Pertinenze e impertinenze* [Naples, 1960], 194–203 [the page numbers in the text refer to this edition]).
Marsh, T. E. 1979. "*Magic, Poetics, Seduction: An Analysis of 'thelgein' in Greek Literature*." PhD diss. State Univ. of New York at Buffalo.
Martin, R. 1970. "Le sens de l'expression 'Asinus aureus' et la signification du roman apuléien." *REL* 48: 332–354.
Mason, H. 1971. "Lucius at Corinth." *Phoenix* 25: 160–165.
———. 1978. "*Fabula Graecanica*: Apuleius and His Greek Sources." In *AAGA* 1978, 1–15.
———. 1983. "The Distinction of Lucius in Apuleius' *Metamorphoses*." *Phoenix* 37: 135–143.

———. 1994. "Greek and Latin Versions of the Ass-Story." In *ANRW* 2.34.2: 1665–1707.
Massaro, M. 1977. "'Aniles fabellae.'" *SIFC* 49: 104–135.
———. 1978. "Un'incertezza di lettura in due passi oraziani (*patiens/sapiens*)." *Atene e Roma* 23: 173–86.
Massimilla, G. 1996. *Callimaco. Aitia. Libri primo e secondo.* Pisa.
Mastrocinque, A. 1998. *Studi sul mitraismo (il mitraismo e la magia).* Rome.
Mattiacci, S. 1985. "Apuleio poeta novello." In *Disiecti membra poetae,* ed. V. Tandoi, 2: 235–277. Foggia.
———. 1996. *Apuleio. Le novelle dell'adulterio (Metamorfosi XI).* Florence.
———. 2003. "Apuleio in Fulgenzio." *SIFC* 96: 229–256.
Mattingly, D. J. 2004. "Being Roman: Expressing Identity in a Provincial Setting." *JRA* 17: 5–25.
Mattingly, D. J.–Hitchner, R. B. 1995. "Roman Africa: An Archaeological Review." *JRS* 85: 165–213.
May, R. 1998. "Köche und Parasit: Elemente der Komödie in den *Metamorphosen* des Apuleius." *GCN* 9: 131–155.
———. 2006. *Apuleius and Drama: The Ass on Stage.* Oxford.
———. 2007. "Visualising Drama: Oratory and Truthfulness in Apuleius *Metamorphoses* 3." In Rimell 2007, 86–105.
———. 2008. "The Metamorphosis of Pantomime: Apuleius' Judgement of Paris (*Met.* 10.30–34)." In *New Directions in Ancient Pantomime,* ed. E. Hall and R. Wyles, 338–363. Oxford.
Mayer, R. 2005. "*Sleeping with the Enemy: Satire and Philosophy.*" In Freudenburg 2005, 146–159.
Mazza, M. 1999. *Il vero e l'immaginato: profezia, narrativa e storiografia nel mondo romano.* Rome.
Mazzarino, A. 1950. *La Milesia e Apuleio.* Turin.
Mazzoli, G. 1990. "L'oro dell'asino." *Aufidus* 10: 75–92.
McCreight, T. 1998. "Apuleius, Lector Sallustii: Lexicographical, Textual and Intertextual Observations on Sallust and Apuleius." *Mnemosyne* 51: 41–63.
———. 2006. "Psyche's Sisters as Medicae? Allusions to Medicine in Cupid and Psyche." In Keulen–Nauta–Panayotakis 2006, 123–167.
Merkelbach, R. 1962. *Roman und Mysterium in der Antike.* Berlin, Munich.
Mignogna, E. 1992. "Aesopus bucolicus: Come si 'mette in scena' un miracolo [*Vita Aesopi* c. 6]." In *Der Aesop-Roman: Motivgeschichte und Erzählstruktur,* ed. N. Holzberg, 76–84. Tübingen.
———. 1996. "Il mimo 'Leucippe': un'ipotesi su PBerol inv. 13927 [Pack2 2437]." *RCCM* 38: 161–166.
Millar, F. 1981. "The World of the Golden Ass." *JRS* 71: 63–75.
Mora, F. 1990. *Prosopografia isiaca.* Vol. 1: *Corpus Prosopographicum Religionis Isiacae.* Leiden.
Morales, H. 2004. *Vision and Narrative in Achilles Tatius' Leucippe and Clitophon.* Cambridge.
Moreschini, C. 1978. *Apuleio e il platonismo.* Florence.
———. 1990. "Le *Metamorfosi* di Apuleio, la 'fabula Milesia' e il romanzo." *MD* 25 (= *Studi sul romanzo antico,* ed. D. P. Fowler and M. Labate: 115–127.

———. 1994a. *Il mito di Amore e Psiche in Apuleio*. Naples.
———. 1994b. "Elio Aristide tra retorica e filosofia." In *ANRW* 2.34.2: 1234–1247.
Moretti, F. 2001–3. *Il romanzo*. Vol. 1: *La cultura del romanzo*, 2001; vol. 2: *Le forme*, 2002; vol. 3: *Storia e geografia*, 2002; vol. 4: *Temi, luoghi, eroi*, 2003; vol. 5: *Lezioni*, 2003. Turin.
Moretti, G. 2002. "Suscitare o no le passioni? Il ruolo di Rutilio Rufo." In *Papers on Rhetoric*, ed. L. Calboli Montefusco, 4: 205–222. Rome.
Morgan, J. 1991. "Readers and Audiences in the *Aithiopika* of Heliodoros." *GCN* 4: 84–103.
———. 2001. "*The Prologues of the Greek Novels and Apuleius.*" In Kahane–Laird 2001, 152–162.
———. 2004. *Longus, Daphnis and Chloe*. Oxford.
Morgan, J. R.–Jones, M. 2007. *Philosophical Presences in the Ancient Novel*. Ancient Narrative suppl. 10. Groningen.
Muecke, F. 1993. *Horace, Satires II*. Warminster, U.K..
Müller, K. 1995⁴. *Petroni Arbitri Satyricon reliquiae*. Stuttgart-Leipzig.
Münstermann, H. 1995. *Apuleius. Metamorphosen. Literarischer Vorlagen*. Stuttgart-Leipzig.
Murgatroyd, P. 2004. "The Ending of Apuleius' *Metamorphoses*." *CQ* 54: 319–321.
Murray, P. 2002. "Plato's Muses: The Goddesses That Endure." In *Cultivating the Muse: Struggles for Power and Inspiration in Classical Literature*, ed. E. Spentzou and D. Fowler, 29–46. Oxford.
Napolitano Valditara, L. M. 1994. *Lo sguardo nel buio. Metafore visive e forme grecoantiche della razionalità*. Rome, Bari.
Nauta, R. R. 2006a. "The *Recusatio* in Flavian Poetry." In *Flavian Poetry*, ed. R. R. Nauta, H.-J. van Dam, and J. J. L. Smolenaars, 21–40. Leiden, Boston.
———, ed. 2006b. *Desultoria Scientia: Genre in Apuleius' Metamorphoses and Related Texts*. Leuven, Paris, Dudley, Mass.
Nehamas, A. 1999. *Virtues of Authenticity: Essays on Plato and Socrates,* Princeton, N.J.
Nenci, G. 1978. "*Graecia capta ferum victorem cepit:* Hor. *Ep.* II 1,156." *ASNP* 8: 1007–1023.
Nicolai, R. 1999. "*Quis ille?* Il proemio delle *Metamorfosi* di Apuleio e il problema del lettore ideale." *MD* 42: 143–164.
———. 2004. *Studi su Isocrate. La comunicazione letteraria nel IV sec. A.C. e i nuovi generi della prosa*. Rome.
Nicolini, L. 2000. *Apuleio. La novella di Carite e Tlepolemo*. Naples.
———. 2005. *Apuleio. Le Metamorfosi*. Milan.
———. 2011. *Ad (l)usum lectoris. Etimologia e giochi di parole in Apuleio*. Bologna.
Nicoll, A. 1931. *Masks, Mimes, and Miracles: Studies in the Popular Theatre*. London, Bombay, Sydney.
Nimis, S. A. 2004. "Oral and Written Forms of Closure in the Ancient Novel." In *Oral Performance and Its Context*, ed. C. J. Mackie, 179–194. Leiden.
Nisbet, R. G. M.–Hubbard, M. 1970–78. *A Commentary on Horace, Odes*. Book I: 1970; Book II: 1978. Oxford.
Nock, A. D. 1933. *Conversion*. Oxford.
Norden, E. 1898. *Die antike Kunstprosa*. Leipzig.
Noy, D. 2000. *Foreigners at Rome: Citizens and Strangers*. London.

O'Brien, M. C. 2002. *Apuleius' Debt to Plato in the Metamorphoses.* Lewiston, N.Y.-Lampeter, U.K..

Oliensis, E. 1998. *Horace and the Rhetoric of Authority.* Cambridge.

Oniga, R. 1985. "Il canticum di Sosia: forme stilistiche e modelli culturali." *MD* 14: 113–208.

Pabst, B. 1994. *Prosimetrum: Tradition und Wandel einer Literaturform zwischen Spätantike und Spätmittelalter.* Cologne-Weimar-Vienna.

Panayotakis, C. 1995. *Theatrum Arbitri: Theatrical Elements in the Satyrica of Petronius.* Leiden, New York–Cologne.

Panayotakis, S.–Zimmerman, M.–Keulen, W., eds. 2003. *The Ancient Novel and Beyond.* Leiden-Boston.

Pape, M. 1975. "*Griechische Kunstwerke aus Kriegsbeute und ihre öffentliche Aufstellung in Rom.*" PhD diss., Universität Hamburg.

Paratore, E. 1942². *La novella in Apuleio.* Messina.

———. 1948. "La prosa di Apuleio." *Maia* 1: 33–47.

Parry, H. 1992. *Thelxis: Magic and Imagination in Greek Myth and Poetry.* Lanham, Md.-New York-London.

Paschalis, M.–Frangoulidis, S., eds. 2002. *Space in the Ancient Novel.* Ancient Narrative suppl. 1. Groningen.

Pasetti, L. 2007. *Plauto in Apuleio.* Bologna.

Pease, A. S. 1935. *Publi Vergili Maronis Aeneidos liber quartus.* Cambridge, Mass. Reprint, Darmstadt, 1967.

Pecere, O. 1990. "I meccanismi della tradizione testuale." In Cavallo–Fedeli–Giardina 1990, 297–386.

Pecere, O.–Stramaglia, A., eds. 1996. *La letteratura di consumo nel mondo greco-latino.* Cassino.

———. 2003. *Studi Apuleiani.* With "Note di aggiornamento" by L. Graverini. Cassino.

Peek, W. 1952. "Polystratos, n. 8." In *RE* 42, cols. 1833–1834.

Pellegrino, C. 1986. *T. Petronio Arbitro, Satyricon.* Vol. I: *I capitoli della retorica.* Rome.

Penwill, J. L. 1975. "Slavish Pleasures and Profitless Curiosity: Fall and Redemption in Apuleius' *Metamorphoses.*" *Ramus* 4: 49–82.

———. 1990. "*Ambages Reciprocae:* Reviewing Apuleius' *Metamorphoses.*" In *The Imperial Muse: Flavian Epicists to Claudian,* ed. A. J. Boyle, 2: 211–235. Bentleigh, Victoria, Australia.

Perry, B. E. 1967. *The Ancient Romances: A Literary-Historical Account of Their Origins.* Berkeley, Los Angeles.

Pfeiffer, R. 1949. *Callimachus.* Vol. 1: *Fragmenta.* Oxford.

Picone, M.–Zimmerman, B., eds. 1997. *Der antike Roman und seine mittelalterliche Rezeption.* Basel.

Pinotti, P. 2003. "L'Asino, il Re, la Fanciulla Gravida e il Cigno. Metamorfosi del mito e prefigurazioni del romanzo nella scrittura platonica." In Guglielmo–Bona 2003, 49–78.

Plaza, M. 2003. "*Solventur risu tabulae:* Saved by Laughter in Horace (*S.* II.1.80–6) and Apuleius (*Met.* III.1–11)." *C&M* 54: 353–358.

———. 2006. "*Nomen omen*—Narrative Instantiation of Rhetorical Expressions in Apuleius' *Metamorphoses.*" In Keulen–Nauta–Panayotakis 2006, 68–85.

Pontani, F. 2005. *Sguardi su Ulisse. La tradizione esegetica greca all'Odissea.* Rome.

Prosimetrum e spoudogeloion. 1982. Genoa.

Pucci, P. 1979. "The Song of the Sirens." *Arethusa* 12: 121–132 (later in Schein 1996, 191–200).
Putnam, M. C. J. 1970. *Virgil's Pastoral Art: Studies in the Eclogues.* Princeton, N.J.
Questa, C.–Raffaelli, R. 1990. *"Dalla rappresentazione alla lettura."* In Cavallo–Fedeli–Giardina 1990, 139–215.
Rabau, S. 1996. "Le roman d'Achille Tatius a-t-il une fin? Ou Comment refermer une oeuvre aperte?" *Lalies* 17: 139–149.
Reardon, B. P., ed. 1989. *Collected Ancient Greek Novels.* Berkeley-Los Angeles-London.
———. 1991. *The Form of the Greek Romance.* Princeton, N.J.
———. 1996. *"Chariton."* In Schmeling 1996, 309–335.
Regali, M. 1983. *Macrobio. Commento al Somnium Scipionis, libro I.* Pisa.
Reich, H. 1903. *Der Mimus. Ein litterar-entwickelungsgeschichtlicher Versuch.* Berlin.
Richter, G. M. A. 1913. "Grotesques and the Mime." *AJA* 17: 149–156.
Riedweg, C. 1987. *Mysterienterminologie bei Platon, Philon und Clemens von Alexandrien.* Berlin, New York.
Rimell, V. 2005. *"The Satiric Maze: Petronius, Satire, and the Novel."* In Freudenburg 2005, 160–173.
———, ed. 2007. *Seeing Tongues, Hearing Scripts: Representation and the Modernity of the Ancient Novel.* Ancient Narrative suppl. 7. Groningen.
Ritook, Z. 1989. "The Views of Early Greek Epic on Poetry and Art." *Mnemosyne* 42: 331–348.
Robertson, D. S. 1971–72[4]. *Apulée. Les Métamorphoses.* Ed. D. S. Robertson and trans. P. Vallette. 3 vols. Paris.
Robiano, P. 2000. "La citation poétique dans le roman érotique grec." *REA* 102: 509–529.
Roca Ferrer, J. 1974. *"Kynikòs trópos:* Cinismo y Subversión Literaria en la Antiguedad." Barcelona.
Rosati, G. 2003. *"Quis ille?* Identità e metamorfosi nel romanzo di Apuleio." In *Memoria e identità. La cultura romana costruisce la sua immagine,* ed. M. Citroni, 267–296. Florence.
Roscalla, F. 1998. *Presenze simboliche dell'ape nella Grecia antica.* Florence.
Rossi, L. 2001. *The Epigrams Ascribed to Theocritus: A Method of Approach.* Leuven.
Rothaus, R. M. 2000. *Corinth, the First City of Greece: An Urban History of Late Antique Cult and Religion.* Leiden-Boston-Cologne.
Ruiz-Montero, C. 2003. "Xenophon of Ephesus and Orality in the Roman Empire." *Ancient Narrative* 3: 43–62.
Russell, D. A. 1964. *'Longinus,' On the Sublime.* Oxford.
———, ed. 1990a. *Antonine Literature.* Oxford.
———. 1990b. *"Greek and Latin in Antonine Literature."* In Russell 1990a, 1–17.
Sandy, G. N. 1974. *"Serviles voluptates* in Apuleius' *Metamorphoses." Phoenix* 28: 234–244.
———. 1997. *The Greek World of Apuleius: Apuleius and the Second Sophistic.* Leiden.
———. 1999a. *"Apuleius' Golden Ass: From Miletus to Aegypt."* In Hofmann 1999, 81–102.
———. 1999b. "The Tale of Cupid and Psyche." In Hofmann 1999, 126–138.
———. 2001. "A Neo-Platonic Interpretation of Heliodorus." In *OPORA. La belle saison de l'hellénisme. Études de littérature antique offertes au Recteur Jacques Bompaire,* ed. A. Billault, 169–178. Paris.
Sanzi, E. 2003. *I culti orientali nell'Impero romano: un'antologia di fonti.* Cosenza.
Scarcia, R. 1964. *Latina Siren: note di critica semantica.* Rome.

Schein, S. L., ed. 1996. *Reading the Odyssey.* Princeton, N.J.
Schepens, G. 1970. "Éphore sur la valeur de l'autopsie (F Gr Hist 70 F 110 = Polybe XII 27.7)." *AncSoc* 1: 163–182.
Schlam, C. 1970. "Platonica in the *Metamorphoses* of Apuleius." *TAPhA* 101: 477–487.
———. 1992. *The Metamorphoses of Apuleius: On Making an Ass of Oneself.* London.
Schlam, C. (†)–Finkelpearl, E. 2000. "A Review of Scholarship on Apuleius' *Metamorphoses* 1970–1998." *Lustrum* 42 (monographic issue).
Schmeling, G., ed. 1996. *The Novel in the Ancient World.* Boston-Leiden.
Schmeling, G.–Montiglio, S. 2006. "Riding the Waves of Passion: An Exploration of an Image of Appetites in Apuleius' *Metamorphoses*." In Keulen–Nauta–Panayotakis 2006, 28–41.
Schmidt, V. 1982. "Apuleius *Met.* III 15 f.: die Einweihung in die falschen Mysterien (Apuleiana Groningana VII)." *Mnemosyne* 35: 269–282.
———. 1997. "Reaktionen auf das Christentum in den *Metamorphosen* des Apuleius." *VChr* 51: 51–71.
———. 2003. "Is There an Allusion to the Christian Eucharist in Apuleius, *Met.* 9, 14–15?" *Latomus* 62: 864–874.
Schouler, B. 1987. "Les sophistes et le théâtre au temps des empereurs." In *Anthropologie et théâtre antique*, ed. P. Ghiron-Bistagne and B. Schouler, 280–283. Montpellier.
Scivoletto, N. 1963. "Antiquaria romana in Apuleio." In *Studi di letteratura latina imperiale*, 222–253. Naples.
Scobie, A. 1975. *Apuleius, Metamorphoses (Asinus Aureus). Book I: A Commentary.* Meisenheim am Glan.
Sedley, D. 2004. *The Midwife of Platonism: Text and Subtext in Plato's Theaetetus.* Oxford.
Segal, C. 1983. "*Kleos* and Its Ironies in the *Odyssey.*" *AC* 52: 22–47 (later in Schein 1996, 201–221).
Shanzer, D. 1986. *A Philosophical and Literary Commentary on Martianus Capella's De nuptiis Philologiae et Mercurii, Book 1.* Berkeley, Los Angeles.
Shumate, N. 1996. *Crisis and Conversion in Apuleius' Metamorphoses.* Ann Arbor, Mich.
Slater, N. W. 2002. "Space and Displacement in Apuleius." In Paschalis–Frangoulidis 2002, 161–176.
———. 2003. "Spectator and Spectacle in Apuleius." In Panayotakis–Zimmerman–Keulen 2003, 85–100.
Smith, W. S. 1972. "The Narrative Voice in Apuleius' *Metamorphoses*." *TAPhA* 103: 513–534 (later with "Afterword 1997," in Harrison 1999, 195–216).
———. 1996. "The Satiric Voice in the Roman Novelistic Tradition." In *Unity and Diversity: Proceedings of the Fourth International Conference on Narrative*, ed. J. Knuf, 309–317. Lexington, Ky.
———. 1998. "Cupid and Psyche Tale: Mirror of the Novel." In *AAGA* 1998, 69–82.
Smith, W. S.–Woods, B. 2002. "Tale of Aristomenes: Declamation in a Platonic Mode." *Ancient Narrative* 2: 172–193.
Solimano, G. 1991. *La prepotenza dell'occhio. Riflessioni sull'opera di Seneca.* Genoa.
Soverini, P. 2004. *Cornelio Tacito, Agricola.* Alessandria.
Stahl, W. H. 1952. *Macrobius. A Commentary on the Dream of Scipio.* New York-London.
Stanford, W. B. 1954. *The Ulysses Theme.* Oxford.
Stephens, S. 1994. "Who Read Ancient Novels?" In Tatum 1994, 405–417.

Stramaglia, A. 1996a. "Fra 'consumo' e 'impegno': usi didattici della narrativa nel mondo antico." In Pecere–Stramaglia 1996, 97–166.
———. 1996b. "Apuleio come auctor: Premesse tardoantiche di un uso umanistico." *Studi Umanistici Piceni* 16: 137–161 (later in Pecere–Stramaglia 2003, 119–152 [the page numbers in the text refer to this edition]).
———. 1999. *Res inauditae, incredulae. Storie di fantasmi nel mondo greco-latino*. Bari.
Summers, R. J. 1970. "Roman Justice and Apuleius' *Metamorphoses*." *TAPhA* 101: 511–531.
Susanetti, D. 2005. *Favole antiche. Mito greco e tradizione letteraria europea*. Rome.
Swain, S. 1996. *Hellenism and Empire: Language, Classicism, and Power in the Greek World, A.D. 50–250*. New York.
Takács, S. A. 1995. *Isis & Sarapis in the Roman World*. Leiden.
Taplin, O., ed. 2000. *Literature in the Greek and Roman Worlds: A New Perspective*. Oxford, New York.
Tatum, J. 1979. *Apuleius and the Golden Ass*. Ithaca, N.Y., London.
———, ed. 1994. *The Search for the Ancient Novel*. Baltimore, London.
Tentorio, G. 2009. "Sirene sofoclee (Soph. Fr. 861 Radt) e manipolazione argomentativa in Plutarco (*Quaest. Conv.* 9.745f)." *SIFC* 102: 5–55.
Thibau, R. 1965. "Les *Métamorphoses* d'Apulée et la théorie platonicienne de l'Erôs." *Studia Philosophica Gandensia* 3: 89–144.
Thomas, R. F. 1993. "Callimachus Back in Rome." In *Callimachus*, ed. M. A. Harder, R. F. Regtuit, and G. C. Wakker, 197–215. Groningen.
Tilg, S. 2007. "Lucius on Poetics? The Prologue to Apuleius' *Metamorphoses* Reconsidered." *SIFC* 100: 156–198.
Tomberg, K.-H. 1968. *Die Kaine Historia des Ptolemaios Chennos*. Bonn.
Too, Y. L. 2001. "Losing the Author's Voice: Cultural and Personal Identities in the *Metamorphoses* Prologue." In Kahane–Laird 2001, 177–187.
Torelli, M. 1975. *Elogia Tarquiniensia*. Florence.
Trapp, M. 1990. "Plato's *Phaedrus* in Second-Century Greek Literature." In Russell 1990a, 141–173.
———. 2001. "On Tickling the Ears: Apuleius' Prologue and the Anxieties of Philosophers." In Kahane–Laird 2001, 39–46.
Trypanis, K. A. 1958. *Callimachus. Aetia, Iambi, Lyric Poems, Hecale, Minor Epic and Elegiac Poems, Fragments of Epigrams, Fragments of Uncertain Location*. London-Cambridge, Mass.
Turcan, R. 1975. *Mithras Platonicus: Recherches sur l'hellénisation philosophique de Mithra*. Leiden.
———. 2003. "*Fani quidem advena, religionis autem indigena* (Apulée, *Métamorphoses* XI, 26, 3)." In Defosse 2003, 547–556.
Vallette, P. 1908. *L'Apologie d'Apulée*. Paris.
van der Paardt, R. Th. 1981. "The Unmasked 'I.'" *Mnemosyne* 34: 96–106 (later in Harrison 1999: 237–246; the page numbers in the text refer to this edition).
van Mal-Maeder, D. 1997a. "*Lector, intende: laetaberis:* The Enigma of the Last Book of Apuleius' *Metamorphoses*." *GCN* 8: 87–118.
———. 1997b. "Descriptions et descripteurs: mais qui décrit dans les *Métamorphoses* d'Apulée?" In Picone–Zimmermann 1997, 171–201.
———. 2001. *Apuleius Madaurensis, Metamorphoses, Livre II*. Groningen.

Van Mal-Maeder, D.–Zimmerman, M. 1998. "The Many Voices in *Cupid and Psyche*." In *AAGA* 1998, 83–102.
van Thiel, H. 1971–72. *Der Eselsroman*. Vol. 1: *Untersuchungen*, 1971; vol. 2: *Synoptische Ausgabe*, 1972. Munich.
Veyne, P. 1965. "Apulée à Cenchrées." *RPh* 39: 241–251.
Vidman, L. 1969. *Sylloge inscriptionum religionis Isiacae et Sarapicae*. Berlin.
Vössing, K. 1997. *Schule und Bildung im Nordafrika der Römischen Kaiserzeit*. Brussels.
Walbank, F. W. 1967. *A Historical Commentary on Polybius*. Vol. 2. Oxford.
Walker, J. 2000. *Rhetoric and Poetics in Antiquity*. Oxford.
Wallach, B. P. 1975. Review of Giangrande 1972. *AJPh* 96: 211–214.
Walsh, P. G. 1968. "Was Lucius a Roman?" *CJ* 63: 264–265.
———. 1970. *The Roman Novel*. Cambridge.
Waszink, J. H. 1974. *Biene und Honig als Symbol des Dichters und der Dichtung in der griechisch-römischen Antike*. Opladen.
Watson, L. C. 2003. *A Commentary on Horace's Epodes*. Oxford-New York.
Weinbrot, H. D. 2005. *Menippean Satire Reconsidered: From Antiquity to the Eighteenth Century*. Baltimore.
Wesseling, B. 1988. "The Audience of the Ancient Novels." *GCN* 1: 67–79.
West, D. 1974. "Of Mice and Men: Horace, *Satires* 2.6.77–117." In *Quality and Pleasure in Latin Poetry*, ed. T. Woodman and D. West, 67–80. Cambridge.
White, D. A. 1993. *Rhetoric and Reality in Plato's Phaedrus*. New York.
Whitmarsh, T. 1999. "Greek and Roman in Dialogue: The Pseudo-Lucianic Nero." *JHS* 119: 142–160.
———. 2001. *Greek Literature and the Roman Empire: The Politics of Imitation*. Oxford.
Wille, G. 2001. *Akroasis. Der akustische Sinnesbereich in der griechischen Literatur bis zum Ende der klassischen Zeit*. 2 vols. Tübingen-Basel.
Willis, J. 1975. "Martianea V." *Mnemosyne* 28: 126–134.
———, ed. 1983. *Martianus Capella*. Leipzig.
Wilson, N., ed. 1992. *Fozio. Biblioteca*. Milan.
Winkler, J. J. 1982. "The Mendacity of Kalasiris and the Narrative Strategy of Heliodoros' *Aithiopika*." *YCS* 27: 93–158 (later in *Oxford Readings in the Greek Novel*, ed. S. Swain [Oxford, 1999], 286–350 [the page numbers in the text refer to this edition]).
———. 1985. *Auctor & Actor: A Narratological Reading of Apuleius's The Golden Ass*. Berkeley.
Wiseman, J. 1979. "Corinth and Rome I: 228 B.C.–A.D. 267." In *ANRW* 2.7.1: 438–548.
Witt, R. E. 1975. "Some Thoughts on Isis in Relation to Mithras." In *Mithraic Studies: Proceedings of the First International Congress of Mithraic Studies*, ed. J. R. Hinnells, 2: 479–493. Manchester, U.K.
Wlosok, A. 1969. "Zur Einheit der *Metamorphosen* des Apuleius." *Philologus* 113: 68–84 (later trans. into English in Harrison 1999, 142–156).
Zanker, P. 1997. *La maschera di Socrate. L'immagine dell'intellettuale nell'arte antica*. Turin (first published as *Die Maske des Sokrates. Das Bild des Intellektuellen in der antiken Kunst* [Munich, 1995]).
Zimmerman, F. 1961. "Chariton und die Geschichte." In *Sozialökonomische Verhältnisse im alten Orient und im klassischen Altertum*, ed. H. J. Diesner et al., 329–345. Berlin.
Zimmerman, M. 2000. *Apuleius Madaurensis. Metamorphoses, Book X*. Groningen.

———. 2002. "Latinising the Novel: Scholarship since Perry on Greek 'Models' and Roman (Re-)creations." *Ancient Narrative* 2: 123–142.

———. 2005. "Les grandes villes dans les *Métamorphoses* d'Apulée." In *Lieux, décors et paysages de l'ancien roman des origines à Byzance: actes du 2e Coll. de Tours, 24–26 Oct. 2002*, ed. B. Pouderon and D. Crismani, 29–41. Lyon.

———. 2006. "Echoes of Roman Satire in Apuleius' *Metamorphoses*." In Nauta 2006b, 87–104.

index locorum

The abbreviations used are from the *Greek-English Lexicon* by H. G. Liddell, R. Scott and H. S. Jones and from the *Thesaurus Linguae Latinae*, with a small number of personal variations and integrations.

Accius
   Trag. **173**, 151n43
Achilles Tatius
   1.2.2, 38–39, 39n121; **1.2.3**, 18n50;
   1.5.6, 42n131; **5.17.3**, 83;
   8.14.2–4, 59n16
Aelian
   NA **5.13**, 19
Aelius Aristides
   28.144, 24n68; **34.16–18**, 29
Aeschines
   In Ctes. **228**, 36
Aesop
   195, 10n23; **282**, 84
Anthologia Graeca
   5.57, 112n187; **5.179**, 112n187;
   6.120, 16n41; **6.164**, 83n93;
   7.42, 16n41; **7.190** (Anyte), 17;
   7.192, 17n47; **7.193**, 16n41;
   7.194, 16n41; **7.195** (Meleager),
   17; **7.196** (Meleager), 17; **7.197**,
   16n41; **7.198**, 16n41; **7.297**
   (Polystratus), 170; **9.92**, 16n41;
   9.203.7–10, 130n237; **9.284**
   (Crinagoras), 172; **9.434.1–2**
   (Theocritus), 8; **11.130.1** (Pollianus), 4n10; **12.80**, 112n187;
   12.91, 112n187; **12.98**,
   112n187; **12.132**, 112n187;
   16.151, 197n103; **16.151.9**,
   197n109
Anyte. See *Anthologia Graeca*
Apollonius Rhodius
   4.893, 19n52; **4.893–4**, 34
Appendix Vergiliana Dirae
   26, 155n54
Apuleius
   Apol. **4**, 88, 189n73; **4.1**, 175; **9**,
   13n33, 97n134; **10.6**, 14n36,
   37n115; **23**, 187n69; **24.1**,
   165n1; **26.5**, 21n58; **31.5**,
   150n39; **38.3**, 150; **43**, 190n74;
   55.8, 67n42; **61.6**, 189n73;
   61.7, 189; **63**, 189; **64.1**, 188;
   64.3, 189; **64.7**, 188; **74**, 83n92;
   84.3–4, 193n86; **98.8**, 165n1,
   197
   Flor. **3.3**, 14n36; **3.9**, 150n39;
   9.8–13, 159n66; **9.14**, 12n31;
   9.24, 150n39; **9.27–29**, 12n31;

INDEX LOCORUM

13.1, 19; 17.4, 182; 17.9–19, 23, 26; **18–19**, 150n39; **18.1–2**, 199; **18.14–16**, 201; **20**, 202, 205
Frg. **8**, 151n43
Met. **1.1**, 132; **1.1.1**, 3, 7n17, 10n24, 28, 30, 35, 43–44, 46, 52, 164, 185; **1.1.2**, 37, 43–44; **1.1.3**, 15n38, 28, 52, 174, 185; **1.1.4**, 52, 152, 174, 185; **1.1.5**, 7n17, 28, 52; **1.1.6**, 7n17, 10n26, 28, 52, 164, 175; **1.2.1**, 73, 140n15, 190n75; **1.2.3**, 137; **1.2.6**, 135–36, 163n82; **1.3.1**, 21, 78, 136; **1.3.2**, 136; **1.4.5**, 158n63; **1.4.6**, 136, 163n82; **1.5–19**, 135; **1.5.1**, 136; **1.5.3**, 73; **1.6.1**, 139; **1.6.4**, 58, 135; **1.7.6**, 73; **1.7.7**, 151n43; **1.7.9–10**, 78; **1.7.10**, 58; **1.8.3–5**, 78; **1.8.4**, 77; **1.13.3**, 163n82; **1.15.2**, 83n92; **1.18.8**, 135; **1.20.1**, 78, 136; **1.20.2**, 163n82; **1.20.3**, 136; **1.20.5**, 114n192, 136, 138; **1.22.4**, 166n2; **1.23.6**, 12n31; **1.24.3**, 73, 180; **1.25**, 119n201; **1.25.1**, 180; **2.1.1**, 150n38; **2.1.2**, 21, 152n47, 163n82; **2.1.3–5**, 140; **2.2.1**, 180; **2.2.8–9**, 134; **2.3.2**, 73; **2.4.3**, 158n63; **2.5.4**, 77n75; **2.6.1**, 78; **2.7.4**, 179; **2.10.2**, 73, 178n42; **2.12.3**, 166n2; **2.12.5**, 128n233, 159–60, 163n82; **2.15.5**, 73n62; **2.19.5–6**, 206; **2.20.7**, 163n82; **2.21.3**, 44; **2.25.1**, 15n38; **2.31.1**, 163n82; **2.31.4**, 73n62, 151n43; **2.32**, 141; **3.4–5**, 195; **3.5–6**, 194; **3.8.7**, 73n62; **3.15.3–5**, 77n76; **3.15.4**, 67n41; **3.19.6**, 151; **3.24**, 141; **3.24.3–6**, 78n77, 127; **3.24.5**, 136; **3.24.6**, 153n49; **3.27.2–3**, 63n25; **3.27.4**, 73n62; **3.29.3**, 26n73; **3.29.5–8**, 63n25; **4.2**, 63n25; **4.14.3**, 158n63; **4.27.5–8**, 109; **4.27.6–7**, 5–6; **4.27.8**, 4, 24, 30, 95, 110n178, 137, 163n82; **4.30.1**, 188, 190; **4.32.5**, 120; **4.32.6**, 44; **4.35.2**, 151n43; **5.6.1**, 21; **5.8.1**, 147n31; **5.9.8**, 83; **5.18.4**, 190n74; **5.24.1**, 113, 115; **5.30.6**, 83; **6.4.1**, 186, 202; **6.4.5**, 204; **6.8.2**, 181; **6.8.4**, 152n47; **6.24.3**, 159n68; **6.24.4**, 74n67; **6.25.1**, 30, 95, 110–11, 112n184, 160; **6.27.5–6**, 115n193; **6.29.3**, 10n25, 158, 160, 163n82; **6.29.5**, 127; **6.30.5**, 168n12; **6.32.3**, 145n28; **7.1.5–6**, 63n23; **7.2.2**, 73n62; **7.10.3–4**, 81, 121; **7.12.1**, 81n86; **7.13.2**, 157; **7.15.2**, 63n25; **7.26.3**, 168n12; **8.1.3**, 13–14; **8.1.4**, 160; **8.2.1**, 152n47; **8.3.3**, 158n63; **8.7.3**, 152n47; **8.8.4**, 152n47; **8.10.1**, 21; **8.16.3**, 168n12; **8.17.3**, 158; **8.23.5**, 140n16; **8.24.2**, 79; **8.24.2**, 80n85, 84n96; **8.24.2–6**, 67n41; **8.25**, 159n68; **8.25.5**, 79; **8.25.6**, 79; **8.27.8**, 80; **8.28.1**, 158n63; **8.28.6**, 80n81; **8.29.2**, 80n82; **8.29.6**, 80; **8.30.1**, 80; **8.30.5**, 80n84, 81n85; **9.3.3**, 58; **9.3.4**, 146; **9.4.1**, 58; **9.4.4**, 163n82; **9.8.1**, 80; **9.8.1–6**, 80n82; **9.9–10**, 80n81; **9.12.1**, 140n16; **9.13.3**, 141; **9.13.4**, 142, 145; **9.13.4–5**, 141; **9.13.5**, 149; **9.14.1**, 146, 161, 163n82; **9.14.5**, 79, 111n182; **9.15.5**, 112; **9.15.6**, 145; **9.16–21**, 146; **9.16.1**, 111n182, 119n201, 146, 161, 161n74; **9.17–21**, 111n182; **9.17.2**, 163n82; **9.22.4**, 161n74; **9.23.5**, 163n82; **9.24.4**, 80n83; **9.28.4**, 191; **9.30.1**, 160, 161n74, 182; **9.39.2**, 196n101; **9.39.3**, 168n9, 196; **9.39.4**, 196n101; **9.42.4**, 140n16; **10.2.1**, 158; **10.2.4**, 158n64,

162; **10.7.4**, 158n65; **10.13.7**,
150n38; **10.15.5**, 140n16;
10.16–17, 127n232; **10.18.1**,
169n13; **10.18.2**, 151n43;
10.18.3, 73; **10.19.1**, 166;
10.29.2, 63; **10.29.4–10.34.2**,
156n57; **10.30.1**, 159n68;
10.33, 121; **10.35.3**, 166;
11.1, 57; **11.1.4**, 58n15, 59;
11.2, 57; **11.2.2–3**, 64; **11.6.2**,
69n51, 90n11; **11.7**, 57; **11.7.1**,
57n11; **11.8.4**, 168n12; **11.9.1**,
63n22; **11.9.4**, 80n85; **11.9.6**,
63n22; **11.10.1**, 82; **11.11.1**,
188; **11.12.1**, 64; **11.13.1**, 115;
11.13–14, 57; **11.13.1**, 63;
11.14.1, 52, 56, 132; **11.14.2**,
63; **11.14.4**, 57; **11.15**, 75,
81n86, 109n173, 115, 119;
11.15.1, 115; **11.15.1–2**, 115;
11.15.1–4, 59–60; **11.16.2–4**,
60; **11.16.3**, 61, 63; **11.16.3–4**,
62; **11.16.4**, 61n20; **11.19.1**, 70;
11.20.3–4, 87; **11.20.6**, 73n62,
163n82; **11.21.1**, 72; **11.21.3**,
73; **11.21.4**, 70; **11.22.3**, 59, 64,
70; **11.23.1**, 59, 70; **11.23.4**, 72;
11.23.5, 152n47; **11.23.5–6**,
161; **11.23.5–7**, 77n76; **11.24.6**,
70, 151n43; **11.25**, 87; **11.25.3–4**, 77; **11.25.6–7**, 70; **11.25.7**,
67n41; **11.26.1**, 166; **11.26.2**,
205–6; **11.26.3**, 74n65, 206;
11.26.4, 74n66, 75; **11.27.2–9**,
68; **11.27.7**, 192; **11.27.8**, 70;
11.27.9, 53n1, 121n205, 152,
186, 187n67; **11.28.1**, 70;
11.28.3–4, 78; **11.28.5**, 82;
11.28.6, 72, 87n107; **11.29.1**,
70; **11.29.2–3**, 74; **11.29.4–5**,
74; **11.29.5**, 192n83; **11.30.2**,
72; **11.30.4–5**, 206n128;
11.30.4, 73n62, 87n107, 88,
152, 192n83; **11.30.5**, 75n67,
82
Soc. **14**, 71; **18**, 148n33; **22**, 71; **24**,
148

Aristophanes
  Pl. **287**, 24
  Ra. **159**, 80n83; **389–90**, 125
Aristoteles
  Po. **1447b**, 41n125
  Rh. **1405a**, 32n97
  In Aristotelis Artem Rhetoricam Commentarium **161**, 29n88
Arnobius
  Nat. **7.33**, 84
Artemidorus of Daldi
  1.22, 83n93
Athenaeus
  Deipn. **1.24**, 112n184, 125n222, 148
Augustine
  Civ. **18.18**, 187n68, 193n87
  Conf. **1.13.33**, 197n103
  Epist. **138.19**, 185, 194n91, 201n114
Boethius
  Cons. **3.1**, 22n62
Callimachus
  Aet. **1.20**, 9; **1.29**, 19n52; **1.31f.**, 9; **1.32**, 20n57; **112.8f.**, 9; **192.11**, 10n23
Calpurnius Siculus
  4.2, 18n50
Chariton
  1.1.1, 39n121; **1.5.4**, 194n94; **1.7.6**, 178; **5.7.10**, 178; **8.1.4**, 38, 162n78; **8.7.9**, 178, 199n109
Cicero
  Agr. **2.87**, 170; **2.102**, 26n72
  Brut. **40**, 32n100; **58**, 11n27
  Caec. **9**, 26n72
  De orat. **1.28**, 18n50; **2.25**, 122
  Fin. **5.48–49**, 147–48
  Leg **2.7**, 18n50
  Mur. **90**, 26n72
  N.D. **1.34**, 122n213; **3.12**, 99; **3.91**, 170
  Off. **3.46**, 170
  Orat. **25**, 27n78; **57**, 27n79; **65ff.**, 32n97; **163–164**, 27
  Planc. **29**, 159n66

Sen. 31, 32n100
CIL 1².189, 181
Clement of Alexandria
    Strom. 1.3.22.5, 29n88
Crinagoras. See *Anthologia Graeca*
Curtius Rufus
    8.2.19–8.4.20, 67n39
Dictys Cretensis
    1.20, 151n43
Dio Chrysostom
    32.101, 24n68; 37.25–26, 173n24;
    37.42, 173n25
Diodorus Siculus
    1.1.2, 143; 1.1.4, 143; 1.4.1, 143;
    1.83.9, 143; 3.27.1, 170–71
Diogenes Laertius
    9.17, 124
Dionysius of Halicarnassus
    Dem. 35, 36
Donatus
    Vita Verg. 26–27, 155n54
Ennius
    Ann. 1.5, 16n41
Epiphanius
    Haer. 3.333, 29n88
Eunapius
    VS 6.5.1–2, 36n113; 7.3.4, 65
Eusebius
    De laudibus Constantini 1, 29n88,
    41, 46–47
Eutropius
    4.14.2, 172
Florus
    1.32.1, 170; 2.7, 190;
Fronto
    Ant. 2.16, 26; 4.3, 26
    Aur. 1.9.3, 27n78, 28n82; 4.3.2,
    131n240
Fulgentius
    Myth. 1, 30n92, 105–6; 3.117, 106
Gellius
    2.29.1, 108; 5.14.4, 144n24;
    9.4.13, 144n24; 9.9.3ff., 12n31;
    10.22.1, 123n216; 16.3.1,
    34n109; 17.17.1, 165n1;
    17.20.4, 178n42; 20.9.1, 27n78
Greek Anthology. See *Anthologia Graeca*

Heliodorus
    2.22.3, 141–42; 3.1.1, 156–57;
    3.3.1, 162n77; 3.4.7, 157;
    3.4.11, 157; 4.4.2, 137n10;
    5.16.5, 178; 6.2.2, 137; 10.39,
    66–67, 109n173; 10.41.4,
    162n78
Heraclitus
    Frg. 16M., 150n40
Hermogenes of Tharsus
    Peri ideon 2.4, 41
Herodotus
    2.36.1, 82; 2.37.2, 82
Herondas
    8, 16n41
Hesiod
    Th. 92, 32n98; 94–96, 9; 98–103,
    33
Hieronymus
    Comm. in Isaiam PLD 24.409d, 48
    Epist. 119.1, 11n27
    Ruf. 1.17, 48–49
    Historia Augusta
        Alb. 11.5, 48; **Alb.** 12.12, 23,
        44, 48, 96, 185n61
Homer
    Il. 1.248, 32; 2.219, 84; 2.538,
    205n126; 3.1, 4n10; 15.1,
    4n10; 16.432, 203
    Od. 1.5, 151; 1.13, 151; 1.57, 33;
    3.103ff., 33; 3.264, 32; 3.485,
    205n126; 5.306, 171; 6.1,
    4n10; 8.83ff., 135; 8.169ff., 32;
    8.500, 178; 9.96–97, 151n44;
    9.515, 147n31; 9.520–25, 178;
    10.81, 205n126; 10.240, 150;
    10.254, 153n48; 10.301, 143;
    10.341, 153; 10.347, 153; 11.1,
    4n10; 12.1, 4n10; 12.5–7, 153;
    12.40, 33; 12.44, 19n52, 33,
    34, 153n48; 12.183, 19n52,
    153n48; 12.184, 153; 12.184–
    91, 148; 12.185, 35; 12.187,
    33; 12.188, 35; 12.189–90, 33,
    35, 153; 13.399, 85; 13.431, 85;
    14.1, 4n10; 14.387, 32; 15.193,
    205n126; 16.195, 32; 17.514,

32; 17.521, 32; 18.282, 32;
  18.354f., 86; 19.1, 4n10; 20.1,
  4n10; 24.62, 19n52
Hymni Homerici
  H. Ap. 546, 9n21
  H. Cer. 495, 9n21
  H. Merc. 580, 9n21
  H. Ven. 293, 9n21
Horace
  Ars 99–100, 22; 129f., 159n66;
    333f., 22, 104; 338, 104n156;
    343f., 22
  Carm. 1.6.1–9, 7n16; 1.7.1–10, 7;
    1.10.3–4, 188; 1.10.19–20, 188;
    1.17.17–20, 15n38; 1.31.9–15,
    7n16; 2.1.25, 205n124; 2.1.26,
    205n124; 2.2.26ff., 205n127;
    2.20, 184n56; 3.13.9–12,
    15n38; 4.2.25–32, 7n16
  Epist. 1.2.23–26, 149; 1.16.14f.,
    104n156; 1.16.26, 27n78;
    1.19.6–8, 30n93; 2.1.199,
    24n68; 2.1.210–213, 31;
    2.1.212, 34n109; 2.1.213,
    164n87
  Epod. 16.60, 152; 17.16, 152
  Sat. 1.1, 104n155; 1.4.34ff.,
    104n154; 1.10.81ff., 122; 2.2.1,
    103n153; 2.3.291, 58n15;
    2.6.77–79, 101–3; 2.6.79, 103
  Inscriptiones Graecae
    12.8.87, 124n220; 22.3814,
    191n79
Hyginus
  Fab. 125.2, 151n43
Ioannes Chrysostomos
  De sancta Thecla martyre 50.748,
    29n88
Isocrates
  Evag. 9ff., 32n97
  Panath. 1, 41n125; 4, 40n122
Josephus
  AJ 18.65ff., 71n55
Justin
  Apol. 2.2, 190
Juvenal
  5.171, 84; 6.522ff., 58n15; 6.532ff.,
    83n90; 6.539ff., 71n55; 12.81f.,
    83n93
Laus Pisonis
  64, 32n100
Livy
  1 *pr.* 5, 6; 1 *pr.* 6, 41; 34.4.4,
    172n20
[Longinus]
  Subl. 34.4, 178n40
Longus
  prol., 42n131; prol. 1.2, 37n114,
    162n78; prol. 1.3, 39
Lucan
  4.1, 4n9; 9.1, 4n9
Lucian
  Demon. 12, 29
  Herm. 86, 83n93
  Hist. conscr. 29.3, 144n25
  Merc. cond. 1, 83n93
  Philops. 4, 41n125; 34, 76n72
  Pseudol. 25, 164n85
  Salt. 2, 164n85; 54, 164n85
  VH 1.1, 45n143; 1.2, 38; 1.3, 144;
    1.4, 108, 162n78
[Lucian]
  Amores 1, 45; 1.1, 3
  Onos 6, 177–78; 11, 151n43;
    35–41, 80n84, 191n80;
    44–45, 196n101; 54, 58n12; 55,
    162n78, 168n9, 187
Lucilius
  frg. 261 M., 11
Macrobius
  Somn. 1.2.8, 23, 39, 96–97, 106,
    163n83
  Sat. 2.7, 159; 5.17.5–6, 197n103
Manilius
  3.29ff., 7n17
Martial
  1.1.2, 183n56; 1.72.8, 83; 3.58,
    18n50; 3.74, 83; 5.7, 83;
    6.39.15f., 85; 7.88.1ff., 183n56;
    8.3.13, 162n80; 8.3.4, 183n56;
    8.3.17–19, 8; 8.61.3–5, 183n56;
    10.83, 83; 11.3.3, 183n56;
    12.2.2, 183n55; 12.28.19,
    83n90; 12.2.1–2, 183n56

Martianus Capella
  De nuptiis **2.100**, 49; p. **997.1**, 105
Meleager. See *Anthologia Graeca*
[Moschus]
  Epitaphium Bionis **93f.**, 8
Nicolaus
  Prog. **3.491**, 154n51
Novum Testamentum
  1 Tim. **4.7**, 110n177
  Lc. **21.1–4**, 71n56
  Mc. **12.41–43**, 71n56
Ovid
  Am. **1.8.74**, 83n90; **3.10.1**, 83n90
  Fast. **1.13**, 7; **6.33**, 204n123; **6.37**, 204n123; **6.45**, 205n124; **6.45–49**, 203–4; **6.51–52**, 204
  Ib. **232**, 11n27
  Met. **1.716**, 34n109; **4.1**, 4n9; **5.555**, 35n112; **5.561**, 27n78, 34; **8.824**, 15n38; **11.179**, 24; **14.121**, 137n10; **14.158**, 152; **15.487ff.**, 137n11
  Pont. **12.1**, 4n9; **18.27**, 15n38
  Tr. **1.1.1**, 183n55; **2.1.358**, 27n78; **2.1.354–58**, 35, 41; **2.1.413f.**, 48n149; **2.1.443f.**, 48n149
Pacuvius
  Trag. **173**, 151n43
Pausanias
  2.31.3, 16n41; **7.16.10**, 171
Persius
  1.56, 86; **1.56–57**, 84; **1.121**, 24n68; **1.134**, 164n85; **2.15f.**, 58n15; **2.68f.**, 71n55; **3.9**, 11n28; **3.54**, 86
Petronius
  1.3, 33; **2.2**, 33n103; **5.1.15f.**, 33; **15.4**, 83n94; **32.2**, 83; **46.4**, 107n169; **50.5**, 172n21; **103.1–2**, 83; **107.6ff.**, 83n93; **109.9–10**, 83n93; **127.5**, 153n48
Phaedrus
  1 pr. 3–4, 107; **3 pr. 10**, 107n168; **3.16**, 19; **4.2.1–7**, 107
Philostratus I
  Her. **7.9**, 144n24; **7.10**, 99; **10.5**, 157n59; **25.13**, 144n26; **33.8**, 144n26; **43.1**, 36n113
  VA **5.14**, 132n247; **5.14.1**, 98, 108; **5.14.2**, 108; **5.14.5**, 108; **8.7**, 86n102
  VS **1.491**, 29, 34n109; **1.503**, 36; **1.511**, 31
Philostratus II
  Im. **1.15**, 99; **1.17**, 157n58
Photius
  Bibl. **72.36a**, 144n25; **86.66a**, 159n66; **94.73b**, 40; **109.96b**, 41; **129.96b**, 42–43, 91; **166.111b**, 2; **183.128a**, 40; **190.147a**, 147
Plato
  Ap. **27e**, 132n247
  Chrm. **157a**, 21n58
  Grg. **523a–526d**, 98; **527a**, 97n137, 98; **527e**, 98
  Hp. Ma. **285e–286a**, 97n137
  Ion **534a–b**, 16, 20n57
  Lg. **10.887c–e**, 97n137, 98
  Ly. **205d**, 97n137
  Phdr. **227d**, 137; **228b**, 137; **229c**, 138; **230a**, 138; **230b–c**, 18, 39n120; **230d**, 101n149, 127n230, 137; **237a**, 19n52, 135; **238d**, 31n94; **241e**, 31n94; **242d**, 31n94; **242e–243a**, 138; **245a**, 30n93; **245c**, 138; **247c**, 138; **248aff.**, 113; **248c**, 113; **250e**, 116n195, 117; **251e**, 117; **258d–e**, 116; **258e**, 18; **258e–259a**, 19n51, 21n58; **259a**, 140n16; **259a–d**, 41; **260b–c**, 132n247; **277a**, 137; **277b**, 138
  Phlb. **11b**, 67n41
  R. **1.350e**, 97n137; **2.377a**, 97n137; **2.377a–378d**, 97; **5.450b**, 38n120; **6.495e**, 84; **8.563c**, 132n247; **9.587c**, 116; **10.617b–c**, 36n112
  Symp. **173b**, 137n10; **180d ff.**, 46n145; **208b**, 37n117; **209e f.**, 116n195; **210d**, 116n196; **212d**, 123n214; **215a**, 123, 126n227;

215b–c, 128; 216a, 128; 216d, 129; 217a ff., 128; 218a, 129n234; 221e, 132n247; 221e–222a, 123; 222b, 153n47; 222c, 126n227; 223d, 126n227

Tht. 146a, 132n247; 147a ff., 140n16; 149a, 105n162, 123; 153a, 140n16; 154b, 140n16; 155d, 37n117; 158e, 140n16; 161e, 140n16; 176b, 97; 201b–c, 142n19

Tim. 26b–c, 97n137, 98, 105n161

[Plato]

Amatores 133c–139a, 150n40

Plautus

Amph. 118, 159; 149, 156n57; 154, 156n57; 155, 195n95; 456, 28n83; 462, 83

Cist. 149, 111n181

Curc. 76–77, 111n181

Pseudol. 35, 157n59

Pliny the Elder

Nat. pr. 7, 122; 10.136, 15n38; 11.266, 19n52; 30.9–10, 92n118, 93n122; 33.149, 172n20

Pliny the Younger

Ep. 14.1, 47n147

Plutarch

Crass. 32.4, 206n129

De poet. aud. 194ff., 112n184

De Is. et Os. 352c, 82

De r. rat. aud. 38a, 162n77; 41d, 29, 31, 162n77; 44b, 37

De superst. 3.166a, 57

Flam. 1.11, 171

Quaest. conv. 2.7.641b, 92n121; 9.2.737a, 171; 9.14.745f, 36n112

Quaest. Rom. 20.268e, 181

Quomodo adul. poetas audire debeat 17a, 41; 19e ff., 125n222

Alex. 58.3.5, 67n39

[Plutarch]

De prov. Alex. 32, 24n68

De vit. Hom. 126, 25n71, 149

Vitae X Orat. 838c, 36

Pollianus. See *Anthologia Graeca*

Pollux

Onomasticon 4.144ff., 84, 84n97

Polybius

1.4.11, 39n121; 12.12.3, 7; 12.27.2, 41; 12.27.3, 142n19; 12.27.10, 142; 12.28.1, 143n22; 39.2, 171

Polystratus. See *Anthologia Graeca*

Propertius

2.1.45f., 7, 9–10; 2.27.1, 4n9; 2.28.61, 83n90; 2.33.1, 83n90; 2.34.32, 16n41; 3.3, 16; 4.1.61f., 7

Quintilian

1.8.2, 29n87; 1.8.19, 99n140; 1.8.21, 99n142; 1.11.1, 28, 30; 2.4.2, 99; 2.12.6, 13n34, 27n78; 9.4.116, 27n78; 10.1.31, 41n125; 11.1.48, 27; 11.3.57–60, 27; 11.3.60, 27n78; 11.3.91, 28; 12.9.9, 11n27; 12.10.52, 27n78; 12.10.64, 32n100

Rhetorica ad Herennium 3.21.34, 151n43

Sallust

Cat. 3.2, 6

frg. 4.54, 11n27

Seneca

Ben. 1.3.5, 100n145; 1.3.8, 100; 1.4.5–6, 41, 100, 132

De vita beata 7.7.3, 116n195

Epist. 88.5, 125n224; 88.22, 154; 90.28, 159n66; 114.1, 28, 33n102

Her. f. 575, 34n109

Servius

In Verg. Buc. 6.11, 155n54

Sidonius Apollinaris

Epist. 7.2.9, 49

Silius Italicus

7.293, 15n38; 11.288ff., 27n78; 15.1, 4n9

Sophocles

Aj. 148f., 26n74

Statius

Theb. 1.718–20, 66; 2.30, 15n38; 3.1, 4n9

Stephanus of Byzantium
  Ethnika **193.6**, 124n221; **357.3**, 124
Stobaeus
  1.49.60, 25n71
Strabo
  1.1.1, 150n40; **11.11.4**, 67n39;
  8.6.28, 171; **16.2.29**, 124
Suetonius
  Iul. **45**, 84
Suidas
  Δ **1603**, 29n88
Synesius
  Enc. calv. **6.3**, 86; **11**, 86
Tacitus
  Ann. **1.1.1–3**, 7
  Dial. **12.1–2**, 32n97; **13.2**, 155n54;
    13.5, 19n52; **16.5**, 32n100;
    20.5–7, 32n97
  Hist. **1.1.1–3**, 7
Tertullian
  Apol. **50**, 197n103
  Castit. **13**, 197n103
  De an. **23.4**, 48
  Mart. **4**, 197n103;
  Spect. **8.6**, 181
Themistius
  Or. **28.341c**, 36
Theocritus
  1.1, 12, 14, 16, 22; **1.2–3**, 13; **1.80**,
    13; **1.148**, 19n53; **7.35–36**, 136
Theodoretus
  Interpr. in Ez. **81.917**, 29n88
Theodorus Priscianus
  Euporista **2.11.34**, 42n131
Thucydides
  1.1.2, 39n121; **1.22.4**, 39, 40;
  3.28.4–7, 157n62
Valerius Flaccus
  1.299, 15n38; **2.140**, 15n38; **6.1**,
    4n9; **6.201**, 155n54; **8.1**, 4n9

Valerius Maximus
  8.10.2, 159n66
Valgius Rufus
  2.4, 32n100
Varro
  Ling. **5.10.69**, 204n123
  Men. **490**, 86n101
  R. rust. **3.16.7**, 16
Virgil
  Aen. **1.4**, 204; **1.7**, 205; **1.12–16**,
    203; **1.36**, 204; **1.47**, 203;
    1.153, 32n101; **1.283ff.**, 171;
    1.419, 205n125; **1.495**, 179;
    1.613, 179; **2.774**, 179; **4.1**,
    4; **4.97**, 205, 205n126; **4.265**,
    205; **5.464**, 32n101; **5.769**, 152;
    6.836–37, 171n17; **7.65**, 19n52;
    7.754f., 15n38, 32n101; **8.309**,
    136; **8.370ff.**, 21; **8.380**, 152;
    10.607, 203
  Ecl. **1.1**, 15; **1.5**, 16; **1.53–55**, 14,
    20n57; **1.51–52**, 15–16; **1.65**,
    16; **3.85**, 155; **5.77**, 19; **9.64**,
    136 **10.16**, 13; **10.19**, 13
  Georg. **2.475**, 19n52
  Vita Aesopi **6**, 16; **7**, 17
Xenophon
  Hier. **11.15**, 39n121
  Mem. **1.3.7–8**, 149
  Resp. Lac. **1.1**, 4
  Symp. **1.1**, 4, 126n226; **1.11**,
    126n226; **2.6.9–10**, 128; **2.6.31**,
    128; **2.12**, 127; **2.17**, 126n226;
    3.11.16–17, 128; **4.6–7**,
    125n224; **4.19**, 126n226, 127;
    4.29, 126n226; **5.5**, 127; **5.5–7**,
    126n226; **5.6**, 127; **5.7**, 87n104,
    127; **6.6**, 126n226
Xenophon of Ephesus
  1.10.3, 142; **5.5.4**, 83

general index

Achilles Tatius, 42n131, 74n67, 154, 159n66, 163n85
Aelius Aristides, 28, 91n114
Aeschylus, 41
Aesop and Aesopic fable, 84, 98, 101–3, 108–9, 112, 120n202, 132. See also *Life of Aesop*
allegory, 23, 25, 54, 56, 100n145, 105, 106n166, 110n178, 112–13, 129–31
ancient novel: ancient reception, 1; and theater, 1; birth of, 1; fictional character, 1–2; Greek and Roman, 175, 178n41; names of, 1–2, 40; poetics of, 38–42; readers of, 1–2, 38–39, 122, 122n209, 176n33, 199n108
anilis fabula. See old wives' tales
Antonius Diogenes, 2, 37n114, 39–40, 92
Apuleius: house at Ostia, 68–69, 192; trial in Sabratha, 182
Apuleius' *Metamorphoses: Africitas*, 193; and the *Apology*, 188–90, 192n86; and the *Florida*, 184, 200n112; edition *in usum Delphini*, 30; manuscript tradition, 185; narrator of *Cupid and Psyche*, 5–6; prologue speaker, 3n4, 4–5, 10–11, 44n137, 52n1, 174; readers of, 3–7, 10–12, 17, 21–25, 37, 41–42, 51, 54–58, 61, 64, 71, 74–75, 81, 87, 89–92, 98–99, 102, 111–15, 118–22, 129–31, 145, 154–64, 166–69, 173, 180–82, 184, 187, 194–95, 197–200
Aristides of Miletus, 3, 5n12, 42–50, 102n151, 162, 206n129
Aristomenes, 21, 24n69, 58, 73, 78, 114n192, 119, 127n231, 134–40, 160, 163n82
Asinius Marcellus, 68, 70, 74, 152, 192
astonishment, 36–37, 62–63, 179

baldness and shaven heads, 55, 66, 73n60, 79, 82–90, 134, 139n12
bees, 15–20, 33
bilingualism, 165, 173n23, 175–76
Bolus of Mendes, 92
bucolic poetry, 8, 13–22

Caelestis, 202, 204, 205n124
Callimachus, 8–12, 19n53, 20n57
Calypso, 33–34, 151
Carthage, 48, 96, 170, 182n51, 183–86, 192, 193–94, 197–99, 201n117, 202–5, 207
Ceionius Rufius Volusianus, 65
Charite, 5, 13, 14, 21, 81, 107n167, 110,

236

110n178, 115, 115n193, 121, 127,
   137, 152n47, 158, 159, 163n82,
   196, 196n102
Christian religion, 71, 79n78, 110n177,
   130, 190–92
cicadas, 9, 10–12, 14, 17–22, 36, 41,
   129, 138, 140
Circe, 25, 148–53
Corinth, 70, 85, 144n25, 151n43,
   166–75, 186, 197, 205
Cupid and Psyche, 4, 5, 12n31, 24, 30,
   44, 47n148, 48, 66, 74n67, 95,
   101, 105n161, 106, 106n166, 109,
   110–23, 131, 137, 159, 163n82
curiosity, 21, 24n69, 53–55, 59–61, 75,
   76n70, 91, 106, 107n167, 112–13,
   117, 120, 129, 132, 135–36,
   138–39, 141, 146, 147n31, 150,
   152, 152n47, 160–61

Dea Syria, 59, 66n34, 67n41, 76, 76n71,
   79, 80, 84, 190–91
Dido, 179, 196–97, 201, 203
Diophanes, 76, 128n233, 159
dreams, 5, 16, 16n41, 20n57, 55, 70–72,
   74, 87, 88, 106, 115, 127, 152, 154

Ennius, 7, 16, 30n93, 165, 193n88
epic poetry, 4, 7, 8–9, 11, 30–34, 41,
   107n167, 109–10, 122, 125n223,
   130, 133, 142, 146–54, 170, 179,
   197, 203–5
Eudocia, 40

fabula Milesia, 2–3, 5n12, 23, 24n77,
   28, 42–50, 53n1, 56n7, 75, 96,
   104n158, 107, 118n199, 120,
   127n231, 131n240, 162, 186, 194
Favorinus of Arles, 29, 32, 34n109, 173,
   175
Fortuna, 59–63, 75
forum Cupidinis, 180, 182
Fulgentius, 23, 30n92, 90, 105–7,
   110–11, 129–31, 151n43

Harpokration of Alexandria, 92
Heliodorus, 2, 25, 39, 66, 130, 142,
   144n24, 154, 156–57
Herodian, 42n131
historiography, 2, 6–7, 32n97, 38–39,
   41, 41n125, 53, 99, 113, 133,
   141–46, 154, 157n62, 161n76,
   201n115
Hypata, 85, 140, 166, 180, 194–95, 206

Iamblichus, 2, 40, 42n131, 92
Isis, 17, 52, 54, 71, 75–78, 80n85, 82,
   90, 112n85, 116, 120, 132, 167–69,
   173, 190n74, 206
Iuno, 112n185, 203, 204, 205n124

laughter. *See* ridicule and laughter
lex Cornelia de sicariis, 194–95
Life of Aesop, 16–17, 20, 22, 90, 93–94
listening and reading, 3–4, 4n11, 5,
   7n17, 10n25, 12–14, 16, 21, 24–25,
   27, 32, 34–36, 111–12, 114n192,
   115, 128, 137–40, 142, 146–47,
   154–64, 198n106, 199n109
Longus, 42n131, 74n67
Lotus-eaters, 36n113
Lucilius, 11, 121n207, 122
Lucius of Patrae, 40–50, 91, 176, 187

Macrobius, 23–24, 39–40, 95n130,
   97n134, 106, 108, 114, 131, 163
magic. *See* witches and witchcraft
Marcus Apronianus, 65
Meroe. *See* witches and witchcraft
metae Murtiae, 181–82
Midas, 24, 111n183
Milesian Tales. See *fabula Milesia*
Mithras (god), 64–69
Mithras (priest), 59–70, 74–75, 81n87,
   109n173, 115–20, 153n47
Mithres (slave), 65
mulcere and *permulcere,* 3, 8n17, 13n34,
   15, 17, 21n58, 22n62, 23, 24,
   26–28, 30, 31, 32n101, 34–35,

39–40, 46, 81n85, 96, 100, 129, 153n48
Mummius, 169–73, 175
Muses, 8–9, 16–20, 31, 31n96, 34–35, 46, 202

Nestor, 32, 33, 125n224, 148n33, 173
Nicetes of Smyrna, 31
nostoi, 33, 112n184, 125n222, 167–68

Odysseus, 19, 20n56, 25, 25n71, 26n74, 32, 32n100, 33, 35, 85–86, 125n224, 128, 135, 142–54, 167–68, 178
old wives' tales, 6, 23–24, 30, 48, 95–118, 119n201, 121
orality, 26, 112n84, 154–64
Osiris, 66, 70, 73n60, 78, 87, 88, 90, 129, 152, 167n6

Pamphile. See witches and witchcraft
Panthia. See witches and witchcraft
parody, 13n35, 56n7, 61, 79, 91–93, 122, 127n232, 139, 145, 157, 178
Persius, 5n13
Petronius, 2, 23, 33, 39, 48n149, 83, 96, 97n134, 104n155, 121n203, 121n206, 122, 125n223, 153, 155, 163, 175n30, 197n104
Philip the philosopher, 25, 25n70, 130–31
Philippus of Amphipolis, 42n131
Photis, 54, 76, 77n76, 80n85, 112, 117n197, 141, 145, 151, 178n42, 179
plane tree, 17–18, 135, 138, 140
Plato and Platonism, 18–20, 22, 24, 36–37, 46n145, 48, 51, 54n5, 56n7, 66, 68–69, 75n67, 93n122, 97–103, 106, 111–142, 155n55, 157n60, 189, 190n74
Plutarch, 37, 56n7, 57–58, 92, 126n227, 140n15, 141, 171, 181, 190–91
Polemo of Thasus, 29n89

programmatic statements, 5–25, 30, 38–45, 108, 143
prose and poetry, 4, 11n30, 34, 40, 41n125, 53n2, 199n109
providence, 59–61, 69, 72n58
pseudo-Democritus, 92, 93n122
pseudo-Lucian, 42–50, 80, 91–92, 166–68, 176–77, 186–87, 191, 196n101
Ptolemy Chennos, 147

reader, identification with Lucius, 21n60, 24n69
reading and listening. See listening and reading
recusationes, 7–8
rhetoric, 2, 11–12, 15, 22, 25–36, 38, 40–41, 46, 88–89, 116n196, 129–30, 154n51, 155n52, 156, 157n62, 184, 189, 194, 200; "Bacchic" style, 31; "singing" style, 27–31
ridicule and laughter, 5, 29, 29n88, 43, 58, 81, 84–86, 88–89, 91, 93, 106–7, 123–26, 134, 140n16, 195
Rome, 6, 27–29, 32, 41, 53n1, 64–66, 68n46, 69–73, 84, 88, 166, 168–76, 180–86, 190–94, 197–98, 200–206

Sallustius (subscriptor of F), 131, 185
Sarapis, 65–66
satire, 4n8, 15n40, 38, 52–58, 61, 71, 75, 79, 81n86, 82–87, 89–91, 94, 96, 97n134, 100–106, 109, 111, 113, 118–26, 133, 139n14, 140n15, 175, 176n34, 187, 199
self-irony, 92, 101–2, 104, 106, 109, 109n175, 111, 111n182, 112, 121, 123, 140n15, 175, 187
seriocomic, 56, 94, 107, 110, 113, 118, 123n215, 124–26, 128 132, 133, 149
sermo cotidianus, 6
sermo Milesius. See *fabula Milesia*
Seth, 69, 90, 167n6

Sextus, 190–91
Sileni, 87n104, 88, 122n213, 123, 126–27, 129, 134
Sirens, 19–20, 31–36, 46, 128–29, 146–54
Sisenna, 5n12, 44, 46–47, 48n149, 131n240, 162, 206n129
sleep, 15–20, 22, 140n16
Socrates (character), 58, 73, 77, 78, 134–40, 151n42
Socrates (philosopher), 18, 20, 21n58, 31n94, 36n113, 37n117, 75n68, 86–89, 93, 97–98, 101–103, 105, 110–111, 116–117, 122–24, 126–29, 134–140, 145n27, 149, 152, 153n47, 157n60
Socratic dialogue, 124, 133–40
spoudogeloion. See seriocomic
susurrus, 3, 5, 11, 12, 13n34, 14–17, 20–21, 23, 26, 26n77, 30, 35, 41, 44, 46, 145n26, 155

theater and theatricality, 1, 26, 31, 85, 86n103, 94, 125n225, 133, 135n4, 154–64, 194, 198–99

Thelyphron, 15n39, 44, 114n192, 160, 163n82, 195
Thessalonica, 166–68
Theocritus, 13–17
Thersites, 84–85
Thessalus of Tralles, 92–93
Tlepolemus / Haemus, 81, 121
tragic messengers, 13n35

utile and *dulce,* 7n17, 12–50, 100, 104, 104n56, 107–8, 149, 161n76

whisper. See *susurrus*
witches and witchcraft, 21, 24–25, 28n83, 31, 33, 34n109, 36n113, 42, 47, 55, 58, 63, 66, 75–79, 91, 112, 114n192, 128–29, 131n242, 135–36, 140, 148–49, 151n42, 151n43, 152n47, 164, 189–90, 192, 193n86, 200n112
writtenness. See listening and reading

Xenophon of Ephesus, 39, 74n67

www.ingramcontent.com/pod-product-compliance
Lightning Source LLC
Chambersburg PA
CBHW030110010526
44116CB00005B/175